JUNGVOLK

JUNGVOLK

The Story of a Boy Defending Hitler's Third Reich

By
WILHELM R. GEHLEN
and
DON A. GREGORY

CASEMATE
Philadelphia & Newbury

Published in the United States of America in 2008 by
CASEMATE
1016 Warrior Road, Drexel Hill, PA 19026

and in the United Kingdom by
CASEMATE
17 Cheap Street, Newbury, Berkshire, RG14 5DD

© 2008 by Wilhelm R. Gehlen & Don A. Gregory

ISBN 978-1-932033-87-8

Cataloging-in-publication data is available from the Library of
Congress and from the British Library

Printed and Bound in the United States of America

For a complete list of Casemate titles, please contact

United States of America
Casemate Publishers
Telephone (610) 853-9131, Fax (610) 853-9146
E-mail casemate@casematepublishing.com
Website www.casematepublishing.com

United Kingdom
Casemate-UK
Telephone (01635) 231091, Fax (01635) 41619
E-mail casemate-uk@casematepublishing.co.uk
Website www.casematepublishing.co.uk

CONTENTS

PREFACE

This book was written more than fifty years after the events described within it happened; therefore, I ask the reader to excuse me if, in some instances, I have my dates or places confused after such a long lapse of time. I have also deliberately changed the names of a few persons, units and places to protect the privacy of those who might still be living among us.

This book describes my life as a young boy as a member of the Deutsches Jungvolk (German Youth) and Hitlerjugend, Bann 39 (HJ; Hitler Youth, Regiment 39), based in Dusseldorf, during and immediately after World War II. The Jungvolk was a branch of the Hitler Youth for younger boys, ten to fourteen years old. My story should not be looked upon as a glorification of National Socialism. I have avoided, wherever possible, descriptions of tasteless or gruesome events that are sadly found all too often in publications about the war.

To the reader it might seem rather amazing and unbelievable that the Nazis required children to do their bit for so-called "Führer, Volk, und Vaterland," and work toward a final victory for Germany, but that is exactly what happened. Our lessons in school, apart from a basic curriculum, revolved around aircraft identification (friendly and enemy), scrap collecting, herb collecting, parades and inspections, and messenger and light antiaircraft (AA) duties. Even collecting Colorado beetles in potato fields was regarded as "victory work." In those years, the Hitler Youth were in the fields all summer long, and it can be assumed that the eradication of this pest in Germany is mainly due to the efforts of the school aged boys and girls that collected them until 1948. The Colorado beetle today is not found in Germany.

In 1943 I was ten years old, and at the age of ten we Jungvolk knew how to change the barrel on a 20mm gun. We loaded magazines and ran messages, often under fighter-bomber fire, between gun emplacements or to headquarters (HQ), when telephone communications had been shot to ribbons. A Hitler Youth knew the sound of a P-38 or a Typhoon making a beeline toward him with cannons blazing. He knew where to take cover in the nearest foxhole. He stood steadfast by the light of AA's, handing magazines to the loader, when around him all hell was breaking loose. It was a total war, where everyone was involved, especially after the Normandy landings—because Germany, from that date, was waging a war on two fronts.

In the eyes of our parents, we were still kids; in the eyes of Hitler, we were a convenient substitute for older flak (anti-aircraft) personnel sent to the front to make up for the terrible losses at Stalingrad. It can truly be said that the Hitlerjugend proportionally took as many casualties from fighter bomber attacks as any other Wehrmacht division. The Hitler Youth organization was, in fact, the second oldest paramilitary group in the Third Reich, founded one year after the Sturmabteilung (SA), or Storm Division, the paramilitary organization of the Nazi Party in Germany. Jungvolk and Hitlerjugend also dug up thousands of soccer fields to be used as vegetable plots. They excavated tank traps, and not with heavy equipment either, but with pick and shovel—working, for the most part, on all of these jobs under the constant threat of fighter bomber attacks.

I did not consult any reference books in writing this memoir, but wrote down what I could remember. I would like to say a big "thank you" to my wife Barbara, who encouraged me in the first place to write all this down, and to Beverly Niekerk for typing the first draft of my notes. I would also like to thank Craig Gottlieb and Vera Crist for the reproduction of a Kreisseiger medal in their collection featured on the book's cover.

Lastly, I dedicate this book to all the soldiers of World War II, and to their friends and relatives, both Allied and Axis, who lost their lives in the line of duty. You are not forgotten!

WRG
Telford, Tennessee
2008

I met Will Gehlen some three years ago and soon after making his acquaintance, I began to urge him to tell his story so that others could better understand what things were really like for young boys growing up in Nazi Germany, as experienced by someone who was really there. He finally grew to know me well enough to admit that indeed he had written down some of the things he could remember about that time, and that he would like to see his story published as a book. Being a university professor with an attitude much like Will's Brother Len, whom you will soon meet, I "knew" I could handle this bit of writing in the span of a few months. Over two years later, it was finally finished. I don't know who was gladder, Will or me.

Will indeed had some notes that had been typed on a typewriter, but these had to be scanned page by page and interpreted. I saw my job as involving more than help with modern hardware and software. I wanted to turn Will's notes into a book that would be readable and informative, as factual as Will and I could make it, and maybe even a bit entertaining. Luckily for me, Will is a fascinating conversationalist, and was always ready to retell a story that was not written down quite right; so a portion of this book is my interpretation and rewriting of his notes, and information I gained from multiple interviews and correspondence.

Will's English is very good, but it was learned by listening to the English of those around him, and sometimes they were not the best teachers. For this reason, some of the notes required further interpretation. This I have done, while trying my best to keep the spirit of the notes and what he told me untouched. Much of the book is written as conversation because that is the way he remembered the events. I have very much enjoyed communicating with him during the preparation of this book, even though it was often difficult to explain to him why I was having so much trouble with the simple task that I told him I could handle so quickly and easily. I would certainly like to acknowledge the assistance of Sean Anderson and Kira Patty for solving some difficult scanning and formatting problems that I could not handle.

You may not recognize the name, Wilhelm Gehlen, but you do know the name of his father's cousin, whom Will called Uncle, Reinhard Gehlen, better known as the chief of the Gehlen Organization and the true father of America's CIA.

DAG
Huntsville, Alabama
2008

CHAPTER 1

Home, Family and Herr Meyer

I have often been asked what it was like to grow up and live in the Third Reich under the leadership of the NSDAP (the National Socialist or Nazi Party) and Adolf Hitler, and to experience a devastating war of destruction, not only of the Wehrmacht (the armed forces) but also of civilians. The aftermath of World War II was in a way, as terrible as the war itself. The constant hunting for something to eat, trying to keep warm in the cold winters of 1945-46 and the rebuilding of our homes and lives is as much a part of history as the war itself. However, to a boy of my age, the war was much of the time, an adventure. The adventure was interrupted often, however, by the realities of what was happening all around us and the losses we experienced.

Born in the year of Hitler's ascension to power (1933), I cannot remember anything about the early years of the Party or the effect it had on my family. I was too young, and what I know of it now, I learned from my parents and from my brother, Len. Brother Len was a true Hitlerite through and through. He will accompany me in this book right to the end.

We lived near what was then a small town in the Rhineland called Mönchengladbach, often referred to as just M-G, a dozen or so miles from the Dutch border, so the opening stages of the war more or less bypassed us in 1939. Not until April 1940 did we realize that the war was also coming to our area. This occurred in the middle of an ordinary April night. As usual, a few planes were flying high overhead. Nothing to worry about, we thought. Herman Goering had reassured us many times in his speeches that no enemy planes would enter our air space. So why worry? But alas, that night we heard loud bangs in the distance to the south of town. By the time we all jumped out of our beds and ran

1

into the road to see what was going on, all was quiet again except for
the receding noise of engines in the night sky.

"Probably a stray bomb from our own planes," remarked Brother
Len. "There was no warning siren so it must have been ours, and
besides, the Tommies (English) wouldn't dare fly over the Reich," he
added. Ah, well, Brother Len knows everything, and he's right I thought,
and we all went back to bed. Next morning came the news from friends
and neighbors that two bombs had fallen on a farm about three miles
south of us, and reliable sources said that they had not been dropped by
our planes. Well, if not ours, that leaves only the Tommies, I thought.
So Brother Len and I had a walk to the farm to see the terrible destruction first hand. It was an anticlimax. Only the barn had taken a hit.
There was not much to see, but nevertheless, half the town had turned
out to gawk at the mess.

We overheard a bystander saying, "Now, we can blame Herr Meyer
for that."

"Meyer who?" someone asked.

"Herman Goering," the bystander replied. "He said last year that
we could call him 'Meyer' if ever an enemy plane flew into the Reich."

We walked home after an hour of fruitless searching for souvenirs.
Brother Len was not very happy about the planes being Tommies.
"They ought to do something about that. I will take it up with my Hitler
Youth leader," he said. Len had been a proud member of that institution
since 1938 and was coming up for promotion to group leader.

At the time, my Dad was in Poland with the Wehrmacht. He had
driven a streetcar, one of those electric street trains with overhead
cables, up to the time the war broke out. He had always been the driver
for the Number 10 car from the town of Süchteln to Lurrip, a distance
of about 14 miles. He was already 38 years old when World War II
began. Hitler called all men between the ages of 18 and 45 to arms, and
Dad was called up into the Wehrmacht and assigned to a tank destroyer (TD) in a Sturmgeschütz battalion of the 39th Infantry Division. I
suppose being a streetcar driver also made him, in the eyes of the
Wehrmacht, a good driver for a 26-ton tank destroyer. He no doubt
protested that there were a lot of differences between a streetcar and a
tank destroyer, but the Wehrmacht would have none of it. Everyone did
as they were told, no arguments. After all, this was war.

We lived in a modest house that was owned by what we called the
"food factory," a food processing and packaging plant located across

the road. We lived with Granddad Willem and Aunt Carol, whose husband was already missing in action in Poland. She was my Dad's sister and had no children, so Mom had taken her in to comfort her and give her company. Granddad Willem, my Dad's father, had lived in the house ever since it was built in 1909. He had helped Mr. Kersken (not his real name) build the food factory, and although the factory now employed a lot of people, and had grown to a huge concern with branches in many other towns, Mr. Kersken and Granddad Willem were still the best of friends.

Mom's Dad, Granddad Zander, was from a small town in northern Luxembourg located in the Ardennes, and had come to Germany in the mid-1920's searching for work. He was a toolmaker by trade and soon found a job earning a good wage in a large truck manufacturing company in Nuremberg. However, money wasn't worth much in those days in Germany, as inflation was rife. I was told that one day a loaf of bread would cost you three million marks, and the next day you could just about get a postage stamp for the same money. Every town and city had a money press and people lit the fires in their homes with the notes. Mom married my Dad in 1928 and in 1929 Brother Len was born. Dad was lucky during the depression when six million people had no job or income. Streetcars had to run—people still had to get from place to place, and there were very few cars in those days.

Granddad Willem (Dad's dad) was a simple bricklayer, road paver, and jack-of-all-trades. In the mid-1920's he even went around town pushing a small cart, selling herrings out of a barrel. Every 200 yards he stopped and praised his herrings to the eager customers. In between times, he was the foreman of the crew that built the food factory for Mr. Kersken. It took the two of them two years and a lot of sweat and useless money to build the place, and Granddad Willem stayed in Mr. Kersken's service until the day he died.

Granddad Willem had been a soldier himself in the Great War of 1914-18. He served in a Westphalian Fuselier Regiment under General von Zwehl and fought at Chemin des Dames and Verdun. His regiment had the distinction of capturing the important Bois de Caures and the town of Besonvaux on February 21, 1916. On November 11, 1918, he walked all the way home from the River Sambre in Belgium, a distance of 170 miles. After World War I, he wore his four medals every Sunday. His Dad, my great granddad, had also fought the French, and in 1871, he was at Sedan when Napoleon III called it quits. It was natural that my Dad would also become a soldier in turn, but the German Reichswehr, after World War I, was restricted to 100,000 men by the Treaty of Versailles, and better men than my Dad were queuing up to get into this formation. Besides, streetcar drivers were hard to come by.

In the early 1930's, the NSDAP became a force to be reckoned with, but our family stayed out of the street brawls that daily occurred between communists, Nazis, and a host of other minor parties. As far as I know, neither Granddad Willem, Mom or Dad ever voted, not even after World War II when Germany became a federal republic. Granddad Willem was a monarchist anyway. He would have gladly supported a new Kaiser—or King, for that matter. He had no time for the Nazi Party. He loved to talk about Hindenburg, Ludendorff and Kaiser Wilhelm and what good soldiers and statesmen they were. He always said that Germany only lost the Great War because of the no-good Austrio-Hungarians, and that now Germany had an Austrian corporal as the leader of the government.

The sad fact was that during the depression, six million unemployed people roamed the streets of Germany, and people would vote for any-one they believed could turn their lives around for the better. That's how Hitler and his Nazi Party stepped in. Much has been written about the intrigues, power struggles, assassinations and other events leading to Hitler's election as Chancellor of the Third Reich. But one thing is clear; Hitler came to power in the middle of a depression. He inherited from Hindenburg six million unemployed people and an occupied left bank of the river Rhine, a legacy left over from the Great War. Then came his election as the Führer of the Third Reich in 1933. Suddenly, in 1935, with the stroke of a pen, everybody had a job, and it was not forced labor either, although some of that did come in 1939.

It was Hitler's intention to make Germany great again and turn it into a prosperous nation. To achieve this, for instance, he approved the creation and building of the Volkswagen, or early "Beetle," a design that did not change much for half a century. He wanted a car that all German people could afford to buy. He also knew that to put the nation on wheels, he needed a network of roads. In the mid-1930's, the road system was in no better shape than it had been ten years earlier during the Weimar Republic. There was just no money available to pay private enterprises to remedy the situation. That minor detail did not bother Hitler. He had something far more valuable than money. He had the hearts and minds of the people.

CHAPTER 2

Everyone Works

Adolf Hitler, with the aid of his devoted followers and a stroke of the pen, created the RAD, the Reichsarbeitsdienst (Reich's Labor Service), whereby any male from the age of 18 years had to serve for two years improving old or constructing new communication lines, roads, railways, and airfields. Huge RAD camps were set up along designated roads and motorways, and young RAD men, equipped with shovels and picks, set cheerfully to work—and work they did. In a year's time, the first few hundred miles of motorways, or "Autobahns" as they were called, were opened to the public, accompanied with the usual parade of Nazi dignitaries.

Germans could then get from place to place in no time. From Allenstein, deep in East Prussia, to Berlin and on to Munich, Nuremberg, Stuttgart, Hamburg and the industrial Ruhr—all came within the Autobahn sphere that now covered Germany from all points of the compass. Of course, it was also Hitler's idea, in the event of another war, that the new highways would become a convenient way of transferring war material or motorized divisions from one end of the country to the other. In 1945, when the allies entered Germany, they used the Autobahn exactly in this way, to the dismay of the German high command.

But all this war talk was unknown to us. We could only see the roads, new factories and railroads being built. The radio, a pet manufacturing project of Josef Goebbels, the Nazi propaganda minister, reminded us every day of how great the Third Reich had become under the leadership of Adolf Hitler.

My cousin Hans told me once about his RAD life, when he visited on a ten-day leave pass: 6:00 AM reveille and beds squared away, exercise in the yard for half an hour, rain, shine or snow; a hearty breakfast at the mess hall; then marching in columns of four off to work or, if road construction had advanced too far, being transported by truck. What a sight it must have been to see 50 trucks loaded with RAD men going to work, lustily singing "Die Fahne Hoch" ("Raise High the Flag," the Nazi Party anthem), or some other Nazi song. They had reason to be a happy lot; three good meals a day, uniforms and working overalls free, 26 Reichsmarks per month and weekend liberty into the nearest towns, where the Bund Deutscher Mädel girls (the BMD, or League of German Girls, the female equivalent of the Hitler Youth) were only too willing to spend time with a strapping RAD man. Home on leave, the men were admired by everyone, and strutted through town like peacocks in their steel gray uniforms adorned with colorful Nazi emblems. Cousin Hans was killed in action on the third day of the Russian campaign, "für Führer und Vaterland," —for our leader and our country—said the letter, to which a posthumously awarded Iron Cross 2nd Class was attached.

On the first of April 1939, I started school, and what a day to remember it was! It was a brand new school built by the RAD, a building contractor, and the Organisation Todt (OT), a civil and military engineering group responsible for many engineering projects in Germany and occupied territories during the war. The old school we had in our section of the town had been erected in 1870. On Hitler's decree in 1936, many new schools were built; ours was a huge affair, as it had to accommodate children from two other sections of town. Moreover, like other schools in the late 1930's, it was designed with foresight. Taking into consideration the Nazi doctrine that every German mother should give birth to at least three children, it was constructed to accommodate the influx of offspring, which every good German woman was expected to contribute. We all agreed our school was special because it was designated by the name "Adolf Hitler School" and the Führer himself was to visit the inauguration on that fine April day.

For two days before the school's grand opening, Mom washed and scrubbed us until our skin nearly came off. Brother Len sported his brand new Hitler Youth uniform. I meekly showed off my white shirt and black shorts on suspenders, but I was given a paper swastika flag to wave vigorously when the Führer arrived. We got to school at 9:00 AM. Hitler was not due to arrive until 11:00, but we nevertheless had to line up outside among a throng of other people who had come to support the great man. Ebullient SA storm troopers were trying their best to bring some sort of order into the chaos. A sprinkle of black and silver uniformed Schutzstaffel (protective squadron or SS) men, guns at ready, lingered on street corners, treating every sightseer with suspicion. The SA marching band had been on their feet since 6:00 AM and was blasting away on their tubas and trumpets, playing fanfares as if the Führer could already hear them. He was, at 9:00 AM, just boarding a plane 250 miles away.

The town was awash with party officials, Hitler Youth, soldiers on leave, BDM girls, Todt Organization engineers, and a host of other more or less important people, but they all had one thing in common: a desire to see the Führer of the Third Reich.

Tension mounted at around 10:45 AM when word came that the Führer and his entourage (the Führer Begleit Kommando or FBK) were only two miles away. We stood to attention on the new school playground, the teachers all in their best dress, by the main gate. Swastika banners were flapping in the early spring breeze. Then a cheer rose up in the distance, "Sieg Heil! Sieg Heil!" and got nearer and nearer. The gates swung open at the playground and a huge Maybach limousine with high-ranking official dignitaries inside entered the site. Another car, Hitler's FBK, followed, and then the Führer himself entered, sitting on the back seat of an open topped Mercedes Benz with Herman Goering, the Reich marshal and commander of the Luftwaffe at his side. More cars followed and as far as I can remember, there were Dr. Goebbels of the Propaganda Ministry, Sepp Dietrich of the SS, Gauleiter Florian, and Robert Ley of the German Workers' Front, who, after all, was responsible for building the new school in the first place.

Four hundred and fifty school children stood to attention. A shout went up, "Heil Hitler!" as the Führer slowly walked along the front of the assembly, shaking hands here and there or asking a question. We each received a signed photograph. Then it was the teachers' turn to be honored. One thing that has always stuck in my mind is that Hitler, on official visits, always greeted and attended to the children first. Then came the unveiling ceremony. High up on the wall of the school was a curtain attached to a rail, with a silver cord dangling down. The Führer pulled the cord, and the curtain fell, revealing the words "Adolf Hitler School" in Gothic lettering. Ohhhhhh's and ahhhhhh's went up from the watching crowd, and the Sieg Heils started all over again. He then spent another 20 minutes or so inspecting the new school, looking into classrooms and the gardens. Then it was all over. The whole cavalcade sped into town for lunch at the Nazi Party headquarters.

Of course we had the rest of the day off, but we were told to go into town to hear the Führer's speech. The older Hitler Youth had no choice anyway. They marched in unison straight from school to the town square. I can't remember much of what the Führer said in his speech, but it was something about the Sudentenland being rightfully German, like Austria and a few other faraway places like Danzig, Memel Land, Alsace-Lorraine and Eupen-Malmedy. (Wherever that is, I thought at the time.) Hitler also declared that he didn't care at all what France and England had to say. "If France and England want war, let them fire the first shot," he stated. "Our mighty Luftwaffe, under the leadership of the great Herman Goering, will smash their countries into submission!" This was followed by applause and approval from Goering. Then it was Dr. Josef Goebbels' turn to speak, but he only elaborated on Hitler's speech. At 4:00 PM, most of the circus got back into their respective cars and left.

Brother Len and I walked home, proud to be part of this great time. "Sieg Heil! Sieg Heil!" we still could hear in the distance.

"We ought to be the Great German Reich," Brother Len remarked. "The English are sitting on their paltry little island and they call it Great Britain, so rightfully we should be called 'great' too!"

Well, Germany was soon to be the "Gross Deutsche Reich" after the occupation of Poland. We then had the name our country deserved, or so we thought at the time. For the time being, however, we went home after the eventful day at our new school, clutching our Führer pictures with both hands.

Long after dark, when night came over the town and all the dignitaries had finally departed, the SA bands were still marching around. Torch lit processions of storm troopers and OT men, goose-stepping along the cobblestone streets went on late into the night. The pubs and bars were open until 4:00 AM. No doubt the Führer and his entourage were at that time somewhere in deepest Germany planning their next move to enlarge the Reich even more.

If so, Minister Goebbels was not among them. He had taken a few days leave to visit his old hometown of Hochneukirch, located just a few miles from us, where he had lived until he moved to Berlin around 1926. Josef Goebbels, only five feet four inches tall with a clubfoot, was not exactly Hitler's idea of a six-foot blond, blue-eyed Aryan superman, but what Goebbels lacked in height and appearance, he surely made up for with his mouth. When he really got going during one of his speeches, his mouth looked like a small steamboat funnel covering three quarters of his face. His ears stuck out like sails on a rigger.

By 1939 there were no Jewish businesses left in our town. Goebbels with his speeches had seen to that, and the situation was the same all over Germany. Kazenstein's Department Store, before 1938, was a respectable business supplying the town folk with all sorts of things for their daily needs at a reasonable price. It was taken over by a Nazi enterprise that had no clue about how to run a store. The new owners had been railroad workers. They were given the store as a reward for being loyal Nazis.

Contrary to common belief today that all the Jews were put in concentration camps, I can tell you that this was not so. Mr. Hersch, a Jewish man who lived in our neighborhood, went about his work all throughout the war. Of course he had to wear a yellow star on his coat, but he was nevertheless a respected member of the community, having lived there all of his life. He was about 60 years old, and since the food factory first opened in the late 1920's, he had been employed as the chief wine and food taster, wine blender and appraiser. I suppose the local Nazis, being fond of good wine and food, couldn't do without him, and therefore left him in peace. Or perhaps they had simply forgotten about him.

Every morning at 7:30 Mr. Hersch walked to the factory gate, lifted his hat, and said a "good morning" to the other workers. He stayed at his job throughout the war and after March 1945, when the town was occupied by the 24th and 102nd US Infantry Divisions. He later retired and tended his garden as if there had never been a war, and millions of his compatriots had not been exterminated by the Nazis. Of course we didn't know about the concentration camps at that time. All we knew and were told by the Party was that Jews, communists, and gypsies were bad people and had to be treated accordingly. Mr. Hersch wasn't bad, I thought, but if Hitler and the Party said they were, then there must be something to it. Our town was a small place compared to nearby larger cities like Krefield, Cologne, and Aachen, so most people knew and respected each other.

Opposite from us lived Mr. Jacob Lanz, whom we had known for years. He was not really a bad person, but he was a communist.

I didn't know what a communist was in those days, only that according to Party doctrine, communists were bad people. Yet Mr. Lanz was left in peace, despite the fact he made fun of the Nazis at times. There weren't many Nazi parades in our section of town, but if ever the occasion did occur, Mr. Lanz would lean out of a top window and make funny faces or shout abuse at the marching troopers. They regarded him as a fool, and in a sense he was, so the Nazis left him alone.

We called him Horse Shit Jacob. In those days there were quite a few horses pulling all sorts of carts, and if any horse came by and dropped a pile, Mr. Lanz, who was a dedicated gardener, came out like lightning and scooped up the mess. "Good manure for the garden," he used to say. And right he was. He grew the best vegetables and tomatoes for miles around. Later, when food was getting harder to come by, many people went into competition with Mr. Lanz for the manure, but no matter how fast other people got their bucket and shovel, Horse Shit Jacob beat them every time.

"Communism stinks," Granddad Willem used to say, and the habits of Horse Shit Jacob are where he got the expression. We shrugged our shoulders and emptied our septic tank to fertilize the garden while Mr. Lanz leaned out the window and held his nose.

CHAPTER 3

Bombings & 88s

After those first bombs dropped by the British demolished the farm shed, Herman Goering was known only as Herr Meyer in our house. It was a hectic time around the area. Air raid sirens were installed on several schools and public buildings, and basements were converted into shelters. Some people constructed their own bunkers in their gardens, and the school cellar was made into temporary classrooms.

Then one day a convoy of Hanomag halftracks appeared in town, towing menacing-looking 88mm flak pieces. Two of them swung off the road near us and went across a field to set up camp. Several truckloads of RAD men arrived with two dozen Polish POWs, and started digging gun emplacements for the 88s. Concrete shelters and bunkers went up in no time, electricity was installed via a huge generator, and before the week was out, the flak crews came to settle into their new home. The other two 88s had meanwhile set up shop in the south end of town, about four miles from us. Next, two searchlights arrived. These were mounted on concrete bases about a mile from the 88s. Thick cables were laid underground from the generators to supply the electricity. We gawked in wonderment at all this and asked thousands of questions during the installation.

Later, a most puzzling piece of new equipment was brought up. We didn't know what the contraption was at first. It looked like an oversized ear with a swivel seat in it. We asked the flak men what it was, and were told it was a "Horchgeraet," or listening device, which could hear the noise of approaching aircraft 40 miles out, or even more. We lived on the western outskirts of the Ruhr area. At the time, the Ruhr was the largest manufacturing area in the world, about the size of the state of Rhode Island, so it was only natural that our district was given the

11

honor of shooting down the bombers that dared to enter the Ruhr from the west.

In early 1940, apart from a few Polish POWs, the demolished farm shed, and the odd air raid warning, we hadn't seen much of the war. Even the newly installed 88s hadn't yet fired a shot. One day about this time, a huge truck stopped outside our house. We all stumbled outside to see what was going on and why it had parked by our front door. The canvas cover on the back lifted and there was our Dad, fresh from the Polish front. He jumped over the tailgate with a smile all over his face. Mom nearly fainted. We climbed all over him asking questions. Brother Len in his Hitler Youth uniform even managed to stand to attention and shout a hearty "Heil Hitler!"

Dad glanced at Len with a peculiar look on his face. "No Heil's now," he said. "I'm on a three-week leave, and this is a private affair with no 'Heils' or standing to attention unless there is an official occasion." What he meant by that I soon found out. A German staff car with an officer inside drew up, and after a smart "Heil Hitler," the driver asked Dad for his papers. After he had satisfied himself that they were in order, he saluted again and went on his way. Then Dad unloaded some boxes from the back of the truck. When Mom asked what was in them, Dad put his forefinger to his lips. "Spoils of war, Agnes, just a few presents from Poland," he said.

After the truck left, taking other soldiers to their destinations, we dragged the boxes indoors. Then the unpacking started. There were stockings, shawls, two pairs of shoes, shirts, cardigans and pullovers, followed by cans of food and seven loaves of bread. Although we had so far not experienced any real shortages, the bounty was nevertheless welcomed, as the ration card never seemed to have enough coupons for all the things our family needed. The most amazing thing he unpacked from one of the boxes was a nearly new Lowe Opta Radio. It was not one of those little "Volks radios" either, but a large wood-encased thing. It even had a "magic eye," the exposed end of a vacuum tube that glowed when the radio was on and tuned, an innovation I had never seen before. In awe we looked at the scale on the radio, medium and long and short wave, and the names of radio stations we had never heard of—Beromunster, Hilversum, Kalundborg, Stockholm, Nantes, and the BBC.

"Where is the BBC, Dad?" I asked.

Len snapped, "It's a Tommie station in England, if you must know."

Oh well, Brother Len naturally knows everything, I thought.

"Okay," Dad said, "you two are not to play with the radio. Only Mom and I select the stations. Is that clear?"

We nodded agreement.

"Can we look at the magic eye when the radio is on?" I asked.

"Of course you can but do not touch!" came the reply.

Listening to a French or English radio station was forbidden during the war, but most people tuned in at times to hear what London had to say. There were a few neutral stations to which we were officially allowed to listen, like the Swiss Beromunster, or Stockholm or Reykjavik in Iceland, but not understanding the language, we soon got tired of them. The best thing on the radio was the so-called "Drahtfunk." It was an official German detecting station that gave coordinates of enemy planes entering our air space from a westerly direction. Of course the coordinates were given in code, but we soon figured that out; in any case, each air defense section later received the appropriate code.

Dad had won the Iron Cross 2nd Class during the Polish campaign and we pestered him to tell us how. He told us, in very few words, that his unit of tank destroyers and assault guns had shot up a whole Polish cavalry division; seven tank destroyers had been pitted against 7,000 horse soldiers, and Dad's outfit had won. Dad didn't look very enthusiastic when he told us this. I could not understand why; after all, 7,000 horsemen was a force to be reckoned with. I told our teacher at school about this and he just shook his head in disbelief.

When Dad visited the local pub, people crowded around him, shaking hands and slapping shoulders, wanting to know how things were shaping up in the east, and whether there would be any more fighting now that Poland had been defeated. Were the French and British calling it quits and suing for peace? Dad wasn't so sure about that, but he did say that he would rather drive the streetcar than spend a winter at the front, wherever the front might be.

His wish came true a few days later, at least for a while. The local transit authority had gotten wind that Dad was home on leave, so the director visited us one morning to ask Dad to drive the Number 10 for the duration of his leave on the early shift from 6:00 AM to 1:00 PM, since they were short of drivers. Dad agreed and wages were worked out then and there. He took his old driver's uniform out of the closet and Mom gave it a good brush up. The next morning at 5:30, he rode his bicycle to the tram depot to take the number 10 to L Street. He must have had a good day. He was supposed to be back home at 2:00 PM, but it was after 5:00 when he finally rolled in, singing at the top of his voice, "Rosamunde, give me your heart and your soul."

Of course he was drunk. He had met some of his old friends after work, and instead of making his way home, they all went for a pub-crawl. So it went for a week or two, but soon it was time to say good-bye. One evening, Dad cleaned his army boots and uniform. We all gathered around. "I'm leaving in the morning at 5:00 AM," he said. "You two," he addressed Len and me, "look after Mom. No messing with the radio, and feed the rabbits and chickens so you have something to eat if times get bad. I don't know when I'll be back, but I hope soon; it depends."

"Depends on what?" Mom asked.

"Well, it depends on how the French and British behave," was his reply.

At 5:00 AM we were all up and about saying our goodbyes, but no truck came. It was a cold and frosty morning as we all stood outside, waiting for Dad's transport. Finally at 7:00 AM, the big truck, which had brought Dad three weeks earlier, roared up the street and stopped, keeping the engine running.

"Hurry up Lou," the driver shouted, "We're late!"

"I can see that," Dad answered. "Where have you been? It's 7:00 AM!"

"The diesel fuel froze, and I had to warm up the fuel lines before I could start this damn cow," the driver, a corporal, replied.

After a last kiss for Mom and a hug for Len and me, Dad jumped into the back of the truck, where he was greeted by a few other soldiers. The driver gunned the engine and down the hill they went. Mom dried a few tears and we went back indoors. "Off to school now," she said, and we obediently trotted off to lessons, sad that Dad was gone and that we did not know when he would come back.

With spring came warmer weather. After school we visited the newly installed 88s in their gun pits. The flak men of the 64th Flak Battalion, based in Dusseldorf, were a friendly lot, only too pleased to give us candy or a mess tin of goulash soup. In return, we gave them the addresses and names of girls whose boyfriends were at the front or watching the Tommies and the French along the border. One Saturday morning, a flak colonel arrived at the guns. He told us to move to the other side of the road or go home, because there was shooting to be done and he didn't want kids near the battery. He said, "This is target shooting. We are using live rounds, and 88 shrapnel has the nasty habit of coming back to earth, so you better take cover and watch from a distance."

We didn't know what he meant by target shooting, since there were no planes or anything else to be seen up in the sky, but we took the officer's advice and moved about half a mile away, into the shelter of an open barn. We were eager to see the guns opening up for the first time and did not want to miss the action. A stiff easterly breeze was blowing that day. From our vantage point in the shed we could see the gunners running about, some with shiny 88mm rounds in their hands, and nasty-looking things they were. The barrels of the two 88s were swinging to all compass points. Then one guy pointed to the eastern sky. Looking in that direction, we saw the target coming up. It looked like a gigantic hot-dog about 5,000 feet up, but as it got nearer we realized it was an unmanned barrage balloon. Such balloons were installed above the Ruhr, suspended on steel cables to protect the factories from low level attacks.

This particular balloon most probably had been deliberately cut loose from its mooring cable for the sole purpose of giving the flak crew some practice. The sausage headed straight for us. Then all hell broke loose. "Wham! Wham!" The two 88s had spoken for the first time. We kept our eyes glued to the sky. Two small black clouds appeared near the balloon, and we heard the "plop plop" of the exploding rounds far above us.

The contraption was still sailing happily in a westerly direction and was almost overhead. The next two rounds exploded right above us because the barrels of the guns were now almost at their highest elevation point, but still the balloon sailed on unharmed. A new sound now reached our cocked ears. A high whistling pitch came from above. The shrapnel from the rounds came back to earth. We stood under the roof of the barn, relatively safe but nevertheless a bit concerned about hot metal bits raining from the sky. Some bits hit the tin roof, while others fell into the grass with a sizzling sound. The next two rounds from the guns missed again, and the balloon was now well out to the west. We heard our colonel shouting, "Cease fire!" There was no point wasting any more shells at the receding target.

Brother Len and I went in search for shrapnel pieces. I found one about three inches long in the grass. When I tried to pick it up, it burned my fingers. It was almost red hot, and we had to wait a few minutes before we could it or any of the other pieces. Then we collected all the bits we could find. Len even climbed on the shed roof and, as usual, he got the bulk of the fragments, even two bits that fit perfectly together. Lucky swine, I thought. He always manages to come out better.

We got home with our treasures. Len immediately got to work mounting his pieces on a board in the shape of a swastika and hung it up in his bedroom. I only found three pieces, so I hid my meager collection under the bed waiting for the day I could get my revenge on Len by finding a bucket full of shrapnel. I'm going to fasten them to a board and make a picture of Dad's tank destroyer out of it! I thought.

CHAPTER 4

88s in Action

April 20, 1941 was Adolf Hitler's 51st birthday and according to tradition, we anticipated special celebrations and glittering parades. School was off for the day, but we were asked to go into town where a high-ranking Hitler Youth official was going to speak to us. I had meanwhile joined the Jungvolk, a younger division of the older Hitler Youth. We were as proud of the unit as our older compatriots: our uniform was the same, minus the traditional dagger. Well, you can't have everything, we thought, not realizing that we were not yet old enough for daggers. Meanwhile, we sure had a nice flag, with a single black rune stitched in the center, forming sort of a half SS banner.

The visit we were expecting was postponed until late evening so we could have a traditional torch light parade, but some other uninvited visitors came instead. I went home when it got dark and soon Brother Len came in as well. We had grown tired of waiting for the visitor. We sat by the radio and stared at the magic eye blinking at us. Then a voice came over the speaker: "Achtung! Achtung, Drahtfunk! Enemy planes approaching PQ 161!" We knew of course that PQ 161 was the code for our area, but whether the planes meant to do business in PQ 161, nobody knew. They were just entering the area, so their target was anybody's guess.

Night turned nearly to daylight as the two searchlights switched on and probed the sky. Other searchlights from further away joined in. Then we heard the drone of aircraft engines coming at us from a westerly direction, getting louder with every second. A distant 88mm flak battery fired a few star shells to further illuminate the sky. A searchlight from the northern part of the Ruhr finally got a plane in its strong beam about five miles from us.

17

Mom was shouting at us to get into the cellar we used as an air raid shelter, but the cellar door, a flat contraption level with the floor, had ten sacks of potatoes stacked on top of it. We decided the doorway lintel at the front of the house was as good a shelter as any, and better than none at all. The searchlight meanwhile had lost the plane. Somehow, the enemy had made a crash dive and got out of the deadly grip of the hundred thousand watt beam.

Soon enough, the crews found another aircraft in their search, much nearer to us. More beams got into the fray, and there was no escape for the plane. Now the 88s across the field opened up, this time for real. This was no harmless sausage balloon—it was an enemy plane with a deadly load of explosives in the bomb bay.

The plane in the beams was about 7,000 feet up. A shell from the 88s exploded close to the plane. Now the 88s had found the range. The flak crew knew their business. Shell after shell left the gun, exploding with short plop nearer and nearer the intruder. Then a little flicker of flame could be seen from one of the wings. The flicker got bigger, and a whoosh of fire set one of the wing tanks ablaze. The plane started a lazy dive toward the ground, no doubt bound for destruction. The searchlights let go and probed the sky for the next victim. The plane was well on fire, gliding in at a 45-degree angle toward the center of town.

We lived on top of a hill about two miles from town, so we had a first row seat for the spectacle unfolding before our eyes. Lower and lower the plane went. There was no sight of any parachutes. We lost sight of it momentarily as it went low behind some high rise buildings, and then we caught it again, but seconds later we heard a tremendous explosion. Sheets of flames went skyward, and more explosions followed as bombs went off in the blazing inferno. We watched speechless—we had just witnessed the destruction of one of our enemies.

"Heil Hitler!" Brother Len said with a deep breath.

"He had nothing to do with it. Our flak crew got him," I replied.

Len had no answer to that. Meanwhile, firing went on for several more minutes, and in the east, searchlights were still probing the sky for more intruders. Finally it was all over, except that downtown a big fire was raging, somewhere near the cinema we thought.

Back in the 88 gun pits, there was a great commotion and other happy noises—not without reason. It was they who had downed the enemy plane, a Bristol Blenheim twin-engine bomber, we were later told. The next morning, the first white ring appeared on the barrels of the two guns. Liberty for the crew was reinstated. All were happy. Even the two party girls we had recommended to the crew before the balloon fiasco had a share of the good time.

We, of course, were eager to get into town the next morning to survey the damage or find souvenirs from the plane crash. It was school in the morning for us and there was no way out until 1:00 PM, but news often travels by mouth faster than by telephone or telegraph.

During the 10:00 AM break at school, we heard that the town center was a disaster. Over 1,000 people had been killed, and six crewmembers of the plane had vanished. By 11:00 AM, the list had shrunk to 100 killed, one block of houses demolished, and six crewmembers dead.

School ended at 1:00 PM. We made our way home as fast as we could in anticipation of getting into town to see for ourselves. Mom told us to be careful, and not to get too near the site and hinder the fire or rescue operations. Len was instructed to keep a wary eye on me. We knew more or less where the plane had come down, but when we got near the site of the crash, the road was blocked by police. All we could see was a smoldering heap of debris 200 yards away. Brother Len, he who knew everything, knew a way over a fence behind the cinema. We climbed over and onto a lean-to shed roof, from which we had a grandstand view of the site. From bystanders we heard that the other wing of the plane had scraped the wall of the cinema before hitting a lady doctor's house where it exploded. As luck would have it, the lady doctor was not at home, but a next-door neighbor lost a hand. Later, the rescue crew found a ten-year-old girl dead among the ruins. The five 100-pound bombs aboard the plane had demolished the doctor's house and severely damaged another four dwellings.

Results were a bit of a disappointment for us. No blocks flattened, no deaths in the hundreds, and as the score stood, just one girl killed, one man with a lost hand, six crewmembers dead, and a few houses more or less destroyed or damaged. On the way home we mused over the result again and came to the conclusion that, after all, it wasn't a bad score: one and a half to six in our favor, plus a Blenheim bomber. What are a few demolished homes against a Blenheim? Houses can be rebuilt, wrecked Blenheims cannot (or so we thought); and besides, our 88 crew had its first white ring now for all to see. Before the war ended, the barrels would have 15 more rings. Right now it was one ring, good old Deutsches Reich, we thought. Eagerly we awaited the arrival of the next lot of Blenheims or Wellingtons but something else arrived first.

Since the early days of the war, two hours per week of school time had been devoted to military matters by order of the Nazi Party, which, after all, had a say in all school matters. From maps we learned where the glorious Wehrmacht now stood and the places we had occupied, and from pictures we learned to identify different calibers of cannons and tanks. Aircraft charts showed the silhouettes of all aircraft involved in the war, and these were constantly updated as new planes took to the skies and flew their first mission. I guess we were better updated in that respect than the common soldier sitting in his trench somewhere along the Siegfried Line.

One day, a fast twin-engine fighter-bomber made a low-level run onto our 88s. There was no time for the crew to lower the elevation of their pieces sufficiently to get in a shot. The plane came too low. It was British—it did not drop any bombs, but the guys in the plane did let loose at the 88s with eight cannons in their wings and fuselage, although they did not do any real damage. When the plane gained altitude after its low-level run, we could see the silhouette and knew it was the newest Bristol Beaufighter, a fast and well-armed fighter-bomber. Only two days previously, we had been shown this type of plane on our school chart. At the time, even the 88 crew did not know what had nearly hit them.

The end result of this episode was the conclusion that no 88 mm battery was safe against low-level attack. The elevation of the gun was limited because of the protective embankment around the pit, but the main limitation was that the gun, although electrically operated, was unable to fire a constant stream of shells. To overcome this handicap, several batteries of quad 20mms were brought in and installed around the outskirts of town. These were deadly, quick-firing guns with four barrels each, which theoretically could throw up 6,000 rounds per minute. Practically speaking, it was more around 800 rounds, because magazines had to be changed out. Those 16 guns around our area mustered 64 barrels between them—enough, we thought, to deter any would-be flyers from coming too near the 88s or the town. That was wishful thinking, as we soon found out.

No more Tommy bombers came that April. Instead, the might of the German Wehrmacht arrived. Halftracks, guns of all calibers, trucks, and tanks rolled into the area, from the puny Mark II tank (Mk II) to the latest Mark VI (Mk VI). There were also tank destroyers and assault guns mounted on Mk VI chassis minus the turret.. Horse-drawn wagons arrived with immensely large artillery pieces of 210 mm and above. Troops arrived by the divisions, all setting up camp wherever there was a square yard of free space to be found. Field kitchens were lit and stew was cooked on hundreds of so-called goulash cannons to feed the hungry army. Most armor was camouflaged with netting; overhead flew a constant patrol of Messerschmitt Me-109s and Me-110s to deter any enemy plane from coming too near the armada.

We asked our teacher at school what this was all about, but he knew no more than we did, or if he did, he wasn't telling. Our teacher was not what you might call a "good" Nazi patriot. He had fought in the Great War, had been wounded at Ypres in Belgium, gassed at Vimy Ridge, and had had his bellyful of glorious wars. Apart from the ritual "Heil Hitler" each morning, he never said much about the Party or our Wehrmacht. He never praised the Führer either. If we met him on the road after school hours, our duty was to greet him with a "Heil Hitler," but he just used to smile and say "Good day." We didn't mind. He was a good teacher. He never punished us too much. Besides, we were going to win this war with or without his blessings.

CHAPTER 5

Dad's Home Visit

On the last Friday in April that year, school was suspended at 11:00 AM because of a teachers' conference. Len and I walked home slowly, gawking at the trucks, tanks, cannons and other war material parked on every main road and side street. It was nearly 12:30 PM and we were still not home. We turned around the corner by our house and there was a menacing contraption parked right outside our front door. We could see it was a TD (tank destroyer) with a long-barreled 75mm gun. What nerve, we thought, parking this thing right under our bedroom window!

But this was no ordinary TD—it was Dad's! He had been transferred from Poland to the west. The armor had been brought up by train and unloaded in the town marshalling yard. As luck would have it, his unit was assigned a sector in our area so he had taken the opportunity to come by and say hello. He had a weekend pass, and for good measure he had come in his TD with one other crewmember. We were absolutely delighted and of course, very proud. Not everybody had a TD parked by his front door, and of course Len and I considered the monster to be ours alone. Everything that belonged to Dad was ultimately ours as well. We wanted to climb all over it and inspect every nook and cranny, but that's where Dad drew the line.

After dinner, Granddad Willem lit his pipe and asked Dad what all the commotion was about with all the troops and armor around and the skies full of German planes. Dad said that he thought we would now finally get to grips with the Tommies and the French. I thought it funny, really. France was 200 miles away, and here we were, a dozen miles from the Dutch border with all the Wehrmacht in the world around us. Later we went to bed happy in the knowledge that soon the Tommies and the French would come to their senses and make peace, and Dad would be home for good.

The next morning we had to go to church. It was Sunday and there was no way around it. Mom was a strict Catholic and she always made sure that we went to church. The Nazis, of course, frowned on church-going, but Mom would have none of that. Mom's word was the law at home, not Hitler's. Monday morning came soon enough, and then it was time to say goodbye again. At 6:00 AM we got up and went outside. Dad was gassing up the TD from five-gallon cans attached to the armor plates on the side. At 7:00 AM, Dad's crewmember arrived. Mom asked him if there was a chance for him to come home the following weekend.

"We're on high alert as of tomorrow," Dad said, "so I can't tell, but if I find out anything, I'll give our battalion milk runner a message. We are only ten miles away in Bracht."

The milk runner was a corporal driving a two-ton Opel Blitz who was detailed to fetch the milk and butter from the creamery in our town. Once a day he took the stuff to the various quartermasters of the battalions

"If you can't make it, I can come to Bracht and stay overnight with Aunt Adele," Mom said.

"I'll let you know before Friday, Agnes," Dad shouted from the open TD flap. An almighty roar came from the 12-cylinder Maybach engine, and off he went. We could hear the clattering of the tracks for quite a while.

On Friday evening we had a small parade of the Hitler Youth and the Jungvolk in town. Brother Len was promoted to Jungzug Führer, a sort of platoon leader. He proudly showed off his dark green shoulder cord. It was pitch black that night when we walked home. The black-out was strictly enforced and not a light could be seen except for the glow of cigars and cigarettes as soldiers stood smoking around their tanks or trucks. Someone in one of the factory offices switched on a light without pulling the blackout curtain. Mr. Vink, the local air raid warden, was soon on hand. "Lights out, dammit!" he shouted. "Switch those lights out now!"

"May I throw a stone through the window?" I asked Mr. Vink.

"You just leave things to me and get home," he replied.

In those days it was fairly common to have a brick thrown through your window if you violated the blackout regulations.

We got home and Mom switched on the radio. There were no planes in PQ 161 that night, but the announcer said that there was an infiltration of a few enemy recon planes in PQ 52, which was to the north of us over the Ruhr area. Far off to the north, we later saw some searchlights probing the sky. We finally went to bed at 11:00 PM. The next day would be Dad's birthday, so we wished him a happy birthday in our dreams.

Banging, crashing and engine noises woke us up about 4:00 AM. What in hell was going on? Len and I ran downstairs. Mom was shouting "Air raid! Get into the cellar!" Before we could open the hatch of the shelter, the noise increased. Planes were flying overhead in a westerly direction. We realized there was something else going on. This was no air raid.

Outside, hundreds of truck and tank engines roared into action. At long last our mighty Wehrmacht was on the move again, no doubt to tell the French to mind their own business. Columns of trucks and armor formed up on the road. Dim blue lights were shining from concealed lamps. Mr. Vink was heard shouting "lights out," but nobody took notice of him. It was now 4:30 AM, May 10, and Dad's birthday. Heck, what a birthday he must be having. Slowly the armor and trucks formed into line with field police directing the traffic. Dispatch riders on their heavy Zundapps or BMW motorcycles, machine guns mounted on sidecars, weaved in and out of traffic. Riders on small solo DKW bikes, hell-bent to get there first, wherever they were going, raced well ahead of the avalanche of other vehicles. High above, planes by the hundreds were heading west—Stukas, Flying Pencils, the dreaded Dornier Do-17, Heinkels, HE-111—all protected by a swarm of Messerschmitt Bf-109s and Bf-110s.

West of us, only 12 miles away, was Holland, and I thought it was funny that all the might of the Wehrmacht was rolling and flying in that direction. What had the Dutch done to us? We had some good friends in Holland, in Venlo, Tegelen and Roermond. We had often visited them and shopped in the towns where coffee and other goods were cheaper than in Germany. Of course, if you bought too much coffee or tobacco in Holland, the border guard on the German side sometimes confiscated the goods, but we lived not far from the border crossing and the guards knew most of us so they closed their eyes. At times we even used to smuggle the stuff across. We knew every cow path in the densely wooded area along the border, and never got caught in an illegal border crossing. Surely, I thought, our Wehrmacht is not going to attack Holland because some shopkeepers had sold a few pounds too much coffee to an honest German?

The 6:00 AM news on the radio told us all about it. Hitler, then Goering, then Goebbels spoke. They told us that the Tommies were hell-bent on violating Dutch territory and had landed some divisions on the coast of northern Holland. They said that the Tommies were going to attack Germany from that direction. Hitler then said that our mighty Wehrmacht was coming to the aid of the Dutch people and on and on it went. We had heard it all before six weeks earlier, when Germany had invaded Denmark and Norway under the pretext that Britain was going to occupy those countries. Of course there was no school that day, so we watched the goings from the garden. There were no comings. The last column of hardware left our section of town at daylight and everything went quiet nearby, but to the north of us, on the main highway two miles away, the armor was still heading toward Holland. The air traffic never did stop that day. At 10:00 AM we could hear some rumbling, like far off thunder, out to the west. It was no doubt artillery fire, coming from somewhere in the vicinity of Venlo on the River Maas, just over the border in Holland. We realized at once that somewhere in that direction a battle was going on, but at 6:00 AM Goebbels had told us on the radio that the British had landed on the northern Dutch coast, and that coast was over 200 miles from us. Now it was 10:00 AM and a battle was being fought somewhere about 15 miles west of us. How did the British army manage to cover 200 miles in just four hours? We shook our heads in disbelief.

At the dinner table, Granddad Willem was not so sure about the British around Venlo. "I bet you, the Nazis are attacking Holland," he grumbled. As I said before, Granddad Willem was a true Prussian. He would have gone through hell and high water for the Kaiser, but he had no time for the Nazis and told anybody so, if they cared to listen. It was not yet all that dangerous to denounce the Nazis, so he knew he was still relatively safe as long as he spoke his mind inside the house or discussed events with good friends. By the time the Nazis started arresting people for defeatist talk, Granddad Willem had died.

The next news broadcast was a different story. Goebbels said that the Dutch had actually allowed the British into Holland and had taken up arms to blow the Reich to bits, and that Germany was only rightfully retaliating and things were going well. A bridge near Venlo had been blown sky high by the Dutch, but our Pioneers (engineers) had thrown a pontoon bridge across the river and now the Wehrmacht was advancing right on schedule. Venlo was captured and our tanks were already far to the west of Roermond.

Granddad Willem just shook his head and mumbled something like, "They'll never sell us any more coffee or tobacco in Venlo."

"Stop smoking," Mom answered. "It's better for your health anyway."

Granddad stormed out of the room and went over to Aunt Carol's place, thick blue smoke coming from his pipe.

Day after day the radio brought more optimistic news. In school, we followed our Wehrmacht's advance on our atlases. Eben Emael, the mighty Belgian fort on the Albert Canal, had been captured by a handful of our paratroopers. Sedan, Brussels, and Rotterdam had all been taken. Our army had the British surrounded near Dunkirk. The Dunkirk news we heard on the radio was unbelievably good: 1,000 British tanks captured, 1,000 airplanes shot down, 1,000 Knight's Crosses awarded to German heroes. Where was it all to end? No mention was made of any German losses. Maybe Dad was having an easy time in France, we thought. We knew he was in France by now because we had a letter from him dated June 10, saying all was well. However, on June 11 near Abbeville, Dad was stopped in his tracks by a British 22-pounder antitank gun. The gunner died but Dad and the commander got out lightly wounded.

We had not heard from Dad since the early part of June, but knowing full well there was a war going on, we just hoped from one day to the next to get mail from him. On a Sunday morning in midsummer, a letter arrived. (Yes, mail was delivered on Sundays in those days.) The letter was not from Dad, but from Granddad Zander, Mom's Dad, who was, as mentioned earlier, employed as a toolmaker in far off Nuremberg. His wife, Mom's mother, had died in 1937 and he now lived in a small apartment near the MAN (Maschinenfabrik Augsburg-Nürnberg) industrial factory where he worked. He told us that he had four weeks leave coming, and with Luxembourg now occupied by the German army, there was no point in going there. If we didn't mind, he would get a train to Düsseldorf and a tram from there to us.

Mom sent a telegram and told him to come straight away. She had not seen her Dad for two years and she was surely looking forward to having him visit. The spare bedroom was cleaned and tidied up. I had not seen Granddad Zander for several years and couldn't even remember him, so I asked Brother Len, who knew everything, what Granddad Zander was like.

"He's okay, but he talks funny," Len said.

"You mean he's got a hair lip?" I asked.

Len laughed out loud. "No," he said, "he speaks Luxembourgish German and it sounds quite funny."

Three days later Granddad Zander arrived with two suitcases full of surprises. He had saved quite a bit of his wages so there were presents for all of us. Granddad Willem was presented with a new pipe and a pound of Landwyk Luxembourg tobacco. That made him smile from ear to appetite. I got a Schuko toy car, one of those wind-up things that will not run off the table. Mom got a winter coat, two shawls and a new coffee grinder. He had even brought a few ounces of coffee beans. God knows where he found them. We hadn't seen any real coffee for ages. There was none to be had in any store, and going to Venlo in Holland for a visit was out of the question for now. Besides, I doubted if there was now any coffee left in Venlo. Dad probably had all of Venlo's coffee in his TD to bring home on his next leave. Aunt Carol received ten yards of curtain material from Granddad Zander. I have forgotten what Brother Len got. It must have been something unimportant.

During school vacation that summer, we played in the ripening wheat fields with the farmer chasing us out if we got caught. We let our kites fly, attended Jungvolk parades or lingered around the 88 guns. We had also by now made friends with the crews of the nearest quad 20mms. There were two of them, about a mile away on a small hill above an unused sand pit. Once every day the crew had to test fire all eight barrels to make sure the complex mechanism of the quads was working and that in an emergency the cannons would fire when required.

The quad 20mm (or, to call it by its real German name, the Leichte Flak Vierling Model 38), operated in principle the same way as an automatic pistol, where the recoil opens the chamber for the next round to be pushed in from a spring-loaded magazine. The gun was first developed as a single barrel cannon on a two-wheel chassis that was towed behind a halftrack. A good crew could be ready to fire in 12 seconds. Speed is essential in a fighter-bomber attack, and the guns were first developed for that purpose. Later, the gun was also used in ground operations and was quite effective, especially when the mobile quads came into use. Enemy infantry was fearful of the quads because of their high rate and concentration of fire.

When home-based air defense became critical, after the first British sorties into German airspace, the 88mm gun took a heavy toll on the high-flying attacking bombers. To counter the losses, Britain created the Intruder low-level fighter-bomber to attack known 88mm positions. The 88s were literally useless against this type of attack, so the 20mm gun was designated as protection for its big brothers. For even more firepower, quad 20mms were installed in concrete gun pits near 88mm positions. The quad was mounted on a turntable that could, with the turn of a wheel to the right of the number one gunner, swivel 360 degrees in about 12 seconds. Elevation was an astonishing 110 degrees, 20 degrees above the overhead point, a movement the number one gunner made by using a wheel on his left.

Firing the gun was by foot pedals. One pedal fired two diagonal barrels. By pressing two pedals, all four barrels fired. The gun could also fire one barrel at a time by pull of a lever. The rate of fire was, of course, determined by several factors: the number of planes in range, the time taken to change the magazines, and the time taken to bring the magazines up to the loaders. The loaders sat on metal stools mounted to the gun on either side, and swiveled in their chairs when the gun was in operation. The magazine handlers had to follow the movement of the gun to keep in touch with the loaders.

I can say that in an average attack, our quads could fire about 800 rounds each per minute. We could throw up a curtain of fire of nearly 2,000 rounds per minute, which the fighter-bomber pilots knew and tried every conceivable means to defeat. The ammunition was 20mm tracer rounds tipped with a fuse such that the round exploded on impact. Thousands of rounds, of course, missed, and to avoid a hail of shells raining down on our own population and towns, missed rounds disintegrated after a certain time or distance, usually four to five miles. The empty brass cases ejected into a metal box at the front of the quad. Depending on the action, the box had to be emptied quite often, and the shells collected for reuse.

The number one gunner, called the K-1, sat in the center behind the gun. Coordinates and range information was given to him by a rangefinder who stood well away from the piece. In charge of the two quads was an NCO or a lieutenant, a sergeant acted as a gunnery sergeant and also as chief mechanic responsible for the function of the weapon. When I first visited the quads, the test firing was usually done around 10:00 AM. I loved the noise and racket of all the barrels going off and usually I shouted for more. The gunner, more often than not, obliged.

They had a lazy time up there in 1940. There wasn't much fighter-bomber activity around. The main bomber stream did not come within the range of the quads, and our 88s and fighters could take care of them. The quad crew would have plenty of work to do later, though.

At long last a letter arrived from Dad. We crowded around Mom to hear the latest news, where he was and what he was doing. I was anxious to hear whether he managed to get any coffee beans and chocolate out of Venlo, but it wasn't good news. Mom's face was going pale, but soon she recovered and told us to sit down and listen. She said that Dad had been wounded near Abbeville, receiving a minor gash on the head and a few small shrapnel wounds in his left leg. He was now in a military hospital in Flushing, Holland but he was going to be transferred to a hospital in Bottrop. Bottrop was in the Ruhr area of Germany, only 40 miles from us, and Mom said that she would go there as soon as she could find out how to get there. Transport by train was not very reliable and timetables had been unreliable since 1939. Of course we wanted to go as well, especially me, as I was going to ask Dad about those coffee beans. He hadn't mentioned anything in his letter about them.

Mom was adamant. She wanted to go by herself. She said that maybe we could visit later if Dad was going to be in Bottrop for a while. Granddad Willem said that his friend, Mr. Kersken from the food factory, had a delivery truck that ran twice a week to Oberhausen, not far from Bottrop. He would go over to Mr. Kersken's and find out the details. Later Granddad came back and told Mom that a truck was leaving at 8:30 AM for Oberhausen and Gladbeck in the Ruhr and Mr. Kersken had given instructions to the driver to drop Mom off at the nearest tram that went to Bottrop.

Mom packed a few clothes and things for Dad, saying that she would only stay a few days and perhaps the next delivery truck could pick her up. Granddad Willem said that he would arrange it with Mr. Kersken, but that Mom should telephone the factory from the hospital so the driver would know where and when to come and fetch her. Later that night in our bedroom I asked Brother Len, who knew everything, if he had any idea what happened to Dad's TD and the Dutch coffee beans.

"Probably shot to pieces, coffee beans and all," he said.

I was a bit annoyed about Dad having his TD shot to pieces. He was only the driver, and what was his gunner doing at the time? Counting coffee beans, I suppose.

Mom left the next morning for Bottrop, leaving our two Granddads in charge of us and the house. She took the letter from Dad as well, just in case a funny Nazi official wanted to know what she was doing in a factory truck on delivery business. Len and I went over to the 88s across the field. On the way there we picked a sack of greens for the rabbits, filling it with clover and dandelions. We now had quite a collection of the little crunchers, maybe thirty, and Granddad Willem was always busy with hammer and nails adding more hutches. We also had eight chickens. Real chicken feed was not obtainable in those days, so Granddad Willem developed his own: boiled potato peelings, some bran from the food factory, stale bread and crushed eggshells. That was all mixed with some water and the chickens loved it—eventually. Mind you, in the beginning they looked suspiciously at this concoction, but I guess they soon realized that there was a war on, so they pecked at it and got used to it. They even laid eggs.

One day, we were sitting on the parapet of the 88s loafing about, when the telephone rang. There was a bell above the bunker entrance so the man in charge could hear the phone ringing inside. There was also a loudspeaker outside, and the signalman inside could flip a switch so the crew at the guns could hear the caller. The caller was the guy in charge of the listening device we called the "big ear." He told the gunner that he could hear some really strange noises that he had not heard before at 50 kilometers due northwest approaching PQ 161.

"What do you want me to do? I can't report this. I don't know what it is," he said to the lieutenant in charge of the guns.

The lieutenant lifted the receiver on his field phone and told the guy to keep his ears cocked at the device and keep giving distance and direction. "Meanwhile, I will get in touch with Battery HQ and find out more," the lieutenant replied. He dialed Battery HQ, said something into the phone that Len and I couldn't understand, and then said, "Yes sir, understood." He turned round and shouted, "Alarm! On your positions!" Turning to Len and me he said, "You two need to get out of here. Things will be getting hot around here in a minute."

We dashed across the field toward home, forgetting the sack of rabbit food. Granddad Willem was in the garden picking gooseberries and

Granddad Zander was not to be seen. We didn't say anything about the incident at the guns, because we didn't want him to send us into the cellar for shelter. We hated going into the cellar. We explained to him that we had forgotten the rabbit food and would fetch it later.

From the northwest we now heard what we first thought was the sound of truck engines. We usually could determine from the sound of the engines what type of plane was approaching. There were, of course, different plane types that happened to have the same engines, but the silhouettes were different and our recognition was seldom wrong. We usually knew what was coming, but this sound we hadn't heard before. Granddad Willem did not care about aircraft or engines. His military knowledge went no further than a machine gun, or at most, a 210mm artillery piece made in 1914.

All of a sudden, the air raid sirens started up. Granddad looked up and motioned us under the doorway, our very own grandstand. Then we saw them, about 45 four-engine bombers accompanied by a swarm of twin Vickers Wellingtons. We knew the Wellingtons, but their big brothers were unknown to us as yet. Our 88s roared into action. The quads above the sand pit followed suit in the forlorn hope that, sooner or later, one of the planes would come into their range.

"They got one, they got one, our 88s got one," Len was shouting at the top of his voice. Yes, sure enough, the 88s had found the mark. A big four-engine bird was well ablaze. A wing trundled down to earth and hit the ground half a mile away in a field. Four parachutes, like huge white blossoms, opened up. Then the stricken plane crashed into a field about four miles away with an ear splitting bang. The four parachutes landed not too far from the 88 gun pits and we saw seven or eight men from the crew running over to them, pistols at the ready. An open Volkswagon Kübel came racing by with several soldiers in it. They had cocked rifles in their arms and turned into the field where the crew of the 88 had meanwhile surrounded the airmen and were marching them toward the main road by our place. When they reached the tarmac road where the VW was waiting, we noticed that one of them was bleeding from his left arm. Clad in a sort of brown uniform with leather hats, they didn't look much different from our airmen, I thought. They were standing with their hands up and probably waiting for a truck to take them to a POW camp. These were the first enemy soldiers I had seen since the war started. Of course, we had seen Polish POWs working on roads around the area, but this was different. This was personal,

I thought. They had come to bomb our homes and now we had witnessed their doom. I threw a handful of gooseberries at them. Granddad Willem slapped me behind the ears.

"Stop this nonsense boy, or else," he said (and I knew what the "else" could be). "They are soldiers like our soldiers, but just happen to be fighting on the other side."

A truck soon came up to take the four men away. We wanted to get to the site of the wreck to find out what sort of plane the 88 had shot down, but the authorities had cordoned off the site and guards stood watch. The 6:00 PM news on the radio told us all about it. A fleet of about a hundred enemy bombers had penetrated the Reich's air defenses in broad daylight and had attacked the Remscheidt and Solingen Steel works with minimal success. In the attack, 17 enemy bombers had been shot down, eight of them Vickers, the others four-engine Halifaxes. So there, we had another plane to put on our chart. I thought Halifax was a funny name for a plane. It sounded like a new brand of toothpaste or soap powder.

So our 88s had deservedly gotten another white ring on their barrels. Another flak battery to the north of town had also scored and shot down a Wellington that crashed a few miles away, barely missing Dad's street car shed and a hospital. Nobody survived that crash.

Mom came home that Friday from Bottrop with the news that Dad was on the mend, that he would be given convalescent leave and would be home shortly. "And guess what?" she added. "He's been awarded the bronze wound badge and the KVK (War Merit Cross) 2nd Class, and he will be considered for a sergeant's course in due time!"

"Is he getting a new TD?" I demanded to know.

"I don't know about that," she said, "but let's all be happy that he is alright."

So life went back to what we accepted as normal. There were still 50 pounds of gooseberries to be picked and red currants too, and Mom and Aunt Carol had to can them.

To us the summer of 1940 was a happy one. Holland, Belgium, France and, sadly, Granddad Zander's Luxembourg, had been occupied by our Wehrmacht. Soon it would be England's turn, we figured. Surely after that, we thought, peace would reign in Europe with Germany the dominant nation.

We spent the last two weeks of our summer holiday near Kleve in a large Hitler Youth camp, a sort of Boy Scout Jamboree, but with stricter

discipline and military-related education. We learned orienteering, cam-
ouflaging, more aircraft identification, football and volleyball, and how
to stand to attention, march, and that sort of thing. The older boys even
took rifle practice and shot with live rounds. By the third day, Brother
Len, who knew everything, could tell us exactly how many parts there
were in a 98 K carbine. At night we guarded the camp, not that we
expected any intruders. There were none, but the youth leader said it
was good training. We sat around campfires when no air raid was on
and sang endless Nazi songs, slept in tents and got up at 7:00 AM for
flag parade and breakfast. What a time we had. Our usual morning
shout of "Heil Hitler!" was twice as good as in school. I loved it and
could have stayed there until the end of the war.

On the fifth night in camp I was assigned guard duty from midnight
to 2:00 AM. My job was to guard the water well, one of those round
brick built structures with a roof over it. A bucket on a chain could be
lowered by turning a handle on the side. The bucket would fill up down
in the well and could be raised again. This was our sole water supply in
camp and during daylight hours there was constant coming and going
at the well to fill milk churns with water. The camp leader supervised
the water distribution and on one occasion he found two cigarette butts
in the upcoming bucket. Everybody had to attend a special parade that
day. Pockets had to be emptied and the contents displayed in front of
each boy. Strip searches, luckily, were forbidden. There were limits even
for the troop commanders. Needless to say, no cigarettes were found at
the parade. The culprit had obviously left them in his pocket, but from
that night on, the well had to be guarded.

At five minutes to midnight our troop leader took me to the well to
relieve another member of our troop. The troop commander told me
that absolutely nobody was allowed near the well. He even gave me the
password for the night, "Bettlaken" (bed sheet).

"If anyone unauthorized approaches the well, what am I supposed
to do?" I asked the leader.

"Shoot him and then ask for the password," he said.

"Sir," I asked, "shoot him with what?"

He handed me a broomstick that was leaning against the wall surrounding the well. With a grin on his face, he then gave me a smart
"Heil Hitler" and was off.

All campfires had by then been doused. British bombers did not
arrive over Germany until after midnight in those days, but no bombers

came. What did come was a crouching shadow. I could see it coming between the bushes and I nearly peed myself. Then I realized that I was responsible for the welfare of several hundred compatriots, so I grabbed the broomstick and shouted, "Bettlaken! Who goes there? Give us the password!" Oh my, I thought. I had just given the password away! But the answer from the dark shadow was "woof, woof," and a big black dog came up to me, tail wagging. Well, that was my contribution to defending the Third Reich's water resources, but no more cigarette butts were found. We took the train home after two happy weeks. School was to start the following Monday and the summer of 1940 was coming to an end.

The latest news from the front told us that Herr Meyer (a.k.a. Goering) was still sorting out the British, who by now, he told us, were using up their last Spitfires and Hurricanes to defend the island. After that, he continued, the great invasion of England would go ahead. The news sounded to us like what we had heard before, after the episode at Dunkirk. He had promised us the same thing then, and now it was September and the Luftwaffe was still no where near defeating the Tommies. Everyday the newsman on the radio told us that the British had lost another 50 or 60 planes. I did a quick reckoning. If our Luftwaffe had shot down 50 or 60 planes a day since the Dunkirk fiasco, that would add up to about 4,500 planes, give or take a few. Good Lord, where did Britain get all their planes? Not to mention the pilots and ground crews necessary to keep them up in the air! And they also had a respectable bomber fleet that was harassing our country in ever increasing sorties. So it was that another nagging doubt was lodged in my mind about Herr Meyer's victory proclamations.

CHAPTER 6

On to England

November brought some more good news over the radio. This time the announcement was an honest one. Even the magic eye seemed to smile. Our Luftwaffe had finished a mass attack on the English industrial city of Coventry and completely destroyed it, or so we thought. "Now let the invasion of England begin," the radio announcer said. But the Führer had things on his mind other than invading England, so it seemed. We thought he might now go for the Balkans or Sweden but nothing came of that.

November was wet, nasty, and cold. We had already started digging in the garden, getting it ready for an early spring planting. The broad beans had to be planted in December but the garden turned into a mud bath. My uncle gave Brother Len a lovely little white Spitz dog as an early Christmas present. He was beautiful and ran all over the place. Mom said something about having another mouth to feed, but Dad persuaded her to let us keep it. He was small and could live on scraps. Besides, we argued, he could watch the potatoes and vegetables in the shed, sort of a guard dog.

The following night we had some excitement, but sadly two of our neighbors died in it. Dad was on the trolley's working a late shift and it was 11:00 PM. He hadn't come in yet, and was no doubt in a pub somewhere with his mates. Brother Len and I were sitting at the table playing a game called Ludo. I was sitting with my back to the window. We were in the middle of an argument. Brother Len was a number one cheater and never could, or would, loose a Ludo game. The radio was on Drahtfunk standby with the green magic eye twinkling when an announcement came.

"Achtung! Achtung! Enemy planes approaching PQ 161!" the announcer declared. We knew that was us, but it didn't bother us much. Every night a few planes, or sometimes a single recon plane, came into PQ 161 or PQ 52 near us. Most were harmless intruders taking night photographs of industrial complexes or communication lines. We heard an aircraft, and it was coming in quite low, maybe 2,000 feet up, judging by the noise of the engines. Single recon planes had been given the nickname "Iron Gustav." The flak never bothered with them because they had no bombs, as we knew from experience. Machine guns and speed were their defense. Even the German night fighters usually left them alone. Why waste precious aviation gas on a recon when the main bomber stream was the real danger?

The small plane kept circling. Maybe he was taking photos of the railroad track leading to the food factory. He was now gaining altitude we noticed, but still going in circles. We stayed inside. We always had the funny notion that a recon plane could see an individual person at night, but of course this was utter nonsense. Then all of a sudden we thought the end of the world had come. There was an almighty explosion. Window glass flew everywhere. A flowering Begonia pot on the windowsill behind me hit my head and knocked me out stone cold. When I came around after a few minutes, I had a lump on my head half the size of a hen's egg. Nobody knew what had happened at first. We had not heard the characteristic whistling of a bomb coming down. Mom held a wet towel on the bump to stop the swelling.

The 88s now opened up belatedly. They had been quiet while the recon was circling and now the culprit and initiator of this commotion had gotten clean away. Ambulances and fire engines were racing past outside. Mom went outside to check for any damage but only a few windowpanes were broken. Dad came rushing in, nearly taking the door with him, telling us that something big had exploded just to the west of us and he was going to investigate. We wanted to come as well, but Dad got really angry with us.

"You two stay where you are and don't move from the house until I get back, understood?" he said. We nodded in obedience with mouths and lips set at twenty past eight. We were too excited to go to bed. It was Saturday anyway and Mom said we could wait for Dad. He did come back at 1:00 AM, filthy and dusty with a grim face.

"Mr. and Mrs. Ahlen got killed. Something big blew their house up," Dad said.

We were shocked. The Ahlen couple had been good friends of our family and Dad had played cards with Mr. Ahlen in the pub only the night before. They were both in their early sixties. What was it that hit their house? Nobody had an immediate answer. The following day an investigating team from a bomb disposal company arrived to search for clues. Later that day we had the news. Dad had that Sunday off and was able to be present at the site in his capacity as a member of the Wehrmacht.

A searchlight had momentarily gotten hold of the recon plane the night before, but the operator had let go of the plane when he noticed something falling out of it. The guy said he saw a parachute open with what looked like a huge gray steel cylinder slung underneath it. The searchlight operator could not follow the mysterious parachute because the light could not be angled low enough. Seconds later came the explosion, and a huge flame shot toward the sky. The investigating team came to the conclusion that this was one of the new aerial mines dropped from low altitude suspended on parachutes. The British had tried them out a few days previously on the Krupp works in Essen. They called them "blockbusters," and Mr. and Mr. Ahlen had been on the receiving end of this one.

We walked over to what was left of the house. It was only a few hundred yards away. The mine probably was dropped to hit the factory railroad but had missed by half a mile. There was a huge crater filled with dirty water, and a heap of still smoldering rubble. A policeman was standing on guard duty. The Ahlens had been found dead in this mess early in the morning.

Tuesday was the funeral and the whole neighborhood was present in church. In church I vowed to God that once I became old enough to be a soldier, I would pay those English back for sure. I still had a big lump on my head from the begonia pot, so on the way home from church I asked Dad if he could put a word in for me at the Party or Air Defense Command. I might be eligible for a wounded medal.

"If the war goes on like it is now, there might come a day when every living German will have a wounded medal," came Dad's answer.

We were able to save our coal ration during the summer because Mom did the cooking on a wood fire. There was still plenty of wood around in 1940. In many parts of Germany lignite could be found from as shallow as six feet deep. Lignite, or "brown coal," is made of decayed wood like ordinary coal, but normal coal is like stone (appropriately called "stone coal" in Germany), while lignite is soft and brown. It is a very good substitute for normal coal. Huge power stations in Germany, even now in the twenty-first century, are fired with brown coal. It is dug out in open cast mines that are somewhat like gravel pits, and mixed with water. Then it is compressed into brick sized blocks and dried.

These bricks, or as they are called in Germany, "briquettes," are sold by the hundred weight to households. In World War II special coal ration cards were used, and we would stack up the bricks in the coal shed. Thermal unit for thermal unit, they were not as efficient as stone coal, but they were better than wood and stored longer as well. We collected our ration from Mr. Nelles, the coal merchant, and filled up our shed in anticipation of a bad winter to come, but as happens so frequently, one expects the worst and reality is different. Winter came late, well into February, and by that time we were already looking forward to spring.

Christmas had been a quiet affair. Mom received the usual presents—shawls, slippers and warm stockings. We had a few new board games to occupy our minds. Dad got hold of a bottle of Schnapps and a bottle of real French brandy, spoils of war I reckoned. Dad also bought Mom a new carpet beater. We didn't have an electric vacuum cleaner in those days. Ordinary folks couldn't afford them. Only privileged Party people and the awfully rich had them. Hitler would have had more support from the women if he had authorized the manufacture of a Volks-Hoover instead of the Volkswagen or the Volksempfänger, the small Nazi radio that was also called the "Goebbels Schnauze" (Goebbels' big mouth).

The carpet beater was of nice wicker stick construction with a pattern in the center. It was first tried out two days after Christmas—on me. Brother Len and I had gotten into a pillow fight and I hit Mom's big flower vase that had been a gift from Aunt Carol on Mom's wedding day back in 1928. It broke into a lot of pieces. As a result I was on the receiving end of the carpet beater. Mom saw that it worked well for this purpose, and so did I. Brother Len got away free as usual. He knew everything, even how to avoid a thrashing from Mom.

What I can remember about Christmas 1940 is that we had plenty to eat; candy, chocolate, boxes of cookies. There was sweet lemonade, ice cream and puddings, not to mention the good dinners. Granddad Willem put the tree up. He was in charge of that every year. He had always managed to cut a tree in the dead of night in some local forest without being caught. He was a genius in that respect. With eyes like an owl and a nose like a terrier, he could smell a forest ranger at midnight a mile away.

Great Granddad, who helped kick Louis Napoleon's butt at Sedan back in 1870, had left us his porcelain nativity set. Granddad Willem told us that it was bought in 1852 and ever since it had been displayed at Christmas time. Granddad Willem had the knack of making a beautiful scene around it with the manger, sheep, small trees and even little chickens made from clay. Neighbors used to knock on the door at Christmas time and ask to see the display. Even Father Urban, the local priest, used to come and admire it. (I'm glad to say that the nativity set is still in the family. I have it now and set it up every year.)

The day after my mother gave me the beating, I was still nursing a sore behind. I was seriously thinking about reporting Mom to the local Nazi Party leader for maltreating a valued future member of Hitler's Wehrmacht, when a Volkskübelwagen stopped outside. It was a military vehicle with a small triangular pennant mounted on the hood displaying a green field with an Edelweiss flower in the center. From the back emerged a tall thin person dressed in a high-ranking officer's uniform. We had just fed the rabbits when the car stopped. I nudged Dad. "There's an officer by the door, Dad."

Brother Len, who knows everything, whispered, "It's a General from the Gebirgsjäger" (or Mountain Troops).

Dad must have recognized the officer because he went to the door and shook hands with him. No one shouted "Heil Hitler." We gathered around and Mom came and told us to wash our faces and hands first, but we stayed put. We were eager to know who the officer was. We all went indoors and Dad then introduced the person as Emil, a relative who had married Mom's cousin Veronika. Uncle Emil (as we called him) was in charge of the Mountain Troops in Norway and was on his way to observe a troop maneuver in the Eifel Mountains. We were awestruck and admired all his medals. What a pity school was not in session! We would have loved to take Uncle Emil to school and show him off. Not everyone had a high-ranking officer in the family—and a Mountain Troop Officer at that, not a simple infantry or artillery guy! What a time to live in, I thought.

Inwardly I was thanking the Führer for giving us a general in the family. He said he could only stay overnight and asked if we had room for his driver. We gave Uncle Emil the room Granddad Zander had vacated and the driver was put up at Aunt Carol's place next door. The staff car was parked in the factory yard and Granddad Willem made sure the gate was locked. We all sat up until 1:00 AM. They talked about relatives and old times but not about the war. I found that rather distressing, but then Mom dished up a first class dinner with pudding and real coffee and it was Christmas all over again.

Only after dinner did the talk float to war matters. Dad asked how things were shaping up in Norway, and Uncle Emil. told us that the British, at least for the time being, had given up the idea of landing in Norway. The battleships Scharnhorst and Gneisenau, in conjunction with the cruiser Hipper, had given the British a bloody nose in a sea battle just south of the island of Jan Mayen, and had sunk the fleet carrier Glorious and a destroyer. The British claimed heavy damage to the Gneisenau, but that was nonsense. The Gneisenau had hit a mine but was now in Kiel for repairs and would soon be underway again. Scharnhorst was back in Germany too, and soon the mighty battleship Tirpitz would be moved to Norway. Tirpitz and Bismarck had just been commissioned and it would only be a matter of time before they joined in the fray against the British. This was all war talk between a corporal of a TD (and now, for the time being, a street car driver) and an officer of the Mountain Division, and we didn't understand much of it. I did ask though if the Scharnhorst and Gneisenau had given the British real hell, and he said he was pretty sure they had.

I said, "Good, because those Tommies killed Mr. and Mrs. Ahlen the other night with a parachute mine."

When Dad explained to him the details of that incident, Uncle Emil said there might be worse times to come and that he was glad to sit out the war in Norway. They finished the bottle of French brandy, but I was already asleep, dreaming of Mountain Troops riding on parachute mines with swastikas painted on the sides. Next morning, in a light drizzle, they departed for the Eifel Mountains to inspect the troops. Dad said to call anytime he happened to be in the area. Then with a slight salute they sped down the road.

"What a nice man," Mom said. She had never met him before and only knew what Veronika had told her in letters. Sadly, we never met him again. He was killed in an air raid in June 1944 somewhere in Romania.

On New Year's Eve, Mom, Dad and Granddad Willem went to a pub just half a block away. Dad left us the Drahtfunk on the radio and told us to fetch him if an alert came for PQ 161. We were allowed to stay up until they came home and we could play Ludo if we wanted. I wanted to draw pictures of parachute mines, edelweiss flowers, TDs and coffee beans, but Brother Len was hell bent on Ludo so I gave in, knowing full well that Len was going to win the contest as usual with his cheating. We had had the game for two years now, and I hadn't won once because of his cheating, but saying this openly into Len's face was to invite a kick up the backside, so I kept quiet as usual. The first game I lost, naturally. Halfway through the second game, I was already two points behind when the loudspeaker on the radio crackled and the magic eye blinked at us.

"Achtung! Achtung! Enemy bomber formations approaching PQ 161 and PQ 55!"

"Thank you, British bombers!" I cried. "You have saved me from yet another Ludo defeat!"

We stormed outside, forgetting Dad's orders for a minute. Far to the north, searchlights were probing the sky and the faint hum of aircraft engines reached our cocked ears. This wasn't our area. It was in PQ 55 to the north, so why spoil Dad's New Year's Eve party? Besides, our 88s had not fired yet.

All seemed quiet across the field in the gun pits. The crew was probably having a good time in the pub and had left just a skeleton crew with the guns. Some flak had opened fire many miles away toward the Ruhr, but the distance was too great to hear the firing. We could only see the flashes of exploding shells in the sky. We watched in silence until a bright light lit up the sky. The far away 88s had stopped their fire and now we noticed some red and green flares high up in the sky. This was the sign, as we knew, that our Messerschmitt night fighters were up. The flares told the flak crews to cease fire to avoid hitting our planes, which were busy breaking up the bomber formation.

The commotion high up to the north now shifted slightly toward us. Orange and green tracers crisscrossed the night sky as bombers and night fighters exchanged cannon fire. The searchlights had switched off to avoid lighting up our own planes. All of this was happening in total silence. The fighting above was, as yet, too far away from us to be heard. It was like watching a fireworks display from five miles away.

All of a sudden we saw a plane on fire, about 8,000 feet up, drifting slowly in our direction. We watched for about a minute as the plane circled and got lower and nearer. Then it abruptly changed course and made a beeline straight for us. Now it was high time to alert the partygoers and break up the festivities in the pub. It was 11:45 PM when we burst through the door. The party was in full swing with only 15 minutes to go before 1941 arrived.

"There's a plane on fire and heading this way!" Len shouted at the top of his voice. There was one second of silence, then beer mugs, schnapps bottles and sandwiches tumbled to the floor. Everyone made for the door.

"Couldn't those dirty English bastards have waited until after midnight?" a flak soldier screamed. "Look at the place now!" and he pointed at the broken bottles littering the room.

Once everyone was outside, Dad and Mr. Vink took charge of things. The burning plane was still 1,000 feet up and a few miles away, but it was getting dangerously closer with every second.

Dad shouted at the flak crew, "You men get to your guns and see if you can get a range and keep the other bombers away from here." Then he turned to Mr. Vink and said, "Now let's see where he is heading. If he keeps on that track, he will end up somewhere near the cemetery behind the church."

The plane, meanwhile, was too low for the 88s to have a good shot at it, so we all watched in fascination as it came nearer and nearer. It was maybe 200 feet up when it silently glided by us, just a short distance away. It was a twin engine and the propellers were feathered. Only the crackling flames and sparks were audible. There was something familiar about the shape of the plane, we thought. Then we noticed it. Yes, it was the black and white cross on the fuselage we could see in the light of a burning wing. It was one of our own ME-110 night fighters.

"Hit the ground," Dad shouted and we made ourselves as small as possible.

The plane glided smoothly into a field of clover just short of the cemetery, and lay there burning fiercely.

"Don't get near it," some Flak man shouted. "There'll be no bombs on board our fighters, but there'll be but plenty of tracer ammo and magnesium flares."

It was all an anticlimax. There was no explosion, just a few crackles as the plane burned. He had probably spent his ammunition on the bombers. A fire engine came racing up the road and turned into the field. Belatedly, the alert sirens started to blare away as the fire fighters pointed their strong lights at the burning wreck.

"Lights out!" Mr. Vink shouted.

What a farce! There was a burning plane that lit up half the town and this idiot was shouting lights out. With foam and some portable CO_2 jets, the fire crew soon had the blaze under control. It was now just a smoldering wreck but there was no sign of any of the three crewmembers. At a respectful distance, so as not to hinder the fire crew, stood half the town discussing what had to be done next.

"Happy New Year," came a loud voice from the 88 gun pits.

"Shut it, man," Dad replied to the greetings. Turning to us he said, "We nearly got us one of our own planes there. Oh, never mind. Happy New Year then!" He gave Mom, who was standing next to him, a kiss on the cheek. "You people stay away from the wreck. I'm going over to the factory to get the night porter to phone the air defense commander," he said.

"It's been taken care of, Lou," replied a firefighter. "We alerted them before we moved out."

A few men now searched the field in the dark to see if they could find any clues about the missing crew, but without results. Half an hour later, a Wehrmacht Opel Blitz drove up. The canvas on the back was lifted and out stepped the disheveled but happy crewmembers to survey their once mighty fighting machine.

"Lucky lot you are," someone said. "We nearly took a bead on you." It was a flak man who had uttered the remark.

"No harm done," a crewmember with the insignia of a NCO answered. "We bailed out over yonder and landed smack in the middle of a Wehrmacht camp that wasn't exactly pleased that we dropped in during a party."

"You ruined ours too," Dad said, "but never mind. Happy New Year! How come you were shot down?"

"Sorry," the pilot said, "I have to make a report first for my station commander, but let me tell you one thing. When you are up there in pitch darkness searching for bombers, you can't see them until they are only 100 feet away. They can muster eight cannons against our four."

"I see," Dad said, "but we sure are glad you made it safely back to Earth."

Another staff car drove up now with a Luftwaffe colonel inside. He stepped out and walked towards the flyers who stood to attention. Without the "Heil Hitler" salute, he shook hands with his men, and we could see that he was glad they had come down from heaven without a scratch.

Most of the sightseers had dispersed by now. The colonel came over to Dad, who saluted smartly. "Thank you for looking after things here and organizing things. Are you the Air Warden here?" he asked.

"No, Sir, I'm on a six months convalescent leave from my unit. Corporal Lou Gehlen, Assault Gun Battalion. I'm driving the local tram just now because they are short of drivers. I have permission from my commanding officer, sir."

The colonel smiled and said, "I believe you, Corporal. Well, we must be off now. Sorry to have interrupted your New Year celebrations. Happy New Year and Heil Hitler." He walked to his staff car where the crewmen were waiting, anxious to get back to base to have a celebration drink themselves.

Dad shook his head. "Happy New Year and Heil Hitler," he said all in one sentence. "Now let's get home and get some sleep. Festivities are postponed until one year from now."

It was 10:00 AM on January 1, 1941 when I woke up. It was a beautiful clear but cold winter morning. Len and I took a stroll over to the ME-110 crash site. A Hanomag halftrack with a recovery crane on the back was busy loading the bits and pieces of the downed plane onto a trailer. There wasn't much left, really, that was in one piece except maybe the two engines. The rest was just charred remains. We asked the sergeant in charge of the salvage operation if we could have just one small piece as a souvenir.

"Go and help yourself. But no flares or ammo," he said. "There might be some still lying around."

I got myself a piece of aluminum from the fuselage. It was not much to look at, but Brother Len, he who knew everything, naturally, and true to his ability, found the burned out gyroscope. He stuffed the thing into his pocket, grinning all over. He always manages somehow, I thought.

School was out until January 10, so we had plenty of free time on our hands. With our neighbors' kids, we played endless games of soccer using a deflated tennis ball. The games were played six versus six, in the parking lot outside the food factory. There was no traffic about, so we had lots of room. Later, after we ran ourselves stupid behind that little tennis ball, we got our little wooden spinning tops out and, with a string whip in our hands, we threw our tops all over the parking lot.

One of our friends named Karl had a top that we used to call a "window jumper." Amazingly, if one hit the top just in the right place, it would take off like a golf ball and fly 50 yards or more. Where Karl found the thing he would not say. It was shaped like a small mushroom or a sock darner. Karl said that I could have a go hitting it, and that I had to give it a good whipping when the top hit the right speed. What he meant by that I did not know, but I gave it a few good whips and the window jumper did take off. Yes, it took off and it hit a window in the factory office.

"Now look what you have done!" Karl shouted, as bits of glass came raining down. Luckily the top bounced back, so we took off like greased lightning.

The Winterhilfswerk (WHW), the winter welfare organization to aid the Wehrmacht, came along that evening, knocking on doors and peddling little Bakelite airplanes for 20 Pfennings apiece. Len got a DO-17. I took a ME-110 in memory of the shot down plane from the night before. I asked if there was a Vickers Wellington in the box, as I wanted to play night fighter versus bomber, but the women said that they did not sell enemy planes.

Snow fell on January 9, the day before school started. We usually woke up at 7:00 AM from the clattering of horse-drawn wagons or a cart being pushed along the road. That morning the sounds were muffled. We looked out the window and there it was, a white winter wonderland. There were no snowplows in Germany in those days, so the white stuff just stayed where it fell and that was it. Everyone coped with it. The few trucks still running had snow chains around the wheels. We threw ashes on the pavement to make walking a bit easier. It was also a good way to get rid of the ashes.

There was no rabbit food to collect out in the fields. They had to live on hay, boiled potato peelings and bran, just like the chickens. I often wondered if those rabbits were going to lay eggs one day since they ate the same stuff as the hens. Granddad Willem had made a sled for us earlier that winter from an old wooden butter crate, which we appropriately named the "butter box Mercedes." It didn't have the fine looks of the mass manufactured sleds, but what it lacked in beauty it sure made up in performance.

We lived on top of a hill and it was about a mile to the bottom near downtown. With no traffic on the roads, we had the hill all to ourselves.

About a hundred kids assembled daily on those snowy winter days with their sleds, racing downhill and screaming at the ascending mob to get out of the way. Our butter box Mercedes beat them all by a mile. We went the farthest and fastest, usually ending up downtown by the butcher shop. Uphill we were the slowest. The thing was cumbersome and not easily pulled up a mile-long hill. The other kids could even carry their sleds on their backs, but it was out of the question with our contraption. The thing was simply too heavy. We asked Granddad Willem to drill some large holes into the wooden sides to take a bit of weight off but he said that was not possible. The butter box had to be strong, and later he fit us some iron rails under the wooden runners. That made the thing even faster by ten seconds, but heavier by five pounds as well. Brother Len had to help pull the sled uphill if he wanted a ride down. On my own I couldn't move it anyway.

Then school started. We stomped through two feet of snow, throwing snowballs at each other and at innocent people going about their business. On January 12, the teacher made an announcement. In the name of the Führer, Volk and Fatherland (and possibly a few scrap dealers as well), a collection of aluminum was to be held to aid in the building of aircraft. We were to bring to school any pots and pans or other stuff made from aluminum and deposit it all in the bicycle shed. Nobody had a bike, so the shed was as good a place as any. Then he added that those who brought any aluminum were exempt from a day's homework. Our cooking pots at home were made of cast iron, and I very much doubted that Mom would have given one of her pots to supplement the building of warplanes even if we had one in aluminum. I searched the field where the ME-110 had crashed a few weeks previously and found about a bucket full of small pieces, two pounds exactly. Well, better than nothing, I thought.

"Well done," the teacher said to me when I hauled my treasures into the classroom the next day.

"Am I excused from homework today, Sir?" I asked.

"Of course you are," he said.

I was elated and forgot to say the obligatory "Heil Hitler" to Miss Jansen who had just entered the classroom. Miss Jansen, an overt Nazi, was a very thin and bony person who taught the 8th grade girls. She looked something like a spider with two legs missing and her voice was as sharp as an SS dagger. She gave me a dressing down and a reminder that as a good Jungvolker, I was required to say the obligatory "Heil

Hitler" as a show of respect to a teacher every time I happened to meet one.

"Understood?" she asked.

"Yes, Miss Jansen," I said.

The snow melted eventually so the butter box Mercedes was stored away in the shed.

One day, a letter came from my Uncle Peter who was an NCO, a 1st sergeant in a flak unit in Konigsberg, East Prussia. He was Mom's brother, and the year before he had married a local girl named Gisela in that far away eastern corner of Germany. He had not been home since he had left for the east in 1939. He had met Aunt Gisela at a "victory over Poland" party. Aunt Gisela was a Protestant, which raised a few eyebrows in our strongly Catholic community when Mom told everyone. The letter said that he would be going to Nuremberg first to see Granddad Zander and after that he would visit us for two weeks, as he had four weeks leave coming. "Konigsberg is a long way from home," he said in the letter, and he would be glad to see the home folks again for a while.

Uncle Peter arrived in February, with Aunt Gisela in tow. As far as I remember, we had never met a Protestant person, so we naturally looked her up and down. We found that she didn't look any different than a normal person. Mom was really excited by their visit. Uncle Peter was in charge of an 88mm flak gun and had been awarded the flak medal for ten kills. That is, his gun had downed ten enemy planes in the Polish campaign. Dad dragged him to the pub the very first night to show him off to his mates. Aunt Gisela was at first treated with suspicion, but when everyone found out that she was a normal person, the same as the rest of us, they accepted her.

Uncle Peter and I walked over to the gun pits of the 88s and he introduced himself. They all shook hands and exchanged experiences. He noticed the two rings on the barrels.

"Two rings, 'ey? Well done," he said.

"Those Tommies are not easy shooting for us," one of the men said. "They come in at an altitude where we just about can't reach them."

"How high?" asked Uncle Peter.

"About 18,000 feet sometimes," the crewmember replied. "The crews use oxygen, you know."

"Well, ask your gunnery supply officer to get those new HB (high altitude exploding) rounds." Uncle Peter said. "I see you still use the older type HT (low altitude exploding) shells. The new ones reach 20,000 feet."

"Wow!" the guy exclaimed. "I'll remember that. We've heard of them, but so far we are still using what you see here. It's like throwing marbles at a tank. Of course our night fighters manage to get quite a few of them."

"And all the glory too," interrupted another gunner. "Your 88s shot down ten, you said? What were they?"

"Fokkers," came my Uncle's reply, resulting in a somewhat startled look. Another gunner shouted, "Fokkers are Dutch-made planes sold to Poland after 1918."

Uncle Peter and Dad got along well and they hung around the pub almost every night when Dad was on early shift and sometimes after the late shift as well. The pub was open until 1:00 AM. In a way, we were glad when Uncle Peter left. We hadn't seen much of Dad during his stay.

March was coming up fast and gardening work would start then. The rabbits were pretty busy too. We had almost sixty by now. It was a lot to feed when there were no greens about and potatoes were getting scarce.

There was a turnip bed in the field covered with straw and a foot of earth. "Go and dig some turnips from out behind the shed," Mom told me.

"It's too cold to dig," I whined, and besides, the ground is frozen solid"

"Look boy, we have to feed those chickens and rabbits," she said. "They can't eat old socks. Now get going!"

I would have gladly given those rabbits my old socks for dinner on that cold day just to avoid digging, but Mom was looking at the carpet beater. That made me pick up a spade and depart for the turnip bed. I managed to dig out two buckets full before I gave up, cold and exhausted. We chopped the turnips into little pieces and the rabbits were happy. It was a welcome change of diet after having bran and potato peelings for months. The result was another bunch of little bunnies a few weeks later.

This rabbit business was getting beyond a joke and putting a strain on our free time, not to mention the food we had to find for them. We asked Dad to kill a few for the dinner table, and for once he agreed. To make double sure that there would be no rabbit population explosion, he selected two bucks to be slaughtered. That would leave 13 little bunnies without a Dad and two does without a husband, but we didn't lose any sleep over it. We had to eat as well, and as for the two bucks? "Killed in action," we called it. There was a war on, after all.

Dad, knowing he had to pick up his soldiering duties and that it would probably be a long time before he came home again, gave Brother Len instructions on how to kill and dress a rabbit.

"I'll be away and Granddad Willem won't live forever, so you better make sure you know this business," Dad said.

The trick was to hit the rabbit with a heavy stick in a certain place right behind the ears. Dad showed Brother Len where it was. Well, it's hard to miss seeing a rabbit's ears, but Len made a mess of it. He hit his leg, missing the buck altogether, but in time he became quite an expert, a killer so to speak.

CHAPTER 7

Dad's Assignment

In mid-March, Dad's marching orders finally arrived. He was to report to his old unit, the 17th TD Battalion, which was somewhere near the town of Posen in what was once Poland. The Germans now called this the General Government of Warsaw. He had three days to get his things squared way, get his uniform cleaned, and say goodbye to his friends and family.

Mr. Abels of the Transit Authority was unhappy when Dad told him, but his job would be there for him whenever he came back. The local Wehrmacht quartermaster issued Dad a new pair of jackboots, and after inspecting Dad's orders, he also gave him a railroad ticket and wrote down our address. He issued Dad a pay book to give to Mom so she could collect his military pay once a month. Soon the last day of Dad's leave arrived. We didn't say much about it. We felt he wasn't eager to go, but war was war, and orders were orders. We all walked to the station with him to say our last goodbye, which was short and sharp, I thought. A hug, a kiss, and that was it. He boarded the train and pulled down the window on his compartment.

"Be sure you stay safe and out of trouble," Mom said with tears in her eyes.

"You too, Agnes, and good luck," Dad replied.

"Bring some coffee beans next time!" I shouted, but the train was already on the move. We waved until he disappeared behind the next bend.

Easter came and we got a letter from Dad. Yes, he was okay and had reported to his TD unit, which was in a first-class camp near Posen. He had another assault gun as well, and a new one at that—a 50mm anti-tank gun on a Hetzer chassis. The chassis originated in Czechoslovakia.

53

When the Germans occupied the country, they took over the Tatra Armament Works and were now busy building armor for their own use. They were really under-gunned and the armor was nothing to shout about, but what they lacked in protection and firepower they surely made up in speed. The monster could move at 35 miles an hour, whereas the twelve-cylinder Maybach-engined Mark IV was only capable of 30 miles an hour. Dad said in his letter that he had heard rumors that there would probably be another campaign somewhere soon, but his unit was still under-strength. It would be another two months before that was remedied; meanwhile, he was having a lazy time.

Granddad Willem read the letter at the supper table that night. "Our Lou is right," he said, "That Adolf Hitler certainly has something up his sleeve, mark my word. Hitler is quite fond of that Mussolini who has attacked Albania and Greece. I wouldn't be surprised if our Wehrmacht has to pull him out of the fire he started there."

"You think so, Granddad?" asked Len.

"I sure do," he said. "That Duce is all fat and mouth with no punch behind him. He got beat in Ethiopia by a mere handful of Tommies mixed with a bunch of natives and halfwit monkeys. The Greeks will give those Italians hell, you just wait and see."

"Mind your language, Dad. There are kids sitting at the table," Mom said.

Granddad Willem lit his pipe and blew a cloud of smoke across the table. "And go outside in the yard with that smelly stuff you smoke. It's not healthy for anybody," she added.

But Granddad Willem was right. The radio said so a few days later. Our Wehrmacht crossed into Yugoslavia, bombed Belgrade to smithereens and came to the aid of our Italian brothers in arms.

"Is that fat ass big mouth Duce unable to win a war on his own?" I asked Granddad Willem.

"Will you shut your mouth!" Mom screamed. Turning to Granddad, she said, "Now look what you have done! Even the kids are learning your foul language."

"I only spoke my mind the other day," Granddad answered.

"I have noticed, Dad, and so have the kids," Mom retorted. Turning to me, she admonished, "Anymore of that language and I lay the carpet beater on your backside, understood?"

"Yes, Mom," I said. "I'm sorry."

That night, tucked nicely under the blankets, I told Len that if I ever got my hands on that fat ass, big mouth Duce, I was going to shoot him with my slingshot.

"Shhhh, Mom might be listening," Len replied.

"I don't care if she is!" I said, but inwardly I was thinking of the carpet beater.

"Where do you pick up all those words?" Len asked.

"Granddad Willem," I said. "You ought to hear some of them I haven't even said yet."

There was a pause for a moment, then I asked, "What is a bordello, Len?"

Brother Len, he who knew everything, didn't know. "Why?" he asked.

"Well, Granddad told me the other day that fat ass big mouth Italian was a schweinhund and the product of a bordello." I said.

"I think it's a town in Italy," Len said.

I promised myself to ask Granddad where in Italy Bordello was so I could look it up on my atlas. Then I went to sleep. Three days later we had geography lessons in school with Mr. Konder. The subject of the lessons was the Mediterranean and adjoining countries and the Balkans. I was searching in vain on my atlas for the town of Bordello, and hadn't followed the lesson. Mr. Konder nudged me. I looked up and he asked, "And where exactly is the seat of our ally, the King of Bulgaria?"

"In Bordello!" I exclaimed.

Mr. Konder nearly dropped his atlas onto my head, and his eyes got as big as saucers. "Who on earth told you that?" he demanded.

"My Granddad, Sir." I replied. "What was the question, Sir?"

"Where is the seat of the King of Bulgaria? His home or his castle?" The teacher asked again.

"Sofia, Sir," I replied, relieved that I knew the answer.

Whew, I nearly could have had a beating there. The teacher did not ask any further questions of me. We heard a lot about the war in the Balkans, and quite openly talked about the Duce, Ciano and the rest of the Italians and what a bunch of cowards they were, needing our Wehrmacht to help out against Greece. I still referred to the Duce as fat ass and big mouth when Mom was out of earshot, and I asked Granddad where in Italy Bordello was, but he wouldn't say. He told me to be careful with my words. The carpet beater was always within Mom's reach.

In May our paratroopers captured Crete under the command of

Luftwaffe General Kurt Student, and many iron crosses, German crosses and other awards were given out. Hitler was handing out awards a
bit too lavishly, I thought. Since Brother Len knew everything, I asked
him about that. Len said that they were given for valor in combat and
to soldiers who had distinguished themselves in battle.

"Fat ass and big mouth got one the other day from Hitler. The radio
told us so, remember? What has he done to deserve one? Our
Wehrmacht and Luftwaffe had to finish what he started in the Balkans.
I think Dad ought to get one too. After all, he fought in France and
Holland and captured all their coffee beans, then he got wounded and
all he got was a Second Class Merit Cross. Where is the fairness there?"
I asked Len.

"Shut up about the stupid coffee beans, will you?" came the answer.

By mid-1941, ration card books had become a bit smaller, not to
save paper, mind you, but there were fewer coupons in them by then.
Some of them, like the butter coupons, were for show and absolutely
useless anyway. There was no butter to be had with or without coupons.
I wondered what had happened to all the butter. There was still the
same number of cows grazing out in the fields. Surely their udders had
not dried up, or had they? Meat was rationed to two pounds a week per
adult and half a pound for children under 14, but we managed quite
well on our rabbits.

When I think back, it still amazes me how Mom could manage to
feed four (that included Granddad) with at least one good meal a day.
She was able to stretch a roasted rabbit or chicken over six days. Only
on Sundays did we use the meat rations we got with our cards. Potatoes
and vegetables were the least of our worries, but chocolate and candy
disappeared from stores. Our beloved sausage was rationed and included in the meat. Later, by 1944, we were happy to have mashed potatoes
on sandwiches.

Not only food, but other everyday commodities were only obtainable with card points. For a pair of shoes it was necessary to go to the
town Party offices and apply for a Bezugschein (permit). The shoes had
to last for eight months, whether your feet were growing or not. Shoe
repair services and cobblers did a roaring trade until they ran out of
leather. Then they made soles cut from old car tires and heels from
wood. A march downtown and back on wooden heels was enough to
wear them down to a sliver.

Granddad Willem was an expert in clog making. You could give him a block of willow wood and in three days flat he would produce a pair of reasonably fitting clogs. I say "reasonably," because even though left and right fitting footwear had been invented in the mid-1800s, Granddad Willem had obviously never heard of it. The right clog fit the left foot and vise-versa. There was never a mistake. You slipped your foot into either clog and that was it. We had blisters like light bulbs on our feet, which after a while turned as hard as tortoise shells. If the weather was nice we played barefoot, but to school and to the Hitler Youth assemblies we had to wear shoes.

One day in mid-June, we all heard the shocking news that Hitler had decided that the pact he had made with Russia in August 1939 wasn't worth the paper it was written on and he had invaded the Soviet Union.

"Now we're in shit up to our eyebrows," Granddad Willem lamented. 'This man is a lunatic. Has he never heard of Napoleon and Borodino?'

"Tell us Granddad," we begged.

"Well, Napoleon invaded Russia back in 1812 and came to a stop at a place called Borodino where half his army froze to death in the Russian winter. Here, read it for yourself," and he handed Len the book War and Peace. "Hitler is telling us all about history, but he must have missed the lessons in school when Napoleon was the subject. He knows about as much about history as a cow knows about making coffee tables."

"Surely Granddad, we'll get to Moscow before the winter. It's only June and besides, Hitler says that the Russkys are only a bunch of peasants," Len replied.

"To Moscow and then what?" he asked. "I'm not a fan of communism. Far from it. I leave that to Horse Shit Jacob across the road, but Moscow is only the start of Russia. There are over 6,000 more miles to go before the Russians' backs will be to the sea, like the Tommies were at Dunkirk, and that was only 200 miles from here. The next sea would be the Bering Straits up near Alaska. Who is going to walk all that way? Our men can't march 6,000 miles on clogs."

"We got trucks and tanks," Len argued.

"So have the Russkys," he said, "and I bet you they are not going to leave a single truck or gallon of gas lying around when and if they retreat." Granddad Willem was getting sort of excited. "Just think of it. Our Wehrmacht is advancing at a rate of 15 miles a day in Russia. At the moment the Russkys are on the run. I admit that, but they have another 6,000 miles to go before they end up at the Bering Sea. How long do you think it will take our glorious Wehrmacht to get to the end of Russia? I tell you, it will take over a year—and that is if the Russians keep on running, but they won't. Just wait, and God help our men when winter comes. Russia is a cruel country at any time, but even more so in winter."

"If we get to Moscow and capture Stalin, we can rest there and wait for next summer," I barged in.

"Yeah," Granddad Willem said, "and he's just going to wait there until our soldiers arrest him? Don't talk such rubbish!"

"Will you all stop talking about war!" Mom shouted from the kitchen. "I have enough worries thinking about your Dad. You're not making it any better."

"It has to be said, Agnes. That man Hitler is a loony," Granddad answered.

"It won't get any better or worse by keeping on about it," Mom said. "All I hope is that Dad is okay. We've had no mail from him for two weeks."

In March, Mr. Lanz (a.k.a. Horse Shit Jacob) approached Granddad with a problem. He mentioned that as of late, there weren't many horses doing their business around, and those who did were skinny and underfed. Therefore, he had to empty his septic tank. His tank was in his backyard, but with no access to it except through the front door and hallway, so he asked Granddad for advice. The way Mr. Lanz had figured it, in order to fertilize his garden down the road, he had to carry the mess in buckets through his kitchen and hallway out to the road. "And then what?" he wondered. "I can't carry them 200 meters down the road. I'm 73 years old after all."

Granddad, in a fit of good will to all mankind, told Mr. Lanz, communist or no communist, that when the time came to do this messy job, he would lend him a barrel. The day we got the news of Hitler's invasion of Russia was also the day that Mr. Lanz cleaned out his septic tank. Granddad lent him our four-wheel cart for the job as well. The barrel was placed on the cart, and Mr. Lanz got to work busily emptying buckets into the barrel. Already two cartloads of the concoction had gone down to his garden, sloshing over the rim and onto the road. The smell was awful. The cart, our prized possession, was covered in the mess as we watched the procedure from our garden.

"I want that cart smelling like roses when you're done with it!" Granddad Willem shouted across to Jacob. Jacob mumbled something and went indoors, bucket in hand, for the next load. On the return journey thorough his kitchen, full bucket in hand, the news came that Hitler had made what turned out to be his biggest mistake and had taken on Stalin. In his excitement, Jacob dropped the full bucket onto the kitchen floor. We heard him shouting, "That idiot has finally done it! Good old Adolf! Now you'll get some real action in the east! Thank you, Adolf Hitler!"

Of course his kitchen was a mess and Mrs. Lanz was not too pleased about it, but nevertheless, true to her husband's beliefs, she joined in the shouting as she swept and mopped the stuff out of the hallway into the road. After this was all finished, he brought back our cart, but it didn't exactly smell like a rose.

"The Nazis have dug their graves with this stupid move. What is a mess on the kitchen floor compared to a kick in the butt of your Führer by Comrade Stalin?" Jacob asked.

"I wish I had that guy's nerve," Granddad later said. "We have a two-front war on our hands. This is something the most brainless general could have warned against, and now Hitler has made himself overall commander of the Wehrmacht—him, a corporal from Austria! God help us all if we lose this war."

"Dad is a corporal, Granddad," I mused.

"You don't have to remind me of your Dad's rank in the glorious Wehrmacht, boy," said Granddad. "But he sure as hell would make a better commander in chief than that Austrian painter and decorator who talks with his backside. Your Dad has more brains in his little finger than Hitler and Goering have together in their ugly heads. With the best determination in the world, our soldiers won't win this war before Father Winter arrives in Russia. We should have marched in the spring. We would have had a reasonable chance of getting to Moscow by November. It is 5,000 miles of hard going, and Siberia is between us and Moscow."

"Yes, Granddad, we should have gone in April," I said, "but we had to rescue that fat ass and big mouth Duce, so now we are in the shit up to our eyebrows." I repeated Granddad's words, but I did make sure that Mom was out of earshot. I didn't fancy a beating.

It then rained for three days. It was good for the garden, settled the dust, and washed the last remains of Horse Shit Jacob's septic tank down the road drain. What a relief to breathe fresh air again. The next day, on Mr. Lanz's upstairs window a red hanky appeared. On one corner, he had painted a hammer and sickle in ink for all to see where his loyalties were. It hung there for three days, but then he had to take it down. Even the Nazis, who only considered him a stupid fool, had finally had just about enough of his sympathies for Stalin. They told him in unmistakable terms to take it down or else, 73 years old or not. What the "else" meant, he probably knew. Down came the communist hanky banner.

We stuck our tongues out at him and called him a "commie." He called us a bunch of Nazis and said that the day of judgment surely was to come for us. Granddad told us not to bother him and said, "To say the least, he is honest about his beliefs, and he might be just a little bit right."

After a quiet time of several weeks with no air raids, one night the Drahtfunk crackled again.

"Achtung! Achtung! Enemy aircraft assembling in quadrant PQ 12!" We knew that was far out over the sea near the Dutch coast, and nothing to worry about since it was 150 miles away. Thirty minutes went by. Nothing else happened, only the magic eye twinkling at us as if to say, "Go to bed, you fools." Then the voice came back on again.

"Achtung! Achtung! High alert in quadrant PQ 161! High alert!" Although our cellar was also our air raid shelter, it was mainly used as a storeroom for non-perishable food and for the coal and briquettes. Only a few days earlier we had received a half-ton of lignite bricks. We had not yet stacked them up, and they lay in a big heap on the floor. There was no way for the five of us (including Aunt Carol) to get in there. Besides, so far, the bombers had more or less left us in peace. There were more promising targets 50 miles east in the Ruhr area than there were in a small town with a food packaging factory. There was not a worthwhile target anywhere near us, excluding the railroad yard and the branch line to the factory. So we switched off the lights and opened all the windows. Ever since the parachute mine that killed Mr. and Mrs. Ahlen blew some of our windows to smithereens, we had opened them during air raids to minimize the blast effect. Whether it helped or not, I never found out. We then took shelter under our favorite place, the front door lintel, and waited.

CHAPTER 8

Krefeld

As we huddled under the lintel, the air raid sirens went to full alert. Searchlights were switched on, and we could dimly discern the two barrels of the 88s swinging back and forth out in the field. From the distant west, we now heard approaching engine noises—Halifaxes, Stirlings, and a sprinkle of Vickers Wellingtons. Nine searchlight beams, some as far away as Krefeld, swung into action. There were so many planes up there they could hardly miss them. All the 88s in the vicinity and further afield now opened up. On the bombers came, as if nothing could stop them. They brushed through the smoke of exploding shells as if they were swarms of flies. Flying right above us, they continued eastward toward the city of Krefeld about 20 miles away.

From our house on the hill, on a clear day, we could see all the way to the city and make out the twelve huge chimneystacks of the steel mill. It was Krefeld's turn that night. The bombers dropped incendiary devices that lit up the city from end to end. Then came the bombers with high explosives, like a stoker tending a furnace. We watched in horror at the spectacle from our vantage point. We could not hear the explosions of the bombs, but we clearly made out the flashes when they went off. The sky was so lit up for miles around that we were able to see the time on the church clock tower half a mile away. Some flames shot up so high that we could see their reflection on the underside of lower-flying bombers. The 88s and even the quads did their very best to bring at least some of the attackers down. They tried to break up the formations by creating a flak corridor of exploding shells, but there were just too many of the bombers. Where in hell was our night fighter force? That night, there were none to be seen. Why?

The British had hoodwinked the night fighters by feigning an attack on Berlin first. Only a handful of Tommies made their way to Berlin, but Herr Meyer had ordered all the night fighters from stations west of the capital to the Berlin air space. By the time he realized what the Tommies really were up to, the ruse had worked. Krefeld was a blazing inferno. The night fighters turned 180 degrees, eager to catch at least the rat-tail of the bomber stream. But their fruitless patrol over Berlin had left them short on gas, so they had to disperse to their stations to refuel. It took two hours to get airborne again, and by the time the Messerschmitts arrived in quadrants PQ 161 and PQ 55, the horse, so to speak, had bolted. Herr Meyer had left the stable door open.

A few of the bombers did get caught, but they were stragglers with no bombs left. Our 88 downed a Vickers Wellington that crashed near the border of Holland with no survivors, a sure third white ring for the crew. We didn't ask Mom if we could go to Krefeld to see the destruction. She surely would not have given her consent, and besides the tram might not have been running that far. For two days we observed a grayish brown cloud hanging over the city. An easterly breeze brought a smell of burned wood. Five hundred people had been killed that night, and half the city center was in ruins. We now agreed with Granddad Willem when he said, "This lunatic Hitler and his disciples are going to kill us all one day."

This first mass attack, witnessed from a more or less safe distance, had opened our eyes a bit. "How could this happen?" we asked ourselves, "How?" Still, our soldiers were marching deeper and deeper into Russia. One hundred thousand Russkys had been captured at Smolensk, and more at Vyasma and Bryansk, and it wasn't even winter yet. Meanwhile, here on the home front, cities were being bombed. Innocent civilians were dying by the hundreds, and Goering did not even bother to come to view the destruction or give comfort to the dazed survivors.

This did not mean our sympathies had changed and that we now sided with the British—far from it. The British were still bombing Germany nearly every night, but what really made us angry was that neither Hitler nor Goering would or could take countermeasures. Of course, at the time of the Krefeld attack, we knew neither about the night fighter fiasco over Berlin, nor that Hitler and his entourage were sitting it out in deepest East Prussia, far from the maddening crowds (and air raids) in a place with the bombastic name, "the Wolves Lair." The wolves should have been in PQ 161 that night, not 600 miles to the east in a bunker. Meanwhile, 600 miles to the west, 500 civilians died in a firestorm. What an upside down world, I thought.

I sat at the kitchen table and opened my school atlas. History and geography were my favorite subjects at school. I was the best student in class on this, whereas math was a book with seven seals to me. At the teacher's request, I could rattle out 50 or more countries and their capitals. When history was the subject, I could tell teacher the most important battles fought in the last 200 years. Granddad's Uncle Valentine, my great grand uncle, had emigrated to America back in 1850 after the first unsuccessful revolution, and had settled down in a state called North Carolina near the town of Asheville. I could not find this town on my atlas, so I thought it must be unimportant. I knew where Canada was. I knew all the South American countries and the Asian ones as well. There were not many towns I could not find if they were on my atlas. Well, there was Bordello, which I had not found in Italy so far, but I kept on searching. Granddad Willem came in and looked over my shoulder.

"Look Granddad," I said, "here is the Bering Sea." I pointed it out to him. "And here are our soldiers now. Surely we will have those Russkys at the end of Siberia in no time, don't you think?"

"That Siberia you're pointing at in your school atlas is ten trillion times the size of our kitchen table," he said.

I didn't know how big ten trillion was, math not being my strong point. I pointed to the Bering Strait on my atlas and declared, "According to the scale here, Granddad, it's only 50 miles to Alaska. Dad can drive his TD all the way down through Canada into the United States and see if any of our relatives still live in North Carolina."

Granddad laughed out loud. "We will soon be having trouble with America too. Just wait. They won't let any Germans in to visit their relatives."

"You mean to say we might have to go to war with America too, Granddad?" I asked.

"Yes, I think so," he said, "with all their 48 states. They are a mighty nut to crack for anyone, not like the tiny countries in Central America."

"We could get our navy to bring our Wehrmacht to America and land somewhere there," I suggested, pointing on my atlas at a place called Virginia.

"Our navy? Did you say 'our navy'?" Granddad sighed. "In 1914, we had a good navy, nine battleships, twelve battle cruisers and a host of other war vessels. At Jutland they sunk three British battle cruisers and our only loss was the Seydlitz. Your Grand Uncle Leo served on the Derfflinger and a cousin of mine on the Von der Tann in that battle. That was a navy to be proud of. What have we now? Two pocket battleships holed up somewhere, a few under-armed cruisers, the Tirpitz in Norway doing nothing and the Bismarck on the bottom of the Atlantic, and the rest you can forget. Hitler is not a navy man."

"We have U-boats, Granddad," I objected.

"They can't take a million men and their equipment across 3,000 miles of ocean. Be sensible, boy," he said.

"But Granddad, let's assume if," and I felt like a field marshal, "we can land there, then we could join up with Dad's TDs, march on to Mexico, and cross the Mississippi here." I pointed to Vicksburg.

"General Lee or Grant would have given an arm and a leg to have you as a commander," said Granddad.

From history lessons in school, I knew Lee and Grant were two generals who had fought each other in the American Civil War at a place called Gettysburg. My history book also told me that the blue side, that was the north, had beaten the gray rebels and had chased them all the way to the Gulf of Mexico. Brother Len, he who knew everything, told me once that the rebels, when they got to that Gulf of Mexico and could retreat no further, had tried to swim to Cuba, but were all eaten by sharks. I thought that was sheer butchery, as I reported to Granddad.

"War is always butchery, boy," he said. "There are no losers or winners, just dead people. Now shut up about America, will you? We are not yet at war with them, and let's pray it never comes to that."

"The boy is entitled to his opinion, Dad," Mom said.

"Opinion!" Granddad exclaimed. "Agnes, you're encouraging him now at his young age to become like one of those Nazi cronies."

"Look, Dad. I didn't start this war," she said, "and I hate it as much as you do, but boys are boys. They all like to play soldiers."

"Yea," he said, "and in a few years' time, if the Nazis last that long, that boy can play real soldier like we did in 1914-18. But today, it seems that war is glorified by the Party that started it in the first place in 1939."

"War, war, that's all I hear in this house," Mom complained. "Get out, all of you, and start cherry picking. I have canning to do."

I climbed up the cherry tree and started picking, still musing over what Granddad had said. Oh yes, Granddad had been a soldier in 1914-1918, but then the Kaiser's army never got anywhere near Paris. Now we have the whole of France, and for good measure Belgium and Holland too, I thought, and according to Minister Goebbels, our army was 200 miles from Moscow and still advancing. Slowly, yes, but nevertheless advancing, and it wasn't winter yet.

At 5:00 PM the factory across from us closed for the day. Mr. Hersch, our neighbor with the yellow star, the factory's food and wine taster, stopped by our kitchen window. Ever since his wife had died back in 1938, Mom had felt sorry for him and washed his shirts once a week. He always wanted to pay her, but Mom would not hear of it.

"Jew or no Jew, the man is our neighbor," she used to say.

The Nazis, knowing that a first class food taster, even a Jewish one, needed clean shirts too, had never interfered. There were still hygienic regulations in force, laid down by the food ministry long before Hitler became the Führer. Food had to be healthy and clean. No army is able to march across Siberia to the Bering Strait with bad bugs in their bellies. Mr. Hersch, of course, had access to all the different foodstuffs that were produced in the factory, and he sometimes slipped Mom a tin of corned beef or a pound of margarine through the window, wrapped in his dirty shirts. On occasion, he even got us a candy bar or two and we were always grateful for these things. I asked him that evening when he stood by our window about our chances of beating the Russkys before winter.

"I'm not allowed to have any opinion, boy, you know what I am," and he pointed at the yellow star on his jacket, "but let me tell you something. There might be days in the not so distant future when the Third Reich lives on home grown vegetables and water and food tasters become surplus labor, if you understand me. Until that day arrives, I will do my duty as I have been told, and try not to upset the National Socialist Party." I noticed he said "National Socialist Party," not "Nazis," and he rose a bit higher in my esteem. "Surplus labor" was something I did not understand, but I sensed a sinister undertone in his voice. With a tip of his hat, Mr. Hersch trundled home, clutching his two washed shirts under his arm.

Twice a week Mom went downtown to the butcher store. The butcher, Mr. Kamper, gave Mom a job as the store cleaner, mopping floors, cleaning tables and counters and, in general, making sure all the choppers and knives were in tip top condition. He paid Mom 20 marks per week, which was good money for six hours work. Sometimes he would give Mom a pound of meat or bacon as an extra bonus. He was quite young, only 26 years old, but because of very bad eyesight, he was exempt from military duty. He ran a first class butcher store and did his very best to satisfy his customers.

All things were rationed by now except a few items that we could hardly use or could not eat, like clothes line pins or scouring powder made from sand. We were getting thinner by now for lack of vital vitamins, except for Mom. She had put on weight lately and looked healthier than ever. Granddad Willem took us aside one day and told us that Mom was having another baby that would arrive sometime in November. Of course, we knew all about babies. Nazi Party doctrine and education had made sure to shoot down that the idea that the stork delivered babies. We knew babies were delivered from mothers, not from the beaks of birds.

I was delighted to hear the news—another playmate, I thought. Brother Len wasn't so sure. "That will be another mouth to feed, and we are on short rations as it is," he said. I didn't want to get into an argument with him about our as yet unborn family addition, but I told him politely that now that Mom was having a third child, she was entitled to the Mother's Cross in bronze. Hitler had created this award with foresight in the 1930s. The more children a German mother had, the better the award. In this way, Germany would produce more babies, more men to become soldiers, or more girls to produce more babies, and so on. Three children were worth a bronze Mother's Cross; there was a silver Mother's Cross for six children, and gold was for mothers who had given birth to eight babies. We had a nickname for the Mother's Cross, which we called "the Order of the Rabbit," in honor of our forever breeding crunchers out in their hutches.

Mrs. Platen, who lived up the road from us, had 12 children. She should have received a Gold Cross with diamonds and oak leaves, but that was not to be. The gold cross was the limit, eight babies or 20. I often wondered how Mrs. Platen could manage her mob and where they all came from. Her husband was a corpsman in an infantry outfit and hadn't been home since 1939, but she had a baby every year.

"Why not make it a Party decree that a woman should give birth after six months instead of nine?" Brother Len said. "That way we can double our population in no time, and Mom can make the Golden Cross as well."

"And live happily on vegetables and water," I added, remembering Mr. Hersch's words.

Two letters arrived from Dad. I was anxious to know if he was getting near the Bering Strait, but he had only gotten as far as Velikye Luki, somewhere northwest of Moscow. Velikye Luki was even shown on my school atlas, so I marked it with a nice swastika for Army Group North. There were also a few photographs of Dad in the letter showing him and the crew lazing around the gun. There was another showing him loading a shell into the breach of the 75mm gun. He had won another medal, the Tank Battle award. Since June, his two guns had knocked out three KV-1s and two Tatra tanks. Germany had given the Tatra tanks to Russia as a goodwill present back in September 1939 for helping out in Poland. Now the Russkys had turned them around against us. It was only good and proper that we should smash them to pieces.

Dad also said that they might not get to Moscow before the winter. The going was slow, and the Russians were stubborn fighters. He said he might have to stay the winter in Solnechnaya (now called Solnechnogorsk) if he couldn't get leave for Christmas. There goes my Bering Strait strategy, I thought. My field marshal brain has to do some calculations now in figuring out how to get to Alaska. Perhaps our southern front could make it. According to the news, our army is deep in the Ukraine—in fact, past the Moscow longitude. Well, we'll see, I thought.

What worried me more than my military strategy was the bitter news that Dad would not be home for Christmas. What about the baby due in November? Should I write to Adolf Hitler and ask him to let Dad come home? Just for a week would help. Then I thought better of it. Our Führer might get millions of letters every day, and he was too busy with the Russians anyway to read my begging letter. And besides, I thought, he might get angry if I bothered him too much, and Mom might not get her bronze cross and I would get a beating for messing things up. Ah, well, we could not always have good times. There was a limit to enjoyment. War is war, so why not look forward, even to a Christmas without Dad? It was only September, and a lot could happen before Christmas.

When school started, it was still quite hot for late September and the beginning of October. In fact, the thermometer went up to 28 degrees Celsius (83 degrees Fahrenheit) and lessons finished early because of the heat. There was no air conditioning in those days and with 60 pupils in a classroom, things could get quite unpleasant. Our vegetable garden was a dustbowl. The rabbits were puffing in their hutches like mini locomotives. Only the chickens seemed to enjoy it. They dug even deeper into the dusty soil and pecked the leftovers from our meals.

Cloudless nights also brought the air raids on again. More frequently now, and at least two times a week, bombers crossed over toward the Ruhr. We could see the glow in the night sky far away where cities were burning to cinders, and hear the never-ending drone of aircraft engines. Our local 88s had an easy time for a week or so. Not many bombers strayed into quadrant PQ 161. The British had a new bomber by now, something we had not heard of, which our school identification chart showed as a huge four-engine monster with dual rudders similar to our ME-110. It was the new Lancaster, with a crew of up to 11 and a dozen cannons and machine guns, some of which were mounted in revolving armored turrets.

With this sort of defensive armaments, they could take on anything we threw at them, but their vulnerability lay, of course, in our 88s. If they could manage to stay outside a flak corridor, they had it more or less made. To counter this, the German home defense command installed more 88s, 50mms and the larger 120mm cannons, slowly encircling the whole Ruhr area. The 120s were installed as twins on huge concrete flak towers on top of air raid shelters, 17 to 20 stories high. These shelters could accommodate 10,000 people comfortably or 15,000, if you stacked them in like herrings in a barrel. Two of those concrete monsters with twin 120mm guns atop were built in M-G, six miles away. This was a respectable addition to sector PQ 161.

Something else also appeared. One day, we noticed that overnight each house had letters painted with phosphorescent paint next to the entrance like VR, VL, HR or HL. Soon we were told that those were the coordinates where our air raid shelter was situated. Ours was VR, meaning "Vorne Rechts" (front right). Not that it mattered much. We couldn't use our shelter anyway. It was full of briquettes, wood, canned fruit and vegetables. Besides, a direct hit by even a medium bomb would have pulverized the cellar. We kept using the front door lintel and Granddad maintained that the best shelter was out in the open fields in a five-foot ditch, or if no ditch was there, just to lie flat on the ground.

Some bad news came. Our local carpenter had two of his sons killed at the Russian front. Mrs. Caspers across the road lost her husband in the Ukraine, killed in action for the Führer and Fatherland.

Dad's next letter came early in November. He was in Selicharevo now and was hoping he could sit out the winter there. It had snowed, then thawed and then snowed again. He asked if we could send some warm winter clothes, like socks and a pullover.

Mom was ballooning out now. The doctor came one day and told Mom that he would send a midwife along the next day. On November 11, little Fred was born. He screamed. We screamed. We all wanted to hold him but the midwife would not have it.

"When does Mom get her bronze medal, the Rabbit Cross?" I inquired.

"In good time, boy," the woman answered. "She gets it when she goes to register the baby, but for now she has to stay in bed for nine days."

Nine days! My oh my, I thought. That meant we had to do all the housework! Well, me mostly. Brother Len was too occupied with his Hitler Youth unit, and besides he was bigger than me and gave the orders. Granddad Willem was useless. He wouldn't even rinse a dinner plate, but Aunt Carol helped out, so the problem was solved. We also received another ration card for Baby Fred, but there were only milk, sugar and oats coupons on his card. I suppose a baby four days old was not entitled to sausage, meat, hard black bread or a broomstick.

Those were hard days for me when Mom was in bed. Brother Len, as usual, found every excuse to get away from the housework. We still had to go to school, baby or no baby, but the teacher let us go home early because of the circumstances. Aunt Carol was there in the mornings. After I did my homework, I washed dishes, fed rabbits and chickens and the dog, fed Granddad and myself—usually with potatoes in the jackets and a pickled herring. Granddad loved it. Brother Len had to fend for himself, the lazy swine. But he did manage to light the fire in the morning before Aunt Carol came over. Washing was out of the question, so it piled up, awaiting Mom's revival. Even Mr. Hersch had to leave his dirty shirts on for a few extra days. By the end of the month, Mom was back on her feet again and all was great. She went to register the new arrival at the town offices.

"Well done," said the registrar. "Our Führer will be proud of you." He filled in the registration forms. The boy's name was to be Frederick, I suppose, in honor of King Frederick the Great of Prussia who, in the Seven Years War, had kicked Austria's backside. He also gave Mom 100 marks as a gift from the Nazi Party and the Rabbit Cross in bronze.

Mom got a baby carriage, a 1920s vintage contraption, from Mr. Hersch. God knows where he found it, surely not between the wine bottles and food boxes at the factory. I had the honor of taking Baby Fred out in the carriage. I wanted to paint a swastika on each side to make it look like a TD, but Mom said no.

Christmas 1941 was approaching fast now. Sugar rations were increased, as was flour and some other foodstuffs so people could have something extra for the festivities. Mom had saved six pounds of flour, five pounds of sugar, 18 eggs, four pounds of margarine and some spices, enough to make a few tins of cookies. Special coupons were released by the food minister that entitled us each to a bar of chocolate, a box of gingerbread men, and a bag full of candy. Each family received two pounds of hazel nuts and walnuts. Baby Fred was not entitled to nuts, so he received an extra bag of oats and a liter of milk. We had apples and pears ourselves. There were almost 200 jars full in our shelter, so we had no shortage of fruit.

One day, Mom met Aunt Kathrin in a store downtown. Aunt told her that she had quite a few things for us, plus some extra rations we could have for Christmas. Aunt Kathrin was my godmother at my christening. She and her husband, my Uncle Herman, lived at the other end of town, and had no children. Uncle Herman had been in the Great War of 1914-18 and was wounded at the battle of Notre Dame de Lorette in France. On his return from the war, he was unfit to work in the factory so he took on the job as overseer of the cemetery.

On her return from the stores, Mom told Len and me to take Dad's bicycle over to Aunt Kathrin's and fetch the things she had promised us. The front wheel was flat, as we found out, and needed repair. So Brother Len, who knew everything, even how to mend a puncture on a bicycle tire, took the wheel off to find where the problem was. By then, it was 5:00 PM and almost dark. A lone airplane was flying overhead. By the sound of the engine, it was a British Vickers Wellington. No air raid, no alert, no 88 fire. One plane wasn't worth the trouble in those days.

Brother Len had meanwhile located the leak on the tire and was busy attaching a patch on the rubber tube. A high pitch whistling sound came from somewhere. I turned around to see what Len was up to, thinking for a moment that he was spinning the wheel on the bike. He was lying flat on the shed floor, fingers in his ears and mouth wide open. I realized a bomb was coming down and fell flat on the ground as well. A split second later, there was an almighty explosion. The lights went out, glass was breaking somewhere, and I heard Mom shouting at us to get under the door lintel. Then all was quiet again. The lone plane had gone, the engine noise receding into the distance. Next I heard people running outside on the road and shouting. A fire engine raced by and I looked outside. The bomb must have fallen quite near but there was no fire to be seen, so it obviously must have been an HE (high explosive) bomb.

We followed the running and shouting mob, turned the corner by our soccer pitch, the parking lot of the factory, and there it was. The lone raider had done a good job with this one bomb. The storeroom next to the factory office had taken the hit, but there were no casualties. The workers had vacated the place only a few minutes earlier. The worker's canteen was also damaged, but because of rationing, workers brought their own meals to the factory, so the canteen was closed anyway. The storeroom was a shambles. The wall toward the roadside had caved in and a crater six feet deep was in the pavement. Granddad Willem and his gang had built this part of the factory years ago. Now it was gone, just a pile of rubble.

An SA group with Polish prisoners of war shortly appeared at the scene. Shovels were distributed and the crater was filled in. The storeroom had been full of the canteen's dinnerware, cups, saucers, plates and coffee pots, all boxed. A lot of it was now broken and strewn all over the road. But about 50 boxes, undamaged, were still stacked up in one corner. The Nazi SA men did their job, got the shovels packed up, and lined up the prisoners. Some SA men were loading the boxes with chinaware into the back of the truck when Mr. Kersken, the factory owner, arrived. Granddad Willem walked over to Mr. Kersken. "Look Jupp, look at those Nazi vultures helping themselves to the china."

"Get my property off that truck right now, or I will call the army command," Mr. Kersken shouted.

He turned to Granddad, "Willem, as soon as the road is clear, please distribute the rest of the china that's not broken to our local people. The canteen won't be reopened, not in this war."

The SA leader tried to argue with Mr. Kersken, telling him that the stuff was to be given to needy people, obviously meaning themselves.

"We are all needy people in this war," Mr. Kersken said, "and this is still my property and not the Party's, so get moving. Your job is done here. Thank you and Heil Hitler." The SA men left red faced, with their prisoners.

"You want me to clear those bricks and stack them up, Jupp?" Granddad asked.

"No need for that, Willem," he said. "I think I'm going to retire after New Year's and leave the running of the place to Walter, my son. Honestly speaking, Willem, I've had just about enough. I created this business 25 years ago, and without your help it would not have grown to what it is now. Now this damn war is wrecking the place and all our work is for nothing. You and I are too old to start all over again." He looked up at the wall behind his desk. There hung Granddad's old spirit level, the same one he had used when he built the place. Years ago, after the factory had been completed, Mr. Kersken asked Granddad for a souvenir, a sort of memento to remember the building of the factory. Both had forgotten where the corner stone was laid a quarter of a century before, so Granddad gave him his old spirit level. Mr. Kersken had it highly polished and mounted it on the wall in his office.

Mr. Kersken then addressed me, "Boy, go home and get that little four-wheel cart of yours, and don't come back until 10:00 AM, okay?"

"Yes Sir! 10:00 AM with wagon, Sir," I said, and left the office.

At 10:00 AM sharp, I showed up with my wagon. I knocked on the office door and took my cap off. "I'm at your service, Sir, waiting for further orders," I stated.

"Okay," Mr. Kersken said, "I'll show you two something now, but it's strictly between us three at the moment, okay?" He took a bunch of keys from his pocket and led Granddad and me out the door. "Get the wagon and follow me," he said.

Granddad and I followed through a side door. To the right was the plant where the wine was bottled, then labeled and corked. When got to the back of the canteen, Mr. Kersken opened a steel door and told me to leave the wagon outside. The room apparently had been the food store at the time the canteen was in use. There were two huge refrigerators with doors wide-open and empty shelves. To the right was an eight-foot high stack of boxes and sacks were standing in the other corner on wooden pallets.

Mr. Kersken motioned Granddad nearer. "There's all sorts of tinned and bagged food in there. Take a box from each stack," he said, and we did.

By 6:00 PM it was all finally done and Granddad and I went home with our wagon full of goodies, Granddad pushing and me pulling. Brother Len, as usual, was nowhere to be seen until we got home. His excuse was that he had been to his Hitler Youth meeting, but he did help us get the boxes inside. Granddad got a slip of paper from Mr. Kersken that said he had received his Christmas bonus from him. We never were asked by anyone how he had managed to get a four-wheel wagon full of bonus. Also on the slip, Mr. Kersken had written that he had to sack Granddad because he was "surplus to requirements." I remembered having heard Mr. Hersch use those exact same words not long ago.

At 10:00 PM we were still stacking things up in the air raid shelter. The flour and the noodles went into Mom's kitchen cupboard. We had found a box of 24 cans of condensed milk as well, so Baby Fred was not forgotten. I had a large candy bar as a reward that night. Mom was so happy she even let Granddad smoke his pipe in the kitchen. We went to bed that night in the knowledge that Christmas 1941 was to be a good one.

After school the next day, I took six Bismarck herrings to Mr. Kersken and received another candy bar.

"Tell your Granddad that Eric, I mean Mr. Vink, is coming over to your house at 5:00 PM with a couple bottles of wine to thank you for the herrings," he said.

After almost two days delay, we finally got around to going to Aunt Kathrin and Uncle Herman's to get the things she had promised Mom when they met in town. On the way home, pushing the loaded bicycle uphill, we discussed the latest events from the eastern front. I asked Len if we were going to beat the Russkys before the year's end. Len said he was pretty sure about that. Maybe not by the new year, but he said that he heard from reliable sources that our Wehrmacht was having a good winter rest in Russia only 18 miles from Moscow, and the reason our troops had not advanced any further was because the Luftwaffe was busy clearing runways of snow. He also said that the Russian government was now out of town on Christmas leave, and that our army was waiting for them to return so they could surround the whole lot of them.

"The British won't do much except send a few bombers over, and our new fighter, the FW--190 will take care of them," he said. The Americans, he added, would stay out of it. "They are too far away, and besides they are only a bunch of gum chewers and jitter buggers."

"What's a jitter bugger, Len?" I asked.

"I don't know," he said.

There was quite a lot lately that Brother Len didn't know, I thought. We got home at 6:00 PM. Supper was ready and Granddad Willem was fiddling with the radio to find the Berlin station with the news.

"Here is a special bulletin from our Führer in Berlin," the announcer said. "After several months of intimidation and humiliation by the American imperialist government, our Japanese allies have picked up the sword to defend their rights and homeland. The glorious Japanese forces are engaged in a deadly struggle with the American enemy in the Hawaiian Islands. Latest reports from the Imperial Japanese high command state that four aircraft carriers and six battleships have been sunk at the US naval base in Pearl Harbor. More news will be announced as it comes in." There was not a word about who started the attack.

I addressed Len. "Those jitter buggers are at war now, maybe with us, too. The Japanese are our allies."

There was no answer from Len but Granddad said instead, "Jupp was right. He has a nose for bad news. I'm beginning to look at this war like an observer of a chess game. It's Hitler's move now. Let's see what his answer will be."

With all the hard work we had behind us that day, we went to bed early. No alerts came. The British in all probability were celebrating the good news from the other side of the world that the Americans were joining the war finally. Granddad's faint hope that Hitler was going to show some sense and stay out of the American-Japanese conflict was shattered the next morning when the news told us that Germany would fulfill her obligation and stand by its Japanese allies, and therefore Germany was at war with the United States of America. The Japanese had so far not helped us in the two-year long war, so what was the big deal? I wondered. Why were we taking the Amis (as we called the Americans) on now? Anyway, I thought, America was a long way off.

"Not so," granddad maintained. "It's just across the channel, boy. Britain will be the future aircraft carrier for the Americans. Hitler is heading for big trouble."

On December 14, to our great surprise, Granddad Zander arrived unannounced with two big suitcases full of presents. Mom was glad to see her Dad again, especially since he was staying over Christmas. Because of the bitter cold weather, we broke off school on December 16. The December of 1941 turned out to be a real killer. The temperature fell to minus 20 and it snowed for days on end. We rehauled our butter box Mercedes, built snow castles, and endlessly dug for turnips beneath the snow. Granddad Willem went in search of our Christmas tree. He got a fine five-foot high specimen out of the cemetery. I reckoned Uncle

Herman, the gravedigger, had given Granddad some advice where he could find one in the middle of the night and get away with it.

Mom, as always around Christmas, was busy with cake and cookie making. Three rabbits were to be killed for the festivities. We had almost sixty, so it was time to reduce the population. Hay, turnips and potatoes don't last forever and winters are long. There were still meats and bacon to be had on the ration cards, and Granddad Zander had his card with him as well. A local farmer we had helped the previous summer to thin out turnip plants, presented us with a slab of two pounds of real butter. Christmas Eve we all sat around the table, including Aunt Carol, and had our dinner. Thanks to Mr. Kersken's generosity, it was first-class. Then we opened our presents. Aunt Carol got an overcoat and Granddad Willem got a tin of tobacco and a new pipe. Brother Len got a pocket watch and a pair of new Hitler Youth boots, and I was presented with a set of molds to make lead soldiers.

Granddad Zander had made the molds at the factory where he worked when he was on night shift. He even brought a few pounds of lead, and said he was going to show me how to make figures in a day or so. Lead was another metal that was hard to come by in those days. The Nazis needed all the metal they could get to carry on the war effort. Len also got a new Ludo game, but I wasn't particularly happy about that. I was the only one who played with him and I knew I was going to lose, so what was the point of being elated about a stupid game? Aunt Carol gave me a 250-piece jigsaw puzzle and I loved it. Len immediately wanted to assemble it, but I told him to keep his mitts off. Baby Fred got nothing. He was only a few weeks old so he wouldn't have appreciated it anyway, but he must have sensed that he was being left out because he screamed for hours on end that night. If only Dad had been home it would have made a perfect Christmas.

We sat around the radio and listened to Hitler's and Goebbels' Christmas messages. They said that things would be getting better by the New Year, and our spring offensive toward Moscow would resume as soon as weather permitted. Hitler also said that our soldiers were in warm winter quarters with plenty of food and clothing and nothing to worry about, and that they wished us all a Merry Christmas.

"Listen to this idiot, just listen to him!" Granddad Willem said. "I can read between the lines. Our men are freezing to death out there. It's minus 40 in the east and warm winter clothing was never issued to our troops. Why? Because Hitler thought the campaign in Russia would be over by September. Now we have the WHW (winter help program) knocking on our doors and begging for blankets and coats."

"Yes," Granddad Zander chimed in. "And I hear they give each soldier a medal for spending a winter in Russia. 'The Order of the Deep Freeze' is what the soldiers are calling it."

"A medal won't keep our men warm," Granddad Willem said, blowing pipe smoke across the table.

Fortunately the Tommies had Christmas too that night, so there were no PQ alerts. We stomped through a foot of snow to midnight mass. It was a peaceful night with snow falling. The night was still with no traffic on the roads or lights to be seen anywhere, except in church where candles were burning behind blackout windows. Even Mr. Vink attended mass. There was no need for him to be patrolling the deserted streets.

A few days later, I asked Granddad Zander to make me a few lead soldiers. There was only enough metal for about a dozen. We found a rusty cast iron pot in the old pig shed and Granddad Zander made a fire out in the yard. He made a fire grate for the pot to stand on. It took almost two hours before the lead was good enough to pour into the molds. The wood fire was just not hot enough, Granddad Zander said. He nevertheless managed to make six soldiers and two horses and cannons. Better than nothing, I thought, but that stopped my progress in creating my own army. Any thoughts of becoming a field marshal went out the window for the time being.

Mr. Kersken called in the morning of December 31 and invited both Granddads, Aunt Carol and Mom to the pub for a New Year's drink. There was no chance of having an air raid. The weather was too bad. Even the Royal Air Force had limits in what they could do and what they could not. Len and I had to baby-sit, but Mom came home at 11:00 PM to fetch us for the last hour of 1941 and to have some apple cider. Aunt Carol would look after Fred for a while.

In Germany, children of any age were allowed in pubs as long as an adult was with them. The pub was crowded and the air thick with smoke. Most of the guests were of advanced age, too old for service. A few soldiers were there on home leave and naturally the crews of the quad 20s and 88s were there. Mr. Hoffman was there with his wife. He was a captain in the artillery and we looked in awe at his medals; Iron Cross, War Merit Cross, VA in bronze and Close Combat Clasp. He told us that he had gotten the clasp for stopping a bunch of Ivans from getting his cannon. The talk in the pub revolved around the war. Most agreed that it was a terrible time for our men to sit it out in deepest Russia, but that surely in the spring our soldiers would get to Moscow.

Horse Shit Jacob, who was standing near the open fire in the chimney corner, spoke up. "They won't get anywhere, winter or no winter. Stalin will see to that."

"Keep your commie mouth shut, Jacob," said Captain Hoffman. "One of these days you'll get into trouble for sticking up for Stalin."

"I'm not sticking up for anybody," he said. "I feel as bad for our men as the rest of you, but my political views and opinions are different from yours, and no Hitler can change that."

By midnight most everyone was too drunk to realize it was almost 1942. Some sergeant from the quad 20s was lying on the floor, beer stein in hand, singing "Lili Marlene." The NCO of the same crew, a giant of a man standing 6 feet 6 inches, was dancing on a table barefoot. Everybody was wishing each other a Happy New Year. Around 1:00 AM we walked home in the knowledge that 1942 was to be the year we were going to end this war with a huge victory.

"I wonder what Dad is drinking tonight?" Len asked.

"Vodka, I suppose." Granddad Zander said. "They don't have anything else."

In mid-January the snow came down and was three feet deep in places. There were no snowplows to clear the roads. We had to shovel our way to the rabbit hutches and chicken pen. We cleared the pavement, but that was all. The rest had to stay where it was. People struggled to get to work as best they could. Even getting to school, just a mile away, was a 45-minute journey. Granddad Zander had gone back to Nuremberg by then. He said he might be up again in the spring.

Three letters arrived from Dad. He was in a small village just to the north of Vjasma, reasonably warm, in a farmhouse. He said he would put in for leave to be home for Easter and Whit Sunday. Mom, being a devout Catholic, had decided that I should have my first holy communion on Whit Sunday, the Sunday following Easter, when children went in pairs to the altar to receive their first holy communion. The tradition was to invite as many relatives as possible and hold a two-day religious festival. Presents of money were given to the communion child, and church services had to be attended twice a day. Dad had therefore applied for communion leave and it was in the cards that it would be granted. The Nazi Party never interfered in these rituals. "God with us," it said on every soldier's belt buckle, not "Hitler with us." So all throughout the dark winter days, preparations went ahead. Mom obtained 250 cloth coupons to have a local tailor make me a new dark blue suit.

In February, we helped Granddad Willem trim the fruit trees in the garden. Some neighbors had the same idea, so all up and down the street the pruning was in full swing. At 11:00 AM that day, the air raid sirens went on a pre-warning alert, meaning enemy planes were still far off, but on their way to the Reich. We didn't take much notice. Just another pinprick daylight raid on some distant city, we thought. No need to stop the pruning and seek shelter.

Around 11:30 we heard engine noise in the distance. The 88s across the field raised their long barrels in anticipation of things to come. Nearer the raiders came, too high to identify them correctly, but we were sure they were Wellingtons and Lancasters. The sirens went to full alert. Mr. Vink, who was also attending to his trees, dropped his saw and went indoors to get his steel helmet and whistle. We decided to carry on with our pruning. From the direction the planes were coming, we surmised they were on the way to the southern Ruhr area, probably looking for bigger fish than our humble town. Several 88 batteries in the vicinity opened fire, including the one in the field behind us. The flak threw a furious barrage up into the air, but the planes held their course, droning steadily on in a southwesterly direction. When the angle of the 88s in the field got to about 70 degrees, we decided to seek shelter under the door lintel. Flak shrapnel can kill if you haven't got a tin hat on.

Two gardens up the side street, our friend Herbie, who was the same age as Brother Len, had taken shelter under an apple tree. He waved to us with his handsaw. He had just used it to cut some branches off. We waved back. Flak shrapnel was whizzing through the air now, plopping into the ground all around us. No plane was hit and we felt a bit of disappointment with the performance of our 88s, despite the fact that they had fired as fast as they could get new range coordinates.

Then we heard a high whistling sound. At first I thought it was Mr. Vink with his whistle, but then I realized it was something else. It was not a bomb—they made a deeper sound. It was time to hit the ground. There was a sharp crack of an explosion somewhere, then nothing. By that time, even the 88s had stopped firing, and the planes were receding into the distance. No bomb, we thought, thank God! As we picked up our saws and pruners to get on with the job, we heard shouting and commotion, and saw it was coming from Herbie's garden. His Mom was shouting for help. We jumped the two fences dividing our gardens, and neighbors did the same. When I got nearer I saw Herbie lying in a pool of blood. He was dead—even I could see that. He had played football with us many times. We shared our butter boxes with him many times. Now he was dead.

Mr. Vink came running across, shouting that an ambulance was on the way with a doctor. We all knew that nothing could bring Herbie back to life. Neighbors were comforting his Mom and sister. The ambulance arrived, but all they could do was wrap the body in a blanket and take it to the mortuary.

Later, after an investigation by a flak trajectory expert, we found out what had killed Herbie. One of the 88 shells had probably had a faulty fuse, and came down hitting the apple tree where Herbie was sheltering. The fuse then activated, exploding the shell just above him and killing him instantly. There was no point in blaming our 88s across the field. Nobody could be certain that they had fired the shell. At the time several batteries were active in the vicinity. Besides, the 88 crews didn't make the shells. They just set the fuses and fired them. That day, we learned the lesson to take proper shelter during an overhead 88 barrage. An 88mm shell was made to destroy an aircraft or a tank in ground defense. It is not a big deal compared to a 500-pound HE bomb hitting the ground, but 88 shells are dangerous nevertheless if they explode near anyone in the open without protection.

Herbie's funeral was two days later. The whole neighborhood paid their respects. The Hitler Youth was in attendance with a platoon, flags and banners waving in the cold February wind. The chaplain read a few pages from the catechism. Then the Hitler Youth stood to attention while a Nazi Party official presented Herbie's Mom with an Iron Cross 2nd Class. A collection was taken up and netted 1,000 marks plus 500 marks from Party funds. Mr. Kersken later sent his condolences with a promise to let Herbie's mom live rent-free until the war was over. Her husband had long ago laid down his life in a forgotten corner of the Balkans. Now she stood alone in life with only a ten-year old daughter. There was no comfort in listening to the speeches of the Hitler Youth and Party men about dying a hero's death for Führer, Folk and Fatherland.

When the first shovels of frozen earth fell into the grave, Horse Shit Jacob left in disgust. "They should hang the Nazi lot," he mumbled.

"For God's sake, Jacob, keep your mouth shut. Those Party cronies are watching you," Granddad Willem whispered.

True to his name, Jacob answered, "and I give a horse shit?" and he stomped across the cemetery toward home. We didn't know it at the time, but Herbie would be only one war victim in our neighborhood in a long list to come. Already the score stood at 11 neighbors who were dead because of the war, including the KIAs on the fronts. Now it was 12. Although technically innocent of Herbie's death, the fact remained that our own flak had been responsible.

We were told in school one day that it was more important to assist the war effort than to learn lessons, so we were required to bring anything useful to school that might help the chronic shortage of raw materials. Of course most aluminum pots, by now, had gone into Messerschmitts and Dorniers, but there were other things to collect: rabbit skins, copper wire, old scraps of wood, rusty barbed wire, bits of brass, and lead. The things on the list that puzzled us the most were wild flowers and plants, which apparently were needed for making medicine. We did the collecting, but whether it was successful or not, I don't know. One thing we did learn, however, was that a lot of good can come from knowing your wild plants. To mention a few plants only, we collected broom flowers, nightshade, foxgloves, elderberry, chamomile and even toadstools. If we managed to bring a paper bag full of these plants to school, we were exempted from homework for two days.

Every Wednesday we had to attend the Jungvolk and Hitler Youth parades, which were usually held in the square downtown. There were speeches to be heard, flags to be raised, medals to be dished out, and plenty of drills to be drilled. Afterward we marched in columns of four into the surrounding countryside to learn tracking, map reading, and digging trenches, or just plain loafed around in the sunshine.

The sunshine, however, also brought the usual air alert, and the field drill would end with a mad dash to the nearest shelter. I remember one of these drills on an early spring afternoon when the sirens sounded an air raid. About a dozen enemy planes slowly approached from the northwest. The 88s had already opened up, but the planes were spaced well apart to minimize the effects of being hit by exploding flak shells. They circled around the area, then all of a sudden, we saw what we thought were big black square parcels coming down from the planes. We ran for cover, expecting to be hit by a new and dangerous weapon. Jumping into the nearest ditch, we waited for explosions. None came.

When we looked up again, the parcels had burst open and released millions of strips of silver foil, about half an inch wide and six feet long. The towns and fields were covered in them. Other parcels opened, raining down leaflets printed in good German telling us that we were going to lose the war, and should not to listen to our leaders. The silvery strips, we learned later, were called "window" and were supposed to jam our radio direction equipment. I took one of the leaflets to Granddad and asked for his opinion.

"The Tommies are doing their best to undermine the morale of the German people," he said.

"Look Granddad, we are now far into Russia," I pointed out.

"I'm not talking about the Russians," he replied. "They are over a thousand miles away at the moment. What I mean are the Amis and Tommies. Their bomber bases are only 250 miles from here, and so are their armies too. If ever they decide to get to us by land, they'll be here before the Russians."

"Our Führer is out on the eastern front, Granddad. What if the Russkys capture him?" I asked.

"He is in the Ukraine," Granddad said, "and surely away from the fighting there. They're not going to get him just yet. At least he is visiting the front there. That's more than some of the higher Party bosses will do. He might not be a great strategist and he wouldn't make a field marshal, but he certainly is not a coward. He won the Iron Cross 1st Class in the last war, and for an enlisted soldier to do that meant he had to perform some truly outstanding achievements, and that he did. If you remember, he was in a military hospital by the end of the war, suffering from gas poisoning."

"What if the Russkys do catch him, Granddad?" I asked.

"Hmm, they might cook him and feed him to the dogs, or they might hang him for all to see, sonny boy," Granddad said.

"And the Amis? If they get him?" I asked.

"Ah, well, they are civilized people, not like the Ivans," he said. But before he could go on, Mom interfered and told us to stop talking about the war.

School was an easy affair now. Our teacher was satisfied if we brought a bag of weeds, a rusty old bicycle, or a rabbit skin to school. The cycle shed in the yard looked like a trash dump. Every two weeks an army truck rolled up with a sergeant in charge of four or five Russian prisoners of war to pick the stuff up. Of course it was forbidden to fraternize with the prisoners, but we nevertheless did. We couldn't understand their language, but sometimes the odd prisoner did speak a few words of German. We slipped them a few slices of bread, and they made us toys out of scraps of metal and wire. The German guard didn't mind. He had an easy life and the prisoners were probably glad to have escaped the hell of war.

Dad got home on the Friday before Easter. He had spent three days on a train from Russia and had a pass for a two-week leave. One good thing was that the next unit he was to report to was somewhere in Saxony. We all crowded around and wanted to hear the news from Russia, but all he wanted to know was the news from home—how the garden was shaping up and how the rabbits were doing. After the hour or so he spent with Mom and Baby Fred, we took him into the garden. He had been away for a long time, so all the work had been done by Granddad, Len and me. Dad was pleased. He inspected the beanpoles Len had nicely set up. The onion sets I had planted stood up like storm troopers in a row.

"Good work guys," he said, and gave Len and me two marks each. There wasn't much to get with two marks, but Dad probably didn't know that yet. We asked him to tell us something about Russia in the winter. "Cold. It was very cold, like living in a deep freezer," he said, and he showed us the Winter Medal he had been given. It already had a new nickname, "Order of the Frozen Meat."

"What about your assault gun? Do you still have that?" Len asked.

"Frozen to death," he said. "Our water-cooled engines are not made for that sort of weather. The cylinder heads cracked and the diesel turned into wax. You either have to let the engine run at all times or keep a bucket underneath it with glowing coals. We lost no end of armor in the winter. Magirus-Deutz has developed a new air-cooled engine that will be a godsend in the next winter if we get them in our tanks and TDs."

"You mean we won't be in Moscow before next winter?" Len asked.

"We might be in Moscow, but that does not mean we'll have beaten the Russians," Dad replied. "There are thousands of miles of hinterland on the other side of Moscow."

"Yes, right to the Bering Sea," I said.

"Now, let's get indoors and see what Mom has made for dinner," Dad said. "We have to send the invitations out for your communion."

"Uncle Pete and Aunt Gisela are coming from East Prussia, and Aunt Theresa, Uncle Leo and Herman are coming as well," I said.

So over Easter we wrote letters to all the relatives we knew, asking them to come to the communion day. We then walked with Dad over to the 88 gun pits to say hello. He also visited Herbie's Mom and asked if there was any help she needed, but her cousin from Pommerania was living there with her and she was okay. The next day, Uncle Pete and Aunt Gisela arrived from Königsberg. Uncle Pete was happy. He had been transferred to a flak unit near Deuren, about 40 miles from us, and had already secured living accommodations in the town. They were glad to be away from East Prussia. He said that it wouldn't be the safest place in the world if ever the Russkys took the area.

Another uncle, Uncle Reinhard, arrived on Thursday, but came without his family. I had only seen him once before, a year ago, when we had gone to Cologne for a day's shopping. He had some business to do there too, so we arranged a meeting. He arrived in a DKW staff car with a driver, but he was in civilian clothes—a rather small and thin person, I thought. If he was in the army he never showed it or talked much about it, but he listened intensely when Dad talked about the war in Russia. He did not stay in our house like Uncle Pete, but had a room at an officer's house somewhere in town. I asked Dad why Uncle Reinhard wasn't in the army like any other good German. Dad said that of course he was in the army, but that the Wehrmacht needed civilians as well to help run things, and that Uncle Reinhard's job didn't need a uniform. Dad said the Wehrmacht couldn't do without him. Only in later years did I find out that he had something to do with security on the eastern front. I never met him again after 1942.

The Sunday after Easter was the communion day. I had to get up at 6:00 AM, and got no breakfast. All our relatives and friends went to church, and other relatives who could not attend sent money instead. Sadly, Granddad Zander was missing. He just couldn't get away from his job. He was helping make U-boat parts that were needed immediately, but he did send 200 marks in a letter.

At 8:00 AM, we formed up outside church for the procession. In front walked the Chaplain with a holy cross, flanked by twelve boys with flags. These were not swastika flags, but yellow and white, the colors of the Catholic Church and the Vatican. Behind came the boys in pairs, then the girls, and finally all the parents and relatives. My partner was my cousin Helmut. The church was full to capacity. What a sight it was, and not a Nazi to be seen! The Nazis were forgotten for a day, and besides, even their children were allowed Holy Communion.

After communion, we all went outside for photographs. High above, a bomber stream was heading eastward, painting condensation trails in the clear blue sky—we may have forgotten about it, but the war hadn't ended while we were in church. Then congratulations came from all sides, and home we went for a huge breakfast. There was real coffee, eggs, bacon and other goodies. Just for that day, I had the head seat at the table that was normally reserved exclusively for Granddad Willem. Everybody gave me cards and gifts of money. I lost count at 500 marks but Brother Len, keeping a beady eye on proceedings, told me later that I collected "1,225 Marks and 50 Pfennings." Brother Len again knew everything.

Mom was put in charge of the money. It was surely going to help next winter. I agreed because there wasn't much you could get even with 1,225 Marks, unless you had ration coupons to go with the money. There was of course the black market, officially forbidden by the Nazi Party, but it existed and was flourishing, nevertheless. The Nazis had everything they wanted, so nobody cared.

After breakfast, the men all went out to the garden, puffing pipes and smoking cigarettes, with their hands full of brandy or beer glasses. The women folk were doing the dish washing and preparing the midday meal. We were sitting in the garden discussing this and that, when I saw Horse Shit Jacob come to the fence. He called me over, congratulated me with a handshake, then put 20 Marks from his meager pension into my hand. I thanked him very much and promised not to call him bad names anymore. A smile went across his face. "Don't worry boy," he said, "you're doing fine. Keep up the good work while your Dad is away. He can be proud of you and Len." With that said, he walked back to his house.

"What a nice man," Uncle Herman said. He had been watching from the garden bench. I was going to say that he was a communist, but thought better of it. You never knew who was listening or who was loyal or not. After dinner, Uncle Reinhard had to leave. He had a long drive ahead of him to Munich, and it was a full day's journey to his office.

On Monday the festivities came to an end. Men had to get back to their jobs: Uncle Herman to his grave digging, Uncle Pete to his new flak battery near Deuren, and Uncle Leo to his railroad yard. For the occasion we all went to the local pub to have a last fling at being together. Even Baby Fred was invited. He was rolled along in his wicker carriage with a bottle of milk at his side. Dad presented Brother Len with a glass full of beer. I got the usual apple cider. Len naturally felt honored and I asked him what it tasted like.

"Great!" he said. "I could drink gallons of it!" I didn't believe him—he was making faces after every sip.

Aunt Gisela had stayed behind too, since Uncle Peter was already on his way to Deuren. Uncle Herman, whom I had never seen drinking anything stronger than coffee, got awfully drunk, and Aunt Kathrin had a real job getting him home.

No air raids had been sounded for several days for PQ 161. It was too good to be true. Was the war coming to an end, or had the Tommies maybe run out of bombs for a while? We heard the reason a day or so later. Enemy planes had attacked the city of Bochum in the Ruhr, but the enemy had sustained heavy losses because of our new fighter, the FW-190. We were told that the British needed time to recover from the raid, and we all hoped they had called it quits for a while. "They'll be back soon enough with more planes than before," Granddad Willem predicted. "They'll find a countermeasure for the FW-190."

The weekend came and Dad had to pack his bags to catch the Monday morning train at 6:00 AM. A few hugs and kisses, and off he went. We all stayed home that morning because of some late sleet and rain. Dad's first letter came a few days later. He told us that he had arrived in Frankfurt just after an air raid. The station and tracks had been damaged and there were no trains going any further that day. He did manage to hitch a lift with an army truck as far as Jena in Thuringia, and from there he took another train to Schneeberg near Leipzig, where he reported to his new unit twelve hours late. The commanding officer understood, accepted the reasons for his late arrival, and even gave him another day off before assigning him to a new assault gun and crew. His new assault gun had one of those Magirus air-cooled engines installed and an improved 77mm antitank cannon. Dad said the engine made a hell of a racket because of the cooling fan, but at least it would not freeze up. Then we knew for certain—the new engines had been developed for the coming winter. The Russian campaign was not over by a long shot.

Brother Len was promoted up another notch in the Hitler Youth. He now had a green and silver shoulder cord.

The postman brought us a letter one day with no postage stamp. It had a big red cross in the corner and "Sverige" (Sweden) printed under it. Mom read the letter and afterwards I asked her whom it was from. She explained that it was from Dad's youngest brother, Willy, who was captured by the British in France in 1940, and now was a prisoner of war in Manchester, England. He was allowed to write two letters each month to his wife and relatives. The letters had to be sent to the Swedish Embassy, which in turned mailed them through the international Red Cross organization to Germany. His wife, my Aunt Christine, lived at the eastern end of town. We had not seen much of her. She had a mother 92 years old living at home plus her two children, a boy named Dieter and a girl named Gertrude. In his letter, Uncle Willy asked us to write to him occasionally. We should give the letters to a Red Cross station, which would send them on to him. It was a long way around but, in fact, this arrangement worked right to the end of 1944. We visited Aunt Christine and showed her the letter, and she said that she received at least two letters a month.

According to the radio news, by July 1942, our Wehrmacht was moving rapidly forward. Not on Moscow, but this time in southern Russia. The Crimea had been taken and our heavy artillery had reduced the Fortress of Sevastopol to rubble. General Reichenau's divisions had taken Kharkov. The Sixth Army, under the command of General Paulus, was on the banks of the Don River. Even in the west we claimed a victory; the British and Canadians had attempted a landing on the French coast near a town called Dieppe, but had gotten a bloody nose in the process. Our army had pushed them back into the Channel with huge losses in tanks and personnel. In Africa, Rommel was knocking on the door to Egypt at Mars Matruh, and Tobruk had finally been taken. Only in Norway could the British claim some success. A commando unit had blown up the heavy water plant in Telemark and also destroyed some fish processing plants in the Lofoten Islands. All was rosy again on our fronts, and Knight's Crosses were awarded by the score. Helmut Rosenbaum, skipper of U-72, got one with swords for sinking the British fleet carrier Eagle off Malta.

Rumors reached us that the Americans had finally decided to throw their weight about by starting daylight raids on German cities, leaving night attacks to the British. This meant that we had to update our identification chart in school. The new menace was the four-engine Lockheed Liberator, B-24. We thought it a rather stubby and pot bellied concoction of an airplane. The fuselage resembled something like an oversized can of condensed milk, so we nicknamed it the "Libby Bomber." The other newcomer was the Boeing Flying fortress B-17, and in a sense it was a fortress. With 13 cannons and machine guns, it could outshoot anything that Hitler sent against it, until the Germans developed the Wolf Pack fighters that attacked the bomber stream en masse. Most impressive of course was the bomb load these monsters of the sky could carry. Their July debut on the marshalling yards of the city of Hamm left the place utterly destroyed. They sustained heavy losses on that raid, mainly from the FW-190, so the Americans installed a few blister turrets and one that revolved in the underbelly with twin cannons. That gave some extra protection, but the ideal solution didn't come until the long-range escort fighter came onto the scene.

We listened to the German bulletins on the BBC radio, too. Although they were officially not permitted, they told us that the Japanese had lost four of their carriers at the battle of Midway in the Pacific. Our own German radio told us differently: the Japs had lost two carriers and the Americans two as well, so the score was even. Also, US Marines had landed on an obscure and swampy island in the Solomons called Guadalcanal, but had gotten a bloody nose from our allies. The Japanese navy had left Rabaul to deal with the situation.

Aunt Gisela had by now moved to Deuren to be near her husband. Uncle Pete was in charge of an 88mm there, taking pot shots at enemy planes heading for Cologne. He soon found out that Deuren and the planes above it were a different kettle of fish from the old Polish Fokkers of 1939 vintage. The bombers came in above 20,000 feet or more and a good deal faster. Lately, they even on occasion brought a fast twin-engine escort with them, a Mosquito. We were told that this was a fast plane made mostly of plywood in a London furniture factory, powered by two Rolls Royce Napier engines and armed with an array of cannons. It attacked 88s and even 50mm guns, so Uncle Peter had his hands full.

CHAPTER 9

Jungvolk Build a Bunker

During the summer school holidays that year, we were told by our Jungvolk leader that we were supposed to have a field instruction course to test our abilities in map reading, weaponry, digging trenches and fox holes, and so on. About digging we knew a great deal. Everybody dug his garden in those days, but I wasn't so sure about weapons. I only had a slingshot, not much to win a war with. I knew how to catch fish or wild rabbits, but guns were something new to us. Of course the main thing was that we were away from home for three days, and we dreamed of far away places in anticipation.

Unfortunately, the far away place was only a mile away. Our leaders had decided that the sand pit below the quad 20mms was the ideal place, so we set up camp and pup tents. Looking up, we could see the eight barrels of the two quads sticking out over the parapet. The troop leader, an 18-year-old Hitler Youth "know it all" like Brother Len, told us to dig an air raid shelter trench. We were each given a short-handled spade. Digging in sand was easier said than done; by the time we were a foot deep, the thing collapsed. Even the troop leader could see the stupidity in that. "We're going to build a bunker above ground, then," he said. We located a few rusty oil drums in the corner of the pit, filled them with sand, and added a few tree branches as camouflage over them. A tent half was the roof. It looked awful. A rain shower could have sent our bunker into oblivion, never mind standing up to an air attack, but we had done our best.

Above us, the crew of the quads was looking over the edge, laughing their heads off. They had concrete bunkers with electricity, a kitchen and even a game room. Their ceiling was two feet thick. Only a direct hit from a 500-pounder could penetrate it, and that was unlikely to come in the foreseeable future. We set up our tents in the square made by the oil drums, and the quad crew threw us down a few cinder blocks, as sort of reinforcement. They also promised us the leftovers from their meals. We had no cooking stove with us, only cold rations and our water, which we had brought in two-gallon cans. That was all. What a life to look forward to, only a few minutes from home. The crew made us some substitute coffee as well and one soldier even brought down a box of apples.

Nice bunch those flak men, we thought, but when our leader decided to raise a huge eighteen by seven-foot swastika flag on a 22-foot pole to show the world around us who was in charge of the sand pit and the castle within, the quad crew drew the line there and then.

"If you want to play heroes, that's fine with me," the NCO said to our troop leader. "You would-be Iron Cross applicants can move a mile or two down the road and raise your flag there. I'm in charge of this area and not the Hitler Youth, so please take the flag down or I'll kick your butt. We have enough problems with air raids without you guys inviting any more. The flag can be seen by any good recon plane from 2,000 feet up."

So the flag came down and the crew above us showed their appreciation by clapping their hands. We built no campfire that night. A constant stream of planes was heading east and the alert was on until 1:00 AM, when all went quiet. At 2:00 AM, Iron Gustav made his nightly round. This was a British Mosquito plane whose sole purpose was to take night photos of the Ruhr area. It also kept us awake when we should have been sound asleep. We called the plane Iron Gustav because the flak could not chase it away, and our night fighters, knowing full well that the Mosquito could outrun them by a mile, didn't even bother to show up. Finally, around 4:00 AM, just before daylight, Iron Gustav called it a day, or night, and headed home unmolested, no doubt with a camera full of film of the towns and countryside around us.

We hoped that our sand castle would not show up on the photos. Our leader had given it the bombastic name of Fort Baldour, no doubt in honor of Baldour von Schirach, the Reich's Hitler Youth leader. I would rather have called it Fort Hess, but then I remembered that the Führer's deputy had taken a ME-110 in 1941 and flown to Scotland to make peace. Hitler had him condemned to hanging, but that was hard to do with him sitting in prison in England, so Hitler declared him a lunatic. So much for his selection of Nazi Party members. People had shaken their heads in disbelief—a loony as Hitler's deputy?

At 6:00 AM, we fell out of our sleeping bags. The ritual test firing of eight 20mm barrels was in full swing. So much for sleeping. We downed a breakfast of bread and margarine with a paper-thin slice of salami and lukewarm substitute coffee, leftover from the night before. This all went down like dynamite, nearly exploding our bowels. Nobody the day before had thought about building a crap house, so we clambered through thorns and bushes to relieve ourselves in a corner of the sand pit, and used the Nazi daily paper as toilet tissue. The place around us soon looked like a minefield and the flak crew above us were holding their noses. It was only 7:00 AM. God knows what it would be at midday in 90-degree heat.

The district commander of the Hitler Youth turned up on a worn out Zundapp motorcycle at 9:00 AM. We stood to attention. "Heil Hitler!" we shouted. He looked our castle over and inspected the tents and the skillfully arranged oil drums filled with sand, and grunted approval. His eyes went over the minefield.

"What is that?" he asked.

We explained to him the lack of proper sanitation and that no arrangements had been made for toilets. He checked his detail sheet. No, there was nothing about that he said. Someone higher up had clearly forgotten that detail. Where people lived, camped, ate and drank, there had to be a crap house.

We dug a trench along the railroad track and buried all the crap piles. Then we did some tracking, map reading, and crawling on hands and knees through the underbrush. We had a mock battle along the track where half of us defended the southern embankment against the group on the northern side. The northern boys were the attackers. We defended with broomsticks as rifles and old drain pipes as mortars but our group was happy in the knowledge that we had the awesome firepower of the eight 20mm barrels behind us. We integrated the quads into our defensive scheme. Of course the crew was unaware of this. We screamed and shouted, imitating rifle fire and mortars. "Bang, bang! Kaboom!" We threw grass sods at each other and hands full of gravel. It was great fun.

In all this commotion we had not heard the air raid sirens in town, but now we heard the 88s out in the field and noticed bombers above heading east. We carried on with our own battle, taking no notice of the air raid. About 2:00 PM, we heard some shouting from the quad pits.

Looking up we saw the gunners and ammo men running back and forth and the barrels swiveling in all directions. Giant (as everyone called him,) the NCO, was shouting something at us and pointing to the east. Turning around we looked toward town, and stopped dead right in the midst of our battle.

There, about 2,000 feet up, coming on a beeline toward our position, was a B-17 Flying Fortress, the first one we had seen close up. The two engines on the port wing were feathered and letting out a stream of white smoke. The monster plane was losing altitude, not much, but enough to make the range finder of the quads call the coordinates every few seconds. The B-17, now about two miles out and 1,500 feet high, veered slightly to the left of our position. This gave the quads a better profile of the plane and a bigger target. We raced to our sand castle to watch the spectacle from what we considered a safe haven.

Above us we heard Giant's command. "Fire!" Four barrels of the quads let loose. "Blam, blam, blam!" A steady stream of tracer-tipped shells framed the wounded war machine, then disappeared into the fuselage. The plane pulled up a bit higher as if to gain altitude. Then we saw eight figures coming from a blister turret. Parachutes opened and the figures floated gently down toward the ground. But the plane had run out of stamina. It dived in a 70-degree angle, well ablaze. Several bombs were released before it hit a factory three miles away and exploded. The factory was a laundry where army and hospital things were washed and cleaned in huge vats. There was a cloud of dust and smoke when the plane exploded, then a whitish cloud appeared over the crash site, shining in all colors like a rainbow. They were millions of soap bubbles. The explosion had released thousands of gallons of detergent. It was like a carnival, but we would have enjoyed it more in peacetime, I thought.

The eight parachutes landed somewhere to the southeast of town and the flyers probably were already in custody. No enemy parachutist gets away in broad daylight, I thought. The quad crew was naturally overjoyed. Although they had not crippled the B-17 in the first place, they nevertheless had given the coup de grace and were entitled to a ring on the barrels. Giant might even get his promotion to lieutenant now. There was no officer on the gun crew at the time. The only officer was a captain and he resided in town, visiting other quads on his rounds.

After the raid, we observed from our vantage point the fruitless work of getting the fire under control at the laundry. Soap bubbles were still floating in clouds around the countryside. Later we heard that eight workers had been killed, plus six members of the plane crew had died.

Test firing all automatic weapons was mandatory at least once a day. Because two or four barrels were simultaneously fired in rapid sequence, the guns needed constant and strict maintenance to avoid jamming or other malfunctions in an emergency. Each two-quad section had a gunnery sergeant who was also a qualified gun engineer attached to the crews. His sole duty was to make the guns work at all times. He was an expert and could take a quad to bits, even at night if necessary. Maintenance was usually done in the late afternoon or at night with the aid of a blue lantern. By morning the piece was ready for a test firing. The amount of shells the eight barrels could use up in a prolonged low-level attack was enormous. Later, in 1944, when fighter-bomber attacks became common, three ammunition trucks had to crawl up the hill to the guns each week, and there still were never enough shells.

We stayed three days and two nights in the sand pit. We were happy when it came time to go home. We filled the slit trench in, emptied the oil drums, rolled them to the far end of the pit, and said good-bye to the quad crew. I asked Giant if I could come sometime and watch, as I lived only half a mile away.

"Sure, boy," he said. "Just don't get in the way during an emergency and if there is an attack, use the bunker over there."

"Thank you, sir," I said and saluted smartly, hand on my Hitler Youth cap, but I didn't say "Heil Hitler." I thought it just not appropriate.

Home I went and into the bath. The dirt came off in pounds. Granddad Willem and Mom were happy that I was home. I think it was because they could leave the rabbit feeding to me again. Granddad also told us that on the day the B-17 crashed on the laundry, easterly winds had blown soap bubbles all over the place and that the cherry trees and currant bushes would have to be washed off if no rain came. No rain came, so I washed the fruit trees down with the garden hose.

Good news was coming in. Dad was still in Saxony and would remain there, so it seemed. He was teaching young recruits how to drive tracked vehicles like tanks, TDs and assault guns, and the newly invented Panzerwerfer, a sort of rocket launcher on an armored halftrack. If he could only stay there for the rest of the year, Christmas leave might be in the cards for him. Kharkov had fallen and our tanks were approaching Voronezh. Further south even, the Sixth Army was across the Donets River on the way to Stalingrad. In the Caucasus, our army was fighting around Batum and Novorossik, the vital oil centers of the area. The war in Africa was not going well though. New Zealand forces had won a victory near a place called El Alamein, and were now chasing our Panzers to the west along the coastal roads toward Tobruk.

"Those Italians are not worth a shit," Granddad Willem said. "They are supposed to keep our supply lines across the Mediterranean open, and what are they doing? Sitting around camp fires, chasing Bedouin women, and eating roasted goat's eyes with those camel riders."

Thank goodness Mom didn't hear that or there would have been a first-class argument in the house.

Len and I walked across the cemetery trying to find Uncle Herman, the gravedigger. We were in search of some good clover and grass for making hay. There was plenty growing between the gravestones, but we needed his permission to pick it. We eventually came across him in the far corner. He and four others were digging the graves for the people who had lost their lives in the B-17 crash. He told us where we could get the stuff we wanted and we filled our sacks.

Just as we arrived back home, a Party official in uniform knocked on the door. Granddad Willem opened the door. Mom was out shopping. The Party man took a folder from his briefcase and took a sheet of paper out of it.

"According to our information," he said, "you are the holder of some domestic animals for human consumption. We are conducting an animal count in the district and we assume you keep rabbits and chickens."

"And a dog," Granddad said.

"Dogs do not come into this count," the guy said.

"Come on. Spit it out. What do you want?" Granddad asked.

"Your household consists of two adults, that is you and your daughter-in-law, and three children under sixteen and therefore you are allowed to keep 26 rabbits and five chickens per year," the man said.

Granddad's mouth was wide open, "I don't believe it," he said. "Who came up with that nonsense, you tell me?"

"The National Socialist Party has decided, and rightly so," the man said, "that all food stuffs, and that includes rabbits and chickens, shall be shared by all the people. How many rabbits do you have?"

"Fifty-six," Granddad said, "and five chickens."

"That makes thirty rabbits over the allowed limit," the Party man said. "I'm afraid we'll have to confiscate those thirty. The law comes into effect on September 1. The five chickens are okay. We won't trouble you about them."

"And you saying that we are allowed 26 rabbits?" Granddad said.

"That's correct, 26," replied the Party man.

"So in three weeks you will call back and take the other rabbits we have over the allowed limit?" Granddad said. "Thank you for telling us Sir, and Heil Hitler."

"Heil Hitler!" the Party man said and left, no doubt rubbing his hands in the knowledge that he had just gotten 30 rabbits for the Party or whoever was going to get them.

"Them no good bastards," Granddad Willem said. "Here we are, feeding those rabbits day in and day out, and when they are fat and ready for the table this Nazi Party man comes along to take them. I'm gonna show those crooks. You just wait."

"What are we going to do then, Granddad?" I asked. "Give them away to other friends?"

"No, boy," Granddad said. "We're going to kill the 30 rabbits and live for three weeks on that meat. If there are any leftovers, Mom can preserve them in jars, gravy and all. Let's start right now."

By the time Mom got home from the shop, four rabbits were already skinned and gutted, ready for the pot.

The next two weeks were sheer murder, but by the end of August we had eaten or canned 30 rabbits. Aunt Carol got one too, and I took one over to Old Jacob, who received it as gratefully as if it had been a 15-pound ham. We took the skins to school for collection and we got a week free of homework. The other pleasure was that I had only 26 rabbits to look after now. More free time, I thought.

On September 1, true to his word, the Party man turned up with another guy in a van full of rabbit hutches. We showed him our 26 survivors.

"Where are the rest?" he demanded to know.

"We ate them," Granddad said.

"You what?" he screamed.

"Ate them, all 30 of them," Granddad said. "If you don't believe me I suggest you go and see the headmaster of Adolf Hitler School up the road and ask how many rabbit skins my grandsons have donated in the last two weeks. It's all on record there."

The Party man shook his head. He could hardly believe the bad news. "Thirty rabbits you ate in three weeks? And with half of Germany starving in this war?"

"Look Mr. Party man," Granddad answered, "I didn't start this war. Without this war, all the German people would be well fed on pork, beef and chickens, and rabbits would be where mother nature had intended them to be in the first place, namely out in the fields. But since this war, we are forced to live on rabbits if we want to survive."

"There are ration cards," the Party man replied.

"Yes, and you invented those as well," Granddad said. "Back in 1938, I could go into any store and get a pair of good shoes. Now in 1942, I can't even get a good piece of willow wood to make clogs unless I have coupons or a ration card and answer a lot of stupid questions."

"This war will end in victory for us one day," the Party man said.

"If you say so," Granddad replied, "but God help us if it doesn't."

"Wow, Granddad! You really gave it to them!" I said.

"Those no-good Party men telling us what we can keep and what we can't do. Well, as soon as that gray doe has her litter," Granddad said, "we'll have to kill a few more of the older rabbits. That Nazi sod might come snooping around here again one day."

In mid-September, Granddad Willem went to see Mr. Kersken at the factory to ask him for some wood panels. A few rabbit hutches needed urgent repair. He stayed for several hours there in the old carpenter shed and found some good pieces about three feet square. He told me to fetch them with the four-wheel cart. Brother Len was supposed to help me, but as usual he was nowhere to be seen, probably hiding in the Hitler Youth office downtown. Granddad was not feeling very well so he couldn't help me. He said he was going to lie down and that I had to get the boards on my own.

The next day, Granddad was still in bed at 11:00 AM. This was very unusual for him and he looked very pale in the face.

"I'm going to call the doctor," Mom said.

"No, not to worry. I'll be fine tomorrow, Agnes," he said.

But by the following day he was still lying down and was getting weaker. We went to school thinking about him and hoping he would be up by the time we got back. It was not to be. The doctor had come at 11:00 AM and told Mom that he needed to go to the hospital for tests and observation.

The doctor told Mom that Granddad had cancer of the liver and the most they could expect for Granddad was three weeks. The liver was shrinking by the day and there was no cure for it. Late that afternoon, Mom sent a telegram to Dad telling him the bad news and asking if he could come home. His answer came the next morning. "Will arrive in M-G station on the 15th, time of arrival 16:45. Dad."

That meant Dad would be home in two days. Mom went to the hospital the day before Dad's arrival to tell Granddad that he was coming. Aunt Christine and Aunt Carol went along to see him. At 6:00 PM on September 15, Dad arrived. A staff car gave him a lift from the station to the house after he explained the situation to the station commander. There was no celebration of Dad's homecoming that night, even less talk about war. Dad had got a temporary special assignment pass from his commanding officer. That meant that he was still on duty for the Wehrmacht, but in reserve, and that he was hereby stationed in his hometown until new orders were issued. He had to report twice a week to the local army commander, but this was only a formality.

The next day, Mom and Dad went to see Granddad. What the doctor told them was not very encouraging. Granddad was dying. They stayed at the hospital for most of the day. Len and I meanwhile worked like slaves in the garden and orchard, picking pears and beans and planting winter cabbage, just hoping to forget all the bad news for a while. An air alert brought some diversion in the afternoon. An American Libby Bomber dropped two leftovers in town, blowing a department store to smithereens and killing two people.

A week later Granddad Willem died peacefully in the hospital. His death did not really hit us until the day of the funeral. Every relative who could manage to come attended. Granddad had made many friends in his life and those still living all came from near and far. Mr. Kersken made arrangements for a proper hearse with two horses, and Granddad's old World War I comrades paid for the coffin. A detachment of World War I Verdun Fighters from the Ritter von Epp Jaeger Regiment was the guard of honor. Poor Uncle Herman had to dig the grave. We buried him on that cool blustery September day in 1942 at 2:00 PM. High above, a flight of enemy Libby Bombers were eastward bound, as if to give the old anti-Nazi veteran a last farewell. No flak was fired. The crew was at the funeral as well.

Life had to go on, but something now was missing in our lives. We were dreading the day Dad would have to get back to his old unit, but no orders came. Winter was approaching fast and there was a lot of work to do. Mom and Dad kept us occupied to help us get over

Granddad's death, but it took quite a while. Dad reported to the army commander in town twice a week as ordered. The commander stamped his pass, wished him a good day, and that was all.

Two weeks after Granddad's funeral, a letter came from Army Command West in Düsseldorf. Dad had been made NCO in charge of the local POW camp just outside of town. The POWs were all Poles. Many spoke German well, and they willingly performed tasks other people would not do. The letter stated that this assignment was only temporary and that it could be revoked by the high command at any time.

It was three miles out to the camp. Dad still had his bicycle in the shed so he had no problem getting there and back. There were in all 75 POW's in the camp, surrounded by barbed wire and an eight-foot high meshed wire fence, but the prisoners had no desire to escape. They had their food and shelter in long wooden barracks. Dad had to keep the records up to date. Guard duty was performed by a platoon of soldiers released from duty because of injuries in battle or unfit for service for other reasons. Dad had every weekend off. Because he was in charge and a family man, he was surely entitled to this. The camp had a cook-house and a canteen to serve the guards and POWs. The food was nothing to brag about, but it was better than none at all. Dad came home every night and left at 7:00 AM, taking a few sandwiches with him.

CHAPTER 10

Giant

I walked up to the quad 20s one day after school. It was a beautiful October day. There was no alert and the crew was doing some maintenance work on the number one gun.

"Mind if I hang around for a while? There's nothing to do at the moment back home," I asked Giant, the NCO.

Giant and I had become sort of friends lately. He had even attended Granddad's funeral. In a small community like ours news travels fast.

"Sit yourself down, boy," he said. "How's your Dad doing at the POW camp?"

I sat down on the concrete parapet next to the number one cannon and replied, "Fine, Sir. He has a cushy job and we hope he will stay there at least through the winter."

"I'll bet," Giant said. "It will be no party in Russia this winter."

A corporal walked up and addressed Giant. "Sir, there is a staff car coming up the road and heading our way."

"Anyone important in it, Corporal?" he asked.

"Sir, I can make out a captain," the corporal said. "The other two seem to be some officials in brown uniforms."

"Not those Party loonies again, I hope. I have just about had it up to here with their interference in my duties," Giant said, and pointed to his throat. "Well, we'll see. Get the men busy, Corporal. It looks more impressive." Then he turned to me and said, "I see you have your Jungvolk uniform on so you might as well stay where you are, sort of on official business."

I wasn't sure what official business I had to perform in a quad battery but I stayed, making myself as small as possible, just in case. The captain was, of course, the officer in charge of the local detachment of the 64th Light Flak Battalion, and he was also the liaison officer to the 88 battery in our area. Giant saluted smartly as the captain approached him.

"Any problems up here, Lieutenant?" he asked.

Giant looked a bit sheepish, "You said 'lieutenant,' Captain."

"Oh, I forgot," the captain said. "As of today you have been promoted to 2nd Lieutenant of the 64th Light Flak. Congratulations, Lieutenant."

"Thank you, Sir," Giant stuttered. "As for problems, Sir, I sent my report in three days ago."

The two uniformed Party men were walking around gun number two, poking fingers into well-oiled orifices, but out of earshot of the captain.

"Those guys are only snoopers," the captain whispered. "They want to make sure that in an air alert your guns are ready so they can go and hide."

The two Party guys came back. "Very impressive, very commendable, Lieutenant," one of them said.

Then the other guy asked, "and who is he?" pointing at me.

"Sir, when not in school or performing his Hitler Youth duties for the Führer, he is our runner to the 88s," Giant answered.

The captain, always taking sides with his own men, sensed some sort of argument but decided to stay out of it for the moment, to see how the new lieutenant would handle this. There was always time to interfere if needed.

"You said 'runner,' Lieutenant, am I correct?" Party man number one asked. "Don't you have an open line from here to the 88s?"

"A line we have, Sir," Giant replied, "but open is a different matter. We are on the far end of the supply line up here. Our cannons work well and the ammunition supply is sufficient, but the rest of the equipment is, if you excuse my words, downright lousy."

"What do you mean by that? Please do explain," the Party man asked.

"Can I be frank with you, Sir?" Giant asked.

"By all means, Lieutenant. I would like to know," answered the Party man.

"Well, Sir, it's like this," Giant began, "our water supply line has had a leak since mid-August. Our shower is not working. The septic tank is overflowing, and as for our telephone system, particularly the important line to the 88s, it was outdated before the Great War. It fails most days. It is of utmost importance that we have good communications with the heavy flak, Sir, especially in an emergency, and that's where this Hitler Youth comes in." Again, Giant gestured toward me. "If our phones don't work, he runs over to the 88s with the message. He outruns any rabbit by a mile, Sir, and I assume you agree with me when I say that contact with the 88s is of vital importance in defending this town and the inhabitants."

"Sure, sure, I agree, Lieutenant," replied the Party man.

Then he asked the captain why the other problems Giant had mentioned had not been solved.

"I have reported these problems several times to the local OT depot which is responsible for all repairs and maintenance of flak installations, that is, except the cannons, Sir, but without results as you can see," the captain explained.

The Party man walked over to the phone and dialed the OT office. A woman's voice answered, "What can I do for you?"

"Kreisleiter of the NSDAP Funk here, madam. Give me your chief engineer."

"Sorry, mein Herr, he is out and unavailable at the moment," came the answer.

"To you madam, I'm Kreisleiter, not 'mein Herr,'" the Party man said, "and if I don't get the chief engineer on this line in two minutes, I'll be downtown in your office in one hour. And don't tell me the chief engineer is out. It's 3:00 PM now and he is supposed to be in his office at 3:00 PM. If you can't manage this request then you can consider yourself relieved of duties and I'll get you a job at the local ceramic factory for the duration of this war. Have I made myself clear?"

"Quite clear, Herr Kreisleiter, hold the line."

We couldn't help it, we broke out in loud laughter. Here was a Party man speaking his mind for a change. He might be a Hitler man, but it seemed he could get things done. Of course, he knew that if he kept on good terms with the local flak, they would keep the enemy planes off his ass. So it would be better to be friends than enemies.

The chief of OT came on the line. "Yes, what's the problem?" he inquired.

"Kreisleiter Funk here of the NSDAP," the Party man stated clearly and firmly. "I'm on an official inspection tour of our local air defenses and I'm present at A Battery of the 64th LAA above the sandpit. I assume you are familiar with the location of this battery?"

"Yes, Herr Kreisleiter, I am," replied the OT chief.

"Very well, then," the Kreisleiter continued. "The battery comman-der tells me that he has reported to your department several problems regarding his water supply and drainage, not to mention his inadequate telephone equipment. I assume you have received these reports since the copies are recorded in the battery's logbook."

"Yes, Herr Kreisleiter," the OT chief replied. "We have had prob-lems ourselves here in the yard and some of our private contractors are..."

The Party man interrupted, "Listen Chief, I don't want to hear about your problems. I want a plumber up here on the double to repair a shower and a water supply line. Now, not tomorrow, right this after-noon, up at A Battery. Is that understood?"

"Very well understood, Herr Kreisleiter," the chief replied.

"And while you're at it," The Party man continued, "bring that sludge-pumper tank of yours up here too. The septic tank is full. Get that cleaned out and you'd better do a good job. I want to be able to have my supper in that tank tonight. I will stay up here until your work-men arrive. Is that clear?"

"Yes, Herr Kreisleiter," the chief replied. They'll be up there by 4:00 PM at the latest."

"Well, you seem to get things done around here," the captain said. "We don't even get the Chief on the phone in an emergency."

"He thinks he's something special as an OT chief engineer but he's only a 2nd lieutenant and worthless," the Party man said. "Every day I add more names to my list of worthless people and he just managed to get on it, lieutenant of the OT or not." And he added, "Sorry Captain, but as for the telephone line, there isn't much I can do at the moment. All our phone equipment is needed to replace that destroyed by enemy bombers, but I will see what I can do."

He then turned to me, "You've got yourself an official part-time job as a runner, boy. I can give you that in writing just in case the teacher asks why you're hanging around the battery instead of doing home-work."

"Thank you, Herr Kreisleiter," I said.

"But don't forget, boy," he said, "you can't have it all your way. School is school, okay?"

"Yes, Sir Herr Kreisleiter," I replied, "and Heil Hitler."

He raised an eyebrow. "Just try to be a good German boy. That's all we ask of you."

At precisely 4:00 PM the sludge pumper came trundling up the hill, followed by a small Opel Blitz truck with OT insignias painted on the doors. With drainage pipe, wrenches and blowtorches they immediately set to work. The sludge pumper driver lifted the metal cover off the septic tank and an infernal stink covered the battery. In a short time, however, the tank was empty and washed out with clean water.

"Ready for your inspection, Sir," the pumper truck driver said.

The Party man walked over and looked into the tank. "Not exactly the place to have my supper, but it will do," he said.

"May I be dismissed now, Sir?" the driver asked. "This sludge," and he pointed to the truck's tank, "has to be spread out in a field before dark."

"Very well, please take it far away. Thank you," the Party Kreisleiter replied.

By 5:00 PM, the water lines were repaired as well and the showers were working again.

The OT men gathered up their tools and departed in the Opel Blitz Kreisleiter Funk, and the other Party man and the captain all went back to the staff car.

"Any problems from now on, Lieutenant, you report to me as well as the OT office," the Kreisleiter said.

"Yes, Sir, and thank you," Giant said.

"Thank you, Lieutenant," he said, "for keeping a watch on the sky above us. Good hunting and good night." And downhill they went in their staff car.

"What about that!" Giant said. "Amazing the power a Kreisleiter has, and I thought they were all just big mouths."

It was time for me to go home by then, but I promised to be back the next day to fulfill my duties as the official runner for the 64th Light Flak Battery. I got Dad's approval, but only under the condition that homework would come first, and rabbits and garden next, before running from one cannon to another. Mom wasn't so sure, but Dad said it was only up the road, and most times she could keep an eye on me from the garden anyway. I asked Dad if I could borrow his steel helmet, but he drew the line there. He said he would inquire if there was one available that would fit my head. With this I went to bed feeling proud to be of use to the Wehrmacht, even if only a very small part of it.

Brother Len, of course, wasn't happy and maybe a little jealous. He said my job was just for show. I told him that I was a member of the Wehrmacht now and had better things to do than argue with him. He said I was a creep and just snooping around the cannons. I told him he could have his Ludo game and play it with the other children. He said he would clout me over the head if I didn't keep my mouth shut. I thought better of it and kept quiet, but inwardly I promised myself to tell Giant to kick Len's butt if he ever turned up at the quads. I wished Granddad Willem could see me now, and wondered what he was doing in heaven. I thought he was probably smoking his pipe and observing the war from a safe distance.

Friday, Dad came home early. He had taken a group of POWs up near a small lake not far from town that day. There they had to clear away some underbrush around the huge West Wall bunkers. They had been built in the 1930s all along the western border of Germany, no doubt with foresight of troubles to come. By midday the job was done, so one of the POWs suggested they should try catching some fish in the lake. There were no rods, reels or line available but they soon came up with a piece of string and found a hazel stick for a rod. They bent a safety pin into a hook and there were plenty of worms about for bait.

If we could only eat worms, I thought, all our food problems would be solved.

The Polish guy was an expert. Born and raised in the Masurian Lake country where people fish for a living, he soon had a half dozen carp, and they were a good size too. A fire was made near the embankment and Dad allowed the prisoners to roast four of the fish. The other two were rightfully his, he said. After all, without him, there wouldn't have been any fish at all. The bounty was a welcome change from the usual rabbit meat. We invited Aunt Carol over for supper and she gladly accepted. With our bellies full and Dad gone to the pub, we sat around the radio. Len had permission by now to search for the news stations. American marines, so the announcer said, had landed in the central Pacific on an island called Tarawa, but our Japanese allies had thrown them back into the ocean.

Our Sixth Army was engaged in a deadly struggle for the city of Stalingrad. The newscaster admitted that the 6th was more or less trapped, but General Hoth and his IV Panzer Corps were coming to the rescue, while our Luftwaffe was keeping our troops well supplied and morale was high. Other news was that our Gebirgsjäger or Mountain

Troops had conquered the highest mountain in Europe, Mount Elbruz in the Caucasus, 16,000 feet high. From the announcer's tone we guessed that the situation in Stalingrad was serious for our Sixth Army, but we believed that our Führer might have another trick up his sleeve.

CHAPTER 11

Runner for the Quads

We fetched our coal briquette rations from the coal man. Wood by now was in short supply. Trees don't grow into firewood overnight, but we found another source. Mr. Kersken allowed us to take all the broken beams and lumber from the old shed that had sustained the bomb hit the year before. It was enough to last at least until spring. Mr. Fruman, the local cabinetmaker, gave us six huge sacks of wood chips from his router machine. We put the chips into an old bath tub mixed them with coal dust, added some water and formed the mass into tennis ball-sized shapes. After they dried they made a good lasting fire. We had only the 26 rabbits left now. The chickens were down to four. Two went into our chicken soup. "Better that than the poor creatures die of old age," Dad had said.

We hadn't heard from Granddad Zander for a while, but one day a letter arrived. He told us that he was being transferred to a new job in Schweinfurt at the SKF ball bearing factory, but he said that he would be able to visit on Christmas. With Granddad Willem's death, we were glad to see our other Granddad, although he wasn't as much fun as Granddad Willem used to be. But then, better Granddad Zander than no Granddad at all.

Meager rations were saved for Christmas. Dad received an extra ration of cigarettes and sugar. Toys were out this year—there was just nobody around making any. Stalingrad needed tanks and cannons, not toys. We understood and were satisfied with a plateful of candy and cookies. The week before Christmas, Mom made a big carrot cake. We had plenty of carrots in the bin out in the field. Mom told Dad to take the cake plus two loaves of bread for the POWs. Dad, remembering the recent fish deal with the prisoners, agreed, and the guys were overjoyed.

Mind you, a big carrot cake and two loaves of bread didn't go far with 75 prisoners, but Dad said it was evenly shared by all.

I also did my first runner duty for the quads, but it was the other way round, so to speak. I was hanging around the 88s that day when the outside speaker crackled.

"Achtung! Achtung! Enemy planes approaching PQ 55 and PQ 161!" The guy who was manning the "big ear" listening station came on the line; "Approximately 40 miles but, west northwest, coming in fast and quite low, probably escort or fighter bombers."

"Okay, we copy," was the reply.

"Can you raise the quads?" the 88 man asked the guy on the other end.

"No, the line is dead and I haven't got a runner here," came the answer.

"That's alright, we have one," he said. "Over and out."

The battery commander turned to me, "That damn line to the quads is out again. You think you can outrun those planes and get a message over to the quads? If those bastards out west come in low, we might need every barrel of the 20s they can muster."

"Sure, Sir," I said confidently.

"But make it fast, boy," the battery commander told me. "Those planes are only 30 miles out. They'll be on us in no time, and be careful."

He scribbled the coordinates on a Meldeblock (official Wehrmacht notepad), and tore the page off and handed it to me. "Now off you go," he said. "Just pretend you are a hare and the planes are the hounds behind you."

I dashed across the fields, looking behind me occasionally toward the west. The sirens down in town sounded full alert. A few minutes later I tumbled into the gun emplacement. Giant had seen me coming and took the message from me.

"No need to hurry, son. We have a radio too," he said, "but thanks anyway."

I felt a bit stupid. There I was running like hell across the fields with God knows how many enemy planes on my heels, and he said he had a radio as well. Giant focused his binoculars to the west. The ground to the next town six miles away was flat as a pancake. High poplar trees in the distance intermittently broke the horizon. The crew was already on action stations. K-1 was in his seat behind the four barrels, two magazine loaders sitting beside him on swivel chairs, and K-5 and K-6 stood by with fresh magazines. These two had the worst job because they had to run with the movement of the cannon in the horizontal direction. K-I had his foot on the right pedal, ready to open fire on command. The other gun, a few yards away, was ready too.

Because of the close proximity of the two guns, each piece had a designated field of fire of 180 degrees to avoid hitting each other when the barrels were depressed to a low position. In addition, there was an eight-foot high, strong wire cage separating the two guns. If any gun depressed their barrel below 30 degrees, the wire cage would stop the barrels from going in the direction of the other gun. Above 30 degrees, the field of fire was 360 degrees and the elevation was an amazing 110 degrees; in fact, 20 degrees past the overhead point. It sounds complicated, but the crew knew their business and the Light Flak was one of the best-trained units in the Wehrmacht.

We saw the planes before we could even hear them. I recognized them immediately as twelve Mitchell B-25s accompanied by two Hudsons. I was wondering what the Hudsons had to do with it. We knew they were mainly used by the RAF Coastal Command. The range finder stood about 20 yards away shouting height and distance. As long as the guns were silent, he could be heard loud and clear, but to hear him once the racket of the guns started was impossible.

"Range 6,000 yards, height 500 feet," his voice came over (but he was shouting out distance in meters, of course).

Planes flying low always seem to fly faster than when they are high up, I thought. The 88s were useless against this sort of attack and the 120s were on the flak tower in the next city five miles away. Although for a much higher elevation, they were in the same dilemma. It was up to the quad 20s now and the bombers were closing in fast. The range finder had to be pretty fast with the planes coming in at high speed, but he shouted, "Ready!"

"Fire!" came Giant's command. Both K-1's pushed the right pedal.

"Blam, blam, blam!" The guns were spitting tracers from their two diagonal barrels, and at the same time K-1 was turning the wheel for the horizontal direction to follow the flight path of the attacking bombers. The cannons on the north side of town joined in, but we seemed to be the nearest battery to the planes. Empty brass cases were tumbling into the metal box below the gun. The lid didn't lock and the case flew open, strewing empties all over the pit. No time to sort that out now. The magazine runners were handing full magazines to the loaders, who were pushing them into the feeder slide.

I watched in fascination as tracers framed one of the Hudsons. Then some hit the plane and exploded on contact. Smoke was trailing from the port engine now. The plane made a sharp turn and came right toward the battery, cannons blazing. Two bombs tumbled out of the open bay and landed right by the railroad track, sending rails, crossties and footplates high into the air. The quads were hammering away like enraged demons now. The Hudson was only about half a mile out. The engine on the portside was well ablaze. The crew obviously realized that bailing out by chute from 500 feet was out of the question, so it was all or nothing.

"B gun has a jam! Where are you, Gunny?" Giant shouted over the din, but the gunnery sergeant was already at the cannon with a steel bar to extract a faulty magazine. It took him six seconds and the gun was back in action and again hammering away.

The Hudson had by then stopped firing but it came right over the battery about 300 feet up. Then, diving into a turnip field, it cart-wheeled and exploded about two miles out. There was no time to muse over it. The Mitchells and the other Hudson were still working the rail-road over. Two made another run for the battery with cannons spitting deadly tracers, but luck was with us and they missed. A bunch of 250-pounders had been aimed at the track, but due to the accurate fire of the quads, most missed. A few hit a unused motorcycle track a mile away. The pilots probably had their hands full avoiding our tracers, so the bombardier had to do the best he could.

Some ME-109 German Fighters now showed up, so we ceased firing to keep from hitting our own planes. Now the enemy was in trouble. The ME-109 was a lot faster than they were, so it was a matter of gaining altitude for the enemy and running for home. Our fighters went in pursuit and caught up with them just on the German side of the border of Holland. They shot four more Mitchells down, but the rest escaped.

Now we could look for the Hudson we had shot down, but there wasn't much to see. The plane had disintegrated into a million pieces. The dead crewmembers were retrieved by the POWs, wrapped in tarpaulins and taken away for burial. Dad was with the POWs on the recovery detail and he came up to the battery afterward in the truck.

I went over to B gun and helped collect the empties. We put them into wicker baskets ready to be taken away by the next ammo delivery truck. Down by the railroad track, a crew from the OT had arrived and was filling in the craters and repairing the line.

The captain of the battery came up a bit later and congratulated the crew on the Hudson kill. He also told Giant that by the weekend he would be a 1st lieutenant.

"Any chance of my crew getting a commendation, Captain? We haven't done too bad since we've been up here, and we got the B-17 to our credit as well," Giant said.

"I'll see the colonel about that, but I'm sure he will agree," the captain said. "Meanwhile, tell the men that by the weekend, I hope, they will all advance to the next rank."

That would mean the gunnery sergeant would advance to 1st class, the corporals to sergeants and the others would each get a stripe on their sleeves. I got nothing, but the captain promised me he would look in the quartermaster store to see if there was a small size helmet for me. I went home at five, happy in the knowledge that I had done my part in the raid.

On December 17 school closed for the Christmas holidays. The holidays had been extended because of fuel shortages. Our school was heated by a central boiler fired with coke.

It was the caretaker's job to keep it going in cold weather, but coke was needed for smelting iron, not for warming kids and teachers, so we sometimes shivered through lessons. If the weather was too cold, the school was closed until temperatures were back to normal.

Granddad Zander arrived on December 20 for a two-week vacation. There was no lead to make tin soldiers, but he brought me a Meceano (or Meccano) toy construction set to make cranes, trucks or other fantasy pieces. There were screws, wheels, and pieces big and small, all neatly arranged in a wooden box. Len got a brand new Hitler Youth knife. Granddad Zander had stopped smoking the year before, so Dad got his whole cigarette ration plus a bottle of rum that he had bought on the black market in Frankfurt on his way to our house. Mom was happy with a winter coat and Baby Fred got a wooden duck on wheels. He was growing fast now and already walking around. Uncle Herman supplied our Christmas tree from the cemetery and Brother Len was in charge of setting up the nativity scene. He did quite a good job of it, almost as good as Granddad Willem.

Christmas was cold and dry. As usual, the Amis and Tommies had a day off work as well and left us in peace. What a nice bunch, I thought, leaving us alone on Christmas. After midnight mass, I slept until 10:00 AM. When I got down to the kitchen, Mom had just taken a huge bread pudding out of the oven. Made with a generous dose of raisins inside and sprinkled with Demerara sugar, it was out of this world. The raisins and Demerara sugar were leftovers from Mr. Kersken's canteen from the year before. Mom put a pine tree twig and a small red candle in the center of the cake. "Now you take that over to the quad pits and wish them a Merry Christmas," she told me. "And no picking out the raisins!"

"I won't, Mom, honest I won't," I replied.

I had my mittens on and it took two hands to hold the cake. How could I possibly pick out the raisins?

The quad crewmembers were playing billiards in the game room. A small but nicely decorated Christmas tree stood on a stool in the corner. Some men were reading the latest news from home. The flak crewmembers were from the Rhineland. Some came from as far away as Silesia and Pommerania. They missed their loved ones the same as the soldiers in deepest Russia. At least the crew was stationed on home soil, but it was nevertheless still nearly a thousand miles from home for them. They graciously accepted the cake, and the battery cook took charge of the distribution. Giant came over to me, shook my hand and wished me a Merry Christmas, and I returned the wishes of the season.

"Now then," he said to me, "you stand right there and don't move. We have a present for you."

I was wondering what the surprise could be—probably a bag of candy or a wire toy made by the POWs. Giant went into the small kitchen and came out with a flat box about a foot square. "Attention, all!" he shouted. The billiard players presented their cues like rifles and stood to attention. He then opened the box and out came a 12 by 12 inch Iron Cross made of gingerbread. It looked like an oversized real cross, but minus the swastika in the center. Instead it had the date 1942 there, and there was a large ribbon with it as well.

"I hereby present you with the Iron Cross, sorry, Gingerbread Cross 1st Class," Giant said, "for devoted duty, on behalf of the 64th Light Flak Battery."

He then hung the cross around my neck and wished me bon appétit. The crew was clapping their hands and grinning. Then Giant said, "Attention! Present arms!" Up went the billiard cues. "Dismissed."

I was a bit disappointed, really—a gingerbread cross. Whoever heard of an award like that? I better not tell my schoolmates. But soon I was really surprised to receive yet other presents: a beautiful brown leather belt with a nickel alloy buckle of the Hitler Youth, a small steel helmet with the flak eagle on one side and the black, white and red shield on the opposite side. The helmet fit me perfectly, I must say.

"That helmet is a present from the captain. He has the resources and money to get anything," Giant said.

The last present was an official one-inch wide black armband with "Flakhelfer" (flak helper) stitched in silver on it. This band was the real thing, not a homemade strip of cloth, and it meant I was now an officially appointed messenger of the flak unit. I put it around my left sleeve, and saluted the crew and said my thank yous. Then it was time to go home for dinner.

Dad was sitting at the table watching Mom and Aunt Carol prepare the now familiar Christmas roast, a rabbit. He was fishing with his fingers in a jar of pickled onions for a pre-dinner snack. He nearly choked on the onion when he noticed my gingerbread cross.

"Agnes, Carol, look at that boy," Dad said. "He got himself an award and an edible one at that." He fingered the long ribbon round my neck. "Better look after that ribbon, boy. It sure is a nice one. It's not an Iron Cross ribbon though, maybe an Honor Clasp ribbon." Then he said, "And what else are you hiding behind your back?"

I showed him my new steel helmet and he put it on my head. "It fits too. Look, Agnes," he said.

"That doesn't make him a soldier," Mom replied. "He's only a schoolboy."

"I know, I know," Dad said, "but it is better for him to learn the drudgery of soldiering now than later. We have only one head to lose, and you never know what the future has in store for today's kids who will be tomorrow's soldiers."

"I pray it will never come to that," Mom said. "Clear the table please, dinner is almost ready."

Len and Dad inspected my armband. "You'll be a captain before I'm an NCO," Dad said.

Dinner was served and we all enjoyed it. Mom had even managed to make a vanilla pudding. It was a bit watery I must admit, but milk was getting scarce and it was diluted 30 percent with water, but to us it was paradise food.

After dinner, Dad and Granddad Zander went into the parlor with a glass of rum and a weak beer to discuss the latest strategies and developments on the eastern front. Len and I went over to Aunt Kathrin's and Uncle Herman's for cake and Kathreiner Ersatz Kaffee. Ersatz means "substitute," and Kathreiner was the manufacturer's name. Real coffee was unobtainable, so our coffee was made of roasted barley or wheat, then coarsely ground, packed and sold without ration coupons. Later, when even barley and wheat became scarce, acorns were roasted and sold as an ersatz. The stuff tasted awful. It was bitter and had no resemblance to real coffee at all, except perhaps for the color of it.

I showed Uncle Herman my armband. I told him I was a messenger for the quads now, but I had left my helmet home.

"You be very careful up there in those pits, boy," he said. "Those aircraft machine guns make big holes," he rolled up his left shirtsleeve and showed me the scar where a French Nieuport Fighter pilot had left his mark back in 1917 while he was on the Chemin des Dame near Rheims. "It took four months to heal up and it still hurts when the weather changes," he told me.

We took the short cut home across the cemetery. It was almost dark by now. White gravestones and crosses stared at us like ghosts. I asked Len if he had his knife with him just in case. He said that he did and not to worry. On a rise beyond the cemetery was the hospital. Up on the 2nd floor behind a badly fitting blackout curtain, was a lit-up Christmas tree.

"Lights out!" Len shouted, but nobody took any notice. "I ought to tell Mr. Vink," he said.

"Look, Len," I said, "it's Christmas in England too, so just let them get on with their celebrations in the hospital."

"Okay," he said, "but if we have an air raid tonight, I will tell Mr. Vink about this tomorrow."

There was no air raid that night, nor the following night. It was overcast and thick clouds were promising snow, not ideal flying weather anyway.

Dad was called out to the camp the day after Christmas. A POW had been found dead in a barracks room. A doctor and some other officials investigated and found out that the prisoner had tried to attach a light bulb onto a small Christmas tree by connecting a naked piece of wire to a wall outlet. The guy had gotten himself electrocuted. Dad had to make a report about the incident in detail. In 1942 Germany had over two million POWs, and every prisoner had to be accounted for. It was bureaucracy in the extreme, so to speak. The poor fellow was buried in the far corner of the communal cemetery. His name and hometown were recorded. That was all. No salutes or services, not for POWs.

Granddad Zander also had to get back to Schweinfurt. He packed his bag one day and we said goodbye. Mom cried and nobody knew if or when we would meet again. As a farewell present, I gave him a wing of my gingerbread cross. The other three wings I equally divided between Len and some friends. I kept the center bit with the 1942 on it and, of course, the ribbon.

I met the captain of the battery in town a few days after Christmas. He was searching for some bargains in a store. I thanked him for the helmet and showed him the armband on my sleeve and pulled the ribbon out of my pocket as well. I told him about the award ceremony at the battery pits on Christmas Day.

"Let me see that ribbon, boy," he said.

I handed the ribbon over to him. He fingered it and took a closer look.

"You'd better look after that," he said.

"Why, Sir? It's only an Iron Cross 2nd Class ribbon," I replied.

"No, boy. It is not," he said. "Look at my Iron Cross ribbon," and he showed me his, fastened to his second tunic buttonhole. "Now look at yours. The colors are further apart and the band is wider than mine. Do you know what that means?"

"No, Sir. I don't," I said.

"That gun crew of mine up there gave you the ribbon of a Knight's Cross," he said. "Goodness knows where they got it, but it's real all the same. So you'd better take good care of that, and don't tell the guys up by the guns. They might want it back."

"I won't say anything, Sir, I promise," I told the captain.

"They're a lousy lot up there," the captain said. "They don't even know the difference between an Iron Cross and a Knight's Cross ribbon of their own Wehrmacht. How the heck can I expect them to know the difference between a Mosquito and a Hurricane Fighter?"

"I know, Sir," I said. "The Mosquito has two Napier 12-cylinder engines in line. The Hurricane is a single engine fighter. Both are British made and..."

"Okay, Okay. You win," he said. "Don't give me lessons in aircraft identification. I'll have you as a spotter and range finder by 1955 if the war isn't over. That might give the quad crew something to think about."

"They did shoot the Hudson down, Sir," I reminded him.

"Yes, I know all about it," he replied with a smile. Then he added, "See you later boy, and be careful around those guns. No hero playing or stupidity, okay?"

"No Sir," I replied, "and thank you, Sir."

I went home with the knowledge that I was the owner of a Knight's Cross ribbon, although, by my reckoning, the Cross itself was still years away, perhaps 1955 as the captain had said. I thought about it and decided that I didn't want the war to last until 1955.

Sometime in early February 1943, we were sitting around the radio listening to the latest news from the eastern front. The Sixth Army had been in trouble in Stalingrad for weeks and had fought to the last cartridge against an overwhelming foe. Not a word was said about the 200,000 Germans who were captured when General Paulus surrendered on January 31, and nothing was said about our Luftwaffe that was supposed to be supplying the Sixth Army, and what had happened to General Hoth's VI Panzer Corps that was going to break through to rescue them? Now even our Caucasus army was in full retreat back to the Kuban Bridgehead.

The next day at the quads, the subject of Stalingrad came up at the dinner table in the game room. It was Saturday and no school, so I went up there early in the hope of getting a mess tin full of bean stew later in the day. I did get one. I thought I was important enough now and entitled to a share of the dinner.

"What now, after that disaster in Stalingrad?" a corporal asked.

"I can read maps," another guy chimed in, "and it looks to me like we are in full retreat to the Donets River."

"Yes," said another, "our men did their very best, but it was the Romanians and Italians who ran away when Ivan attacked."

"Those no good Ittys. Hitler couldn't have found a worse ally back in 1939. 'Pact of Steel' they called it. Ha! More like a pact of spaghetti if you ask me," the gunnery sergeant said.

I thought I would put my bid in here since I knew a lot about the Italians. "Yea, that big mouth fat ass Mussolini couldn't even beat a bunch of camel jockeys in the Libyan desert without Rommel's help."

The crew nearly fell off their chairs. They stared at me, astonished. "Where did you pick up those words? Surely not here?" Giant asked.

"No, Sir, not here," I confessed. "My now dead Granddad Willem used to speak like that about Mussolini. He hated them Ittys and he told me once that Mussolini was born in Bordello, but I couldn't find it on my school atlas."

The men broke out in laughter and the gunnery sergeant said, "Well, the boy is right. Rommel is on the run in Africa, thanks to the Italians who can't get supplies to him."

The conversation drifted back to Stalingrad.

"My brother-in-law is with the Sixth Army, one man said, "and we haven't heard from him since the first of November."

The next day, a backhoe came up and dug a 150-yard long trench for an electrical cable for the searchlight that was going to be installed. The platform was a prefabricated concrete base set two feet deep into the ground. A few big logs were piled up around the pit and the backhoe used his dozer blade to pile up a protective mound around it. The searchlight and swivel were bolted onto four large bolts that were set into the concrete base and then the electrical connections were made. The light was about four feet in diameter. By early evening the job was done.

The new four-man crew was due to start their duties the following day. Searchlight crews are only needed at night of course, so they had to sleep during the day. There was plenty of room in the battery to accommodate the men. Only the cook was not pleased. It meant he had an extra four people to feed, so he had to scrounge for extra rations. The next day the new crew for the searchlight arrived—three privates and a sergeant in charge. They tested the piece and found that it worked. Of course the beam couldn't really be seen in daylight, so the real test had to wait until dark. Gunny had trouble that day with the metal box that collected the empties under A gun. He finally wedged a piece of wood between the lid and frame to hold the thing in place, at least until a replacement part was available. Also, the lower left barrel needed replacing, which was done in short time.

"I need a test firing on that barrel, Lieutenant," Gunny said to Giant.

"Okay, Gunny," the lieutenant said, "get on the phone to air alert central command in town and to the captain's office. Tell them we are firing for 20 seconds at 4:00 PM."

This was done to let them know that there was no attack imminent and no need to start the sirens all over town.

Giant turned to me, "You can run over to Lieutenant Giesen on the 88s and tell him we are test firing in half an hour, 4:00 PM exactly; a 20 second burst on one barrel. Got it?"

"Yes, Sir. Can I do the firing? I would love to, and I promise I won't mess things up," I pleaded.

"What do you think, Gunny?" Giant said. "Do you think you can lower the seat enough for his foot to reach the pedal?"

"I'll try. If not, we'll have to do some leg pulling or mount a block on the pedal for him," Gunny said with a grin.

"Okay, get over to the 88s," Giant said, "and come straight back. Gunny here will oversee this operation."

I dashed across the open field, took a short cut through a sugar beet field and delivered my message. I was back at the quads in 15 minutes. Gunny had already lowered the seat.

"Try it out," he said, "but don't push any pedals. It's not four o'clock yet."

I tried and just about managed to reach the pedal. At 3:55, Gunny pushed a lever on the right side. It switched the firing sequence from double to single barrel. Another switch showed that the lower left barrel was in the ready position.

"Okay, boy," Gunny said, "when I say fire, you push the left pedal. Left, not right. I will give you a pat on the head when you should take your foot off the pedal. You might not hear my cease fire command while the gun is in operation." He turned to K-3, the loader. "You ready, Kohnen?"

"Yes, Sergeant," Kohnen replied. "Two magazines in the slide, elevation 45 degrees."

Gunny then turned the wheel to move the gun to point in a southwesterly direction. "You ready now?" he said.

"Ready when you are," I said confidently.

"Fire!" Gunny shouted. I pushed the pedal down as instructed and the left barrel let loose a stream of tracers arcing high into the sky, harmlessly disappearing into the distance. It was all over in 20 seconds. I let go of the pedal when Gunny tapped my head. I felt like a field marshal again. My ears were still ringing from the staccato of the rounds leaving the gun barrel.

"How does it feel?" Gunny asked.

"I could do this all day, Sir," I answered.

"Once I thought along those same lines," Gunny said, "but after we had the first few attacks and saw the first casualties, I quickly changed my mind. This cannon is made for fighting, not fireworks."

"I understand, Sir. Thank you for letting me test fire," I said respectfully.

Giant came over to us. "Well done. Now, this stays between us, boy. Normally this would be against regulations, but in this case, well, you seem to be one of the crew, so to speak."

"I won't tell anyone, Lieutenant," I reassured him.

"You can tell your Dad if you like," Giant said. "He might wonder why we fired that burst."

The rest of the crew had watched the proceedings and were clapping their hands. "We have a new K-1 here by the look of it," Magoley said.

It was dark when I got home. Mom had heard the firing, of course, and was worried. She knew I was up at the quads, but since no alert had been given and the Drahtfunk had been quiet, she had calmed down. I told her about the test firing and my role in it and she warned me to be careful up there. Later in the evening Dad met Giant in the pub. Even a flak commander had to get away from the guns now and again. Gunny was in charge in his absence. The lieutenant told Dad about me testing the gun for 20 seconds, and I heard about the conversation the next day.

"Yes, that boy gets his nose into everything," Dad had said. "If it wasn't for him being so useful, I would tell him to stay away from the quads. But who knows, this war might drag on for a while yet. Maybe all our kids will have to be soldiers as well, and the younger they learn, the better they learn. Len is 14 now and has to learn how to fire a carbine, and 12-year-olds are used on 88s now."

"Well, Lou, as I see it," Giant had replied, "it's not all for Führer, Volk and Fatherland. It may be more or less to save our own skins in time to come. By the way, Lou, how long do you think you'll be staying around here? They leave you pretty well alone here, don't they?"

"The high brass knows where I am, Roland. I have the funny feeling that it won't be long now before I get new orders. My old unit, the 17th TD, is assembling right now in Romania. My commanding officer wrote to me a few weeks ago that they will get brand new 77mm cannons on an eight ton Hanomag halftrack. They have already gone to the Ukraine, I was told. Something is brewing out there in the steppes, Roland."

So went the conversation between Dad and Gunny. They downed the weak beer, shook hands and parted.

Before I went to sleep, I looked out the window toward the quads. All was dark in that direction, but suddenly a brilliant beam of light reached into the clouds. The searchlight crew was trying out the new toy, all 65,000 watts of it. A good job done, I thought, and fell asleep.

Two weeks before Easter, Dad received a letter from the division command. He had to report before a medical examination board in Bielefeld to determine if he was KV (fit for frontline duty). If the report was positive, he had to proceed to Heiligenstadt in Saxony and see Colonel Henseler on May 21. If unfit, he could go back to POW guard duty.

Mom went with Dad to Bielefeld. In Dortmund they ran into an air raid and found shelter in the station bunker. Not much damage was done to the track and the train was on its way again at 11:00 PM. They slept a few hours on the train and at 10:00 AM they got to Bielefeld. As we expected, Dad was determined to be fit for frontline duty, and was given a military travel pass from our town to Heiligenstadt. We had eight days before Dad had to leave. We hurried to get the rest of the garden done while Dad was still there. A replacement sergeant had come to take over guard duties at the POW camp, so Dad had the last week off before leaving.

April 29 was goodbye day. Mom went with him to the station, and on the way there they dropped into the local Wehrmacht office to arrange for her to collect Dad's pay once a week. Len and I stayed at home and planted the last rows of beans and potatoes. Mr. Lanz, previously Horse Shit Jacob, came to the fence.

"Not to worry boys," he said. "The way this war is going, your Dad will be home again soon. Unless, of course, the Allies think otherwise."

"How do you know how long the war will last?" Len asked him.

"The writing is on the wall, Len. If you remember the Wehrmacht was on the Volga last October. Now it's May 1943 and they are back in the Ukraine at the starting line they left from a year ago. There be no more "Forward, march," boy. It'll be "Forward, Comrades," and Germany will have to retreat." With that, Mr. Lanz shuffled back across the road to his house.

"He thinks he knows everything," Len muttered as he put the last beans into the ground.

"Yes," I snapped. "I know a few more people like him."

That evening around the supper table with Aunt Carol in attendance, Mom told us that now that Dad was gone and Granddad Willem was dead, it was up to us to see that things got done. "Our animals and garden come first. Hitler Youth and playing soldier, second," she said. "Neither the Party nor the Wehrmacht are going to help us."

"But Mom, I'm a group leader and have to attend meetings three times a week," Len said.

"I don't care if you are a group leader or the Party boss himself. I'm the boss in this house," Mom said, "and I give the orders. Is that understood, Len?"

"Hmm, yes, Mom." Len admitted.

"I'm the last person who would deny you two any pleasures or free time," Mom said, "but there won't be any until after the work around here is done. I can't do it all and neither can Aunt Carol, and I have the baby to look after too."

Mom sent Dad a birthday cake on May 10. He was still in Heiligenstadt but his recent letters gave a hint of things to come. Most of his unit was in Romania now. The armor had already departed for the Ukraine somewhere to the south of Kursk. It was about that time that we heard the news about the raid on the Moehne and Eder Dams by the RAF. Some distant relative wrote to us about the horror and loss of lives the breaches in the dams had caused. Cologne had also just experienced its first big 1,000-bomber raid, and the city was in ruins we were told. But by far the worst news came from Schweinfurt. Granddad Zander had been killed in an American bomber raid on the ball bearing factory. The fact that 20 percent of the bombers had been shot down was no consolation to us. Mom's Dad was dead, and I had lost my other Granddad now. My loyalty to the 1,000-year Reich took a steep dive. I realized that all was not well with the Party.

Dad was now somewhere near Belgorod in Russia. I consulted my atlas and found the town in the Ukraine south of the city of Kursk. He had a new self-propelled gun, a 7.65mm on full tracks, something like a Panzer howitzer. Summer school holiday came, and with it a new menace cropped up in Germany. Colorado beetles appeared in our potato fields. This was something we had never seen before, and they could destroy our whole potato crop.

Of course the Allies got the blame. We were told that planes had dropped them all over Germany to starve the population. The authorities, however, had forgotten to say that most farmers were on the front, and that the pesticide that normally kept Colorado beetles in check was not obtainable, so the creatures had a free run over the potato fields.

Now, instead of working outside around the house, we had to collect Colorado beetles. We walked along the rows and dropped the beetles we found into a jam jar half full of kerosene, but no matter how many we collected, the next day they were there in force again. POWs came and helped as well, but it was a never-ending job. Only in 1948 was the battle against the pest finally won. Insecticide had taken care of them by then.

CHAPTER 12

The Attacker Becomes the Attacked

Day raids were very common in the summer of 1943. The might of the US Air Force was now thrown against the Reich. Unlike their friends the Tommies, who only raided at night with the assistance of a so-called Pathfinder Force, the Americans specialized in daylight raids. That meant they didn't need a pathfinder or target illumination. A smoke bomb would do the trick. On a good day, and there were many that summer, they could plainly see their objective far below, and just dropped the bombs by visual aim through the bombsight. They nevertheless paid a heavy price, not so much from the 88s, but from our fighters, which had the advantage of operating over Germany from bases that were never far away.

Long-range fighter escorts for the American bombers were not yet available. Only a few Mustang P-51s were as yet equipped with drop tanks to provide sufficient fuel to escort bombers, and even then their range was restricted. Germany also finally had, although two years behind the Tommies, a radar device that could pick up a bomber stream way out over the North Sea, which was the well known assembly point before heading for Germany or the occupied countries. This gave the German Air Defense ample warning to get their fighters ready for take-off. The Allies countered by dropping more "window" to confuse the radar, but it did not work as well as expected. The window foil scattered too much and was easily recognized as such, whereas the bombers always flew in tight formations and patterns.

The Allies also dropped small, six by six inch cardboard pieces with a three-inch diameter circle of phosphorus in the center. In the summer heat the protective wax cover on the phosphorus melted, and once in contact with air, the pieces burned for several seconds. We called them "fire cards." The aim of course was to destroy the dry, golden fields of rye, wheat and barley, but in damp weather the things were useless. Once wet or damp, even phosphorus won't burn. It just crumbles to harmless dust. The cards did keep us on our feet. We had to collect them and bury them four inches deep. Many of us burned our fingers, I remember.

Another letter arrived from Dad. He was still near Belgorod, but something was brewing. He said not to worry. Things were okay where he was. Then came July and "Operation Citadel," as Hitler called it. The soldiers involved remember it as the Battle of Kursk, the largest tank battle ever fought. The German Wehrmacht tried to encircle several Russian armies in the vicinity of Kursk and mustered several thousand tanks, TDs and SPGs (self propelled guns) to trap the Russians. After the Germans had advanced a few miles, Ivan's resistance stiffened and for the rest of the month of July, both tank armies fought for supremacy. The Russians won, but lost many thousands of men, not to mention a great deal of armor. Another one of Hitler's ambitious schemes had died in the steppes of the Ukraine. All we had to show for it was another 50,000 POWs, as if we didn't have enough of them already. There were three camps by now near the town and they helped, or were forced to help, bring in the harvest and clear the streets in bombed-out cities.

By now Aunt Gisela had found a place to live near Uncle Peter. He had rented an apartment in the small village of Wurm near the city of Geilenkirchen. He had turned the old school house into a place to live, and he was stationed only a few miles away with an 88 battery. One day Mom and I boarded a train at M-G bound for Aachen. At Geilenkirchen, which was a few miles east of there, we were told to disembark and make our way to Wurm by foot. Fortunately for us, the train had to stop at a small place called Lindern because of an air raid alert, and we just jumped off. From there, it was only two miles to Wurm.

It was a lovely summer day. I noticed several bunkers and gun emplacements along the sides of the road, but there was not a soul to be seen. This was the West Wall or Siegfried Line. Here, in the 1930s, the Reich's Labor Service had been busy building fortifications on every piece of elevated ground. Dragon's teeth, designed to stop tanks, connected the bunkers for hundreds of miles, but at the time all was peaceful, with only the occasional sentry in the distance. POWs out in the fields were bringing in the harvest. Hay was stacked up on wooden der-ricks, and horse-drawn carts loaded with potatoes clattered along the dirt road. Overhead, a few contrails reminded us that the war was still going on somewhere, but there wasn't a gun to be seen or heard.

What a serene place, I thought. No bomb craters. No flak. No Party officials barking orders. Not even a swastika flag anywhere. In mid-1943 that was certainly rare.

Aunt Gisela had settled into her new apartment in the old school-house. We stayed for the weekend and Uncle Peter came over from Dueren to see Mom on Sunday. I asked him why no Flak had fired at the bombers during the air raid alert when we were on the way from Lindern to Wurm.

"We have to conserve ammunition, boy," he said. "One day, believe me, a big air raid will happen somewhere around here, and we have to be prepared for it. Also, our Wehrmacht in Russia needs all the ammu-nition they can get to stop Ivan."

"Is there anything around here worth bombing? I asked. "I've seen only fields, a railroad line, and a closed sugar beet processing plant, and POWs cutting hay."

"It's not the beet factory or the hay derricks," he said. "We're only 20 miles from Aachen, the largest city on our western border and a big manufacturing center. We're also not far from Euskirchen, the training ground for our tank commanders, and the Roer Dams. All of these are inviting targets that are probably already on their maps in England."

"You think the Amis and Tommies will try to attack us by land from the west?" I asked.

"If we don't have peace in this world soon," Uncle Peter said, "they surely will come one day. Our Atlantic Wall along the French coast won't stop them, and this little line outside they call the West Wall won't either."

"But look at all the bunkers, Uncle!" I pointed through the window at a concrete blockhouse not 200 yards away.

"Those are empty shells, boy," he said. "Even if they were manned and armed they would be useless. The country is too open around here; there are too many good roads. Any attacking force can outflank each and every one of them, given the armor. And that, boy, the Allies will have when the day comes. The Amis don't do things by half measure. They're biding their time right now, but once their war machine starts rolling, there will be hell to pay if we don't stop them."

"Wow, Uncle, you make it sound bad," I said.

"I'm being realistic," he said. "In a year things will change dramatically around here. Well, let's see if Aunty has coffee for us, shall we?"

We took the Sunday night train back to M-G and managed to catch the last tram home. Len had stayed behind to look after the rabbits.

By August we finally knew that the Battle of Kursk was over and lost. Citadel had failed. The radio of course didn't exactly say that the Wehrmacht was in retreat, but we could read maps. The towns mentioned in the broadcasts were well to the west of Kursk and Belgorod. We had not heard from Dad since Citadel had started, but as long as no MIA or KIA letter arrived from the high command, we were pretty sure he was safe somewhere in Russia and just didn't have the time or opportunity to write letters. We also knew that mail trains got attacked or bombed by Russian partisans, a constant threat to our communications east or west.

I hadn't seen the 88 crew for a while, so one day while I was collecting rabbit food, I decided to go over and say hello. The week before I had noticed some work going on at the 88s. Trucks had rolled up unloading stuff and there was hammering and drilling, making me wonders what was going on there. The crew greeted me with the usual "hey, boy" and a candy bar, and asked how things were at home.

"Go and see for yourself," I laughed. "It's only 400 yards away and not out in East Prussia. What are you guys constructing?"

"Protection, son, protection," the lieutenant said.

"From what?" I asked. There were huge steel shields mounted halfway along the gun's recoil mechanism, bent in a 30-degree angle toward the inside. The shield was only 10mm thick, and even I knew that any 20mm cannon shell from a fighter-bomber could pierce that sort of armor. A lance corporal explained to me that the 10mm shield protected them from bomb shrapnel and small arms fire. The bomb shrapnel story I accepted, but I didn't buy that small arms bit. Small arms are carbines and machine guns, machine pistols and anything up to 9mm caliber. "So what's really going on?" I asked.

"Well, you never know, boy," he said. "The Amis might drop parachutes one day and try to capture our guns. The shields will come in handy then."

"Or maybe the Amis and Tommies will one day just march to our doorstep with rifles and machine guns over their shoulders?" I inquired.

"Don't mention that when some Party man or high brass is around, boy. You'll get into trouble," he said, and I knew he was right.

I decided not to tell Len my suspicions about the shields. He would only find a stupid reason to contradict me anyway. Four years of war on the home front had made me a lot wiser than I had been in 1939 when everything was "Sieg Heil, we'll beat the Tommies," and lustily sang, "Germany belongs to us today, tomorrow we'll own the world." Times had changed for certain, I thought.

One day when the coal man delivered our ration of briquettes and coal, he asked Mom if we wanted a few carts of coal dust to make our own briquettes. The stuff was laying a foot deep in his yard and it was free of charge.

"Of course," Mom said. "We would love to have a few loads. I'll send the boys over with the cart later. How much can we have?"

"Well, make it two, Agnes. Some other folks might want some as well."

Len and I went to the coal yard with the cart and shovels. The stuff was bone dry and felt like talcum powder. Great clouds of coal dust floated all around us. We looked like chimney sweeps in no time, but we didn't mind. Another winter was coming and the stuff surely came in handy in cold weather. Granddad Willem had shown us how to make our own briquettes a few years back with wood chips and other things. We shoveled coal dust into the old iron bathtub in the yard, then tore up old newspapers and rags and added them with sawdust and wood chips, courtesy of the cabinetmaker. All of this we mixed with a generous dose of water and stirred for an hour with an old oar we had hanging in the shed. After a while the concoction turned into a stiff substance, something like wet clay.

Then the fun started. We scooped the stuff up with our hands, formed it into briquettes the size of tennis balls, and laid them out in the sun to dry. We sat around the bathtub for hours covered in black sludge up to our armpits, forming briquettes. Even Baby Fred got into the action, and didn't he do well! He was black from head to toe. He even jumped into the bathtub, and screamed when we pulled him out. Then he started to shovel the black stuff into his mouth. Mom decided that things were getting out of hand and she carried him inside, getting covered all over with black sludge herself.

"These homemade briquettes are the best invention since sliced bread," Granddad Willem used to say, and how right he was. They kept the fire going for hours on end and lasted us all winter. We had to wash ourselves down with the garden hose before we could take a bath. The next day we started the proceedings all over again, except that Baby Fred was tied like a dog to the nearby garden bench. He screamed for a while because he wanted to help, but he was banned from the bathtub for the day. As a reward for our good but dirty duty, Len was permitted to attend the Hitler Youth meetings for the next two weeks. I could visit my friends up at the quads, but only after we had done our homework and fed the rabbits. There were times when I hated those carrot crunchers. They surely made a mess of my free time, and I promised myself that once the war was over and beef, pork, and chicken were in abundance, I would kill every damn rabbit in the area.

The next morning I went up to the quads. The crew greeted me like a long-lost relative. I told them about my visit to Wurm and Uncle Peter and said that I had been pretty busy the last few days making winter fuel. I asked Giant if I could hang around for the day since I had Mom's blessings.

"Of course, stay around. You are welcome," he said. "We had a jam on A gun during test firing and Gunny is going to strip it down to see where the problem is. You can watch if you want. It might help you in 1955 when you are a gunnery sergeant," Giant said.

I went over to the cannon. Gunny was inspecting every nook and cranny, checking the slides with a pencil flashlight. He finally found what he was looking for. A rivet had come out of a duralumin (aluminum) strip on the slide and had fallen into the feeder chamber, resulting in a jam at the loading slot. It took him two hours to get the cannon ready again, but Giant said it could wait. "We'll have lunch first." It was pea and potato soup with bacon and a good-sized piece of kommis brot (army bread) with salami.

Halfway through the meal the radio speaker crackled, "Achtung! Achtung! Enemy planes approaching PQ 161 and PQ 55!" The telephone rang. It was the guy on the "big ear" giving us a range of 40 miles west-northwest and closing in. Giant asked him if he had contact with the 88s and he said he had. The fighter base near M-G also had the report from a radar station in Belgium.

"Makes me wonder at what time of the day the enemy has lunch. They always seem to come when it's chow time," Giant said. He dropped his soupspoon, spit out a bite of the kommis bread, and pushed the alert button on the wall. The alarm bell rang and he shouted into the mike, "On your stations now!"

The searchlight crew, who had been fast asleep, fell out of their bunks with bleary eyes, looking for their pants and boots.

"You men can go back to bed," Giant said. "Your time will come at night."

"How the heck can we sleep through this racket?" the sergeant said, pulling his trousers up.

"Want to volunteer? You'll be welcomed, Sergeant," Giant said. "We need more magazine loaders if things get hot around here."

"Naa, I'll be satisfied to watch you," the sergeant said, "and I'll get out of the way if it gets critical around here."

Giant's commands now came in rapid succession. "Lookout, keep your eyes on the western horizon. I want to see them before I hear them." He turned to the range finder guy, who was already focusing his three-foot wide instrument to the sky. "Height and distance as soon as you get a bearing, okay?"

"Yes, Sir," he replied.

The phone rang again. It was a guy from the 88s across the field asking if we had a clean lens for the optic on our range finder. Theirs had gotten damaged.

"Okay, boy," Giant said to me, "now you run over to our big brothers there and take this lens for the range finder. Don't drop it."

Giant picked up the phone again. "I'm sending the boy over with a lens. He's on his way, and good luck."

"See anything?" Giant asked the lookouts.

"Nothing, Sir," came the reply.

I sprinted across the field. It took me just eight minutes to deliver the lens to the 88s.

"Thank you, boy," the 88 sergeant said to me. "Tell the lieutenant he'll get it back after the alert, and I'll make double sure we get one from supply in the morning."

I was wondering where those planes were. Surely they ought to be near us by now, but the lookouts were still searching the western sky.

"Any luck yet?" the lieutenant asked another fellow who was staring up.

"Not a bird to be seen, Sir," the man replied. "That Horchgeraet ("big ear") guy needs his ears washed out and the radar crew in Belgium isn't much better," he shook his head in disgust.

I went back to the quads and got there just as the phone rang. The "big ear" guy was on the line.

"What is it?" Giant asked. "Are planes coming or not?"

"Sure they're coming, Sir," he said. "Not far off, about 12 miles west. They seem to be circling around as if they are looking for something, Sir."

"Hmm, that's why it took them so long in coming," Giant said. "Radar can't get them at this level. They're too low. Well, we'll see."

In the distance, about four or five miles to the west, tracers of another light flak cannon were streaking toward, for us, an unseen target. A row of high Lombardy poplars restricted our view in that direction.

"Damn those trees!" Giant shouted. "I'll have to have a word with the colonel one day to get on to the forestry commission to cut them down."

Giant was right. The quads position was not exactly an ideal place to set up a battery for defense against low-level attacks. To the west we had the poplars, and to the northwest was the food factory with its two high chimneystacks. Only to the south and east did we have an unrestricted view. Our single advantage was that the quads were positioned on the only high piece of ground for miles around, about 60 feet above the plain. Still, it was not exactly a mountain, not even a hill.

"Here they come!" a lookout shouted, pointing to the west.

We heard the high pitch of aircraft engines and then saw them coming, just above the tops of the poplars. They were mean-looking machines. There were four of them, the new American fighter bombers, P-38s or Lightnings made by Lockheed, which could also be fitted with drop tanks and used as a long-range escort. They had the characteristic twin fuselage, and were powered by a pair of turbo-charged Allison engines. We had given them the name "Gabelschwanz Teufel" (fork-tailed devil) on our identification chart a few weeks ago, but this was the first time we had seen them for real. We had been told that their range was insufficient to reach us in Germany, but these devils had drop tanks. They jettisoned them as they came toward us, and the tanks landed in a field of stubble. The 88s were useless against them. They came in too low but we nevertheless did fire at them, probably just to keep up our morale. The P-38s made a turn and came on a beeline toward us.

"Hell, those things are fast!" Hansen shouted over the noise. The quads opened up with tracers heading toward the planes.

"Get into that bunker, boy," Giant shouted. I tried to, but fell over an empty magazine box. The P-38s were now on their run in. Five cannons and machine guns, all mounted in the nose cone, were spitting fire. Thank God no bombs, I thought as I finally dived into the bunker. I heard the "plop, plop, plop" of bullets hitting the concrete roof above me and the clanking of empty brass cartridges falling into the metal bin. Someone screamed, and a rush of wind came through the open door as a P-38 screeched only a few feet above the bunker.

The planes made a wide turn over the town. This time they came from the easterly direction where our cannons had a much better view. I stayed under cover, but through the open steel door of the shelter, facing east, I could see them coming for another attack. Again we heard the whining sound of the turbo charger and the rat-a-tat of the cannons. I noticed that one of our quads had ceased firing. Was it A or B gun? The other one was still going full steam, with all four barrels at the same time. The loaders were working overtime, I thought.

Then I heard someone shouting, "We hit one! We got one of the devils! Look! Look!" I saw through the open door that it was K-1 Hansen on A gun. The engine noise receded, so I came out of my shelter. There sure enough was a P-38 trailing smoke, but too low and too far off to the west to observe the crash. The other three had gained altitude now and were heading to the northwest followed by a barrage of 88s and 20mms from the battery on the north side of town. I heard some shouting from B gun and ran over. Giant was attending to Magoley, who was bleeding from a chest wound. Blood ran into the concrete pit and covered the gun swivel.

"Damn, they've shot the phone line to pieces. We need a doctor and an ambulance," shouted Private Schiager, who was also the corpsman for the battery. The wound in Magoley's chest was something that went beyond a corpsman's ability to treat. Help was needed and fast.

Without an order, I sprinted across the field. A block down the road from us was Doctor Frank's office. He had been retired since 1941 but still attended to emergencies, and this was one for sure. I hammered on the door. Mrs. Frank opened it and I told her in a few words what had happened up in the pits. Dr. Frank came down the staircase. He had overheard my report and his medical bag was already in his hand.

"Maria," the Doctor told his wife, "phone the hospital to send an ambulance up to the Light AA Battery near Mr. Kersken's factory. I'm going up there myself."

I raced back across the field to the quads. The doctor, who had no car, followed at a slower pace. Maybe ten minutes had passed since the end of the attack. I fell back into the gun emplacement. "The doctor is coming, Lieutenant, and the ambulance will be up in a minute, too," I reported, gasping for breath.

"And I thought for a minute you were running away from the shooting when I saw you dashing across the field. Thank you, boy, thank you, but it's too late. Magoley is dead," said Giant. "But we need the doctor anyway. Corporal Kohnen has been shot through the leg."

The doctor arrived and went over to Magoley. There was nothing he could do there. "We have a wounded man over in the bunker, Sir. Our corpsman is in there with him," Giant told him.

Doctor Frank went into the bunker and with the help of the corpsman, he bandaged Kobnen's leg and gave him a tetanus injection. An old Auto Union ambulance came up the hill with a driver and two female nurses. Kohnen was put on a stretcher and the doctor jumped in next to the driver.

"Thank you, boy," the doctor shouted, "you have done a good deed here," and off toward the hospital they went.

The corpsman and a guy from the searchlight team put Magoley's body on a cot in the bunker and covered him with a blanket. It was time now to assess the other damage. A gun was okay, but B gun had a few dents and bruises, and Gunny was already making an inspection and getting to work on it. Giant was writing the report for the local AA commander about the attack, the aircraft involved, the time, how much ammo had been fired, casualties, the usual stuff a battery commander has to write down and, of course, the probable kill of a P-38. I say "probable" because only on official confirmation that the enemy plane had crashed somewhere could the kill be credited to the quads.

"Will you mention me in the report, Sir?" I asked, "After all, I did fetch the doctor, didn't I?"

"Look, boy, according to regulations," Giant said, "you're not supposed to be up here in the battery during an attack, but to set your mind at rest, I'm going to mention it to the captain and it will be in his hands then, okay? But don't be upset. You have done a wonderful job. The men around here can confirm that, and I dare say Kohnen will be thankful once he hears about it."

"Will he be okay, Sir?" I asked.

"Yes, he has a nasty leg wound by the look of it," he said. "Magoley had no chance. He bled to death within minutes."

A truck came up the hill with two corpsmen inside. They unloaded a coffin to take Magoley away. He will probably get a military funeral and a posthumous Iron Cross, I thought. The cannons will get a white ring when the P-38 kill is confirmed. The crew will get a citation, and all I'll get is a beating from Mom when I get home. But then, nobody knew in advance that the P-38s were coming for an attack, and Giant said he would tell Mom later that night about my role in the whole thing.

By 5:00 PM, communications had been restored. Gunny had repaired the broken phone lines and Magoley's body had been taken away. Nobody was in the mood for the interrupted dinner of pea soup with bacon. The captain shortly came on the phone to say he was sorry about Magoley's death and that he would go to the hospital in the morning to see Kohnen. He also told Giant that the battery had their confirmed kill. The P-38 had crashed in flames into a field just outside the village of Born. He would contact headquarters for two replacements for the dead and injured crewmembers. Giant gave him a quick rundown of the attack and mentioned my part in it. The captain said he was pleased to hear it.

"I can't give him a medal," said the captain, "but I will mention it to his Hitler Youth Leader. They might come up with some kind of an award. Anyway, I'll come up the hill myself after the hospital visit. It's too late now. Get things squared away up there and give half the men the evening off. I don't expect any attacks now. It's getting too dark for them. Just leave a skeleton crew on standby."

"Okay, Sir, and good night," Giant said and hung up the phone. Turning to me, he smiled and said, "I bet you're sure scared to go home now, boy. Your Mom isn't going to be very pleased."

I just nodded, thinking of the carpet beater.

"Tell you what I'll do," Giant said, "if you hang around for another half hour, I'll walk you home and explain things to your Mom. How does that sound?"

"Fine, Sir, that would be most appreciated," I said.

Understandably, Mom had been worried to death. The news that a quad crewmember had been killed and another one wounded had spread fast. She knew that I was up there during the attack. Giant told Mom the circumstances and that I was under two feet of concrete the whole time. It was a much safer place than our own door lintel he thought. "But Agnes," he said, "tell him to bring his tin hat next time. The captain is coming up in the morning after the hospital visit. I gath-

ered there will be no school, so please let the boy come up. Our commanding officer would like to tell him thank you."

Before Mom could object, I shouted, "That'll be great! Mom owes
me another day off for making coal cakes."

The lieutenant looked puzzled and Mom told him about our briquette making business.

"We have some coal dust up at the bunker," Giant said. "We use
coal for heating and you're welcome to a load."

"Heavens, no," Mom said. "I have enough washing to do for a
while. That black stuff is hard to wash out, but thanks all the same. If
we do run short of winter fuel, I'll come and ask."

"Okay, Agnes. I must be off," the lieutenant said. "I promised my
gunnery sergeant a beer at the pub. By the way, how is Lou doing?"

"We have not heard from him for a while," Mom said, "but you
know yourself what our field post service is like."

"Let's hope things turn out alright for all of us one day. I must be
off. Good night all." With that Giant walked off into the night to the
pub.

I was at the quads by 10:00 AM. The crew was doing a maintenance
job on B gun. There was none of the usual joking and fooling around.
Magoley's death had dampened their spirits, but the new white ring on
the barrels was already in place.

At 10:30 the captain arrived in a Kübelwagen. After a "good morning" and "Heil Hitler," he read Giant's report. Then he called the whole
crew to gather round. The sun was up and it promised to be a nice day.

"No need to assemble in the bunker now. Just stand at ease," he
said. "I've got something to say and this concerns everyone of us here.
First, let me tell you that no one is sorrier than I over the death of one
of our crewmembers in yesterday's attack. I just came from the hospital. Kohnen is doing fine but he won't be back with us. They're going to
ship him out to a military hospital in his hometown of Frankfurt. His
leg is busted for good and he'll be limping for the rest of his life. As for
Magoley, he will be buried with full honors in Greifswald, Pommerania,
where he was born."

Changing subjects, the captain continued, "I attended a meeting late
last night with the colonel and the command of the district air defenses,
and we came to some conclusions and created some new guidelines. The
low-level attack yesterday was probably a test. Maybe they were testing
our defense against their fast and hard-hitting fighter-bombers, but

what puzzles me is the way they went about it. Normally, if they have
flak suppression, they have a bomber formation overhead at a height
the quads can just barely reach. Then once the quads are busy with the
bombers above, they send in the flak suppressors, and before our guns
can adjust their range and elevation, they have time to hit their targets.
Yesterday, those P-38s had drop tanks. We recovered all of them, more
or less intact. With them the P-38 has an estimated range of about 900
miles. Enough to take off in southern England, fly 300 miles on a beeline to this part of the Reich, and hang around for 30 minutes before
heading back to base."

"Are they able to carry any bombs, Sir?" Gunny asked.

"As far as we can determine," the captain said, "they can carry a
load of 500-pound fragmentation bombs, but with drop tanks their
bomb load is considerably reduced, and those guys yesterday had no
bombs. Their advantage lies in speed and firepower. We haven't seen the
last of them. From now on, we will have a full crew on alert in daylight
at all times. They won't come at night. Flak suppression is a dangerous
business at low level, even for the best pilot. What we do expect now is
something in the range of a medium-level bomber stream, and while
we're busy with them, the flak suppressors will sneak up and throw
whatever they can throw at our batteries."

"Sounds like we could do with more fire power ourselves," Gunny
chimed in.

"That you will get," said the captain. "In the next few days, two
twin heavy machine guns plus six crew members will be assigned to you.
These guys are supposed to be specialists in this sort of attack. The 88s
will get help as well. The problems with low-level attacks will only
increase. We've been up here almost four years, and the enemy has certainly registered every flak position in Germany on their maps by now."

He addressed Giant, "Lieutenant, see that the crew for the machine
guns get bunks somewhere up here. I can get OT to build you another
bunker if you like, but right now they're busy digging slit trenches outside town. Maybe I can get you two replacements for Kohnen and
Magoley in the next few days. Meanwhile, you have to do the best you
can up here. Also you'll be getting a brand new short wave radio set so
you can be in constant communication with all batteries in this area.
Your gunnery sergeant can operate the thing until we get a full time
radioman.

Anything else while I'm up here, Lieutenant? Oh, I almost forgot," the captain addressed me, "the colonel told me to express his thanks to you. No doubt Kohnen's mother will be pleased to hear the story of how her son was saved, and I have a thank-you present for you as well."

He handed me a nice Hitler Youth knife with sheath. It was not new, but it was nevertheless in good shape. "Thank you, Sir. Many thanks," I said.

Giant then said, "And at Christmas we'll give you another gingerbread cross with oak leaves this time."

"Make sure he gets it with the proper ribbon, Lieutenant," the captain remarked.

Giant looked at me. I was just going to tell him the story behind that ribbon remark when the captain winked at me and put his finger to his lips.

"Well, I'll be off, Lieutenant. See you around," the captain said, and he left in his staff car, gunning the engine on the downhill slope.

"You seem to be on good terms with the captain," Gunny commented.

"Naa, it seems like the captain just likes me, Sir," I replied. No way was I going to tell him about the Knight's Cross ribbon.

School started in mid-September. Not until later in the month were the twin machine guns installed. Small pits with a cross layer of concrete was all the protection they got, but the OT did set up a new bunker for the crew. It was one of those prefabricated things, holding six men with a small kitchen and a toilet. Our generator supplied electricity. The OT also brought a round, eight-foot high ammo bunker for them. Our own magazine couldn't hold all the ammo, and leaving it lying outside under canvas was an invitation to disaster in an attack. The six new crewmembers for the twins seemed to be a bit young to me, but they were a happy lot. The youngest one was only 16 years old, but they took their business seriously enough as we soon found out.

We by now had a formidable array of weapons in the vicinity. Four 120mm flak guns on the flak towers in M-G, two 88s in the field, two quad 20mms, plus an array of machine guns, a searchlight, and the "big ear," not to mention the 37mm flak guns north of the town. It seemed to me that the 88s were protecting the 120s, the quads were protecting the 88s, and the machine guns were protecting the quads. Who was protecting the machine guns? Maybe the common soldier with a rifle in his hand or a hand grenade in his belt?

Since the day the P-38s sneaked up on us, the quads had a full crew on duty at all times during daylight. At night there was no danger of having an attack by low-level intruders or fighter-bombers. The captain gave the crew some lessons regarding the types of attacks to expect. He said we would have to make a few distinctions.

"We are dealing with a situation where not all attacks can be regarded as being for the same purpose. It concerns us only that we have to defend our sector, regardless of who the attacker is or for what purpose he is here. There are a few things, however, that I'd like to mention regarding what we are dealing with from our own point of defense. First, we have fighter-bombers. Usually they are designated to attack columns of transport, moving trains, important crossroads and so forth. Second, there is the flak suppressor. His sole purpose is to make sure that we keep our heads down while his big brother does his business. Third, you have the low-level intruder who seeks targets of opportunity. Unlike the fighter-bomber, he attacks anything he thinks is worthwhile. Fourth, and last, is the fighter escort, which usually swarm around their big brothers and seldom venture into our range. Anything else doesn't concern us much. We leave that to the 88s and, of course, our own fighters."

The twin machine guns were mounted on swivels and could easily be taken off. Somewhere, the captain found two large pieces of heavy tarpaulin that could be draped over the guns at night. One good thing was that the twin operator could fire over open sights with no need for a range finder. A central trigger fired both barrels. On either side, another guy fed the ammo belts into the chambers. There was one chamber on the right, and one on the left, sort of mirror images.

Of course, the new crew was a bit suspicious of me at first, as I was just a schoolboy hanging around the quads, but Giant, who by now had overall command of the quads, the twins, and the searchlight, soon straightened them out about my being there. They eventually took me in when I told them where single females hung around in town, and who was or was not willing to have a good time with new arrivals.

The new short wave radio was also installed. It had a 15-foot high antenna above the radio shack that whipped gently in the fall breeze. Gunny, who was operating the radio until a trained radioman was assigned, could raise almost any battery between us and the river Rhine. He had contact with the fighter base in M-G and with the high command of the air defense in our district. Some days, transmission or reception was bad, and it took a lot of twiddling with the dials to find the right frequency, but overall, it was a big improvement over the old system of having just a telephone line that more often than not was out of order. I felt myself sort of out of a job now and I told Gunny about it.

"Ah well, that's progress for you, boy," he said. "Radio signals are faster than your legs. In fact, they're a lot faster, and a bullet or bomb can kill you, but it can't kill a radio signal once it's been transmitted, understand?"

"A bullet or a bomb can kill the radio," I replied.

"Oh yes, I admit that," Gunny answered. "But we can build another radio set. We can't build another you."

"Hmm, I suppose you have a point there, Sergeant."

The rest of 1943 was more or less uneventful. Of course, the air raids continued. Mostly the bombers came in above 20,000 feet, out of our range, but lower-level intrusions were suspiciously absent in our area at least. Giant thought the Amis and Tommies had something up their sleeve.

Late in September, the city of M-G was on the receiving end of a massive air raid by a fleet of RAF Lancasters. Our 88s shot two of them down. The searchlight crew claimed that they were the first to see them. Other heavy flak got another seven, and our night fighters claimed six victories. That brought the score to 15 for the M-G raid. Not a bad night's work for the air defense, but alas, the city was in ruins. Fires raged for several days. The fire fighting system was stretched to the breaking point, and only a two-day downpour eventually stopped further destruction. We were getting ready for the next winter, our fourth in the war. Would it ever end, we asked ourselves.

The 120s on the flak towers and the 88s out in their field emplacements had no respite. The British bombers were aloft every night. The Americans came in broad daylight and now had fighter escorts to keep the ME-l09s and FW-190s at bay. The formidable P-51 Mustang had a range that was getting them almost to Berlin and back—and I emphasize "almost." Not until June 1944, when the Allies captured the airfields in France, were the escort fighters able to reach any part of the Reich.

Only fog or heavy cloud cover gave the flak crews some relief. They had to fire on visual targets, whereas the fighters could reach the bombers above the clouds and fight it out with them. Most of the Allied

bombers now had some sort of air to ground radar, or another device called "Oboe," enabling them to bomb precisely, even in bad weather. The Ruhr area, with most of Germany's manufacturing industry, was the main target. The oil refinery installations around Leuna, Dessau and Bremen were also hit, and manufacturing capacity was profoundly reduced. The huge and sprawling synthetic rubber factory near Marl-Huels one day received a plastering that produced fire and billowing smoke thousands of feet high into the sky. Even we could see it, and we were almost 80 miles away.

Germany, cut off from pre-war natural rubber supplies by the effective Allied blockade, invented the process of making synthetic rubber. Trucks and aircraft needed tires, and the partial destruction of the manufacturing facilities in Marl-Huels was a blow to the country. After that, air defenses vastly improved. No fewer than 17 antiaircraft battalions were ordered to reinforce the batteries already stationed in the Ruhr area. A lot of the machinery from the factories was moved underground, safe from even the largest bombs. With oil refineries, it was a different matter: unable to operate in caves or unused mines, they were therefore defended by nearby fighter bases. The refinery of Leuna, near the city of Jena, for example, had three fighter bases within a radius of 50 miles to protect it, but all to no avail—the bombers still managed to get through. Attacker losses were high, but it was worth it to them. The refinery was never able to operate at full capacity, and by the end of February 1945, it ceased working altogether.

We had received three letters from Dad. The last one, dated October 21, was mailed from Dunaburg, somewhere in Lithuania. He said that he had stomach trouble and was nursing a slight wound in his arm he had received during the Battle of Kursk. The divisional Medic had recommended to his unit commander that he go into a military hospital for treatment. After all, Dad was now 42 years old, an age where most fighting soldiers were released for home duty. Of course, there were men older than Dad serving in the Wehrmacht, but mostly they were high-ranking officers and well behind the firing lines with staff cars or even planes at their disposal. Dad had made it from Kursk to Lithuania mostly on foot, or occasionally in a four-wheel farmer's cart pulled by a sturdy Russian Panje pony. Most of his unit's TDs and SPGs were by now rusted hulks far out in the steppes, shot to pieces by the superior new Russian T-34 tanks. Even our up-gunned Mk VIs couldn't scratch them.

Dad wrote that he was going to be transferred to the old military hospital in Bielefeld again. Of course, this made Mom happy, although it was 200 miles away, but trains did run despite frequent interruptions from track damage or the occasional air raid. Trains were actually forbidden to be in motion during a raid, but even the best locomotive engineer couldn't hear the air raid siren, much less aircraft engines overhead, when their engines were running. Besides, most engineers preferred to be a moving target during a raid rather than a sitting duck.

By mid-November, Dad was in Bielefeld. Mom went to see him, and she later told us it took her almost two days to get there. The whole industrial Ruhr was in ruins. Len and I wanted to go as well, but Mom said that was out of the question. The journey was far too dangerous, and besides, we were busy stocking up for war winter number four.

CHAPTER 13

The Stork

Brother Len was 15 now and spent a lot of time at the Hitler Youth meetings. He was learning how to fire a rifle, and one day he even brought it home, minus live rounds of course. He took it to bits and showed me how to assemble it. He said that in a week or so he would be able to do it blindfolded. Well, Brother Len knows everything, I thought.

We picked flowers and weeds for medicine, but the season was over, so in order to help the war effort, we started our scrap collection again. Everything was to be salvaged, from worn out bedsprings to rusty chamber pots. Brother Len and I found an old cast iron bath tub in a drainage ditch about two miles west of town. We took our four-wheel cart there and got a full load—bathtub, wire and some rusty tins.

It was about 4:00 PM and getting dark as we pulled the cart along a rutted footpath. Out to the east we heard engine noise in the sky. Always alert to an attack, although no sirens had sounded, we took cover behind our metal fortress, the cast iron tub. A single engine German plane, a Fieseler Storch, engine sputtering, was gliding toward the field beside the path. We realized the plane was in some sort of trouble and the pilot was obviously looking for a flat piece of ground to make an emergency landing. A Fieseler Storch could land almost anywhere on a flat bit of ground—a 100 yard takeoff or landing strip was no problem for this versatile recon plane. The pilot made a perfect touch down. The Stork came to a stop not 20 yards away from us. The engine conked out on the last fifty yards. A lieutenant, obviously the pilot, followed by a colonel, climbed out and came walking toward us. The colonel wore the red braids and epaulettes of the Artillery with plenty of medals to show on his coat.

Len clicked his heels and shouted, "Heil Hitler!"

My patience with Len's fanaticism for all this "Heil and Sieg" had been wearing a bit thin of late.

The pilot said they were having a problem with their engine. There was a leak in the oil cooler, and their radio wasn't working. He asked us about a phone so he could contact his base in M-G.

Len pointed in the direction where we lived, about two miles away, and told the pilot that Dr. Frank had a telephone and that he would be only too glad to run to the doctor's house and get a message over to the base. And here I am, I thought. He runs his butt off for those stranded officers and lets me pull the cart full of iron home.

The colonel came to my rescue. "No need for that," he said. "The lieutenant here will walk with the two of you, and you can direct him to the house where the telephone is. Make it fast, Lieutenant, we haven't got much time."

"Couldn't you have made it to the base? It's only seven miles away," I asked the lieutenant.

"No, son. We were too low," the lieutenant replied. "We're on an inspection tour, getting to know the lay of the land from higher altitude."

"Inspecting fields and fences?" I asked.

"Sort of," he said. "One day we might have to dig a few antitank ditches and slit trenches around here."

"What does an artillery colonel care about antitank ditches?" I asked.

"They are dug as protection against tanks, son. When you have tanks, you need cannons to stop them. That's where our artillery colonel comes in. You follow me?" the lieutenant explained.

"So far, yes," I said, "but are we expecting any tanks around here soon? I mean enemy tanks?"

"Sooner or later, yes," he said. "I'll settle for later right now, unless this war ends sooner."

We reached home and Len showed the lieutenant where the doctor's house was. After the pilot called the base, he walked over to us and said, "All clear. They're sending a staff car and a couple of mechanics out in a truck right now. Many thanks for your help. If you see them, please direct them to the field. I must get back to the colonel."

About 8:00 PM we heard a truck stop outside. It was an NCO with pilot's wings. He was talking to Mr. Vink, the air warden. He told him there was no way he could get the Stork airborne unless he had a small generator and some light. Mr. Vink was adamant. "No lights. Sorry," he said, "but you're asking for trouble. This has to wait until daylight."

Mr. Vink brought in a roll of blankets. "Not much," the NCO said, "but it'll keep us from freezing. I called the base and they said it's okay, but to get this plane airborne as soon as it is ready. There is urgent work waiting for us. A few ME-109s need our attention."

The men thanked us and drove back into the night, not looking forward to a cold, uncomfortable few hours in the back of an open truck.

The next morning, we took the scrap iron to school and were given a day off. The teacher probably expected us to deliver another load the next day. We wanted to see the Stork take off, so we raced home at breakneck speed, wagon in tow. We had just about changed into work clothes, ready to dash out into the field, when the alert siren started. It was a full alert, meaning an attack was imminent. We stopped under the door lintel to wait and see what was going to happen.

Across the road from us, Mrs. Schroder was going from door to door with a large cardboard container selling washing powder by the scoop to eager customers. Washing powder was always in short supply, and we always welcomed any extra ration, especially when it was delivered to our own doorstep. She was just dishing some powder out to Jacob's wife, with the cardboard bucket beside her on the pavement, when suddenly, from out of nowhere, came the screaming sound of turbo-charged aircraft engines. I looked up and there he came, just above the roof level of the houses, a P-38 with machine guns blazing from the nose cone.

We stood safe under our lintel and watched the bullets hitting the pavement. It looked like a gigantic invisible needle was stitching holes in the ground. Mrs. Schroder grabbed her precious bucket, darted for the nearest doorway, and almost made it. Almost. A bullet hit her in the right arm, and another pierced the container, spilling washing powder all over the pavement. She let out a scream and fell flat into a doorway, blood spurting from a hole in her arm. Then the P-38 was gone, but we could still hear the engines roaring somewhere in the vicinity and its cannons and machine guns hammering away. Then the quads opened up. The doctor came running up the road with his first aid bag to attend to Mrs. Schroder.

Despite the flak fire and the P-38 still prowling around, I ran across the road and scooped up as much washing powder as I could and put it into my cap. The P-38 came for another run with the two Allisons and Turbos going full blast. I just sprinted back to our safe haven under the door lintel. For a split second I could feel the slipstream of the propeller blades as the plane darted overhead. I looked up and saw the twin boom with the American star painted on the wings. Then he was gone.

Again, we heard the hammering of his cannons in the field somewhere. I thought he was giving the 88s a working over. Then I remembered. Heck, he was after the Stork out in the field! I dared not try to sneak a peek over the hedge separating us from the fields. The P-38 was too close for comfort. Finally the noise of the Allisons receded into the distance and the quads ceased firing.

"Well, well, look at that," Len said. "The swine got the Stork."

I burst out in laughter. It sounded like a line out of a fairy tale—"the swine got the Stork." The P-38 did a first class job. The Stork was a heap of smoldering canvas and metal. For good measure, the enemy pilot had destroyed the truck as well, clobbering the thing into a wreck.

The next day I went up to the quads to hear their story about the P-38 shooting up a Stork right under their noses, but they had a good excuse. The field with the Stork had been to the north of the quads and the factory had been in their line of fire. Any aircraft on a low-level prowl in that direction was invisible to the quads unless the plane was at a higher altitude.

Easter 1944 came, and Len graduated from school and took an apprentice job as a toolmaker in a local machine shop. Before the war, this factory made candy-wrapping machines, but now they turned out parts for submarines. I was glad he had left school. I could roam on my own without him acting like a big brother. His work schedule was from 8:00 AM to 6:00 PM, five days a week. On Saturdays he worked from 8:00 AM to 1:00 PM. He got off early because he also had to attend the Hitler Youth meetings as a group leader of the 231st three times a week. Most of the work at home fell on me.

I made a point of getting up very early in the morning in order to get most of the work done before school so I would have free time afterward. We spent a lot of time in the school air raid shelter now because of the constant alerts. This was a cellar beneath the school that had to accommodate almost 500 children, so there wasn't much room to teach. Luckily, the teachers realized that packing 500 children into a cellar was not really the safest policy, and usually sent us home early.

Dad wrote toward the end of May telling us that he might be transferred to Holland. If so, he would try to get a few days leave for a stopover, but he could not promise anything yet. Air raids also increased at an alarming rate, mainly on communication lines, railroads, road junctions and ship canals. These raids were by medium and high-level bombers. The low-level attackers were suspiciously absent. On one day alone, no fewer than 13 alerts were sounded and the heavy flak had a busy day shooting down a Libby and a Mitchell bomber. Our fighters were not to be seen. Wherever they were, it surely was not near us. Gunny said that if I saw a green plane, it was British; if it was silver, it was American; and if I couldn't see it, it was German.

Iron Gustav visited us every night. Sometimes there were two or three of them. The searchlight crew did their best to get hold of them, but the Mosquitoes were too fast and got out of the beam before the antiaircraft guns could adjust their sights.

Those few days without low-level intruders were almost like peacetime. Had the Tommies and Americans run out of fighter-bombers? I asked Giant what he thought, and he said that a large raid or even an invasion was coming, somewhere in France or maybe even Holland.

"Can't our navy stop an invasion? We have air fields all over France and Holland."

"Our navy is nonexistent, boy," he said. "Where is our battle fleet? The Bismarck is long gone. The Tirpitz is stuck up in Norway, the Scharnhorst was sunk last Christmas, and the Gneisenau is in dock for repairs. Our few remaining cruisers won't be able to stop an invasion, and our air bases in the west are short of fighters and bombers. They're all fighting the Russkys on the Dnieper River."

On my way home from the quads, I met my friend Heinz. He was in the same Hitler Youth group as me, and at times he helped out at the POW camp, doing errands for the guards and checking the perimeter fence.

"Been up at the quads?" he asked.

"Yes," I said, "anything happening that you know about?"

"The OT is going to dig some slit trenches for protection against Jabos (Jagdbombers or fighter bombers)," Heinz said, "and Giant told them to keep out of range of the quads. Have they started digging yet?"

"Not as far as I know," I said, "but I agree with the lieutenant. Let them dig anywhere, but not near the guns. Construction work in any form invites fighter bombers."

"How long is your Dad staying this time?" he asked.

"My Dad is in Holland as far as we know," I said, "and we haven't heard from him for a while."

"Your Dad is in the garden. I just saw him," Heinz said.

"You what?!" I shouted, and ran home as fast as I could. I nearly took the door with me as I burst inside. There, sitting at the table eating Mom's stew, was Dad.

"Well, how's our flak kid?" Dad said. "I see you have done a grand job out in the garden," he smiled, patting my back.

I wanted to ask a hundred questions and needed a hundred answers. "Wait till Len comes home, he said. "All I can tell you is that I have two days at home. I'm on my way to Flushing in Holland and have a 48-hour stopover pass."

Mom, Aunt Carol and half the neighborhood were crowding around, wanting to know how he was.

"Not 100 percent fit," he would say, "but who is nowadays? The doctor in Bielefeld has designated me to be on convalescent leave with limitations. So I won't complain."

I told Dad all about the Stork incident and how Mrs. Schroder's washing powder got hit and her as well. When Len came home from work, we sat around the table for supper. Dad told us that he had been discharged from the hospital a few weeks ago. Several men and officers, including him, were sent to Colbitzer Heide near Hillersleben in Saxony. At Hillersieben was the Wehrmacht's proving ground for test firing a new antitank gun. The cannon, if proven successful, would be installed into the new TDs, but he could not tell us any more.

I asked Dad if he had seen the Dora Gun at Hillersleben. We knew that this super heavy gun had been there since 1942. One like it had been employed at Sevastopol back in July 1942 and had pulverized the Russian forts there. Yes, he had seen the Dora Geraet, as it was called. It was a real monster cannon weighing a massive 1,350 tons, with a barrel length of 95 feet and a caliber of 35 inches, but he said he doubted that it would ever get out of the proving ground. The gun required too many railroad cars to transport and 750 men to operate. The bombers would soon find the monster. "It's not easy to hide 1,350 tons of steel," he said.

Then he told us about the island of Walcheren and the city of Flushing where he was now stationed, defending the port of Antwerp from the British. The next day Dad went to see some old friends, but the pub was closed. They had all closed down by 1944. I went with him when he went to see the local Wehrmacht commander to ask if there was any chance he could get an extra day or two at home, but the colonel told him it was not in his power to grant extra leave.

That evening, the last one at home for Dad during the war, he told us to look after things, and be careful not to get ourselves hurt. He couldn't say when he would be home again. The following morning at 6:00 AM he was off to the station to get a train to Venlo. From there transport was arranged to get several groups of men to Flushing.

Mom was in tears this time. "Will this stupid war never end?" she lamented. "It's going on five years now, and still no end in sight."

"You're one of the lucky ones," Aunt Carol said. "I lost my husband four years ago in Poland, remember?"

At 10:00 AM the radio had an important announcement to make. After the usual rousing martial music, the radio guy said, "The invasion of Europe began this morning at 7:00 AM. Allied forces have landed on the Normandy beaches, but our Atlantic Wall will stop any enemy attempt to gain a foothold. Everywhere our troops are engaged in pushing the enemy back. To us, it will be a victory. To them it will be another Dieppe."

"You see?" Mom said. "Now they will surely get your Dad."

I knew from my atlas where Normandy was and Flushing was almost 200 miles to the northeast. Besides, he was probably still on the train and hadn't even reached the coast yet, I told Mom. Unbeknownst to us, the train had stopped at Eindhoven, Holland, where Dad and the rest of the men who had been at the proving ground were ordered to proceed to Vyborg in Denmark.

On the way to school the next day, I noticed the OT men, assisted by POWs, digging slit trenches 12 feet long and three feet deep on each side of the road, even in the front gardens of the houses. The POWs must have had some knowledge that the invasion of France had begun. They were singing in their guttural Polish voices and grinning as I passed by.

For a few days more, there were no alerts. The enemy planes probably were too busy in Normandy. Giant said that he had not seen the sky that empty of planes for two years. "They are busy getting airfields in operation there in Normandy. I don't believe all that crap on the radio that our Wehrmacht is pushing the Allies back into the sea. Only this morning they said that we are fighting a bitter battle around a town named Caen. That's 20 miles inland."

"If we're pushing, how did the Allies get to Caen in the first place?" Gunny asked.

So a week went by without daylight air activity. Only during the night did we hear the bombers overhead on their missions, and only Iron Gustav was routinely present in our area. Every night he came, usually arriving around 11:00 PM and leaving at 3:00 AM. Occasionally he brought a friend, but mainly he was on his own.

Wilhelm Gehlen, age 8, about 1941 in Jungvolk uniform.

A meal of barley soup (and not very good!) served to Hitler Youth, courtesy of the NSDAP about 1940. Will is staring at his soup, center.

Brother Len (X) and a few of his Hitler Youth friends, about 1941.

Dad and his TD, somewhere near Cholm, Russia, April 1942.

Dad near Vilikye Luki, Russia, 1942.

Hitler Youth on parade in Xanten (Westphalia), 1941. Will is somewhere near the end of the group.

Hitler Youth outing on the Rhine near Remagen, 1941. Will is in the front row, fourth from the left.

Hitler Youth outing at King Ludwig I Church, Bayern (Bavaria).

Hitler Youth hostel, Westwald, Kelheim, 1939.

Another photo from the Hitler Youth outing to King Ludwig I Church. Will is in the second row, fifth from the left.

The Hitler Youth hostel outing, 1939. Will is at the back left with his head just showing.

Hitler Youth camp near Hardt. SS man (in foreground) visiting. Will is somewhere near the rear.

Hitler Youth digging trenches for shelter from bombing, near Krefeld, 1942.

Hitler Youth weekend outing in the Eifel, 1940.

Hitler Youth camp, Durach, Allgau, 1940.

Will (left) and friends inspecting a newly arrived quad 20mm AA gun.

Brother Len (right) with cousin Helmut, who was killed in an air raid in 1944. Both are in full HJ uniforms.

Brother Len in full Jungvolk uniform, early in the war or just prior.

Hitler Youth outing in Seiburg. Brother Len is on the far left, out of uniform, 1943.

Brother Len doing machine gun training in Krefeld, 1944.

German reading primer issued to schoolkids like Will beginning in the 1930s.

Even for first graders, like Will in 1938–39, it was impossible not to know the country's leader.

The Nazis began indoctrination early, though the Jungvolk's tasks became more deadly as the war went on.

Sieg Heil!

9. November.
. Die Fahnen wehen.
.. Die Flammen lodern.
.·. Die Toten mahnen:
:: Seid tapfer und treu!

Hitler made November 9 a national holiday in 1933. Five years later it resulted in the rampage called Kristallnacht.

One of the teachers who was required to accompany the Jungvolk on outings, Eifel, 1940.

Hermann Glaser, Hitler Youth Group Leader, 1940.

Another photo of brother Len doing machine gun training, 1944.

Hitler Youth training, Harz area, 1943. Brother Len is front center.

Hitler Youth getting instruction on how to extinguish a phospohorous bomb, 1943. Will is in a helmet, second row from back, center left. Just behind him in a hat is Mr. Vink.

CHAPTER 14

New Weapons, New Hope

Doctor Goebbels, our Nazi Propaganda minister, announced over the radio that we had invented a new weapon that we were using against England. It was called a V-1, a flying bomb or pilot-less aircraft that took off from a ramp. We had seen some of those ramps on one of our annual Hitler Youth camps in the Reichswald, but at the time we did not know what they were for. The guards would not let us get near them and told us to get lost. It was not a Hitler Youth playground, they said.

We also had a new fighter plane. We had seen one a week earlier, and I was surprised to discover it had no propellers, but made an awful noise. Later, we observed the same plane landing at the fighter base in M-G, a few miles away. The quad crew agreed that this so-called ME-262 was faster than any plane they had seen so far. Given enough of them, we could show the Allies a thing or two in the air.

Then, toward the end of the month, the daylight air raids started again, and low or full alert was on all day. The sirens didn't bother with low alert. It was a full alert all day. The Allies had finally managed to break out from Normandy, and towns like Cherbourg, Le Mans and Falaise were in the news. My atlas showed these towns were still a long way off, but the radio told us that our Wehrmacht was holding this or that town. There was no more talk of pushing the enemy back into the sea. Paris had been lost and American troops were 150 miles from the German frontier.

With less school to attend now, plus the summer holidays, we had more time for the harvest and gathering wood and hay, but it was now becoming a dangerous business. Living under constant alert, we soon learned to walk with one eye on the rabbit food or firewood, and the other searching the horizon for fighter-bombers. The bomber streams above were no worry to us. They had better things to hunt than a lonely rabbit food collector, and at the height they flew, they could not see us anyway. We cheered when AA fire or the odd fighter brought one down. If the fire was in the vicinity above us, we jumped into a slit trench, holding a bit of tin over our heads to avoid getting hit by shrapnel. I used my steel helmet only for parades or at the quads.

The fighter-bombers were a different story. We dreaded these because they had bases in France and were able to carry a cluster of fragmentation bombs. A slit trench was not exactly the ideal shelter. A foot of concrete was the best cover against them.

Some new low-level attack planes came on the scene. The P-47 Thunderbolt was the latest. The plane had a huge radial engine, was very fast, and could fly almost at ground level. We called them "Heckenspringen," or hedgehoppers. They bounced up and down in altitude like racehorses on an obstacle course. Despite their low-level attacks, we did not think they were as dangerous as the P-38s. For one thing, we could hear them coming from a few miles out, which was time enough to find cover.

Another addition was the Typhoon, a British fighter-bomber built by Hawker-Siddeley of Hurricane fame. They also carried air-to-surface rockets, but they mostly attacked railroad yards, trains and road traffic. One day in August, four Typhoons worked over the town railroad yard. I was up at the quads and had a spectacular view of the attack. First two P-38s appeared to act as flak suppressors. They exchanged some fire with the light AA in our immediate vicinity, but mostly with the quads to the north of town. While this was going on, four Typhoons managed to sneak in on a low-level run over the town. All quads and twins were busy with the P-38s.

I was peeping over the edge of the parapet near B gun when I saw some streaks of smoke coming from the wings of the attacking Typhoons. My first thought was that our cannons had hit them. Then I could see the sleek rockets speeding away from the planes toward the railroad yards. There was an ammunition train parked on a spur line, ready to pull out for the western front. The rockets hit the train somewhere in the middle and immediately started a fire. One daredevil guy managed to disconnect eight cars and the engine pulled away with them. The other cars blew up, one after another. We were three miles away from the railroad yard, but the shock wave almost blew us over. One car must have been loaded with Nebelwerfer rockets, because we could see the smoke trails going up several thousand feet.

Some stuff landed dangerously close to us and we sought shelter in the bunker for a minute. The part of the town near the yard was in flames. Several blocks had collapsed and damage was extensive. One car axle with its wheels was found two miles from the explosion where it had landed on top of a closed gasoline station, caving the roof in above the pump. Another huge metal beam came down in the play area of the city park, killing three small children. In all, 16 people were killed and 100 injured. The Typhoons got away. None were even hit.

"What a mess! Look at it," Giant said, "and they're going to blame it all on us again. We're supposed to protect them down there, but we also have to keep the P-38s at bay, and there are no German fighters to be seen." He was right. We had not seen a German plane during the attack. Nobody came to the quads and complained about the attack. Most people probably realized that it was useless.

The Third Reich was in trouble, but the Party still thought they knew best. They still came knocking on the doors and begging for things for the welfare organization, as if we had not given enough by now. What else did they want? When they came to us a few days earlier, Aunt Carol showed them the door. "I gave my husband for the war effort and he died for it. I have nothing else left to give. "Why aren't you at the front?" she asked the party man. "If Hitler Youth kids of ten and 12 are required to help the war effort, then surely you ought to be at the front fighting instead of coming around begging for things."

The party guy left, red-faced. He had no answer to that.

I came back from church the following Sunday. It was a beautiful, cloudless day, ideal for flying, I thought. I had just changed into my shorts when Mom asked me to fetch Baby Fred. Fred by now was three years old. He had figured out where our milkman kept his horse, and ever so often he walked the 200 yards down the lane to look over the fence and talk. Whether it was to himself or to the horse, I'm not sure. We didn't worry too much, because there was no traffic on the roads and we knew where we could find him.

That day, I found him by the fence, talking to the old mare in the field. I took his hand, "Come on, let's go home. Dinner will be ready soon. Yummy, yummy, Freddy." To get home, we had to traverse the huge parking lot in front of the factory, the same one we used to use for soccer play. Just as we started across the parking lot, I heard the screaming sound of Allison turbines. I froze. There was only a three-foot high privet hedge behind me—no other shelter. Home was just 100 yards away, but at that moment, the open expanse of the parking lot looked like 40 acres to me.

I pushed Fred into the hedge and looked up. A P-38 was coming straight toward us, just above treetop height, the nose cannons spitting fire. I heard the plopping sound of bullets on the factory roof, and pushed Baby Fred deeper into the privet and sheltered him with my body. Two small bombs tumbled from the plane and disappeared with a high-pitched sound behind the factory. The next moment I heard the explosions.

Fred was struggling and screaming to get away from me. I couldn't see the P-38, but I could tell by the engine sound that he was somewhere near. I decided to run for home but Fred was only three years old and he couldn't, or rather wouldn't, run. I kept pulling his arm. "Let's go Freddy! Quick, bang bang is coming!" I shouted to him. We had been lucky so far, not getting hit. I thought the pilots were terribly bad shots.

We were just in the middle of the parking lot when a P-38 came right overhead, maybe 50 feet high. I could see the pilot's face as he looked down on us. Was he smiling at our helplessness? He did not fire his guns, and I was surprised to see him actually wave at us. I waved back and before he went out of sight I saw his wings doing a sort of wobble from left to right and back. Was that some sort of greeting? Surely from 50 feet up he could tell the difference between soldiers and little kids. Perhaps he was a father of a son himself, or he simply had spent the last of his ammunition.

Giant told me later that afternoon what the attack was all about. A locomotive at the factory loading area was under steam and some men were busy loading food crates into boxcars. The steam coming up from the engine had given their location away to the prowling P-38s. The two bombs exploded inside a heap of coal, and a piece of shrapnel had pierced the boiler of the engine. No other damage was done and nobody got hurt. The engine was soon repaired and went off, to the relief of the quad crew. Having a steam locomotive parked 200 yards away was just inviting trouble.

Call it a close shave or whatever, but worse things were coming. The war was not going away. In fact, it was getting nearer by the day. In the east, the Russians were knocking on the door of East Prussia. Knowing full well what was in store for them once the Russkys broke the door down, the population of the far eastern provinces was leaving by the millions, clogging the already congested roads even more. Around our area, the refugee problem was not as acute as out in the eastern provinces, although by now the US Army had taken the first big German city. Aachen had been captured after heavy street fighting, leaving the city of Charlemagne in complete ruins.

The Americans were now approaching the Hürtgenwald, a dense forest defended by Volksgrenadiers and a determined SS division. Even I knew that if the Americans took the forest, the road to Cologne and the river Rhine was wide open. Meanwhile, the small river Roer had temporarily stopped their advance. The ground on either side was swampy and the Germans had opened the sluice gates of the huge dams above the town of Schmitt in the Eifel Mountains, adding even more water to the already saturated ground.

A few days later, an order was delivered by a motorcycle messenger. Giant nailed it to the wooden bulletin board and we all gathered around. It was a decree by Hitler himself. The light AA flak was heretofore under the command of the Luftwaffe—as if we didn't know that already. The pay for the antiaircraft crews was upgraded to the same level as the Luftwaffe Field Division. Cheers all around, except from me. Every downed aircraft was worth a 25 Marks bonus to all crewmembers. Signed: The Führer. Countersigned: General Quartermaster. Dated: January 1, 1943.

"1943?" Giant exclaimed. "It's already October 1944!"

One wet and gloomy Thursday in late October, we were told that school was out for a few days. The school authorities were having a conference with all teachers in the district to determine whether it was advisable to close the schools altogether if the weather forecast promised a nice day. Sunshine and cloudless skies brought the fighter-bombers out in swarms like bees on a sunny spring morning. It was just too dangerous to sit in a classroom during an attack with only plaster ceilings and a tiled roof for protection. The cellar could hold only about half the pupils anyway. There was hardly room to move around, let alone putting almost 500 desks in there, and besides, the toilets were outside.

School started at 8:00 AM, so it was still relatively safe to walk the one or two miles to get there, but by 9:00 AM, the Jabo pilots were patrolling the skies. Sometimes they were far away, sometimes in our vicinity, but wherever they were, we could hear them any time of the day. 10:00 AM was break time, when we were allowed half an hour in the yard outside. Many times the big siren on top of the roof would start wailing, aircraft engines could be heard approaching, and 500 children would desperately try to get back under some sort of protection. It was a mad scramble, and often not everyone made it. Those who did not ran to the toilets or jumped into the slit trenches by the side of the playground. Of course, the pilots were not looking for school playgrounds. They were searching the roads for transports, rail tracks, and factories. There were a lot of them around, but we did not know it at the time.

We went home from school that gloomy October Thursday in the knowledge that at least for a few days we had free time, or so we thought. We prayed for good flying weather so that we might have a few more days of free time. The local Hitler Youth leader, who had heard about the teacher's conference, had other ideas. We were told to be at the assembly point on Friday morning 9:00 AM sharp for weekend parades, field lessons, ditch digging and guard duty.

Len, of course, was all for it, but I didn't like the idea at all. I went to see Giant at the quads and asked him if he could have a word with the Hitler Youth leader to say that I was needed at the guns.

"Of course, boy, I'll phone the captain and tell him," Giant said, "and meanwhile, you stay put."

"We have orders to fetch a broken down quad from somewhere, get it up here and break it down for spare parts," Giant spoke to Gunny. "You told me yourself that you needed replacement parts urgently, so here is your chance. We'll get them without begging or bribing the engineering shop with schnapps or bacon."

"Everyone at Borsig-Rheinmetall should be shot," Gunny answered.

"Who's that?" a guy from the crew asked.

"Those are the people who make the guns and are supposed to supply us and everybody else with spare parts, but they don't do it," Gunny replied.

"There is a spare quad to be had from the 76th Battery at a place called Baal or something like that near Linnich. It's not that far, about 30 miles from here," said Giant. "We're going to go get it."

"Linnich? As far as we know, the Amis are somewhere around there," Gunny said. "That place is frontline, Sir. It will be a rather dangerous undertaking, especially in broad daylight and with good flying weather."

"Sergeant, I hope I don't have to remind you," Giant said, "that the so-called 'frontline' goes right through here. And who said anything about broad daylight?"

"What do we get for a transport, Sir?" Gunny asked.

"The captain thinks a halftrack would be too slow," Giant said, "and that we would never make it in the dark, so he's sending an eight-wheeled prime-mover. He can only supply a driver, we have to supply the rest of the men. Be up at 4:00 PM sharp, take two men from each gun, and hope for the best."

"Where the heck is this place called Baal, ever heard of it?" Giant asked.

"I don't have any idea," said Gunny, "but if it's near Linnich, we're sure going to find it—if we don't run into the American lines, that is."

"I know where Baal is Sir. I've been there before," I barged in.

"Do you now?" Giant said. "You're a geographical wizard, aren't you? Well, we're not going to take a Hitler Youth on a trip like this. Your Mom will kill me if something goes wrong."

"I want to go, Sir!" I begged. "You just said that the front line goes right through here, and you need men. You need someone who knows the way, and my Mom won't mind a bit. I'm safe under your protection, she always thinks."

"I'm not going, boy," Giant replied. "Gunny is in charge of this detail and if he and your Mom have no objections, so be it. You have my blessings."

"Thank you, Sir," I said. "I'll go and tell Mom, and if anybody else wants me, like Herr Funk from the Hitler Youth, please tell him I'm on a special assignment."

Giant broke out in laughter. "Special assignment, huh? What's so special about picking up a heap of scrap metal from Baal? But go on, it's 1:00 PM now. I'll see you here before 3:30."

"Yes, Sir," I said and went off toward home.

Mom wasn't at home when I got in so I wrote her a short note, telling her that the captain needed me for an urgent errand, that I might not be home until the morning, and if she wanted, she could go to the quads where the lieutenant would explain. I knew she wouldn't go to the quads and she trusted the men up there—after all, they more or less kept the Jabos off our back. I also told Aunt Carol, then I made sure the rabbits had enough water and hay and went back to the battery.

We reached Baal about 2:00 AM. A military policeman directed us to our destination. It was a cannon park just outside town, not far from the Roer River, which was swollen out of all proportion. Pioneers were busy laying mine fields. Some traffic, mostly trucks, was moving out to the north, loaded with equipment. After we found a place to park the truck, we piled stiffly out of the cab. For the first time, we heard the rumbling of the front, not far away-artillery fire and small arms, and a few mortars but no tank cannons.

"Tanks won't get through this mess. They're on the other side of the river, waiting for springtime," an engineer from the Pioneers told us.

"So what's the mining for then?" Gunny asked. "I see you're putting daisy chains (strings of mines) across some of the roads leading to the river."

"Well, one day this swamp will dry out," the Pioneer replied, "and the Amis will get across the river then, so we will be prepared."

Gunny shook his head in disgust because he knew a few daisy chains wouldn't stop tanks.

"We've got 88mms, 75mms and SPGs too, you know," the Pioneer said tartly.

Who's in charge of this outfit anyway?" Gunny asked. An officer walked up, and in the dim light we could see that he was a captain of the Engineers. Gunny did a smart salute while the others hid behind a rather dejected tank destroyer that was parked to one side.

"Ah yes, Sergeant, you're welcome to the quad," he said after Gunny showed him the transport documents. "It was left in our care by the 76th AA."

Gunny replied, "Where is the 76th now, Sir, if I may ask?"

"Gone into the line near Linnich along with some 88s," said the captain. "They took a heavy pounding around Aachen and only got this one quad out. It's a bit damaged, mind you, but I'm sure you guys know what to do with it. I'll send a sergeant major along to direct your driver and crew." He marched off and soon a sergeant major of the Field Artillery came and directed the flatbed crew deeper into the park. It was a hair-raising trip, but the driver made it.

A winch attached to the back of the cab pulled the quad onto the flatbed, and chains and ropes were used to secure it.

"Not too bad looking, this thing," Gunny said.

"It's dark, Sergeant, you just wait until daylight when you can see what you have," the sergeant major remarked.

"Any spares are better than none at all, Sir," said Gunny.. "Thank you. We must be off, if we are to get home before daylight. Any chance of finding some hot coffee around here before we set out?"

"You must be joking, Sergeant," said the captain, "not at 4:00 AM. If you need to make it home before daylight, I strongly advise you to forget coffee and get a move on. The weather forecast mentioned something of a sunny day."

"Damn, that's all we need now," said Gunny.

In Hardt we managed to get coffee and a slice of dark bread with liverwurst from a field supply kitchen. It was not much, but better than nothing. I was dead tired and fell asleep. Gunny by now knew the way home. We rattled into town at 8:30 AM, safe and sound. Giant greeted us with a broad smile, "Well, you made it. Nice quad you got there, plenty of spares."

The gun didn't look too bad in daylight. Apart from two crooked barrels and a few dents here and there, it was a good bunch of parts that Gunny could bring to use.

"I went over to your Mom's last night," Giant said, "and told her I had to send you to the Russian front."

"No! You didn't, did you?" I said.

"No, no, it's okay. I told her you went with the guys to fetch some supplies from the quartermaster, and since you knew the way, they took you along."

Despite the earlier weather forecast, the sky stayed overcast, so we had breakfast and took care of the gun. The driver was glad to get home too. The captain had phoned a few times in the early hours, wanting to know if we had returned. Usable parts of the quad went into the magazine bunker, and the rest was dumped over the parapet into the sand pit below. "I could have taken that scrap to school with me, Sir," I said. "We collect all scrap metal, and up here we throw it away!"

CHAPTER 15

A Journey
& The Americans

October came and we heard nothing from Dad, but Mom got a letter from one of her old school friends asking if Mom could come for a visit. She had news from Mom's cousin who had been very ill. Mom knew that her cousin had been suffering from liver problems for a long time, and she hadn't heard from her in over a year.

The letter, however, was dated July and it was now the end of October. Mom's school friend lived in a small village on the river Sauer in the Eifel region near the border with Luxembourg, and as far as she could tell us, the Americans already occupied that area. Mom, being Mom, said she would try to get there anyway. After all, she said, "I'm a civilian and I didn't start the war."

I was going to go as well. There was no garden to tend. Len had to feed the rabbits in the morning before work, and Aunt Carol would see to brother Fred and run the house. Mom told her that she would probably be away for a few weeks. Despite the travel difficulties, Mom and I managed to leave on the last day of October. We got a train from M-G, via several diversions and hold ups, to Prum in the Eifel region. Here Mom was told it was the end of the line; no trains went any further. The US Army was only 30 miles away on the western side of the river Sauer in the Ardennes.

A railroad guard told us that although no fighting was going on down there, we would be better off going back home. He said we might run into trouble.

Air activity in the region had been remarkably low due to the atrocious weather. Wind, rain and low clouds had prevented the Americans from making full use of their superior air power.

161

Mom had always been a determined person. Having made her mind up, she decided to get to her school friend and if at all possible, to Wiltz as well, where her cousin lived. Mom asked several army truck drivers if anyone was going down to Dasburg. She finally found a guy who probably took pity on us, and told us to hop on the back. He could take us to a crossroad, not far from our destination. "But," he added, "if we get stopped by the field police, you better have a good excuse ready or you'll be walking."

"Won't you get into trouble yourself for giving us a lift?" Mom asked.

"Why no, you're German, aren't you?" he replied. "And, if you have a good reason to get to Dasburg and we have space available, there's no problem."

"Any chance of running into an air attack?" Mom asked.

The driver laughed. "Not in this weather, and it's getting dark. If we hurry, we'll be there around midnight, so let's go."

The rain had ceased as we left Prum behind us in the dark, but a cold wind was blowing and we were sheltered only by a tarpaulin. The driver either knew the road well or he had owl vision because he made good time. We passed one field police checkpoint, which waved the driver on. In some villages, soldiers were cooking over charcoal fires to avoid any light or flames. Armored cars, halftracks and a few tanks were parked in small alleyways. A few artillery pieces under netting stood in an orchard, just discernible in the dark. I wondered why they parked there, so far from the front, when Germany was threatened from three sides now. At one point, the driver stopped at a field kitchen. He got a mess tin full of stew and handed it to Mom.

"Here, have something warm," he said. "Sorry, no coffee around here."

"What about yourself?" Mom asked.

"Don't worry, I'll get my share too." And so he did. The cook filled his tin up again after we had eaten. Ten minutes later we were on the road again.

Amazingly, we saw quite a few people walking eastward along the road. Refugees who are trying to get away, I thought. Most probably, they were Belgian Nazi sympathizers getting away from the wrath of their own countrymen. Just after midnight the truck stopped at a crossroad. "Dasburg is just a mile down the road. Be careful, you two," said the driver. "You could run into a friendly patrol or even Americans. Just tell them that you're refugees. Nobody bothers refugees much around here. We leave them in peace and they don't harass us. Good luck!"

Mom and I picked up our suitcases and bags and started walking along the river. It was pitch dark. Occasionally we heard some sort of explosion in the very far distance to the north, which I thought were maybe from mortar or small cannons. Star shells lit up the sky to our right across the river at one time, but all went quiet after a while.

Just this side of Dasburg was a small hamlet where Gerda, Mom's friend who had sent us the letter, lived. Mom found the house right by the river. She knocked on the door.

"It's me, Gerda, Agnes! Open up! It's freezing cold out here!"

Gerda came to the door. "My, oh my! Am I glad to see you! Come on in to the warm and have some real coffee and cake. How did you manage to get here with all the Wehrmacht up in the Eifel?"

"It's a long story, Gerda, but your letter, the one you wrote in July, only reached us a week ago."

Gerda poured us some coffee and set a plate with slices of cake on the table.

"Real coffee?" Mom said.

"Yes. I got a small supply from some friends across the river."

They exchanged news over coffee and cake, and Mom said that she wanted to get to Wiltz to see her cousin. "I doubt if you can get there," Gerda said. "The Americans are across the river. Well, sort of. They patrol there now and then, but their line is supposed to be up on the Hosingen Road. They don't venture down to the other side of the river. It has been very quiet around here."

"If you want to go to Wiltz," Gerda said, "you'll have to get across the river. This is not a real problem. Although it's 35 feet wide, it's very shallow. There's a ford down by the old mill and the water level is low right now. You can get across with just getting your feet wet. It's not very pleasant in this type of weather, but it's better than swimming across."

"What about guards?" Mom asked.

"There are none by the mill, as far as I know," Gerda said, "and those by the bridge can't see you. The sentries up on the bunkers a few miles away can't see you going across either. Once you're on the other side, keep in the cover of the trees until you get to the main highway. Turn left there. That gets you to Holsthum and Consthum and on to Kautenbach, but the Americans are somewhere up there. Just hope and pray they don't shoot. Well, you two don't look like German SS grenadiers."

We slept well that night in Gerda's guest room. Daylight came and we took a walk through the village's only street. The bridge was guarded by a few soldiers with rifles slung over their shoulders and potato masher grenades in their belts, but other than that, no weapons could be seen anywhere.

At that point, the river was only ten yards wide. The other side, which was now supposed to be American-occupied territory, was a massive pine forest. The American frontline, if there was one, was several miles away on top of a ridge running from north to south along the main highway from Luxembourg City to Weisswampach on the Belgian border. The river valley was sheltered and impenetrable to the gaze even from the highest points on either side of the river.

"Patrols come out only at night," Gerda said, "but they don't harm anybody. I reckon they will spend a quiet winter around here."

We got to the old mill and inspected the shallow ford across the river. "Why not go now?" Gerda asked. "The guards can't see you from the bridge, and if there is an Ami hiding in the woods across, he won't shoot. He can see you are civilians."

"What about our suitcase and haversack?" Mom asked.

"If you must travel, travel light," Gerda said. "You have your coats and your ID papers, and before dark, you could be in Consthum snuggled in a farmhouse drinking American Nescafe. What about that?"

"That sounds good, doesn't it?" Mom answered. "Trouble is, we have to get to Wiltz and back home again. I have a three-year-old boy there with Carol looking after him. And there's Len—but he always manages somehow."

"If you make it to Wiltz, I'm pretty sure you can make it back again," Gerda said. "Thousands of civilians are on the road nowadays, crisscrossing the frontlines. Neither the Amis nor the Wehrmacht have the time to check their movement now."

We dashed to the river bank and stepped from one rock to the next, getting our feet wet in the ice cold water, but we made it across safely. Not a shot was fired and nobody shouted "stop." At the edge of the forest we turned around and saw Gerda waving to us. We waved back and went into the cover of the fir trees.

"Well, so far so good," Mom said. "I'm not very familiar with this area, but somewhere ahead is a small side road that leads to Vianden.

We can't take that, so we better stay on this cow path until we get on to the road to Consthum."

At 2:00 PM, we came to a paved road running to the west. We hadn't seen a soul since we crossed the river. The countryside was hilly but now, being on some sort of plateau with some open fields, we could see that someone, probably a farmer, had recently worked in the turnip field we were passing. The turnips had been pulled up and were lying in neat rows along the track, ready to be carted away. A recon plane was high overhead, and in the distant east we could make out a German Fieseler Stork circling over a forest.

We stood on this road for a minute, looking left and right. Across from us was a path. A gate with a sign, "Eintritt verboten," blocked the way, forbidding entry. We climbed over the gate, not knowing if a minefield or some other hidden danger awaited us. We had followed the path for about half a mile, when the forest began closing in on us again from both sides. The path had to end somewhere, I thought. Then I saw a small foil-packed satchel lying on the ground. I picked it up. Some English writing was on the side of the unopened packet. "Lemon juice powder," it said.

"What do you think it is?" I asked Mom.

"No idea," she said, "but it sounds like some sort of pulver (German for gun powder)."

"In a small packet like that?" I asked. "No, Mom, it's something else."

I opened the pack and a yellowish white powder came out, smelling strongly of lemon.

"Lemonade powder, that's what it is," I said.

"We had some before the war. It came in small packets like this and was called 'Brause Pulver.' It had sugar mixed with it," Mom said. "If you mix it with water," she added, "you get a reasonably tasty drink for hot summer days."

Some sweet lemon powder would be nice, I thought. I emptied the packet into my mouth and nearly choked.

"What's the matter with it?" Mom asked.

"There's no sugar in the stuff! It tastes like vinegar. It's awful!" I said, between spitting and coughing.

"That will teach you a lesson not to eat just anything that's lying around."

We marched on. The path had narrowed now. Pine trees were all

around us, and we could just make out the next field some distance
ahead, where we saw an old, dilapidated cow shed in a corner of the
field. I was getting tired. It had been mostly up hill ever since we crossed
the river. Our last food had been breakfast at Gerda's.

"Let's rest a minute, Mom," I said.

"Okay, but only a few minutes," she replied. "We have to get to
some sort of civilization before dark. It's 3:00 PM now and we have
about two and a half hours of daylight left at most."

Out to the northwest, a few planes were circling around low in the
distance, but they were too far off to identify.

"We'd better not hide in the barn. We might get into trouble with
the owner if he's about, or the planes might think it's a target worth
shooting at," said Mom. "And we ought to see a living being soon.
We're not far off the Ettelbruck Highway."

From somewhere in the underbrush came a sound, "Brrrrring,
brrrrring!"

"What was that?" I whispered.

Mom put a finger to her lips. We listened intently. It came again,
"Brrrrring, Brrrring!"

"It's some sort of a telephone ringing!" she said.

"What?" I exclaimed, "here, in the middle of nowhere?"

Then we heard talking not far off in the undergrowth. Mom stood
up. "We have to take a chance, now or never. Hello! Anybody out
there?" she shouted in her shrill voice.

We then heard some commotion inside the bushes and half a dozen
figures, clad in uniforms with rifles at the ready, came crashing out of
the forest into the clearing. They shouted something in English that we
didn't understand, but we put our hands up like we had often seen in
the Nazi movies when the Wehrmacht had taken enemy prisoners.

One of the soldiers shouted something toward the bushes, and a
minute later, what I thought was some sort of officer came running, a
revolver in his right hand. "Who are you?" he said in broken German.

"Refugees," Mom answered. "We want to get to Wiltz."

He did not understand, but the men had now lowered their
weapons and the officer motioned us to follow him. We were escorted
to a small camp in a clearing, which was probably a patrol point. A few
tree stumps were lying around, and a field telephone was on one of
them. I now noticed the wire running along the ground. The officer got
on the phone and said something and pointed at us. After a minute of

conversation, he put the phone down and came over and addressed Mom in broken German. "You wait here. Captain is coming in auto. Maybe one hour. Maybe not one hour. Sitzen Du down, okay?"

There was nowhere to sit except on the pine needle-covered ground. "What name?" The officer asked Mom.

Mom gave him her ID card, which showed her name and picture as well as mine. Children under 18 years of age did not require an ID card in those days.

The soldiers, meanwhile, were talking to each other and chewing something. One guy reached into a canvas bag and handed me a small bar wrapped in waxy paper. I looked at the soldier. He grinned and pointed to his mouth. "Good, good," he said.

"Eat it," Mom said. "They surely are not going to poison us."

I unwrapped the bar. It was dark chocolate, something I hadn't seen or tasted for a long while. "Danke, danke," I shouted and grinned back.

Another guy shoved a sandwich into Mom's hand, a thick slice of ham between slices of bread. A steaming tin cup full of real coffee followed. I got one as well, although I wasn't very fond of black coffee without a generous dose of sugar. Nevertheless, it was warming. The Nazi Party had spread the rumor that the Allies would not treat civilians very kindly. Here we were, experiencing the opposite.

The officer was unable to keep a German conversation going. No doubt he only knew a few words, but somehow we understood his assurances that all was okay and that we would be taken care of by a higher-ranking officer soon.

I admired the soldiers' rifles leaning against the trees, but dared not touch anything. To me they did look a bit better and lighter than our 98Ks. There was also a small grenade launcher or mortar, and all the soldiers had pineapple grenades hanging from belts and buttonholes. We called this type of hand grenades "pineapples," and the German ones "Kartoffelstampfer" or potato mashers.

After I had done away with the coffee and chocolate, we were each handed a tin full of hot tomato soup. I hadn't seen a fire going, and was wondering where the hot coffee and soup came from when I saw the so-called cooking stove. It was a small square tin with a white tablet in the center burning with a light blue smokeless flame. The flame couldn't be seen even from five feet away.

We sat in silence for about half an hour, just grinning at each other again and again. One of the guys picked up a pair of binoculars and

went away for a minute or so. The men started packing up their gear
and disconnecting the field telephone. Another one rolled up the cable
and disappeared over a hill. Shortly afterward, a squat little open car
with a machine gun mounted on a swivel came bumping along the cow
path with two men in it. A larger three-axle truck followed the car. The
men all saluted and loaded their gear on the back of the truck.

The little car was obviously a staff car. One of the men came over
to us, an officer, I presumed, but he had no fancy uniform like our officers. He didn't salute or shake hands. He looked at us for a few seconds
and said in good German, "I'm Captain Jäger. My orders are to take
you to regimental headquarters. Our colonel would like to ask you
some questions. Don't tell me anything now. I'll be present at headquarters, so you won't have to tell your story all over again. Have you
got any weapons on you?"

"No," Mom said. "We are not soldiers. We are civilians."

"Okay, then, Ma'am," the captain said politely. "Now let's get
going before dark."

Mom sat in the back of the jeep, and I sat up front next to the driver. There was no point in talking to him, I guessed. He couldn't have
understood me anyway. It was getting dark, and the truck with the other
soldiers had turned off into a small side road a few miles back. At a T-
junction the driver stopped. "Left here," the captain said, but the driver
pointed to the right.

Mom asked the officer, "Where are you taking us?"

"Regimental headquarters in Clervaux, Ma'am, he said.

"In that case," Mom said, "turn right here and then take the first
turn to the left and that road goes straight into Clervaux."

"You seem to know the area quite well, Ma'am," the officer said.

"I lived around here," said Mom, "a long time ago before I married
my husband and before the war."

We rolled around the last downhill bend into Clervaux. The town
was dark. Blackout was enforced but there was a lot of coming and
going. It made me wonder how those guys could see to drive their jeeps
and halftracks on the narrow cobblestone streets. Trucks were parked
everywhere. Jeeps stood in driveways and a bunch of TDs and several
tanks were parked in front of the twin-towered parish church.

The jeep came to a screeching halt in front of the Hotel de Ville, the
headquarters of the local commander. "Please follow me," the captain
said. We stepped into the vestibule of the hotel. Several GIs were loung-

ing around. A desk in one corner was occupied by a radioman with a telephone switchboard behind him. We followed the captain into a large room with several tables and chairs arranged in rows, which was probably the breakfast or dinner room, I thought.

"Take a seat, Ma'am. I'll go see the colonel," the captain said.

The officer then looked first at Mom, then at me and addressed me in a sort of guttural German, "Feeling fine, boy?"

"Yes, Sir, thank you," I replied.

"Want some chocolate?"

"No, thank you. I had some already, Sir."

The two officers smiled and looked at each other. "Now then," the colonel said, "you are...?" He looked at Mom.

She handed him her ID, and he looked through the pages and put it on his desk.

"Okay, Ma'am. I'm Colonel Fuller. I'd like to ask you a few questions. Please be assured this is not a military style interrogation, but you must understand that you two were found behind our lines, and as you came from the German side, we'd like to know how you got through, and above all, why you came."

"We were not found behind your lines, Sir," Mom said. "We just happened to stumble upon your men there. We approached them, not the other way around."

"That's right, Sir," the captain chimed in.

"You make a point there, Ma'am," the colonel said. Then, turning to the captain, "Some of our soldiers think this is a big Boy Scout jamboree."

Mom then gave him a brief description of what had happened and showed him the letter she had brought along telling of her cousin's illness. We did not mention Gerda, but we told him where we crossed the river at midday and that she knew the area quite well from her teenage days.

The colonel then said, "So now you'd like to get to Wiltz to see your sick cousin?"

"That is correct, Sir," Mom replied.

The colonel sighed. "You know, Ma'am, there is a war going on around here. It might look quiet and peaceful to you, but we never know what is going to happen. We're not in the habit of letting civilians roam around in combat zones. We fight soldiers, not housewives and children. We are after the Wehrmacht. I admit Wiltz is in a quiet area now, well behind the frontline, but that still makes it a war zone. How did you intend to get there if our men hadn't picked you up?"

"Walk it, I presume," said Mom, "or find a farmer with a horse and cart to take us there."

"There are not many horses and carts left around here, Ma'am," said the colonel. "The retreating German army made sure of that."

"What else can we do then, Sir?" Mom asked.

"What do you have in mind doing in Wiltz once you get there and see your cousin?" he asked.

"I don't know," Mom said. "It depends on her condition. If needed, I'll stay until it's all over. There will be peace one day. I have a very young son at home. My sister-in-law is looking after him for now."

The colonel looked back at me. "You a Hitler Youth?"

"Not a very good one, Sir." I replied. I thought I'd better not mention the quads and the fun we had shooting at American and British airplanes.

"My son is one of the stay-at-home types. He looks after the garden and the animals and makes sure we have a decent meal at least once or twice a week," Mom said. She didn't mention Brother Len, so I kept him out of the conversation too.

"Some boys your age have been firing at us, believe it or not," the colonel said.

"He couldn't reach the trigger on a rifle, Sir," said Mom. "You're surely joking?"

"No Ma'am," the colonel replied. "I wish I could introduce you to some of our guys that captured Aachen last September. They caught ten-year-old sharpshooters taking pot shots from windows at our men."

He turned to the captain and handed him Mom's letter. "Here Captain. Get on the phone to Dutch Cota's headquarters. Ask someone to check this address out. Tell them it's urgent."

"Yes, Sir." The captain said, and left.

"Now, then," the colonel said, "while we wait, I think it's time for some coffee." He returned to his desk and looked through some papers. Outside in the dark street the clanking of tracks could be heard, either tank or halftrack, I thought.

The corporal came with a wooden tray holding an enameled coffee pot, three cups, a basin with sugar, and powdered milk. We helped ourselves. This American coffee drinking business was getting a bit too much for my bladder. I asked for the restroom and the corporal took me to it. He even walked in with me and brought his rifle, as if I were a POW. By the time I got back to the colonel's office, the captain was back, talking to the colonel in English. Then he turned to us. "Okay, our division headquarters has confirmed the address given is correct. I will issue a travel permit and then you are free to go. But," he added, looking at the large clock behind him on the wall, "it's almost 9:00 PM now. We would gladly give you a ride to Wiltz, but there is nothing going that way until morning. Have you got any relatives or friends in town?" Mom shook her head.

"Very well then, Ma'am, if you don't mind bunking it rough, we can help you out for the night."

"We don't mind, Sir," said Mom. "We are really tired, and we'll lay our heads down on the floor if we have to."

"Not quite like that, Ma'am," said the colonel. "There are a few rooms upstairs with beds in them from a time when this was a peaceful tourist town. You can have one of them for the night. I'll get a sergeant to bring you some blankets. I'm afraid there are no sheets. Your countrymen took them before they left, and they took the covers, too. I'll send a mess servant up with some hot food. You look like you could use some."

"Thank you, Sir," said Mom.

"I will send someone up to wake you at 7:00 AM," said the colonel. "Be ready to board one of our supply trucks at 8:00 AM. They run to Wiltz. If you hurry, we might even get you some breakfast. One more thing, Ma'am. Headquarters in Wiltz has told me that you should go to the Château at once to register. It's a formality we require of any civilians. If the German Luftwaffe leaves us in peace, you ought to have a reasonable rest."

We went up to the third floor. There we were shown a small attic room with two single beds. There was only a mattress on the beds, but another guy brought in four army blankets. A small bare bulb hung from the ceiling, giving a diffuse light. A corporal brought some coffee, again without cream and sugar, and two flat dishes with brownish beans, bacon, bread—all topped with a fried egg. It was like paradise. We hadn't eaten such good stuff in ages, and wolfed the goodies down. I even decided to wash it down with the strong black coffee.

Outside on the street there was steady coming and going, but because of the blackout I dared not lift the curtain. The last thing we wanted was to get bombed by our own Luftwaffe. If only Giant and

Gunny or my classmates could see me now, I thought, they wouldn't believe it.

We had a good night's sleep under the protection of the US Army, of all people. At 7:00 AM, a knock on the door woke us up. We had slept in our clothes, so it was just a matter of combing our hair, spitting into our hands and rubbing them off on the blankets, and our morning toilet was done. How simple life can be sometimes.

Down the hall, coffee and a plate of sardines were waiting and we each ate two. The captain came shortly afterwards, "Ma'am, haven't you got any luggage? Don't tell me you left home without at least a small suitcase?"

"We lost the suitcase crossing the river," Mom lied. "It went down in deep water."

"Okay," he said. "There's a truck outside going to Wiltz. Better hurry. You both can sit up front with the driver. A few more people are going that way too, and they'll be some company for you. And just in case the Luftwaffe wants to spoil things, we have a twin AA taking point."

We climbed into the small truck. The driver was gunning the engine. "Kommen, Kommen, schnell!" he shouted in broken German. He pulled up to the square in front of the church where another dozen trucks were forming into a convoy, all destined for Wiltz. Slowly the trucks snaked their way out of town onto the Wiltz highway. Just outside Clervaux, a halftrack with twin AA cannon took point. Another similar one let us pass and pulled in behind us as tail end cover. The cannon crews were peering into the sky, ready to shoot anything that remotely looked German. We passed a few hamlets with GIs standing around by their trucks. Some civilians waved at us. Incredibly, a few farmers were harvesting the last turnips in a field.

Then the whole convoy came to a halt. A jeep with two MPs inside waved everybody to the narrow right shoulder. A huge flatbed truck came roaring down the road loaded with a tank destroyer. I looked in awe at the monster, but I thought ours were better. But we surely had nothing like that flatbed. If we had, I hadn't seen one yet in this war.

Then we passed an artillery battery, four 10.5 howitzers, the cannoneers lounging around. We rounded the last bend just outside Erpeldange and rolled down into Weidingen, a small suburb of Wiltz. This was where Mom's cousin lived, but the driver was not going to stop. His orders were to take us to the Château for our registration pass.

Although the driver had said two words in German when we left Clervaux, he had not uttered another word during the two-hour journey. I thought he might have been planted by the captain to hear our conversation, but Mom, clutching the travel permit she had been given, had not spoken a word either.

A few Sherman tanks were parked by a small side road near the school. Surely our Panthers and Tigers, weighing 72 tons apiece and armed with an 88mm, outclassed the flimsy-looking Shermans in any fight. But the American tank destroyers and self-propelled guns were a sight to see. I was sure that Dad would have loved one of their TDs. The trucks had meanwhile scattered in town. Not all were going to the Château. Our driver went through an archway and pulled into a large yard, then pointed at a door to our right, and said to Mom, "Go in da." He then drove off without another word.

A sign said something like "Div. HQ, 28th Inf. Div. Enter." Mom told me to wait outside on a garden bench while she attended to the registration.

I watched the comings and goings. An officer in a car with two stars mounted on a tag on the front came rolling into the yard surrounded by other brass. This must be a general, I thought. Much later, I found out that the person I had seen was indeed General Norman Cota, commanding officer of the 28th Infantry Division. In one corner of the yard, I could see a twin AA gun mounted on a tank chassis. I had seen them on halftracks, but this was new to me.

I considered myself a bit of an expert on light AA guns, so I decided to walk over. But before I managed to get off the bench, someone tapped my shoulder. I turned around and nearly fainted. There, with a smile all over his face, stood a big black soldier. To me he looked like he was from the deepest part of Africa. We had always assumed that colored people lived in Africa and dressed in grass skirts, but here was a soldier, an American, and by the expression on his face, a friendly one, too.

I strolled over to the twin mounts. Nobody was near it, but I dared not make a closer inspection for fear of the big black guard. I thought it was a 20mm, like our quads but the magazine mountings were on top of the barrels, whereas ours were on the side. I heard Mom calling, so I went back.

"Everything is alright," she said. "I gave the Amis my cousin's address in case they want us for anything, but I don't think they'll bother us much. They have a war to run and are not interested in playing nursemaid to us. Come on, let's go."

We walked back toward the lower part of the town. Across the valley, toward Derenbach, a few German fighters were having a shootout with six or seven Mustangs P-51s. We distinctly heard the rattling of the machine guns. We saw one plane, American or German, I can't remember, going down in flames, crashing somewhere in the forest to the west.

We passed a few burned out dwellings. Some were shuttered up; the occupants had fled and not returned yet. Outside one house, a woman was cutting firewood with an rusty old bow saw.

Then all of a sudden, the P-51s came racing from the west toward the town. They turned sharply to the east and then came back. I heard the rattling of cannons and machine guns against another sound. The fighters were chasing a German V-1, the pilotless "doodlebugs," as the Tommies called them. It was only a few hundred feet up, engine sputtering as if short of fuel. Before the P-51s could get a good shot at it, the thing nose dived a few miles off into a field near Winseler and exploded with an almighty crash.

That seemed to be the end of the activities for a while because all was quiet. The Mustangs went home to their base for refueling. Only the two trails of smoke in the distance told us that all had not been peaceful around Wiltz.

Almost like home, I thought. War can be great fun as long as your own pants are not on fire. It was turning colder now. By the time we reached the lower part of town, a few snowflakes were falling from the sky. We got to cousin Herta's house, but what a disappointment awaited us. It was all boarded up, the roller blinds were shut, and nobody came to the door when we knocked. After a while, we gave up.

There was a baker's store just down the road so we proceeded there. The shop door was unlocked and we walked in. If this was supposed to be a baker's store, then someone had his bearings wrong. There were some wrapped soap bars on a shelf along with shakers of Ata scouring powder, a box of turnips, and a few other odds and ends, but there was not a loaf of bread to be seen. An elderly lady came through a back door into the store. When she saw Mom, she cried out loud, "Oh my Lord, it's you, Agnes! How did you get here from Germany?"

"It's a long story, Mrs. Knauff, and I'll tell you all about it one of these days. But all we came for is to see Herta." Mom showed Mrs. Knauff the letter she had received. It was seven weeks old by now, and had been written before the Germans retreated to the West Wall lining along the border.

"Dear me," Mrs. Knauff said. "Herta died four weeks ago. They buried her down near the church." She pushed a chair up to Mom and told her to sit down.

Mom couldn't speak for a minute. Tears were in her eyes. Then she said, "And all this for nothing, and too late. Lord help us, what are we going to do now?"

"Okay," began Mrs. Knauff, "down by the brewery is a small hotel. The owner was pressed into the German military when they retreated. His wife is still there. She's from Bitburg, Germany, but they've had the hotel since they got married back in 1929. She has few Americans staying with her at the moment, sort of billeting there. She does the cooking and washing for them. I'm sure she would be glad to accommodate you, if you're not afraid of a bit of cooking and washing for the US Army. At the present, she's doing it all herself."

"How do we know she will agree to it?" Mom wanted to know. "I have only a few Reichsmarks on me and they are surely of no use to anyone around here now."

"Money is not the issue here," Mrs. Knauff answered. "She might be glad to have some help. I can't phone her. All lines are solely for military traffic. The private phones have been cut off. But wait a minute," she said. She turned around and shouted, "Felix, come here a minute, will you?"

A boy about my age came into the store. His crop of red hair was standing straight up like a flaming torch. "Yes, Mrs. Knauff, what is it?" he asked.

"Take this lady and her son down to the Brasserie Hotel," Mrs. Knauff told him, then turned to Mom. "I'll give you a letter to show Thea, that's her name. Felix here will take you. He is the son of our friends. His Dad is fighting somewhere in southern France and his mother is a nurse in a military hospital in Luxembourg City. Sometimes, if she can get a lift with someone, she comes up to see him. Nowadays there's not much public transport around here, so I look after him and he helps out in the house."

"Do you still bake bread then, Mrs. Knauff?" Mom asked.

"Well, as you can see, we're supposed to be a bakery, but there is no flour around for baking bread. The American military command here in town has promised to let us have a few sacks plus some yeast to feed at least some of the locals. There's another bakery in uptown Wiltz. They seem to be better off there. Just being near the brass in the Château makes all the difference."

"Where is Mr. Knauff, then?" asked Mom.

"He took the horse and wagon and went to Bastogne to see if the QM (quartermaster) and district commander will issue a few sacks of flour."

"What? In this weather?" Mom said. "It's eighteen miles to Bastogne!"

"Well," said Mrs. Knauff, "when he left this morning, it looked like a nice day ahead. Nice weather also seems to keep the American planes aloft, sort of a protective cover."

She motioned us out the door and told Felix to keep his eyes on the sky. The snow was coming down fast as we left, with Felix leading the way across the river Wiltz over an old stone bridge. The retreating German army had destroyed the bridge, but they hadn't done a very good job of it. The Americans had made it passable again, even for heavy armor. There was another crossing further on, but that had been blown up good and proper and was being temporarily repaired.

Shortly, we arrived at the hotel near the brewery. Two American trucks were parked outside. One had a small infantry support cannon in tow, something like 75mm, I guessed. Felix went inside first to look for Mrs. Jaques, the owner, and give her the note Mrs. Knauff had written telling her of our circumstances. A minute later the lady of the house came outside and introduced herself. "Just call me Thea for short," she said after Mom had explained who she was and showed her ID card. "Come on in. It's getting cold out here."

We walked in, crossing a small reception hall, and stepped into a nice warm kitchen that was combined with a dining room. Food was cooking in two pots on an old cast iron stove. "Sit down and make yourself at home," said Thea. "I'll get us something hot to drink."

Over coffee, Mom explained our situation, how we got to Wiltz, and how we were unable to get back home, now that the weather had turned bad.

"If you don't mind lending a hand cooking and washing for a dozen Americans, I would surely be glad to have you until you can get back to your family. There are two small rooms upstairs for you and your son. Bedding is there too. I hid mine before the German army got hold of it. There's a washroom next to it, but I'm afraid there is no hot water. If you need a bath, you have to heat the water in the large metal tub on the stove."

"I don't mind," Mom said.

"You any good at log splitting, boy?" she asked me.

"Sure am," I said. "I do it all the time at home."

"Good, you see to that then," she said. "Logs are plentiful in the yard. We're surrounded by a forest. There's an axe in the shed outside, but be careful."

Mom then mentioned to Thea that she could not pay her for our stay, but that she would surely pay once times get back to normal.

"No need for that, Agnes," she said. "These are hard times. We might as well stick together. I'm glad for a bit of help and company."

"How do the soldiers behave?" Mom asked.

"They're quite nice and behave as well as soldiers can behave. Those Americans are supposed to all be frontiersmen, or so we were told, but all they do is drive trucks, brush their teeth, even with snow, and chew that awful gum stuff. None of them can split a log or fetch a bucket of coal."

Felix, meanwhile, had taken me to the side. "Come up to our house to see me when you get the time. We can do some fishing in the river. I'll show you where the best places are."

"I have no fishing gear, Felix." I said.

"Not to worry," he said. "I catch the trout by hand—been doing it for years. It's easy."

"Okay, if my Mom will let me, I'll come," I said.

Felix left for home. The snow was falling heavily by then. To make myself useful, I asked Thea to show me the wood and coal shed. She did, and also showed me the corner of the yard where I could dump the ashes from the fire.

"Come on in now," she said, "it's meal time. The Americans are having beef stew and we get our share of it." She showed Mom the small pantry where the food supply was kept. The Americans had been generous, I must say. There were tins and cans of all sizes, boxes of candy bars, bags of flour and other goodies. It was like an Aladdin's cave.

"Today, it's beef stew and a juicy Georgia peach cobbler for dessert," Thea said. "They love cobblers. The sergeant, who knows German, even written German, gave me the recipe and we have dozens of cans of peaches."

We went into the kitchen. There was a serving hatch to the hallway where tables stood with mess gear laid out. A good fire was burning in the grate. Someone had a wind up gramophone going and strange music was coming from the contraption. About a dozen or so soldiers were sitting around. Some were writing letters, others were reading books or cleaning their rifles.

"Lunch is ready!" Thea shouted in English. She turned to us, "Some can speak German quite well, but they like to hear my broken English. They think it sounds funny."

The soldiers grabbed their mess tins and lined up at the serving hatch. This was not a self-serve affair, Thea explained. But there were no complaints. The men looked Mom over while waiting for Thea to give an explanation. "This lady here," and she pointed at Mom, "is friend mine, name Agnes, helping me to feed you hungry wolves. She not for fun, understand? You touch lady, I go to General Dutch (this was General Cota's nickname) and report you, then you in brig, okay?"

Everyone was served a good mess tin full of beef stew and helped themselves to bread rolls from a huge plate. Some came for a second helping, others demanded their peach cobbler and gave Thea excellent comments on her cooking. The sergeant said that Thea was surely the best cook in the 29th Division, if not in the whole US Army in Europe, and promised that once the war was over, he would take her to Fort Campbell as a chief cook, and might even take her to Washington to cook in the White House.

After lunch was over for the men, Mom collected the dirty mess tins and cups and did the washing up. I took them back in the hall and set them on a table. Then we had our share of the food, and I admit the cobbler was out of this world.

"What are they doing for evening meals?" Mom asked.

"They usually have cold rations," said Thea, "but if we have any leftovers, I don't mind warming that up for them. I do have coffee going at all times, though. Even at night the coffee pot is by the grate ready for them. After all, it's their coffee and food, and we can call ourselves lucky to have such generous guests. Once this war is over and the soldiers have gone, I bet there will be hard times before it gets back to normal."

I went to the coal shed, filled up two buckets, and also took several big logs into the hall and stacked them near the fire. Some of the soldiers were smoking and talking there, others were resting on their collapsible field beds, staring at the ceiling. Others still were playing cards or some sort of game with two dice. It must have been a good game. At times there was great excitement, and money was changing hands.

I asked Thea if there was anything else she wanted me to do. She shook her head. "You're not a slave, boy. Just take it easy. I'm afraid we haven't got a radio. The Germans took that when they left. The soldiers have one, but they only listen to the English stations, and the music is absolutely terrible. They do have plenty of magazines lying around with pictures, but some are not fit for children to look at."

I strolled into the hall to look around, just to make sure there were not any of those lying magazines around. The soldiers were not exactly what you could call a tidy lot. The tables were covered with a mixture of empty Chesterfield and Lucky Strike packets, chewing gum wrappers, clips of ammo for their carbines, cans of weapon oil, and even some live pineapple grenades. One guy was lying on his cot, cutting his toenails with a bayonet. He seemed to be someone higher ranked than the rest, with three chevrons on his jacket. He waved me over with his bayonet.

"You, boy, Luxemburger?" he asked me.

"I nix Jewish, nix soldier, and nix Luxembourg. I vom Germany, Deutschland, and I got here by mistake," I added in good German, hoping that he would understand me.

It turned out he was quite good in German and he told me that I had mistaken his English word "you" for the German word "Jew". Both sounded similar to me. He continued in respectable German, "How did you get here to Wiltz, then? I thought all Germans were 35 miles that way," and here he pointed to the east, "fighting for their Führer and Fatherland."

"My Mom is from around here, and we got lost between the lines," I said, and told him the story of how we came to Wiltz.

When I told him about the telephone ringing in the forest after Mom and I crossed the river, he nearly fell off his cot with laughter. He explained the episode in English to his mates in the room and they all joined in. He told me that the Germans had captured several walkie-talkies and had been listening in on the American traffic. The Germans knew full well how to use the walkie-talkies, and it took a while before the Americans took countermeasures. The simplest one was just a change of frequency. They only had a limited range anyway, and were useless to the Germans once the batteries went flat, because they had no new ones that fit the device.

He then asked me what it was like living in Germany in this fifth year of the war. I said that quite a few of our people were sick of war. Aunt Carol had lost her husband and a lot of our neighbors had lost relatives in the fighting. I told him about Herbie, who had died from our own flak shell. Bombs had destroyed most towns, and food was scarce.

It looked like we would be stuck in that God forsaken corner of the Ardennes until the war was over and done with. But we were safe. There was no fighting, and there were not many air raids either, at least none that were too serious. There was also plenty to eat and Christmas was not far off.

I almost had forgotten about Christmas. If we got stuck there, we would have Christmas without Brother Len, Baby Fred, or Aunt Carol, and Dad was still away somewhere in Europe. He could be dead by now, I thought, and tears came into my eyes.

It had grown dark outside and a few of the guys lit kerosene lamps. A low wattage bulb hanging from the ceiling gave off a diffuse light. Somehow the electricity was working—a sign that somewhere in the depths of the country, a power station was in business as usual. Not bad. I thought, when I considered that only a few weeks before war had hit this part of the Ardennes with a vengeance. The Americans advanced at such a rapid pace that the Germans had no time to demolish the power stations.

Mom came into the hall looking for me. I told her that the sergeant could speak very good German, so she walked up to him. "I made a fresh pot of coffee for your men, and there's leftover stew from earlier if you want," she said.

"Thank you, Ma'am. I'll get word around to the boys. Your son here has entertained me most of the afternoon with tales from Germany."

"I hope you don't take him too seriously, Mr....?

"Tillman, Sergeant Carl Tillman from Salinas, Kansas. Ma'am, my father was German born. He came to America during the Great War as a prisoner, married my Mom in 1919, and I was born in 1920. They are still alive and living in Kansas."

Mom had addressed the sergeant as "Mr. Tillman." She had never been one to respect ranks—to her, everyone was Mr. or Mrs. She had never even said "our Führer." She always spoke of "Herr Hitler," or simply "Hitler."

"Is your husband in the Wehrmacht, Ma'am?" the sergeant asked.

"Yes, well, he was when we saw him last, in June," said Mom, "but we don't know where he is. We have not heard a thing from him recently. The world is upside down."

"Well, Ma'am," said the sergeant, "I'm not a sentimental person, but I do hope things turn out right for you. One day this war will be over and someone has to rebuild Europe."

"It looks like your people have to help there, Mr. Tiliman," said Mom. "It's funny, really First you smash Germany to pieces, then you rebuild it."

"France and Britain need their own countries rebuilt," said the sergeant. "They won't help you, so I presume it will be up to us to see that this part of the world gets back to a reasonable state."

"Thank you, Mr. Tillman," said Mom. "I appreciate your view regarding rebuilding Europe. I'm not a politically minded person, and never have been. I was born in 1900 and lived through the Great War. Now this. I just hope that it all will end soon. Germany and France have been at each other's throats for centuries, and after each devastating war, both nations have risen from the ashes," Mom said a bit pathetically.

The sergeant laughed. "You Germans seem to get on well with the British and Americans when there's no shooting going on, but mention the word 'France' and Germany seems to go crazy."

We had supper in the kitchen. Thea had made spaghetti with fried onions and corned beef. For drinks we had some of the lemon powder. This time it was quite nice—a generous dose of sugar made all the difference. At 9:00 PM, Mom took the heated bricks out of the bakery oven, wrapped them in towels and put one on the foot end of each of our beds. I went to sleep soon after, snug and warm. I woke up once in the middle of the night. High above, I could hear a stream of planes heading east.

"Who might be on the receiving end of their bombs?" I asked myself. "I hope not our town," and went back to sleep.

The smell of frying bacon and boiling coffee woke me up in the morning. I knocked on Mom's bedroom door—no answer. She must already be up, I thought, so I had a quick cat wash, dressed and went downstairs. It was 8:30 AM. The sun was up, shining on a white wonderland. The snow was almost a foot deep. I fetched the coal and fire logs from the shed. Indoors, the soldiers were busy frying eggs and bacon, while Mom and Thea were cutting bread rolls. Coffee was dished out by the gallon. God, I thought, those guys can sure drink some coffee. I wondered if they would like our ersatz stuff, made from roasted acorns and barley.

What a war the Amis were fighting! They had full stomachs, were never hungry, and had more planes and tanks than men to operate them. No wonder they were enjoying themselves, I thought. Of course, what I did not know about was the blood they had spilled so far in the conflict, the anguish and misery they had endured, the homesickness, and the maimed and mutilated bodies of the wounded and the dead.

After breakfast, a lieutenant came into the kitchen. The sergeant acted his interpreter. "We won't be in for lunch. We have some marching to do for a change. It's a nice day and there's plenty of air cover for us. If all goes well, and I reckon it will, we'll be back for supper."

The men loaded themselves with their weaponry and grabbed their carbines. As if by magic, the pineapple grenades had vanished from the table as well and were now dangling like oversized eggs from their pocket flaps and belts. Ten minutes later, they had all departed, taking the road up to Nürtingen.

Soon the floor was swept and mopped, and the tables cleared and washed. Thea opened the window to let in some fresh air. "Smells almost like roses now," Mom said.

"Can I go to see Felix, Mom?" I asked. "It's a nice day. I've cleared the ashes away, stacked logs by the grate, and put two buckets of coal by the back door. I promise to be back before dark. I will, Mom!"

"What do you think, Thea?" Mom asked. "You reckon it's safe for him to go?"

"Of course," said Thea, "let him have a bit of fun." To me she said, "Remember, boy, keep your eyes open. One never knows. The Germans still have planes, and they're only 35 miles away. And look out for those V-1s. You can never tell where they'll end up when they run out of fuel." She then told me that there was a sled hanging in the woodshed I could use if I would take Mrs. Knauff a few potatoes from the pile in the cellar. I filled a small bag, rummaged in the shed, found the sled, loaded the taters and marched off.

A US Army bulldozer was busy clearing the snow off the road, pushing the white stuff down the embankment into the fast-flowing river. Traffic was sparse and I met only a halftrack, coming down the hill from the upper end of town at breakneck speed. They sure had some good drivers, I thought.

We got back to Knauff's store in time to witness the arrival of Mr. Knauff. It had taken him six hours to get from Bastogne to Café Schumann in the snow. At the Winseler turn off, the road was blocked by a huge self-propelled artillery piece that had broken a track link. It took two Shermans to clear the highway, so Mr. Knauff had to spend the night at the crossroads café.

He had received two sacks of flour, a can of dried yeast and baking soda, so he was now able to bake some bread for the people in the neighborhood. Not everyone had the good fortune of having a dozen soldiers billeting in their homes.

Several days went by without much going on. The snow melted again. I did the usual work of looking after the fires. Mom and Thea did the cooking. Once Mom went up to the Château to ask if there was any chance of getting back to Germany, but the colonel with whom she spoke told her that it was impossible to get anywhere near the border. The Germans had mined the whole area and fired on anything that moved—rabbits, deer, soldiers or civilians. The colonel's presumption was that the Germans, sitting snug in their West Wall bunkers, had something to hide.

The common belief was that the war would be over by Christmas, or at least sometime in January, but the real news regarding the end of the war was not very encouraging. The Allies sat on their butts and would not, or rather could not, attack in such bad weather, and the Germans, defending their home soil, just stayed put and waited, cannons and machine guns at the ready, aimed westward. Then in early December, the skies cleared and fighter-bombers were up from dawn to dusk. Medium Mitchell bombers kept plastering the Siegfried Line. The Wehrmacht sat under six feet of concrete and laughed at the fruitless bombardment.

CHAPTER 16

Saint Nicholas Day, 1944

December 6 was Saint Nicholas Day, the day when children in Catholic countries get small pre-Christmas presents. The weather was clear and cold. Mr. Knauff had applied for some extra flour to do some baking for the coming Christmas season, and the commanding officer had authorized the QM in Bastogne to give Mr. Knauff three sacks of flour and some other supplies. Being in a sort of pre-Christmas mood, he also dispatched a small truck with a driver to take Mr. Knauff to fetch the stuff in Bastogne, where he had to sign in person as the recipient of the goods. After all, regulations have to be followed, war or no war.

In all armies, the QM is either the most loved or the most hated person. They're all the same. They always treat the stuff they are supposed to distribute to the needy soldier as if it belonged to them personally. They don't want to part with anything. They are the real misers of any army. Their power is limitless, so to speak. Even the high-ranking brass bow their heads and beg, and never forget to say "please."

Felix and I had permission to go along as well. There was plenty of room in the truck, which had four seats and a tarpaulin-covered back. The sky was clear of planes, friend or foe (the foe this time around being German). Mom didn't mind either. After all, I was under the protection of the United States Army. Protection? All the driver had as a weapon was a sort of large bread knife in a sheath dangling from his belt and a carbine in a rack behind us. If the German army wanted to set an ambush for us, I thought, we'd be in real trouble.

Traffic was minimal along the highway leading to Café Schumann. As we climbed up to the crossroad, we met the first American armor. Three Shermans were parked under some trees to our left. The tankers were busy over open fires making breakfast. Tents were their accommodation, I noticed. At the crossroads, a burly MP stopped us and demanded to see the driver's papers. He looked us over, and waved us on without further word. The driver was fairly good in German and told Mr. Knauff that he was from an American town with the German name of Frankfort. "That's in Kentucky," he said. His parents ran a vegetable stall in the market there and he had learned a bit of German in high school. "Isn't that where the coal comes from in America?" I asked.

"Yes, well, most of it," he said. "There's some in West Virginia, too, but their coal is like dog turds. It won't burn, and for smelting, it's useless."

He used the English word "dog turds" so I asked him what it meant in German. He laughed, "dog shit, Hunde Scheiss, understand that?"

"Ah, I know what you mean now," I said. "We burn coal dust mixed with water sometimes and we call it 'black cow shit.' But lately, we've been mixing the wet dust with wood chips and newspaper and drying them. They get as hard as cannon balls and burn for hours."

"Is that so?" the driver replied. "I'll have to remember that when I get home to Kentucky. There are a lot of poor folks back home. They can probably learn something from your German ingenuity. Know anything else that's useful?"

"Yeah," I said, "make bread with half flour and half sawdust. It's good. Cleans your guts and stops the trots too."

"Yuk, boy," said the driver, "don't tell me you eat this sort of stuff."

"We do," I said, "and we make our own coffee from acorns and roasted barley."

"I better not tell that to the folks back home," he said. "They might think I'm joking."

I told him it had been no joke living in Europe during this war—not when you were on the losing side, anyway.

The driver did not reply to that. He was gunning the engine now. We had a clear run to Bastogne. Near the Winseler turn, a dozer and some combat engineers were filling in a huge crater by the side of the road where a V-I had landed the night before. The road was getting busier now. It was, after all, the main highway connecting Bastogne to Ettelbruck and on to Luxembourg City.

We passed a few burned out farmsteads. At the border, US Military Police and some Belgian patrol officers stopped us once more. Again, they waved us on. The road now went straight ahead into Bastogne.

To our right was the village of Wardin. As we were passing, right by the side of the road, I saw my first German Jagd Panther, the new tank destroyer. This one had seen better days, and was only a burned out hulk. The fighter-bombers had probably seen to that. A Belgian farmer was busy taking bits and pieces useful to his farm machinery off the tank.

"Spoils of war," the driver said, grinning. "I wonder who buried the crew. Probably we had to do it."

I wondered if it even occurred to him that the German crew might have gotten away.

The new generation of German tanks and TDs could take on anything the Allies had on tracks—but fighter-bombers were a different matter. There was not much the tanks could do against them without fighter cover, and that was something they did not have, at least not in sufficient numbers.

Uphill we went into Bastogne, which lies on a high plateau in the Ardennes. Most other towns were built in valleys, but not Bastogne, and in winter it can be the coldest spot in Western Europe. Cold easterly winter storms sweep through the streets, there are no mountains around the city, and the surrounding forest gives only minimal protection. The town, which looked relatively undamaged, was then the headquarters of VII Army Corps, which had captured the area from the Germans in the fall and had sent the Wehrmacht running across the German border.

It was almost noon when we reported to the QM. Amazingly, the guy seemed to be in a generous mood. We got four sacks of flour instead of three, and some other boxes containing cans and packets which we quickly loaded into the back of the truck. He bid us a friendly farewell and we left the holy domain of the QM much elated.

"The man deserves a medal," I muttered.

The driver stopped at the main square. It was lunchtime and soldiers were milling around steaming field kitchens, mess tins full to the brim. A few civilians had lined up as well. The generosity of these GIs knows no bounds, I thought. The driver told us to get into line. Somehow, he got a mess tin and a spoon for each of us and we patiently waited our turn.

As usual, the US Army food was excellent, better than I had ever eaten at the quads back home. I made a mental note to tell Gunny and Giant about that, if we made it back home again. The cook up at the quads had done his best to feed the crew, but nobody can live a healthy life on nothing but sauerkraut and turnips while fighting off enemy planes.

I hadn't seen a turnip since we left home in Germany. Well, not on a table that is. There were some growing in the fields, but most probably they were intended for animal feed. After lunch, we strolled around the square a bit. In peacetime, this was the main shopping area with trees and a small park. Now, most of the shops had lost their window-panes and were boarded up. A conglomeration of trucks, jeeps, TDs, tanks and steaming field kitchens occupied the square, all protected by four light AA mobile twin cannons, one on each corner of the square.

The Amis, so I noticed, seemed to be having a good time. There was no urgency or alertness. If it wasn't for the presence of the army, one could easily take this for a garrison town well inside the hinterland.

At 2:00 PM, we met the driver again. He told us to hop in; it was time to go home. Felix and I asked him if we could sit in the back. The canvas was rolled up now. The driver said it would be damn cold back there, but we didn't mind. We had a better view from the open end of the truck.

We left the city and passed the burned out Jagd Panther tank. The Belgian farmer was still busy taking parts off with hammers and spanners. I wondered if Panther parts fit on Deering Reapers or German Deutz tractors.

The border was no hold up this time. We slowly went by without stopping. The driver must have had a few beers in Bastogne. The way he steered the truck could not exactly be called safe driving. He went hell-bent straight toward the Winseler turn where we had seen the combat engineers filling in the crater the V-1 left. Just before we got to the turn, he pulled over on the hard shoulder under some trees. He jumped from the cab and ran into the bushes, his fly already wide open.

The huge self-propelled artillery piece we had seen earlier on our way to Bastogne was slowly coming around the Winseler turn, headed toward us on the other side of the road, its powerful engine sounding off with a deep roar. Then all of a sudden, we heard another sound from somewhere high up, a high pitched whining noise not unlike the turbos of the P-38s, but more powerful.

In a flash, a silvery green plane shot across the sky, just above tree-top level. I immediately knew it was a German ME-262. We had just enough time to see the marking of the black and white cross on the underside of the wings. There was no mistake. It was truly a sight to behold. The pilot had spotted the SPG. An alert pilot cannot miss something that size from 200 feet up. Our truck was sheltered under the trees, but the monster SPG was in the open. The driver did not notice what was just above him. The roar of his own engine drowned out the plane's jet turbines, and he also had limited vision—his eyes were on the road, not the sky. We waved frantically at the driver to stop, pointing up to the sky, stretching our arms out imitating wings of a plane. Our driver came running out of the bushes, his fly still open. "What the hell was that?" he exclaimed.

We didn't need to explain. Somewhere, behind the fir trees, the jet engine noise grew in volume. We flattened ourselves behind some trees. The SPG driver had understood our signs. He jumped off the gun platform, sprinted across the road, and made it just in time. The ME-262 had the SPG lined up in his cannon sights and came on, fire spitting from the guns, small explosive shells bursting on the road, the clang clang of bullets hitting the protective armor of the SPG. Then he was gone. It had lasted only a few seconds and the sound of the jet engines quickly faded away into the distance. The plane had no bombs, so the SPG had gotten away with a few dents and bruises. We all got up and inspected the minor damage. There was nothing serious—even the engine was still idling.

By the time I got back to Mom and Thea's, it was dark. Clouds had been bubbling up in the west for a while, and a cold wind swept through the empty streets. A slight drizzle had started and I was glad to get into the warmth of Thea's kitchen. The fires were going well, but I fetched some more logs and coal inside anyway. The soldiers were huddled around the grate, slurping piping hot coffee.

"Howdy, boy. Where have you been all day? Your Mom said you went to Bastogne. Some guys have all the luck while we rot here in this place," the sergeant greeted me.

"It wasn't all fun, Sir," I replied. "We got attacked by a German ME-262, one of them jet fighters." I told him the whole story. When I mentioned the truck driver having a pee during the attack, he laughed out loud.

The next few days it rained on and off. By December 11, it had gotten colder again. The next morning it was snowing. Only two weeks to Christmas and my mind went back to our home in Germany. I wondered what Brother Len was up to now and Aunt Carol and Baby Fred. Mom, before we left, had given Len strict orders about feeding our rabbits. There was no way out and no excuses, and Len knew it. He had promised to feed them every day before he set off for work. They were only fed once a day, anyway. The rabbits knew by now there was a war going on, so they were satisfied and did not complain.

There was an uneasiness around the town. We could more or less feel that there was something in the cards. Was it the long-awaited attack on the German West Wall to end the war, or was it something else? We sat and waited.

We had not seen enough armor or troops lately to warrant an attack on the German bunker line. Besides, the weather had turned from bad to worse. If any attack was forthcoming, it would probably be up near Aachen where, as we knew full well, the Americans had a foothold on the Reich. Around us all seemed quiet. Too quiet, I thought.

On the December 15, I came back from an hour at Felix's. A heavy mist hung over the Ardennes. Inside, the GIs were at their usual pastime, playing cards. Tompson, the mortar plate man, was writing a letter. The sergeant was still reading Tolstoy's War and Peace. Oddie, the other mortar man, was engaged in an arm wrestling match with a guy from Nebraska named Pat. On a night like this, one looks forward to a warm brick on the foot end of the bed. After supper was done, Mom made me a cocoa drink and I went into the hall to see how the sergeant was doing with his book.

"Well, Sir," I asked, "has Napoleon beaten the Russkys yet?"

"Hell no, boy." He came unstuck at a place called Borodino. "Ever heard of it?"

"I think I have, Sir," I replied. "If I remember right, our Wehrmacht passed through it in the fall of 1941."

"And came unstuck, as I remember," was the reply.

"Well, not exactly at Borodino, Sir," I answered. "Our Wehrmacht got to within 15 miles of Moscow, something Napoleon didn't accomplish."

About 10:00 PM we heard planes flying overhead, heading in a westerly direction. The sound of their engines was familiar to me, but surely no JU-52s could fly in weather like this. The card game had stopped. Oddie and Pat ended the arm wrestling match and all the men cocked their ears.

"It doesn't sound like our bombers and they're too slow for fighters," the sergeant said, "and besides, our pilots would rather fight with the infantry than fly in that soup up there."

"Those are Junker 52s, Sergeant," I said, "German transports used for parachute drops.

"You may be right, maybe not," the sergeant said. "Regiment is trying to find out something. If it's serious, they'll call us here. Meanwhile, let's all go to sleep and forget about JU-52s. There's no need for alarm. Nobody is going to do anything in this weather, least of all the Germans. They can't afford to squander the advantage they have sitting in a defensive bunker line. Good night, all."

And so it was. The Americans didn't do a thing in that weather, but their assumption that the Germans were doing likewise was wrong. The weather made no difference to the Germans' plans. To the contrary, they rather welcomed it.

About 5:30 AM, I woke up. There was a sort of vibration in the air. Window panes were rattling, and from far off toward the east, I could hear the rumbling thunder of cannon fire. Up in the clouded sky, an unending stream of planes flew in a westerly direction. I tumbled downstairs, pulling my sweater on the wrong way around. Mom and Thea were already busy making coffee and bread rolls. The GIs were standing around waiting for orders from the sergeant and any news, but the sergeant knew as much as they did—nothing.

Cold rations were munched. Grenades and rifles were checked over. Then the phone rang. It was division headquarters. All personnel had to report immediately to their respective regimental command posts in full combat gear. The Germans had made a breakthrough attempt near Dasburg. "And we have to stop them," the company captain said over the phone.

Meanwhile, the artillery barrage that had awakened me had stopped. Only an occasional explosion could be heard. I listened for a few seconds. "German artillery, 210mm," I thought out loud, "effective range about ten miles."

The men then moved out, boarding the truck and the halftrack with its 50-caliber machine gun mounted above the cabin. Woosie, the gunner, let loose a test burst that made Mom and Thea run for cover. Then they roared off.

For the Germans, events up at Dasburg had not gone exactly as their high command and planning staff had predicted. First of all, the bridge over the river there had been blown. The Germans, having brought up a temporary bridge, found out that the newly installed structure could not support Tiger Tanks weighing over 70 tons, so they had to figure out something else to get the monsters across the river. Meanwhile, the German infantry did get over to the other side, but found themselves without the heavy armor support they so badly needed to knock out American strong points. By 2:00 PM, another bridge was finally in place, strong enough to hold the weight of the Tigers and Panther Tank Destroyers, but the Germans had lost a few precious hours.

We didn't know if the American soldiers were supposed to come back to us or not. We cleared the hall as best as we could. It looked like they were coming back, I thought. The cots were still there, and there were some mess tins, and a few canvas bags. Under one cot I found a carbine and six pineapple grenades. I hid it all under a pile of blankets.

Thea made us some breakfast of ham and fried eggs with slices of white bread. We could distinctly hear the sound of battle, and it was getting louder.

All of a sudden a GI stormed through the door. It was Corporal Dellora, the guy from Iowa who had been in sickbay. He was also the machine gunner of the platoon.

"The bastards have left without me!" he shouted.

"You were supposed to be sick," Thea reminded him.

"I sneaked out of the ward. Can't let my buddies go without a gunner, can I?" said the corporal. "Any idea where they were headed? I need to know."

"Why don't you ask headquarters?" Thea asked. "Your buddies left the telephone behind."

"Good idea. I'll do that," Dellora said, and dialed the number. He talked for a minute, then hung up.

"Okay, they haven't gone far," he said. "They were sent up to Derenbach on a recon. I might catch up with them at the ammo dump. They're drawing mortar rounds there. Hell, they even took my rifle. What now?"

"No, they didn't," I said. "We hid it under that pile of blankets there, and your pineapples too. Want some coffee before you go?"

"No," he said. "I might see ya'll later." And with those words, he stormed out through the door. I looked and saw him running like a rabbit up the street toward the church.

By late afternoon, the Germans finally had some of their armor across the river at Dasburg and were heading straight for Marnach, knocking out a few SPGs and Shermans in the process. They did not have it all their way though, far from it. Of course, they had the element of surprise on their side, plus the fact that the American lines were thinly manned with only a strong point here and there at important crossroads. Nevertheless, American resistance by that afternoon stiffened. The narrow, twisting Ardennes roads were ideally made for roadblocks. The huge Tiger Tanks with their wide traction needed all the room they could get to keep going. It was single file, and anyone who broke down held up the whole column. There was no time for repairs. The broken down culprit was pushed off the road by another monster tank.

Darkness came early in December, and the dense Ardennes fog, so characteristic for that part of Europe in winter, suspended armor operations for the night. Only the German infantry cautiously proceeded, followed by a few PaK antitank guns, manhandled by six to eight men. By the morning, they sat across Sky Line Drive, the main north-south highway. This road runs along the crest of the Ardennes from Diekirch in the south to Weiswampach on the border with Belgium. From this vantage point, one can see far into Germany, right up to the West Wall bunker line. To the west were the important towns of Clervaux or Cterf, Kautenbach, and still further west, Wiltz. Here the Americans had set up a few strong points and they did remarkably well inflicting heavy casualties on the Volksgrenadiers, especially at the small farmsteads of Hoistum and Consthum.

From the scraps of information we got from various sources, we knew the Germans had taken Clervaux and were advancing on Wiltz from two directions. The main thrust was centered on the Clervaux-Wiltz highway, where the armor found the best going. The other direction was from Dautenbach, but only some motorized units and foot-slogging grenadiers and parachute troops used this road.

The American defenders of Wiltz had nevertheless installed some sort of roadblock just above town with an infantry support cannon, some machine guns, and a few BAR (Browning Automatic Rifle) men. When the Germans finally broke through into Clervaux, the Americans tried to evacuate the town, but soon realized their mistake. The narrow roads leading out of town were already clogged with military traffic. Putting an extra 1,000 civilians on these roads would only increase the problem, and everyone knew that fighter-bombers, American or German, would attack columns on open roads.

The American air force had not shown up yet. The weather was still very bad, but amazingly, the German Luftwaffe had made a show despite snow and fog. There were a few things the Americans could learn from the Germans. The GIs were cursing their air force, which in turn cursed the foul weather. It was nothing new to the Luftwaffe to fly in poor visibility. They had gained plenty of experience during four years in Russia, where weather conditions were far worse than in the Ardennes. It was well known to us that bad weather would always ground American air support. Of course, the GIs knew that the Germans had the same bad weather, but the German pilots seemed to cope with this handicap just a little bit better than the Americans.

We stayed put at Thea's. One way or another, this storm, like so many we had experienced since 1939, would blow over. We hadn't seen or heard anything of the men who had been billeted in Thea's house. Their gear was still there, by now neatly stacked on the cots. Thea's pantry was bursting at the seams with American supplies. Except for the fresh meat, which had spoiled because her refrigerator didn't work, all the rest was in good shape. There were plenty of canned meats any-way—corned beef, stewing steak, and several bags of flour, sugar, cof-fee, candy bars, canned butter, cookies, eggs, salted bacon and other things. The only things we did not have were cigarettes or liquor, but then, none of us smoked or drank anyway. I rummaged around in the pantry. No GI, I thought, has to fight on an empty belly. I also knew that now the GIs would face the hard steel of the German Wehrmacht.

Thea had a shelter under the house, a sort of cellar, like the things we had back home that always gave me a bout of claustrophobia. In better times, it had been a storage room for empty beer barrels and other things. It was sturdy and reasonable protection from an artillery shell up to 155mm, I thought, but certainly not the ideal place to be if a 1,000-pound bomb from a plane happened to find the spot. We could not afford to be choosy. Thea took some of the food and drinking water into this cellar with a good number of blankets. There was no heat in the shelter.

On December 17 and 18, German artillery shells began dropping on the town. Nothing heavy, 105s, I thought. I had survived three years of aerial bombing by now and any bomb, large or small, beats a "105er" in destructive power, so we didn't worry too much, and there was noth-ing we could do about it anyway. Several German planes came on the 18th and dropped a few bombs in the vicinity, a meager contribution to their efforts to get to Bastogne. Then behold, the American air force showed up, despite the rotten weather. P-38s and a few Thunderbolts did their very best to ward off the German attackers, but without much success. It just was not American flying weather that day.

On the 19th, we heard distant cannon fire, but it was more from a northwesterly direction. The sector around Wiltz was remarkably quiet. I told Mom I was going to see if Felix was okay. I had not seen him for a few days.

"Be careful and get back if there is an air raid," Mom said.

I found him in their back yard, shoveling snow into a heap. "You want to come on an inspection tour?" I asked him.

"Where to?" he asked.

"Anywhere. I'm just nosey and would like to know what's going on in town." I said.

"There isn't much going on. Most of the Amis left this morning, probably to Bastogne," he said. "I haven't seen a truck since 11:00 AM."

"In that case, Felix, we can't do any harm." I said. "If the Amis have given up the town, it means that the Germans are not far behind. We can always hide somewhere anyway. You coming?"

"Ah, why not? Where are we going?" he asked.

"I figure they will come along the Clerf Highway," I said, "and if we hide in the stone barn near the bridge, we'll have a first-class seat to watch the glorious Wehrmacht returning to the town."

"Don't say that when Mr. and Mrs. Knauff are about." Felix said. "They have just about had a belly full of war and the Germans."

We made our way toward the river bridge, but made sure we stayed under cover of the embankment—not that we feared a sniper bullet of course. The Germans were supposed to still be hanging around near Clervaux, but we did worry about the planes. We should not have worried. There were none about. A thick mist hung over the valley and visibility was only a few hundred yards. Surprisingly, a group of Amis were busying themselves down by the bridge. Some were placing small boxes under the parapet. A halftrack was parked behind a stone garden wall. Then I spotted Dellora, the machine gunner who had skipped sickbay a few days earlier. He was sitting on a stone wall by the bridge smoking a cigar.

"Let's give Dellora a fright, shall we Felix?" I said.

"Are you mad?" Felix corrected, "The guy has a .50-caliber machine gun and after what has been happening around here in the last few days, I bet the man is trigger happy."

"I didn't mean to attack him with stones or a broomstick," I said, "we'll sneak around from the back and just say hello. We can't just walk straight up to him from the front. He might let loose with that Browning machine gun before he recognizes us."

We sneaked around several gardens bounded by stone walls. The snow cover on the ground silenced our approach. Then we were upon Dellora. I tapped his shoulder, grinning like a happy gorilla and said, "Hello, Herr Dellora, good day."

He spun around, his eyes and mouth wide open. The cigar had fallen onto his lap and was burning a hole into his dirty pants. "What, what, what the hell are you two doing here? Don't you know that the whole of the German Wehrmacht is coming right down that road any minute?"

"We sneaked up on you to bring you greetings from Thea and my Mom," I said. "They want to know if they should cook any meals for you. You ought to thank us for coming under fire to look after your welfare."

"Thanks all the same," he said. "It's up to the sergeant if we come for supper, but I doubt it. No joking, boys. The Krauts will be here soon and you better beat it."

"What's going on here then? How did you two get here?" the sergeant said as he walked up.

"Walked it, Sir. Mom asked if it's okay to put beef stew on for you?" I lied.

"It's a nice thought, but no thanks," he said. "You two better get out of the way. Find the deepest cellar and get in it. The Germans are coming and there'll be some shooting."

We asked him if we could cross the bridge to get to the other side. We told him there was a short cut home along the river. In fact, it was nearer—but what we really wanted was to get into the field by the stone barn without telling the sergeant. He waved at us to go across and told us to hurry. To the left of the bridge was a small extension of the parapet. Pat and the guy named Oddie were manning the mortar. Ammo boxes lay scattered about. The others were sitting on boxes behind the stone wall. Up on the hill above the gardens in a side street, I saw the barrel of a tank destroyer cannon poking from behind a ruined wall.

There was still the odd American truck or halftrack coming from the direction of Clervaux. Out from the north, we could now distinctly hear the noise of tracks and the deep roar of powerful engines. We went through a side door into the stone barn. The walls were at least 18 inches thick and made from natural stone. They were as good as anything we would find. We found a peephole and waited. The bridge was in full view and so was the Erpeldange Road, at least up to the nearest curve.

At 10:00 AM on that day, December 19, 1944, so history says, General Cota left Wiltz with his staff to report to General Troy Middleton, who by now had left Bastogne and set up shop in Neuchâteau, leaving the defense of the beleaguered city in the capable hands of General McAuliffe. The reason was obvious to anyone who cared to read a map. The Germans had outflanked Wiltz to the north. In fact, they were by now knocking on the gates of the Bastogne defense perimeter. To hang on to Wiltz would have, in all probability, created a second Bastogne. With the forces available, there was no point in holding Wiltz, so it was left to a colonel to organize a rear guard and destroy the bridges and the stores that could not be taken away.

"It's getting rather scary. Should we go home?" Felix said.

"No, not yet," I said. "There's nothing going on out there. I'd like to see what's going to happen next. This 18-inch thick wall is the safest cover we can find in Wiltz."

"Hear that, Felix?" I said. "It sounds like tank tracks, and it's coming from the Erpeldange direction."

"Could be American stragglers," Felix said, "but come on, let's get home."

"Okay, but just one more minute," I said. "If they are Germans, we run. If they are Americans, we stay. Agreed?"

"No," he countered, "I'll wait two more minutes and then I run—Germans, Russians, or Americans."

"Okay, two minutes, Felix." I said.

We did not have to wait two minutes. It was probably only half a minute, and there they came, rounding the top left bend of the Erpeldange Road—three Panther tank destroyers followed by two Mark IVs, the older type of Panzer with a stubby 75mm cannon. It was too late to run. I told Felix if he didn't want to watch, he could crawl under an old wagon that stood abandoned in the corner. He did just that, and sat there holding his ears. Not a shot had even been fired yet. I looked at the bridge. The men there had taken cover. All I could make out was Dellora's .50-caliber, the muzzle poking over the wall. Slowly, the leading Panther came downhill followed by the others, cannons and turrets swiveling, probing and searching.

"Blam!" The American SPG got the first shot in, but missed. The Panther had seen the muzzle flash and replied with an 88mm round, but missed as well. The SPG, motor running, tried to back up further behind the buildings, but the second round from the Panther's deadly 88 found its mark. The SPG blew up in a cloud of smoke. Now it was the Shermans' turn. Three of them were lined up across the river on high ground. The Germans had not noticed them. The first round from the Shermans hit the track of the leading Panther. Before he could come to a stop, the track curled itself over the driving sprocket and fell useless onto the road. The tank came to a halt sidewise, completely blocking the way. To the left was a steep embankment; to the right was a slope of 70 degrees. There was no room to get by until the wreck was out of the way. The crew of the Panther came tumbling out of the hatch. Dellora opened up with his .50-caliber, but he missed too. The Germans managed to take cover behind the next tank destroyer. Without further ado, the second Panther pushed the wreck over to the side into the field below. Meanwhile, the Mk VIs and the third TD was keeping the three Shermans busy, but the score was still even: US, 1 SPG lost; Germany, 1 TD lost.

German infantry could now be seen. They cautiously crept through bushes, crossing back yards and gardens to outflank the men on the bridge, but Dellora with his .50-caliber was on alert. He kept up a steady fire at the approaching Germans and also made sure that none of the tankers dared show their heads above the turret hatches. The Americans' mortar joined in the fray as well. Pat and Oddie were seemingly experts in that respect. Their rounds fell right on target, scattering the grenadiers and forcing them to take cover in the houses above the embankment, leaving their dead and wounded in the open. Of course, the mortar and the .50-caliber were useless against the German armor, and it was only through the sheer heroic effort of the Shermans above town that the German tanks had so far been kept at bay. But how long could it last?

The Germans, in firepower, outgunned the Shermans by miles, but the struggle for the bridge was not over by a long shot. From somewhere high up in town, unseen by any of us down by the bridge, an American M-61 T1 with its 90mm gun had spotted the German armor on the other side of the valley. Now this was a fellow that could take the German heavy stuff on equal terms. With the first shot, he blew a Mk IV to bits. Nobody got out of the burning hulk.

The Germans now tried a different approach, sending the other two Mk IVs back around the bend. In fact, they had to back up. The road was too narrow to turn around. Through gardens and a narrow alleyway the two Panzers crept downhill toward the bridge, their infantry lined up behind them. Dellora could see them coming, but there was nothing he could do. The .50-caliber, although a powerful and fearsome weapon in a shootout with infantry, was no more than a slingshot against the heavy armor of a tank. The remaining two Panthers kept up a steady fire at the Shermans and one of the Shermans got hit. Smoke was coming out of the open hatch but we were too far away to see if the crew got out.

Felix was still cowering under the wagon, asking how things were going out there. I told him that we were going to run for home as soon as the air was clear. Somehow, things outside came to a temporary halt. The Germans were recovering their wits. The Amis were waiting. The next move was up to the attacker, and they did move. Behind the bend from the direction the Germans had come, was a gas station with an attached workshop. They managed to get a heavy machine gun onto the roof, and with the help of the tankers' automatic weapons, they forced Dellora to take cover. The M-61 uptown, for some mysterious reason, had ceased fire, or more likely, had given up and retreated—a serious setback for the defenders. The only weapon that was able to give the Panthers a fright had left the fight.

The Shermans were no match for the Panthers. The Germans were delighted, of course. Now, with the M-61 out of the way, it was just a matter of time before the Amis had to give way. The Panthers hit another Sherman. Now the Americans were in serious trouble. The last surviving tank called it a day and retreated up a side street. Before the Germans could get another shot at it, it was gone, leaving the men on the bridge.

This time the Germans made no mistake. The two Panthers came barreling downhill, cannons and machine guns blazing away, while from the flanks the Mk IVs and the machine gun on top of the workshop kept up a steady covering fire for their advancing grenadiers. On the Panthers came toward the bridge, 200 yards, now 100, only 50 yards to go. Then with an almighty explosion, the bridge blew up right into the faces of the advancing tanks, and they came to a sudden stop. The mortar and the .50-caliber ceased firing. A big cloud of dust hung over the scene, and from our cover inside the stone barn, we were unable to see if any of the Amis had gotten away. Outside, the firing had stopped altogether.

The German armor was unable to get across the river until bridging equipment could be brought in, or they could try to ford it further upstream where it was shallow. Their infantry was still nowhere to be seen. They were probably hiding in the house above, waiting for further developments.

Mist and fog were coming down again and I thought it wise to run for home. We were well covered by the stone barn, and the river embankment was steep and hid us from view as we splashed through the icy water. Soon the scene of the battle I had just witnessed was lost in the swirling mist.

Felix made his way home and so did I, expecting a dressing down from Mom, who had surely heard the sound of firing at the other end of town. It was getting dark. Outside, an American halftrack was parked, engine running. Inside the hall, our American guests were busy bandaging two wounded men. The Nebraska guy had a bandage around his head, but was smoking a cigarette and sitting on a chair. The other wounded man was Oddie, the mortar man. He was in a bad way, bleeding from several wounds in his shoulder and leg. He was on a stretcher, and Mom and Thea were handing bandages to Pat, who was now the acting corpsman as well as the second mortar man. The sergeant was talking to the wounded, but I couldn't understand what he said. The Nebraska guy was quietly smoking, but Oddie was moaning and let out a scream now and then. I did understand the sergeant when he said, "Stop it, Oddie. Stop it. We'll get you out."

Then the men loaded the stretcher with Oddie onto the halftrack. The rest of the guys followed, and without even a goodbye, they roared off in a westerly direction. Was that the last of the Americans we would see? A few minutes later, a small jeep came racing along the street. The driver stopped, came running indoors and looked around. Seeing nobody except us, he turned around, jumped back into his jeep and gunned the engine. He, too, left without a goodbye.

No manners, those Americans, I thought, and after all we had done for them. We kept them warm, washed their dirty socks and fed them— and not even a thank you. Well, the food was theirs, I admit, and they left a full pantry behind, but nevertheless a friendly, appreciative last word would have been welcomed. I did, however, remember later that I had not seen the .50-caliber gunner, Dellora. I wondered why. I told

Mom about my adventure, said that we had been far away from the action. No harm was done.

It was pitch dark by now and outside all was quiet. Only far out to the west could we hear the steady rumbling of artillery. German or American? We didn't care.

"I wonder where the Germans are?" Thea said. "They are surely in town now."

"I reckon they're busy mopping up, if there is any mopping up left to do, but more than likely they're inspecting all the goodies the Americans have left behind," I explained.

Nobody came that night. Not a shot was fired. We sat around the grate eating the leftovers Thea had wisely prepared for an emergency. Nobody thought of going into the cellar for shelter. The war was over, or so it seemed. Now we might be able to go home and have Christmas with our family, I thought.

I was up the next morning at 8:00 AM. I was anxious to see our German troops again and find out how things were in Germany. Since we had been in Wiltz, we had learned no news of what was going on there. I told Mom that I was going to take a walk to uptown. She, as usual, told me to be careful and to not get into trouble. Trouble? As if we aren't in it up to our ears already, I thought. Hadn't we been in trouble since 1939, or for that matter, since 1914? Only in the early years of the Nazi Regime had things been better, for a few years at least, probably up to 1939, but then all the gains had been squandered away by the new war. All I could remember was living in a country that was at war with England, France, Russia, America, and a host of other nations. Our Wehrmacht had been to the gates of Moscow in 1941. The Atlantic Wall was built to stop any invaders from across the sea, and what did we have now? Russians at the Oder River, ready to invade the Reich from the east, and Allies already inside Germany near Aachen. And there was nothing to stop them.

From what I had gathered inside the American occupied area, there was no chance in hell the Wehrmacht could do anything to stop the Allies. Their war matériel was overwhelming—perhaps not so much in quality, but what they lacked in that respect, they sure made up in quantity. Our combat engineers were using wheelbarrows to fill in the shell craters down by the bridge, and the Americans in Bastogne had bulldozers to clear the roads. Well, why worry, I thought, as I walked over to the bridge. New bridging equipment had been brought in, but the

German tanks and TDs were already on the other side of the river. They had found the shallow ford and were now up by the Château, sitting comfortably in the area the Americans had left the previous day, smoking Camels, and eating Spam and corned beef, all washed down with real coffee. The soldiers I saw were mainly from the 5th Parachute Division.

There was hardly a German tank or TD to be seen. They were badly needed further west to strangle the 101st Airborne inside Bastogne. A few trucks and Kübelwagens, motorcycles with sidecars, and an 88mm on a Hanomag halftrack were all I could see. Heavy artillery was absent, but a 75mm cannon, pulled along by four sturdy horses, made its way along the Café Schumann road. Up on Main Street by the mayor's office, a German field kitchen had set up shop. The smell of pea soup wafted across to me. Soldiers stood in line, banging their mess tins with spoons, telling the cook to hurry up. A few civilians were walking along the pavement. A shopkeeper was busy sweeping up the broken glass from his store window. A German soldier was sitting on the stone steps of the Mayor's office. A blanket was spread out in front of him and he was fiddling around with a submachine gun. I walked over to him and said good morning to him in German.

He looked up at me in surprise. "I thought you people speak French here?" he said.

"In the south they do, but I'm German," I said.

I walked up Main Street to the very top by the church. A crowd of German soldiers was milling around an American M-61. That's the same one that knocked out that Mk IV down by the bridge, I thought. Presumably, the crew had run out of ammunition and stuck a phosphorous grenade into the breach, making the thing useless for further action.

When I got to Thea's, they were busy cooking and washing. Without caring for the GIs now, things were easier and Mom had asked Thea if she wanted us to leave.

"Heck no, Agnes," she said. "I'm glad you're here. Besides, where else can you go?"

"Well, Thea," said Mom, "I have a family at home as you know, and as much as I enjoy staying here with you, I'd like to go home as soon as it is possible. Christmas is only four days away and I'm homesick. I'll go tomorrow and find the German commander and ask him if we can leave soon."

"I hope you can make it," she said. "But if not, don't worry. Stay as long as you like. We'll have a good Christmas, I promise you."

The next morning, Mom went off to find the German commander. I decided to see if Felix could come out for a while. Mrs. Knauff told me that he was not in. He was uptown helping some relatives board up broken windows. I made my way over to the bridge to see what was going on there. Two German Volksgrenadiers were on guard, K 98s slung over their backs. One was a young kid, perhaps a couple of years older than me. I bid them good morning. The older soldier grumbled something I didn't understand. The younger one was friendlier. They didn't ask me if I was German, or what I was doing there, but I explained to the kid that I had witnessed the bridge blow up.

"You were here by the bridge?" he said.

"Not exactly," I confessed. "I was in that stone shed you see over in the field."

"Well, well," he said. "It must have been some battle. I only got here this morning from Koblenz. I've not fired a shot yet."

"You're not the only one," I lied. "I don't know the difference between a trigger and a bolt."

"Well, our guys did get one of the Amis, didn't they?" he said.

"How do you know? You told me you only got here this morning."

"There." He said. "Look, just beside the parapet. That's where we buried him."

I strolled over. Sure enough, there was a mound, covered in snow. A crude wooden cross was stuck into the ground, with a chained dog tag draped over the two cross bars. I fingered the dog tag. There was a long number on it and some letters. The bottom half had a name and an address: P. T. Dellora, Sioux Falls, S.D.

So that's where one of our friends ended up, in the cold ground of the Ardennes, 4,000 miles from South Dakota. Tears rolled down my cheek. I stood in silence for a minute and thought of the sergeant, the Nebraska man, of Oddie and Pat and the rest that got away, leaving poor Dellora behind.

"They'll find him when they come back, don't worry," the older soldier said as he stood next to me.

"You think they'll come back?" I asked.

"I'm under no illusions, son." He said. "The Reich is collapsing. Oh, yes, we're advancing now but not for long, maybe another week or so. Hitler is having his last gamble. He wants to play the Americans against the British, and he hopes they'll fall out with each other over the spoils of Germany."

He had a point there. We knew from experience with our so-called Axis allies, Japan and Italy, that a coalition war is a complex business under the best of circumstances, and without a measure of confidence between them, it's almost impossible to agree on certain issues.

"Did you know the guy?" he asked me.

"I met him once in town. He was a nice guy, a machine gunner on a .50-caliber. Now he's six feet under."

"Not six feet, son." he said. "The ground is frozen rock hard. You'd need a ton of dynamite to make a six-foot hole. We covered him with stones and debris from the bridge. His mates will find him soon, don't worry."

I said a last goodbye to Dellora and the two guards and went back to Thea's. Mom wasn't back yet, so I told Thea what had happened to our guest and told her where he was buried. I also told her what the guard had said about the Amis coming back.

"I'm sure they will," she said. "I'll take care of it and see that his friends know what happened and where he is buried."

"Just in case they don't come back, Aunt Thea," I said, "he was from a place called Sioux Falls, South Dakota. His dog tag said so. It's hanging on the cross."

Mom came back later with the news that there was nobody who could help us. The commanding German officer was a colonel. He told her he was a combat soldier, not engaged in administration. Maybe in a few days, if all went well, there would be a proper town commander and he would surely help. He never asked Mom how she got here in the first place from Germany. I suppose, being a combat colonel, he didn't care one way or the other.

"So it looks like we're spending Christmas together after all," Thea said.

"Yes, it does. I almost forgot about that," Mom said, turning to me. "What a Christmas, huh, son? No presents, but also no arguing with your brothers and we do have a pantry full of candy bars and chewing gum."

"Yeah, and no silly Ludo games either, Mom." I said.

Thea somehow managed the next day to get a small Christmas tree. There were millions of them growing in and around town. It was set up in the hall where the fire grate was, and I had the honor of decorating

it with Thea's baubles and silver lametta. She even found a few candles
and their holders. No German troops had bothered us so far. Nobody
had knocked on our door at all. Thea's place was off the main road on
a side street, and there was plenty of room for the few Germans in the
Château and in uptown.

We heard the latest news from Bastogne via my German friends,
who were still on bridge guard. They occupied a downstairs room in a
house next to the bridge. The roof had caved in, the windows had no
glass, and there was a big, man-sized hole in the front wall next to the
entrance. They had a fire going though, and their meager rations were
brought down by a motorcyclist.

I learned that the young soldier's name was Helmuth and that he
was from Cologne. The older guy's name was Eugen Gerstaetter, or
something, and he was from far away Greifswalde on the Baltic coast.
He hadn't been home in three years, he told me, and he said there was
no chance now of getting back there ever again. The Russians had overrun his hometown. He had no wife or other relatives, and he said if he
got out of the war alive, he would try to find a place to live in the
Rhineland. Helmuth had been drafted from the Hitler Youth only
recently, in November. They sent him to Koblenz to undergo basic training and this was his first assignment. He hardly knew how to change a
magazine in his rifle.

What they did have in this dilapidated empty house was electricity
and a working radio. A radio was something even Thea didn't have.
From that, they more or less figured out how things were going, but the
older guy took the German news with a pinch of salt. They also listened
to the long wave BBC German program, and by now they knew that the
victory parade along the French coast was going to be called off. The
Germans never got further than 45 miles west of Bastogne. British and
American troops ended the Germans' dream of a new Blitzkrieg near
Celles, in full view of the Maas River Bridge they were supposed to capture before racing the last 200-odd miles to the Channel coast.

News traveled fast, especially in wartime, so a day or two before
Christmas we heard from someone, who had heard it from somebody
else, who had it directly from Eisenhower, of course, that General
Patton had orders to break through to encircled Bastogne. His army was
far to the south, almost a hundred miles from the happenings, but he
did a 90-degree turn and his armored combat commands went hell bent
on icy winter roads up north to relieve the city. In fact, the "I know

more than Eisenhower" informant told us, of course under strict orders not to spread the good news, that Patton's 4th was already in Martelingen, a dozen or so miles from the perimeter. General McAuliffe was supposedly waiting for him there by the side of the road, drinking German ersatz coffee because the Americans had run out of supplies. The informant further said that the reply McAuliffe gave to the German demand for the surrender of the city was the word "nuts." The Germans, in turn, thinking that the city had run out of chestnuts to turn into ersatz coffee, sent a 10-pound barrel of the nuts into the city as a Christmas present. So we thought that McAuliffe was sitting in Assenois Village, drinking coffee made of chestnuts and waiting for the 4th to come up from the south.

True or not, we began to believe those tales about American gains around Bastogne and Celles. Firstly, every soldier, German or American, agreed that Hitler's Ardennes offensive, which had gone off half-cocked from the beginning, was doomed to fail. It was too little, too late. Secondly, and this was a decisive factor benefiting the Americans, was that the bad weather, which so far had been Hitler's main ally, improved, so Panthers and monster Tiger tanks were now easy prey for Thunderbolts, Typhoons and Lightnings.

CHAPTER 17

A Christmas Story

German troops were now coming back into town, this time from the west. There were no smiles, no words of "forward to Antwerp." They spoke in low voices of heavy losses near Pert and Winseler, of going without food for days, of living on rations they took from American dead and prisoners. Oh yes, they were still taking American prisoners, even at this stage in the battle, but sending them to the rear was a half-hearted effort. Many GIs escaped. The Ardennes was an ideal place to hide.

The days after Christmas also brought about a change in German tactics. Hitler, again in one of his sour moods, had called for his generals to attend a meeting at his headquarters. Rundstedt was there and so was Model, but most of the front line generals had found excuses. They knew that when the Führer had one of his tantrums, heads would fall. They knew that the Wehrmacht had the mobility and the brains behind it to gain ground, but they never had the strength to do two things at the same time, like taking Bastogne while reaching out for the Maas river crossings and the country beyond. After a few heated arguments, it was agreed they would take the front line on the southern sector back to the dominant heights of Sky Line Drive, while the northern Panzer divisions would head for Luttich (Liège).

The dream of reaching Antwerp had dissolved in a cloud of battle smoke near Celles. Only scattered remnants of the once proud Panzer divisions made it back. Jochen Peiper's Panthers and Tigers had run out of gas. The tankers had abandoned their armor and walked 25 miles back through the wintry forest to their own lines. Taking the line back to the heights above the river Sauer could only mean that Wiitz had to be given up as well.

One day after Christmas, several German trucks arrived in town. A Kübelwagen drove through the streets with a guy making an announcement over a loudspeaker to anyone who cared to listen, that all civilians had to be evacuated to a safe area as of that night. Each person was allowed to take two bags with provisions and a blanket. Nothing more was allowed. The reasons given were that the American aggressors were making an all-out effort to recapture the town and it would be in our own best interest to leave before it was too late.

We were told to assemble at the Château at 7:00 PM. Many of the citizens didn't want to leave their houses, fearing, and with good reason, that they would be pressed into the German labor service and might never see their homes again. For them, the better side of the coin was to stay and hide and let the war pass them once again. They hoped they would survive as they had already survived on three previous occasions over the past five years.

Mom was busy putting foodstuff into canvas bags Thea had found for us. I had a small leather rucksack, which I filled with coffee, candy bars and ration boxes. I even managed to get two loaves of white bread into the sack. I filled my pockets with chewing gum packets.

Thea wasn't leaving. "This is my home and I will stay. I might go down into the beer cellar to hide if things get too bad, but I doubt that the Germans will do a sweep of the town. They're in too much of a hurry to get away."

Mom's efforts to change her mind and get her to come with us fell on deaf ears, so we parted at 5:00 PM. Tears were flowing freely. Thea wished us a safe journey. "Come and see me when all of this is over," she said.

"We will," we both promised. "Thank you for all the things you've done for us. God bless you."

We walked the mile or so up to the Château, where a fleet of bussing trucks was waiting with engines running. Halftracks loaded with disheveled soldiers were already leaving in a hurry. It was advisable to travel in the dark. Daylight would bring the Thunderbolts out again, so it was better to get out of the area while the going was good. A line of about a hundred civilians was waiting for orders. A burly NCO checked Mom's I.D. "I see you're a German citizen. Are there any relatives you can go to, or is there any particular place you want to go?" he asked.

"Yes, I have folks living around Krefeld," Mom said. "My husband is in the Wehrmacht in the east, but I have not heard from him since

June. I have his pay book here if you want to check on that."

"No need for that. I believe you," he said. "Please get on that truck over there. You will not be alone. There are a few more German-born people there."

"Where will we be taken?" Mom asked.

"As far as I know, the trucks are heading for Prum tonight," he said. "From there you'll be able to get to Cologne by train, I hope. I'm only responsible for getting this convoy to Prum. You'll be on your own then and have to make your own arrangements for further travel."

Twelve other people were on the back of the truck, mostly elderly or very young. All were huddled in warm winter clothing with blankets across their knees. The truck had a tarpaulin cover, so we were reasonably sheltered from the cold wind.

At 7:00 PM the convoy started on its journey. We crossed over the bridge and climbed up on the Erpeldange road. It was dark, but I could still see the outline of the stone shed to our left where Felix and I had watched the destruction of the bridge. As we reached the hill at Erpeldange, we could see the flaming sky out to the west and hear the rumble of artillery fire. The road was covered with ice in places and the trucks skidded along most of the time. Luckily, some were equipped with snow chains, including the one we occupied. Several times the convoy came to a stop because a truck had run into a ditch or snow drift. A Hanomag halftrack with a steel cable and winch was able to pull the vehicle back onto the road.

It was hard going to Clervaux. The town was a beehive of activity. Loaded trucks, horse-drawn carts, shouting drivers and officers all were trying their best to get away or under cover before daylight.

Midnight came as we crossed Sky Line Drive, heading for the German border. By 4:00 AM we had made it. The West Wall bunkers and dragon teeth flew by. We reached Gemund, a small town crossing the line of the West Wall. We could not see much, but the town had obviously suffered heavy damage from the fighting in early fall. Pioneers were busy fortifying houses and setting up roadblocks. I saw the dark outlines of some artillery piece, and glimpsed a few bluish lights, and then we were on the open road again. A whiff of urgency seemed to hang over the whole area. I thought the decisive battle for Germany would have to be fought here, at the West Wall. Here the Wehrmacht had to stop the Allies. If they failed, then Germany was doomed.

Finally, we reached Prum, or rather, what was left of it. The Allies had bombed the town to smithereens. There was not even any railroad station, just a mound of debris. The truck stopped by a half-destroyed schoolhouse while the rest of the convoy carried on.

"This is the end of the line, folks," the driver said. "You'll be taken care of by the NSV in a minute."

The NSV was a sort of welfare organization run by women. Most of them were dedicated Nazi Party members who proudly displayed a black triangular metal badge, printed with the letters NSV. They greeted us with open arms and a cocky "Heil Hitler," and took us into the schoolhouse. A small cast iron stove was trying its best to give some sort of warmth, but it smoked more than heated. The glass in the windows was gone; some were covered with cardboard, but some were open and a cold wind blew through the room, making the stove send more clouds of smoke to the cracked ceiling. There was a kettle of soup on the stove plus the obligatory pot of ersatz coffee. We were given a bowl of soup—cabbage and potato, I think it was supposed to be. I fished in vain for a bit of meat. There was none, and if there ever had been, it had atomized, vaporized or, as I suspected, been eaten by the NSV Party members, who all seemed to look well fed. The coffee was horrible, but I drank it all the same. I didn't want to arouse suspicion by hinting that we had drunk better coffee in the past few weeks.

Mom looked at me and whispered, "Don't say anything about their food, okay?"

I nodded agreement. Some food, I thought, and my mind went back to Wiltz and Thea's cooking as we slurped the concoction they had offered us, just to warm ourselves up. Afterward, an NSV woman came and asked us several questions about where we wanted to go and where we came from. Mom told her a cock and bull story about getting trapped in Wiltz during the rapid American advance, and said all we wanted now was to get to Krefeld.

There was no way the NSV could check on Mom's story. Communications had broken down since the bombing, and by the looks of it, nobody was going to do anything about it, or even cared. In Prum, the important thing was to just clear the streets and fill in bomb craters to keep the roads open for the Wehrmacht so they could move in whatever direction the war told them to go. To my mind, that direction was east, although perhaps the NSV were thinking differently. The way they behaved, shouting "Heil Hitler" and "Sieg Heil," you would have surmised that our troops were going west, all the way to France once again.

The NSV woman, however, did ask Mom about the Americans in Wiltz and how they had behaved. Mom said they were friendly and no harm had come to any civilians. Other than that, she couldn't say. "We were civilians there and, as such, were treated that way," Mom told her.

The NSV woman then gave us a free traveling pass for the railroad and said, "This will get you to Cologne. That is, if and when the trains start running again."

I looked out the window at the railroad station. Heck, it would take months to get that heap of rubble cleared, not to mention rebuilding the tracks.

The NSV woman continued, "Once you get to Cologne, go and see the station master's office. Someone there will give you advice on how to get to Krefeld." Then, as if she had read my thoughts, she added, "There will be no trains from here. Repairs can take a while. If the bombers let us repair them, that is."

You can say that again, I thought.

"I'll try to get you on an army truck going in that direction, but I can't promise you anything." she told us. "The Wehrmacht has been advised to take civilians out of the war zone if space is available, but I have to remind you that Wehrmacht personnel, ammunition and other essentials have priority. You might have to wait a few days before you can leave."

"What are we going to do in the meantime? Are we allowed to stay here in this place?" Mom asked.

"Of course you can," she said. "We don't have any other shelter. We can give you an army field bed and a blanket or two and we'll try to make one hot meal a day."

'Hot meal,' I thought. They might as well call this stuff dishwater. But I suppose the German people who had not experienced American food were glad to get anything that went down warm into their stomachs, even if it did taste like dishwater. From somewhere outside, a siren started wailing. "Here they come again," the NSV woman said. "We might get bombed. There is no shelter, sorry. We have to take what comes."

We did not worry. We had seen enough artillery and bombs to have become accustomed to them by that time. I looked through the broken window. High up, a flight of Thunderbolts were making their way eastward. A few tracers fingered their way towards them, but they flew on. None of them attacked, although surely they could see the army trucks parked in the streets. Perhaps there were bigger fish to catch somewhere else. Seven people had disembarked from the truck with us when we arrived in Prum. They sat with us on the old school benches and desktops, now all covered in dust. The large blackboard hanging on the wail still had some writing on it in white chalk. "Alles für Deutschland" (All for Germany) it said.

Two of the people who were waiting to travel on wanted to go to Mainz on the Rhine. The other five were bound for Berlin. Berlin was the last place I wanted to be if this war was going to end inside Germany. I visualized what a house-to-house battle inside the city would be like. Something like Stalingrad two years before perhaps, with two million Berliners trapped in the middle of it.

Later, Mom and another woman helped the NSV cook another kettle of that awful soup. A constant stream of civilians kept coming in, begging for a dish of soup and a crust of black bread. All were served. Most of them were local inhabitants who had been bombed out and had nowhere to go. In earlier times, people who had lost their property through enemy action were reimbursed or given shelter in other areas, usually in the countryside far away from the cities.

By the end of 1944, it was impossible for the German authorities to supply even basic needs, never mind rebuilding houses or finding other accommodations for those who had lost everything. It was even worse near the frontline. Most of the higher authorities had fled. They were all Nazi Party members first-class, and knew that the Allies would not pussyfoot around with them if they got caught. Most had something to hide in their past. It made sense to them to leave before the Allies could get hold of them.

Again, I heard aircraft engines outside. I dashed to the window. Three Thunderbolts dived onto the town, cannons hammering away at something a few blocks up the street. People scattered in all directions, searching for cover in ruins like frightened chickens. I heard a scream or two from somewhere. Nobody cared. Mom was getting restless. It was mid-afternoon. She told me to watch our belongings while she went to see if there was any way we could get out of this distressing town. I sat and waited. Then I got up and walked over to the blackboard. I found a broken piece of chalk and drew funny faces around 'Alles für Deutschland.' The people smiled. Some woman said something about me still having a sense of humor in these hard times and that she liked my drawing.

Mom came in shortly afterwards. She took me to the side. "Listen," she whispered, "I found us a small truck and driver who is going to Euskirchen to the depot for spare parts. He said he will give us a lift. He leaves as soon as it gets dark. I offered him a few American ration boxes but he declined. He is allowed to take civilians if they happen to go that way. I told him we are heading for Cologne. That's not far from there. Don't say anything to the others in here. We'll just sneak away, okay?"

"Okay," I said, "but those people over there will surely guess what we're up to if we take our bags and march out that door."

"You're right." Mom replied. "We'll just tell them we are going to find an air raid shelter or some other excuse."

"On the other hand, Mom," I said, "it's none of their business. The NSV will be only too glad to see us gone. We'll make room for the next batch of refugees."

"You're right." she replied. "We'll just walk out with our bag. Nobody cares about us anyway. I'll be glad to be out of this dump."

"Did the driver say how long it will take to get to Euskirchen?" I asked.

"He reckons he can easily make it before dawn." she said. "We can sit in the warm cab with him and get some sleep."

Sleep? I almost had forgotten how tired I was. We hadn't slept since the night before we left Thea's. Later we picked up our bags, said good-bye to the NSV woman, and told her we were going to find an air raid shelter. Nobody asked any questions. We thanked her for the soup and I added a "Heil Hitler" as a parting salute.

The army truck was waiting down by the square, engine running. The driver waved to us to hurry. "I want to get to the depot before morning," he said. "The Amis are working by a precise timetable around here. They show up around 9:00 AM, shooting at everything that moves, and then leave us in peace until noon."

"Must have something to do with their breakfast, you think?" I asked the driver.

"Probably," he said. "At noon they come back for a second time. Then they usually calm down for a few hours."

"Ah, that's when they have their afternoon nap," I added.

"I sometimes wonder what they eat for breakfast," the driver said.

"From what I have seen in Wiltz, they have bacon, eggs, ham and real coffee," I said.

He put the truck into gear and slowly made his way around a half-filled in bomb crater. "They treated you well, then, them Amis?" he inquired.

"Of course they did. Why not? We are civilians, not SS members or Party officials," Mom replied.

I fell asleep in the warm cab as the truck ate the miles through the Eifel forest. Near Blankenheim we ran into an MP checkpoint, their gorgets with the eagle on it glowing yellowish in the dark. I thought of the canary birds Dad was going to breed after the war. The MPs checked our papers, but did not ask any questions, and allowed us to proceed with a "Heil Hitler."

Just before daylight, we rolled into Euskirchen. The town had its fair share of destroyed buildings, but it was nothing like we had seen in Prum. Euskirchen was a garrison town for infantry and tankers, and a lot of military traffic was about. We got off at the railroad station, thanked the driver, and wished him good luck. The ticket window at the station was closed, but I saw a uniformed railroad man in the back. Mom knocked on the glass. The guy came over and opened the hatch. "Yes, Ma'am. What can I do for you?"

"We want to get to Cologne," Mom told him. "Here are our travel permits from the NSV in Prum."

"So Prum and the NSV, eh?" he grumbled. "They haven't got a clue what the situation is around here. We had an air raid yesterday. The Amis blew the track to bits about three miles from here near Bullesheim. The OT is working on it, but it won't be back in service until tomorrow."

"No chance then to get away?" Mom asked.

"Well, there is a service from Bullesheim to Cologne as far as I know," he replied, "unless the Amis have put another stop to it. But you'll have to walk to get to Bullesheim."

"Is there no other way to get there?" Mom asked. " Three miles is a long walk for us in this weather and with our bags to carry as well."

"I don't know, Madam," he responded.

"I suppose we'll have to walk it then," Mom said. "I don't fancy hanging around here until tomorrow."

"Yes, Madam," he replied. "Now if you'll excuse me, I have a railroad to run, trains or no trains. There is a waiting room if you want to stay."

We found the waiting room. A small stove gave a bit of heat. Nobody else was in there and the room was bare except for an old timetable dating back to 1939, when times were good and trains ran on schedule. We sat there for an hour or so and then Mom got up. "Come on, let's go. We can't sit here forever."

"Where can we go? There are no trains. You heard the guy, Mom." I said.

"Somewhere," she said. "It doesn't matter where, but we might head for Bullesheim. It's not that far."

"Three miles, the guy said, and with our luggage it'll take us hours in this weather," I replied.

"I don't care," she said. "We'll walk. It's better than sitting in this dump."

"I'm hungry," I said.

"Open a ration box," she said. "We have plenty."

I did and found a tin with liver cheese. I took a slice of bread from my rucksack and wolfed it down. I felt better and ready to go.

It was 2:00 PM on the station clock as we set out for Bullesheim. We asked a young boy how to get there. "Klein or Gross Bullesheim?" he asked.

"I don't know. How many Bullesheims are there?" Mom asked.

"Two," he answered.

"Well, we need the one where the railroad station is," Mom said.

"Ah, okay then," he said. "Just follow the main road out of town. The railroad track runs more or less along the right side. You can see the Bullesheim church spire when you get to the T-junction. Turn left there. It's about three miles."

"Oh, thank you," she said, "and God bless you."

He looked a bit surprised because we hadn't said "Heil Hitler."

We got to the T-junction. The railroad track was there alright, making a wide curve to the left. In the distance there was a grove of trees and beyond that I saw two church spires, about a mile or so apart.

"Which one? The near one or the one further away?" I asked.

"I don't know," she said. "The boy didn't say."

"Knowing our luck," she said, "the Bullesheim we need won't be the nearer one, but all the same, we can follow the tracks. They will get us there no doubt."

After a while, a small, old clapped-out bus overtook us. It stopped just ahead.

We walked up to the open window. The driver leaned out, "Heading for the Cologne train, you two?"

"We sure are, Sir," I said.

"Okay, hop in. That's where I'm going," he said.

We got in. A few soldiers and some civilians were inside. We seated ourselves just behind the driver, who hammered the bus in gear and put his foot down.

"That station master never told us there was a bus running to Bullesheim," I shouted above the racket of the engine noise.

"He knows nothing," the driver answered.

"How much do we owe you?" Mom asked.

"Nothing, Madam, absolutely nothing. It's all paid for by the NSDAP. Comes out of the Gauleiter's emergency fund."

The other passengers laughed. They were all bound for Cologne, so we gathered. The bus was only going as far as the next railroad station, circumventing the damaged track between Bullesheim and Euskirchen.

The train was there alright when we got to the station, black smoke belching from the locomotive stack. I just hoped the Ami fighter-bomber pilots were having an afternoon nap. With all that smoke, the thing was probably visible from miles up. Because the track was damaged in the direction we had just come from, and no turn table or switch point was at Bullesheim, the locomotive had to reverse the eight carriages all the way back, either to the nearest switch point or to Cologne. In other words, the engine was on the end of the train, pushing the cars.

The compartments were small and dirty but it was reasonably warm. We climbed on board, followed by two soldiers, three civilian men in working overalls and a woman who carried a cage with two live chickens. That made eight of us, not counting the feathered passengers, in a compartment made for six people. Better a bad train ride than a good walk, I thought. It was 30-odd miles to Cologne. Once we all were seated, the woman took the two chickens out of the cage and placed them on top of the luggage rack.

"They've been in that cage since 9:00 AM," she explained. "They need a bit of space to flap their wings. They're for our dinner next Sunday."

The chickens dutifully did what chickens do, dropping a blob of chicken shit into a soldier's lap.

"I wouldn't have minded if it had been an egg," the soldier said, wiping the mess off with his sleeve.

The soldiers then took off their boots and made themselves comfortable. An infernal stink arose, a mixture of sweaty feet, homemade cigars and chicken shit. To open the window was out of the question. It was too cold outside, and the chickens would surely have taken the opportunity to escape the butcher's knife that was awaiting them at their destination. So we had to live with the smell for a while, whether we liked it or not.

We had neither heard nor seen an enemy plane all that day. Trains and railroad tracks had become a favorite target of the Jabos. At 4:30 PM, the engine finally blew the whistle and started moving. At long last, we were on our way home to Aunt Carol, Little Fred and know-it-all Brother Len.

By my calculations, there were about 30 cubic yards of air in the compartment when we entered it. By now it had surely all been converted into carbon dioxide. I felt dizzy. The chicken woman was coughing as if she had first-degree tuberculosis. A guy in overalls suggested opening the window an inch or so, but one of the soldiers protested. "I'd rather die of stink than freeze to death," he said. He lit another of his cigars and gave it to his mate, who thanked him by letting off an almighty fart. There was no escape from the compartment. Third class had only one door, and that opened to the outside.

By 7:00 PM it was pitch black outside. Our train approached the town of Weilerswist and stopped before it reached the station platform. I wiped the grime from the windowpane to see what was going on. All I could make out was a red signal, the arm in horizontal position.

We sat there for five minutes. Then one of the civilian men rose, "Grab hold of those chickens. I'm going to have a look and see what's up." Quickly the woman pushed the chickens back into the cage, and before the Wehrmacht could raise a strong protest, the guy opened the door and jumped down from the running board. The fresh air entering the compartment was like manna from heaven. It almost floored me. After a few minutes the guy came back. "Can't see anything out there," he reported. Then engine behind us let off a short blast of the whistle and slowly started again, only to come to a stop in the Weilerswist station. A railroad guy came along the carriages, a kerosene lantern in his hand. He shouted that the train wasn't going anywhere that night. The Amis had taken care of the track. Repairs were in good hands, but would not be completed until 8:00 AM.

"At this rate we'll be home by 1950, Mom. Is there a waiting room here?" I asked the lantern guy.

"Sure there is, but it's cold. You're better off on the train."

"Not me," I blurted out, "we're not staying in that stinking hole until 8:00 AM. We'd rather freeze in the waiting room. We've got blankets."

Nobody wanted to leave the compartment except Mom and me. That suited me fine. I had already had just about enough of that smelly lot in there. Yes, there was a small waiting room with a 25-watt bulb dangling from the ceiling, a few dusty benches along the walls and the latest issue of the Völkischer Beobachter newspaper on the floor. I read the headlines: "Bastogne will be taken by our grenadiers and tanks, the Führer has promised." Some promise, I thought.

Around 9:00 PM, I heard a car stop outside, and I went to have a look. It was an enclosed Wehrmacht van. On the door were painted an eagle and swastika inside a white circle with the letters FP, for Fieldpost. It was a small pick-up van. The door was open and the driver was throwing two mailbags into the back.

"What in God's name are you doing out here in the middle of the night and in this cold?" the driver asked me.

I told him in a few words about the hold up on our journey to Cologne, and that Mom was half frozen inside the station waiting room. He was on his way to M-G and said we could catch a ride.

I ran back into the station and whispered to Mom to gather the bags and told her that I had found us a ride home. We grabbed our bags, the driver placed them in the back, and we climbed into the cab. The driver gunned the engine and we were off.

"I hope you don't get into trouble if we run into a check point," Mom addressed the driver.

"No chance there," he said. "I'm the mail deliverer. Nobody is allowed to stop the mail, not even the SS. I carry their mail as well, you know. The only thing that can stop us is a fighter-bomber come daylight. So I'll make sure I get to M-G before 9:00 AM." At that time of the year, daylight came around 8:00 AM, but we knew from experience that the killers would not show up until about an hour later.

We told the driver that we had been evacuated from Wiltz while visiting relatives. We did not mention our adventures with the US Army. On and on we went. To the east of us, about 25 miles away, was the city of Cologne, where a red glare was reflected from the sky. The RAF was busy again, plastering the Rhine metropolis with phosphorous and high explosives.

I pointed at the distant glow. "It must be hell out there, living through this. There can't be much left to burn, I should imagine. Cologne has had its fair share of bombing ever since 1942."

"If the war doesn't come to an end soon, all our cities will be gone, erased, burned and smashed to piles of rubble," the driver said.

"Are you from a big city?" Mom asked.

"Hannover, and from what I know, my town is in ruins, too," he said.

"Are you married?" she asked.

"Yes, Madam," he replied, "but my wife and daughter had the sense to leave the city and now live with relatives in the countryside near Bad Oldesloe. I haven't heard from them for a while, but that's the mail today. Not much of it reaches its destination, I'm afraid. The Ami planes swoop onto anything that moves. I make it my business to drive at night. It's safer, and so far I've been lucky."

Just outside the town of Erkelenz, we stopped at an army post, where a few bags of mail and some parcels were waiting. A group of soldiers stood around. There was a farmhouse and a few sheds just across the road.

"We made good time," the driver said. "We're going to have a ten-minute stop. I can do with some coffee if they have any."

We stepped off the van, stretching our cramped limbs. A guy came over with some mess cups full of steaming ersatz coffee. We had better stuff in our bags, but we weren't going to show it. After all, real coffee was a commodity fit for kings and queens in those days, and not to be given away freely. To the west we could see the flicker of artillery fire and hear the far away dull boom of cannons. We slurped the hot ersatz. I asked one of the men where the firing came from.

"It's way over near the Rur (Roer) River," he replied. "The Amis have been sitting there since November. Only the Ardennes battle has stopped them from crossing. And the lousy weather had something to do with it as well."

"How far off are they, then?" I asked.

"About 10 to 15 miles," he said. "We expect them to move any day now. We had a respite for a few weeks, but since they sent our Wehrmacht head over heels back to their starting point, we reckon they will be advancing again soon."

"Any chance of us stopping them, then?" I asked. "I mean, we have tanks and guns."

"Did you say tanks, boy?" the guy laughed. "The Wehrmacht is broke, kaput. We have men, yes, and we have two assault guns over there in the big barn and 26 rounds of HE ammunition, but not a drop of gas. For reinforcements, they did send us a battalion of 12- to 15-year-old Hitler Youths without a rifle among them. The leader had a MP-40 machine pistol, that was all. Now they're busy digging foxholes and antitank ditches near Huckelhoven. If we're lucky, we might get a few dozen Panzerfausts and some antitank mines as a late present from Santa Claus." The Panzerfaust was the German version of the bazooka, with the difference being that you could use the bazooka over and over again. The Panzerfaust, once fired, left the operator with a useless metal tube in his hands. He had to get another one to fire.

A captain turned up from out of the darkness. Behind him marched a group of young kids in uniform with rifles under their arms. The carbines looked taller than the boys.

"Okay, line up!" he shouted. "Sergeant, see to it that this kindergarten class gets some idea what this war is all about. I just fetched them from the replacement pool."

There stood a bunch of kids at 4:00 AM on a lonely stretch of highway near Erkelenz, trying hard to learn weapons exercises in an hour or so that would take real soldiers months to master. "Left, left, left, right, left, right, left, halt, about turn, present arms," the sergeant shouted. If it had not been for the seriousness of the situation, with artillery shells exploding on the horizon, the performance of those boys, no older than myself, would have made a story line for a comic strip. But nobody laughed.

A boy dropped his rifle. Embarrassed, he picked it up, wiping it clean with his cloth cap. In normal circumstances this would have been a first-degree disaster, punishable by two days in the brig and a week of eating, sleeping and living with the rifle in your hand. But these were not normal times, after all, so the sergeant let it go with a warning. Another round of explosions were heard to the west, followed by the stuttering of some automatic fire. It was still too far away to be machine gun fire, so I figured it was probably 20mm or even 40s. I knew that the Americans had 40mm twins. I had seen many of them in the past six weeks.

The driver of the Fieldpost van walked up. "Okay, let's get moving. Daylight will be here in two hours and I want to be at the base by then. I need sleep, too. I've been up for 36 hours now."

We got into the cab and the driver pulled out onto the road. Twenty thousand feet up, in a never ending stream, Lancaster Bombers were making their way home, undisturbed by flak or night fighters, their nightshift over Cologne successfully completed.

We sped along the tree-lined causeway. Anhoven flew by, then another nameless village. The first gray streaks of daylight were appearing in the eastern sky when we reached Rheindahlen and turned left onto the Hardt highway. A bomb crater by the railroad crossing blocked our way. The driver pulled over, drove through three front yards, leaving muddy ruts and uprooted flower bushes in his wake, and regained the road.

At the small hamlet of Koch, we encountered another road obstruction. This time it wasn't a bomb hole, but a huge 155mm artillery piece, towed by an 18-ton Magirus halftrack. Although the snow had melted, there was still the occasional black ice around. The Magirus had skidded into a ditch, leaving the artillery piece sideways across the road, unmovable by man or beast. A mobile crane had to be commandeered from somewhere to get the monster halftrack back onto hard surface. The Magierus was made for cross-country and could plough through almost any terrain. Without the cannon in tow, he probably could have gotten out of the ditch on his own, but it was impossible to unhitch the piece. It was too heavy to manhandle.

There was no way for the Fieldpost van to go through front yards because the houses stood right by the road. The rest of the highway had a deep ditch on either side. We either had to turn back and make a detour of several miles, getting shot at by the American fighter-bombers, or find some other way. Daylight was coming up fast. In another hour or so, the sky would be swarming with twin forked devils and hedge-hoppers (P-38s and P-47s).

The eight-man artillery crew stood around smoking and loudly shouting about what they should do next. Some were cursing. An NCO, both index fingers stuck in ears, tried in vain to quiet the mob. They were blaming the mishap on Hitler, Goering, Roosevelt, Stalin and lesser dignitaries—anyone except themselves. The driver probably had simply been going too fast, hit some black ice and ended up where he was now.

"What now?" our driver said. "I'll take any advice. I don't want to be blown up by a fighter-bomber cannon."

"Okay, Sir, look," I said, "there is an alleyway to the left. Let me just go and investigate. There might be a way around up there. These stores usually have a back entrance for unloading."

"Okay, but make it fast," he said. If there isn't a way around, we'll try to double back to Rheindahlen or go through Venn."

I ran along the alleyway and sure enough, there was a back entry. The alley turned back onto the road passing the obstacle that blocked our progress. It was narrow, but the van could just make it.

"You deserve a medal, boy," he said. "Thanks a lot. We're on our way."

"Been waiting two years for a medal, Sir," I said, "but all I got was a gingerbread cross. I ate it and kept the ribbon."

We were finally back on the Hardt highway. After we left the artillerymen to themselves, the driver said that many Hitler Youths were now awarded the Iron Cross. Medal manufacturers were turning them out en masse.

"You haven't got one, Sir, I noticed."

"No, and by the looks of it," he said, "I will never get one. I'm a humble mail carrier and I'm not sticking my neck out. I'm not in a particular hurry to earn a medal, win or lose."

"You seem to be one of those average-type soldiers who just want to get home in a hurry, victory or defeat," Mom chimed in.

"Yes, I am. Win or lose, it makes no difference to me, Madam." he said. "I have never fired my carbine in anger so far, and that's saying a lot in this, the sixth year of the war."

"You don't sound very patriotic," Mom said, a smile on her face.

As a watery sun rose above the eastern horizon, we rolled into Hardt. "I ought to turn right here and head for the fighter base at M-G," he said, "but there is still time enough before the flyboys come. How far do you live from here?"

"Only five miles, near that church you can see in the distance," Mom told him.

"Okay, sit tight," he said. "I'll get you there."

The places we passed now were familiar to us, and we knew the names of the people who lived on the farms. To my left, far ahead, I saw the familiar barrel of the 88 in the field behind our house. A minute later, I made out the slight rise where the quad was stationed. Finally, at long last, we stopped outside our place.

"Please come in and have some breakfast," Mom invited the driver.

"No thank you, Madam," he said. "I've got 45 minutes left to get to base in one piece. Nice to have had you on board, your company made the time go faster. Have a good day."

"Thank you so much. I hope you get home okay one day," she told the driver.

We gathered our bags and went in the front door of our house.

Aunt Carol almost fell over when she saw us. She rinsed the enamel coffee pot and put a fresh kettle of water onto the hot stove. Baby Fred came dashing in. He had been in the garden talking to the rabbits. We hugged him and kissed him a hundred times. He was delighted and asked for a "sweetie." I fished an American candy bar out of my rucksack and handed it to him. He laughed and dashed out into the garden again. What a life that kid has, I thought. Born in a war, raised in a war, and plays in a war, and he doesn't even know that a war is going on all around him. Brother Len had gone to work already. The rabbits were looking healthy. There were 20 left, so he must have killed a half a dozen for the dinner table. That suited me fine. Aunt Carol said he had been helping her as much as he could. He was knocking off work at 2:00 PM every day now because of his Hitler Youth commitments. They had to do trench digging and target practice on the shooting range with machine guns, carbines and even Panzerfausts.

Little Freddy came running in from the garden, his face covered in chocolate. He climbed onto Mom's lap. "Mama, Mama, Len beat me, Mama."

"Why? Tell me," she said.

"Cuz I pooped in his bed, Mama," Freddy admitted.

We all laughed. Aunt Carol explained that one night she put Freddy into Len's bed when Len was out on a night detail with the Hitler Youth. Freddy had messed in bed, and when Len got home at 6:00 AM and crawled, exhausted, under the blankets, he discovered that little Fred had left something for him between the sheets. He then gave Freddy a smack on his dirty behind.

The town had experienced a few raids while we were away, but none of them had been serious. Aunt Carol had heard that the quads had shot down another American plane, something like a twin-engine bomber. The 88s had two to their credit.

It was time for breakfast and Mom made real coffee, tinned ham and white bread, all courtesy of the US Army. Freddy had another Hershey bar.

Around 9:00 AM, the American Jabos turned up as predicted, but I was too tired to watch their performance. I went to bed and listened to the hammering of their machine guns. A bomb was dropped. It fell into the cemetery, disturbing those who were already dead. What a waste of a good bomb.

I slept all day, got up at 7:00 PM and had a sandwich. Len was nowhere to be seen. Mom and Aunt Carol sat in the front room talking. I went to the "restroom." I thought I'd give our toilet the American name I had learned in Wiltz. One day, sooner or later, the Americans would come to our town, we knew. It might then come in handy if I could show the GIs where our "restroom" was. I went back to bed, dreaming of bridges and mortars, of .50-calibers and Felix.

I woke up with a jolt. It was daylight. Outside a van with a loud-speaker was going up and down the streets. I went into the kitchen for breakfast.

"And you're not going, you hear me?" said Mom.

"Going where?" I asked.

"They want all men between the age of 12 and 65 to assemble forth-with at the school playground to dig antitank ditches or something," she said. "You're not going."

"I've got no intention of digging stupid ditches for a victory that will never come, Mom," I said. "I'm going up to the quads. It's safer under a concrete roof than in an open field digging. If all those kids and old men assemble in the open and dig trenches, the fighter-bombers will have a field day. Did they say all men between 12 and 65?"

"Yes, why?" she asked.

"Hmm, all of a sudden, kids of 12 are 'men.' Before, we used to be called "little brats." We're 'men' now that the Party has to fear for their own backsides."

"Go and feed the rabbits," Mom said. "Then you can go up to the quads, okay?"

"Okay, Mom," I said.

"Where is Len, Mom?" I asked. "I've not seen him since we got back."

"Aunt Carol told me that he has to be out quite often on night exer-cises now. He didn't come back last night," Mom said.

I donned my Hitler Youth uniform and walked along the road. At the turn for the sandpits and quads, a policeman stopped me.

"This way to the school, boy. Just follow the others," he said. There were several older men and boys on their way to the school playground. Some shouldered spades. Others had pitchforks.

"I know where my school is, Sir," I said, "but we're supposed to be off until further notice."

"That's right, boy," he said, "but it's defense work we have to do, not school lessons."

"I'm messenger for the flak quads," I informed him. "Besides, at 8:00 AM this morning a truck with a loudspeaker came by telling us that we were men, not boys."

"What do you mean?" he asked.

"The loudspeaker said 'all men between the age of 12 and 65'; it didn't say anything about boys," I responded.

"Okay, big man," he said, "off you go to the flak guns then, and happy hunting."

It was sunny and clear. The Jabos would have a field day in this visibility. For the Amis it would be like hunting jackrabbits back home on the plains, except that the rabbits were 'men' between 12 and 65.

Up at the quads, not much had changed. There were two new privates, one more white ring around the barrels, and a bunch of Hitler Youths down in the sand pit, without their flagpole, but with a portable toilet.

"Well, well, look what the wind has blown in. Where have you been? Your aunt said something about you and your Mom being in Luxembourg. Is that true?" Giant greeted me.

"Yes, we got back yesterday morning with the Fieldpost," I said.

"What? Not in a parcel, I hope," he laughed.

"No, we got a lift in a mail van," I explained. "It's a long story, but I'll tell you all later. How's everyone here?"

"We had another of our comrades killed in an attack. Pelzer got it this time," Giant explained. "A Mitchell got him with its tail gun, but we got the bastard on his second run in. He crashed over yonder in Neersen. It got us another ring and the Iron Cross 1st Class for me.

Gunny came running over, a broad smile on his face. "I heard you were out west. Seen any Amis while you were there?"

"Plenty man, plenty," I said.

"Meet any generals?" he asked.

"I saw Cota," I answered.

"Who's Cota?" he asked.

"General Norman Cota, 28th US Infantry Division," I said. "And I met a colonel, too. I think his name was Fuller, and then there was the sergeant. I have forgotten his name. There was Pat and Oddie. Oh, and Dellora, but he got killed."

"Who else did you meet then?" Gunny asked. "Not that General Patton we hear so much about here?"

"No, I don't think I saw him," I said. "But I met a black man, a soldier."

"What? You mean really black, from Africa?" Gunny asked.

"No, he was an American," I explained, "but he was friendly. He let me have a walk around an SPG with twin 20mms"

"You must tell us all about it at dinner," he said. "Are you staying for today?"

"Yes," I said. "I don't fancy digging trenches with the HJ (Hitler Youth) and the Volkssturm. I'm going to make you some real coffee now, US K-ration stuff, not the ersatz crap, okay?"

Soon a kettle of water was boiling and I made a large pot of real coffee. It was a bit weak, because I didn't want to give away too much of the good stuff. Then the cook distributed the coffee to the crews. Each one had a small mess cup full.

I noticed several new men at the twins and there were two new ones at the quads. One of the new machine gun men was surely not German. His looks were more like a Mongolian warrior. After the men left the mess bunker and had gone to their battle stations again, I asked Gunny about the funny-looking guy,

"He's a replacement on the twins," Gunny said. "They lost a couple during an attack in early December."

"How did he manage to join the Wehrmacht?" I asked Gunny. "Did he bribe the SS or what?"

"They are short of manpower now," he said. "They're taking volunteers from POW camps who want to fight for the Reich."

"There isn't much of the Reich left, Gunny," I said. "Those volunteer guys won't make any difference. You ought to see what the Amis have in armor to throw against us. It makes your head go dizzy."

Giant got in on the conversation, "Don't say too much about what you have seen while you were away. Somebody might want to know more details, especially those Hitler Youth idiots down in that sand pit."

"Anything going on here, apart from shooting at planes while I was away then?" I asked.

"Well, they transferred a few quads to frontline duty and put 37mms in their place," Gunny said, "but they have left us alone so far."

I told them in a few words about our adventure and added that the Amis were well behaved, had good weapons and ammo, and plenty of it, and that the food was excellent. I looked at the haggard faces of the crew. What a difference from the well-fed GIs, I thought. This bunch looked like spiders with two legs missing.

CHAPTER 18

Our Last Bullet

To the south of us, about seven miles away, the 120mms on the huge concrete flak towers were already busy firing at some bombers high above. Soon the 88s got into the fray and the sky around the bombers was carpeted with small black clouds.

"They can almost walk on that up there," Gunny said. "But they're out of our range. I wonder where the escort is?"

"The less we see of them, the better!" shouted Giant.

I threw the empties into the gun pit, then collected them and had two baskets full. I could not manage on my own to take them to the magazine, but the funny-looking guy was standing near me, his eyes on the sky.

"Gunny, how can this guy be useful to us, if he can't understand what we're talking about? What about orders or instructions?" I asked.

"I can speak a few words of Russian," the new guy said. "I was on the northern front two years and had plenty of contact with Ivan, but this guy here beats me."

"Where's he from in Russia?" I asked.

"He isn't Russian, so he says. That's the whole point of it. He says he's from Samarkant or something, and to him that's not Russia," said the new guy.

"Well, does he know how to fire that thing?" and I pointed at the twins.

"No, but he's learning fast," he replied.

Lunchtime came. We had not had an alert so far. The crew took turns to come in for their meal. I went into the mess bunker. The cook was filling metal plates with some awful smelling stuff. I was glad I had a good breakfast earlier.

The men busied themselves eating the greenish-looking concoction. I asked Giant what it was. He said it was half-fermented sauerkraut soup with three molecules of meat per half pint. It looked like gorilla snot to me.

I walked outside and thought about the food we had in Wiltz—fried eggs, ham, white bread, K-rations, lemon juice powder and chewing gum. Then I remembered and went back inside and yelled, "Hey guys, I have a present for all of you!" I pulled out several packs of chewing gum from my pocket and gave each of them one strip.

"Treat it as your pudding with the compliments of General Cota," I said.

"Who's he? Never heard of him," K-1 commented.

"Some guy he met while he was away," Gunny said. His look at me said, "Be careful with your talk."

"Yeah," I said, "I found it in a parachute container with other food stuffs."

"What if the stuff was poisoned and deliberately dropped for us Germans to pick up?" K-1 asked.

"You've got a point there," I said, "but look, I'm still alive. I've been eating this stuff for the last four weeks and I feel amazingly well. Does that convince you?"

"Okay," K-1 said, "but thanks, anyway."

Soon the men were happily chewing away. Give them a US tin hat and an M-1 rifle, and they would almost look like Americans, I thought.

Down below on the road near the entrance to the sand pit, where the Hitler Youth boys were still busy digging useless foxholes, I noticed a lone figure on a bicycle pedaling up the hill, a carbine slung over his shoulder. There was something familiar about that figure, I thought. I was just about ready to investigate when someone shouted, "Alarm! Enemy planes at four high, due west."

I looked west. Four Mustang P-51s were streaking toward the town at a height of about 1,000 feet. For good measure, they had two Mitchell Twins in tow. The crews were already at their positions, so the command to fire came as an anticlimax. There was no time to get coordinates from the rangefinder. It was fire over open sights. A and B guns let loose on two barrels each, four men changing magazines as fast as they could. Empties clanked by the hundreds into the boxes and spilled out into the gun bed. I had conveniently forgotten to replace the cover on the bin on A gun, so the empties came tumbling out all around me.

With their airbases now less than 100 miles away, the Americans obviously had plenty of time on their hands, and tried to give our area a good plastering.

Then somewhere out of the clear blue winter sky, two ME-262s jets of our own Luftwaffe appeared. Now the odds were in favor of the greater German Reich, so to speak. It was still six Americans versus two Germans, but it was quality against quantity, and that was the difference. The two slow Mitchells were just chickenfeed for the ME-262s. The pilots knew they did not have a chance in hell of taking on the jets, so they made a 180-degree turn and headed west as fast as their twins would let them. They were followed by a stream of fire from our four 20mms, but with no observable results.

We ceased firing. We didn't want to endanger our own jets and we watched the slaughter in progress about 1,000 feet up. With all due respect, the P-51 guys did their very best, but they were outgunned and outrun by planes that were a good 150 miles per hour faster than they were. The ME-262s were also piloted by fanatical Luftwaffe aces who knew their jobs.

The first Mustang was hit by the 37mm nose cannon, and just disintegrated. The second took a few dozen 20mm tracers in his rudder and wing, trailed smoke and came down fast. The pilot bailed out and landed safely at the east end of town. The other two turned sharply to the west, trying hard to make a run for the safety of their lines. The jets easily caught up with them and shot another one down somewhere near the Dutch border.

Surprisingly, the fourth one got away unscathed. The jet pilot, because of his superior speed, had overshot the P-51. The American pilot then managed to get a bead on the jet, but he missed. He took his Mustang down to treetop level, too low for the ME-262, and vanished over the western horizon unharmed. We waved and cheered, throwing our hats and helmet into the air. One jet did a victory roll for us. Then they both turned to the northeast and flew out of sight.

"Well, well, what about that?" Gunny said to Giant. "Wasn't that something?"

"Yes," Giant said, "and I wish we had had a few thousand of them back in 1940. The world would be a very different place now."

"I don't know," Gunny said. "Remember, Lieutenant, every time a new weapon is developed, the other side invents a countermeasure. Mark my word, one day in the near future the Amis will get something that can blast the fastest jet out of the sky; perhaps a rocket of some sort, or even a plane faster than the ME-262."

"Maybe you're right, Sergeant, but I, for one, wish this shooting would come to an end one way or the other. I've been at it now since 1938 when we went to beat the Czechs. Now my wife and kids have died in an air raid, my home is overrun by the Russians, the Amis are less than 35 miles away, and there is no hope of getting out of this hole that Hitler dug for us in September '39."

The captain was standing nearby and overheard the conversation between Gunny and Giant. He walked up. I thought he was going to throw his weight about, as he was the senior officer at the moment, but he instead addressed them in a low voice. "Look, Lieutenant, I don't have to remind you that back in '39, you, as well as the rest of us, and that includes our Hitler Youth here," and he pointed at me, "shouted 'Heil Hitler' and 'Sieg Heil' every time the Führer opened his mouth when we were overrunning Poland, France and the rest of Europe. Now the tables have turned. We'll be overrun sooner or later. There is no such thing as a wonder weapon that can turn the tide in our favor. Our few jets, V-1s and V-2s won't make a difference, and neither will Goebbels' vision of a victory with the help of the Japs. We all swore an oath to Adolf Hitler when we joined the Wehrmacht, and we have to stick to it whether we like it or not. Now get this place cleaned up, Lieutenant. I have to visit the 88s. Good hunting, and, oh, I almost forgot, Heil Hitler." He turned and walked over to his staff car and drove off.

"Sardonic bastard," someone whispered. Was it the lieutenant, the gunnery sergeant, or someone else?

"There was a time not long ago when I thought the captain had seen enough of this war," Giant said. "Looks like I was wrong. The Amis are 30 miles down wind from us, and we have nothing to stop them with apart from the Hitler Youth and a Volkssturm, who are granddads every one of them. And here this captain tells us about oaths and duty to the Führer and showers us with his 'Heil Hitler' confetti."

"Well, I never gave an oath to the Führer, not that I know of," I said, and I walked over to A gun to collect the empties.

One of the gunners from B gun walked over, "Well, boy, in all that excitement I swallowed that gum you gave me earlier. You don't have another strip somewhere do you?"

I took a pack out of my pocket. "Here, give the rest to your buddies as a belated Christmas present," I said, and walked back to Giant.

"I hope the captain chokes on that gum I gave him earlier. That wasn't very polite of him to remind you of your duties and all that nonsense about Hitler and the oath," I said.

"He probably thinks we're on a winning streak, after seeing the P-51s go down. He'll come to his senses one day," said the lieutenant.

With all the excitement going on, I had almost forgotten about the guy on the bicycle I had seen earlier coming up the road before the P-51s roared in. Now he reappeared from a slit trench, picking up his bike and pushing it uphill toward our position, grinning all over his face. Yes, it was Brother Len, he who knows everything, sporting a new uniform of the Hitler Youth, a 98K rifle over his shoulder, and a full ammo belt.

We boxed each other, slapped backs and exchanged the latest news both good and bad. Of course, Brother Len had heard all the latest rumors and knew from reliable sources that the Allies would be stopped three miles west of town. He said they had dug an antitank ditch eight feet deep and several miles long, and 100 Volkssturm were ready and eager to take on the entire 84th US Infantry with their Panzerfausts. One hundred granddads with a single Panzerfaust each should do the trick, when 116 German divisions had failed to do it on D-Day in June. I almost fell over with laughter. Len admitted meekly that 100 Volkssturm weren't much, but it was better than nothing, and anyway, he added, the ditch would stop the tanks.

"Yes," Giant said. "It'll stop them for two hours and six minutes."

Len looked puzzled. "Why the precise time?" he asked Giant.

"Two hours to laugh at the ditch and six minutes to fill it in and get across," he replied. "What are you doing here, anyway? You ought to be by that antitank ditch with those Volkssturm people."

"I went home," Len said, "and Mom was back, so I came up here to say hello to my brother."

"Okay, you said your hello," Giant replied. "Now get back to your post. There's an air raid going on and we have a war to fight."

I gave Len a strip of chewing gum and told him I'd be home at 6:00 PM to tell him about our recent adventures. He gathered his rifle and bicycle and pedaled down to the main road.

"Now there goes a true Hitler soldier," Giant said. "Duty before pleasure."

"I hope not," I said. "When he's away on his duties, I have all the work to do at the house. It's a big job, you know, Sir."

"The way it looks, boy," he said, "we'll all be out of a job before long. We'll end up in a POW camp, if we're still alive by the time they get here."

"You think they'll take me as a POW, too?" I asked. The thought of being taken at gunpoint by a GI, then shipped out to the wilds of Nebraska or Texas did not appeal to me at first, but thinking about it, I changed my mind. I might see some cowboys and Indians for a change, I thought, instead of Nazis and Wehrmacht troops.

By 5:00 PM it was already dark. The sirens finally blared the all-clear, but the war was not forgotten. Far out to the west, flickering lights high in the night sky, and a distant rumble like an approaching summer thunderstorm told us that the ground war was getting closer by the hour. Brother Len was already at home when I got in. He was getting coal and wood for the stove. Outside, it had become bitterly cold, so I was glad to be inside with a warm fire. After a meager supper of fried potatoes and "garden bacon" (fried onions), we sat by the radio to hear the latest news. The radio commentator had a clever way of hiding the truth. Our SS troops were fighting a holding action around the West Wall, he said. "Around" was one way of admitting that the Allies had breached our mighty Reich's protective barrier. The places he mentioned, the villages of Brachelen, Hilfahrt and Baal, were well east of the West Wall. I knew that much.

The nearest bunkers and strong points of our frontier fortifications were about 15 miles west of us, but the sound of battle was more due southwest. So in all probability, the advancing Americans had not yet crossed the river Maas, just inside of Holland.

Len was off to his Hitler Youth duties early the next morning. He was assigned as a guard to a group of Polish POWs digging slit trenches in front yards, often under protest of the house owners, but there was nothing they could do about it. The Führer orders and we follow. That was the motto.

For several weeks, apart from the constant air raids, our sector had been remarkably quiet. This was because German Pioneers had blown the bridge over the river Maas. They had also blown the Roer Dams in the Eifel, and the penned-up waters thus released had swollen the Roer and subsequently the Maas to such an extent that it required special bridging equipment to get across. For mile after mile, the countryside along the rivers had been turned into a bottomless swamp, two miles wide. A mile-wide river with swampy approaches on either side made it impossible to cross by boats, unless the water went down. The Allies, after the Arnhem debacle the previous September, when they had gone, as it was stated, "a bridge too far," were extremely cautious crossing the Maas again under unfavorable conditions. The Americans had by now dubbed the river Maas the "river Morass."

It took several weeks for the ground to dry out sufficiently for the Allied commanders to contemplate the next move. This period was more or less a quiet waiting game for both sides. The Germans sat immersed in the destroyed ruins of the border villages, wet to the bone, hungry and full of uncertainty about what the future would bring. The Americans, for once, weren't much better off. They sat in muddy fox-holes, wet and cold, but at least they were relieved every three days to thaw out and have a reasonable few hours in a dry place and a hot meal. The Germans couldn't afford that luxury. There were just no reserves to relieve the forward troops.

By this time, Germany was literally scraping the barrel for soldiers. The debacle at Stalingrad back in February 1943 had cost Germany over 30 first-class divisions. This loss had to be made up somehow, so by a stroke of the pen, 240,000 home defense personnel, mainly from the light flak, were drafted into the army. The vacuum they left behind was filled by the Hitler Youth. In addition, several hundred 88mm flak batteries were taken away from home defense to replace the awful loss-es that had occurred in the battles for Stalingrad, Kursk and the Dnieper crossings.

Nevertheless, there were still a formidable 250,000 flak cannons dispersed around the Reich, to the dismay of the Allied Air Force, which had to run this gauntlet more or less every day. Heavy flak was some-thing the bombers could not do much about, but the German fighters were having a hard time getting at the B-17s, Liberators and Lancasters of the RAF. The USAAF had finally managed to get long-range escort fighters. P-38s, P-47s, and the P-51s had just recently been equipped with 110-gallon drop tanks, giving them a free run to any target within the shrinking borders of the Reich. There were also the rocket-firing Typhoons from the RAF that could take on anything the Germans threw at them. Swarms of them attacked German supply lines, rail and roads alike, while others went for the light flak batteries. So far, our battery had not been attacked by Typhoons, so we didn't complain.

After the show of the ME-262s and the subsequent destruction and slaughter of the P-51s, the war in the air intensified. High altitude bombing was the order of the day. First, the city of Julich received a plastering that reduced the town to five-foot piles of rubble. Euskirchen was next on the agenda, then Neuss, Krefeld, Moers and a few lesser important towns. We thought that somehow, apart from the fighter-bomber menace, our small town would escape safe and sound, but that was wishful thinking.

Our turn came on February 13, 1945, the same day the city of Dresden was attacked. According to some estimates, more people were killed there instantly than were killed by the atomic bomb dropped on Hiroshima. Unfortunately for us, a diversionary attack was made on our town. The intention was most probably to draw the German fighters away from the main objective. If that was the idea, the ruse surely worked, but we did not know about Dresden at the time.

It was a Tuesday. Brother Len had not gone to his duties. He had a flat tire on his bicycle and was doing his best, or worst, to mend it at 10:00 AM. To march five miles to the place where the trench digging was going on was too far to walk, even for Len. I had been to the sawmill just up the road to get a sack full of wood chips. Out in the yard Len was cursing his bad luck. I stopped and asked," Why don't you call it a day, Len, and help me with the wood chips?"

"Why don't you get lost?" was the reply.

"Ungrateful bastard," I mumbled. "I've dragged two sacks of wood chips all by myself from the sawmill while you were mending punctures."

Out from the west, we could hear the distant drone of aircraft noise. By the sound of it, they were Flying Fortresses, better known as B-17s. I was thinking of running over to the quads, but since I had not heard or seen any fighter-bombers, I decided to carry on with the task of getting the wood chips into the basement.

Then the first wave of bombers were over the town. Len was busy spinning his back wheel to test if it was running smoothly. The shell made a sort of funny whistling sound, I thought. Then I saw Len lying on the ground with his fingers in his ears and his mouth wide open. It immediately struck me that the whistling sound was coming from a bomb that was headed right at us. I threw myself on the ground and heard an almighty bang. It was too late to get into our air raid shelter, and besides the trap door was blocked by bags of chips and odd bicycle parts that Len had conveniently deposited there.

"Heck, Len, that was close!" I shouted.

"There's more to come!" he yelled. "Watch out!"

Mom came running into the yard, telling us to get into the shelter. She hadn't noticed the blocked trap door. The three of us then huddled by the back wall. We heard more whistling sounds, and then the bombing really got going. Since we lived about two miles out of town, we were spared wholesale destruction, but every windowpane went flying. Shingles from the roof dropped on us with a good sprinkle of 88mm shrapnel mixed in. Downtown we saw geysers of black and brown dirt blowing high into the air. A pall of yellowish smoke hung over the area, and the bombers still kept coming.

The attack lasted for just over 40 minutes. To us it seemed like hours. The nearest bomb, the very first one we had heard coming down, hit the back of the factory across the road, but nobody was in that part of the building. It was only used for storing empty wine bottles. Through all this awful din, Baby Fred slept. He was still asleep when the all-clear sounded. From the fires and smoke we could see from our house, it looked like the northern part of town had borne the brunt of the attack. After the all-clear sounded, I asked Mom if I could go over to Aunt Kathrin's house to see if she was okay. Permission given, she told me to watch out for delayed action bombs. I dashed across the fields and turned into the cemetery to look for Uncle Herman, the gravedigger. I couldn't find him, but another horrible sight greeted me. High explosives had fallen among the graves. The cemetery was littered with broken coffins and grave stones mixed with the bony remains of long dead people. I almost got sick, and ran as fast as I could to the back gate.

I almost made it without interruption, but when I turned the last corner before the exit, I heard the beat of drums and singing. There was Uncle Herman, standing by the side of the path, hat in hand. Then I saw why. Around the corner came a procession of Hitler Youth and Party members. Four of them were acting as pallbearers, carrying a flag-draped coffin. The song they were singing was about a Hitler Youth who died in the line of duty for the Fatherland. I couldn't grasp it. Here we were just after a devastating air raid, and these guys were marching and singing in the graveyard.

I walked up to my uncle and stood beside him. There was a freshly dug grave a few feet away. The congregation assembled around the grave and then a Party member gave a rousing speech about how the youngster had been killed while digging a trench to defend our Reich.

He had been shot by a fighter-bomber. He then reminded the funeral guests to do their utmost to save the Reich and Führer. Three salvos by 24 riflemen from the Hitler Youth were then fired and the coffin was lowered into the grave. A woman in black, the mother of the dead Hitler Youth, was crying when the Party leader came over to present her with an Iron Cross. Then they all wheeled about and marched out the way they had come.

Uncle Herman and two aides were already busy filling in the hole. He took me to the side, out of earshot of his two helpers. "Now you know what happens if you stick your nose out too far in this war, so be careful and don't volunteer for anything." He pointed at the fresh grave. "That's the seventh one this week I've tended to, and after this air raid, I'm sure there will be many more."

After all I had seen in the last few months, he did not have to remind me what was afoot. Nevertheless, I agreed and told him I would surely heed his advice. The sun had gone down by then, and I decided to go home. Uncle Herman told me that all was safe up by his house, apart from a few broken windows. I didn't want to go into town where fires were still burning and occasional delayed action bombs were still going off with a huge bang. Besides, I assumed that the police had blocked all roads into the center.

When I got home, Len was still there. He had not gotten his bike mended until late. I told him about the funeral and the Party man's speech. Len naturally knew everything, and tried to convince me that the Hitler Youth would sooner or later decide the outcome of the war. I told him that his views were all nonsense. If the SS could not stop the Allies, who the hell did he think could?

"Do you really think a regiment of Hitler Youth and a bunch of Volkssturm granddads armed with Panzerfausts can stop them?" I asked. "The Amis are now 25 miles to the west of us. The Russkys are on the Oder River 60 miles from Berlin. Between them is what's left of our Fatherland, bombed into mountains of rubble. And you talk of victory!"

"Well," he said, and I noticed an undertone of doubt in his voice, "I'll do my best as I was told, and if all others do the same, we might just have a chance of beating the Amis back to the beaches."

"All others, Len?" I said. "You'd better try and sell that to the Party men and the other pen pushers we have around. I'll bet you anything that they run east and swim across the Rhine when the first GI comes down that road," I continued. "Look, Len, I was in Wiltz with Mom when the Amis were fighting in the Ardennes, while you were taking pot shots with your rifle at P-38s. There was a battle going on and we sat in the middle with no way to run, and you are talking as if you and your outfit can win this war single-handedly. From what I saw in the Ardennes, fighting a war is not just trying to shoot down a Thunderbolt with a rifle or a quad 20mm. No, Len, there are thousands of well-equipped Amis and Tommies out there with an abundance of all sorts of weapons ready to jump on us here. They'll bury you and your outfit, plus the Volkssturm for good measure, in those antitank ditches you just dug."

"Well, we'll see when the time comes," he said meekly. But I was sure that deep down, he knew I was right.

In the next few days after the raid on February 13, we saw a sight that was new to us in the war. A steady stream of bedraggled and wounded German soldiers passed through town, mixed in with horse-drawn artillery, Hetzer tanks and the odd SPG. Even a few tank destroyers and a Werfer battery came rumbling along from the west.

"No, we're not setting up shop here. Your town is not important. Our next defensive line is the Rhine," a soldier told us.

"Did you hear that?" Len cried. "Not important! We've been digging ditches ever since the summer of '44, and all for what?"

"Does that mean that the Führer has abandoned us to the mercy of the Tommies and Amis?" I asked.

"It sure looks like it," Mr. Vink said. "From what I know, your Hitler Youth and Volkssturm will hold the enemy as long as possible, so we can get our armor across the river."

I had a funny feeling in my stomach. If the Amis were to advance on our town, they wouldn't know if a 12-year-old Hitler Youth or a 72-year-old granddad was pulling the trigger. All they would know was that they were being fired at, and that they would retaliate with all they had. The air raid of February 13 had killed almost 350 people in town, including my Aunt Christine and my two cousins.

Three days later, we had another heavy raid. The day before, we noticed a Mosquito reconnaissance plane flying over the town, probably to assess the damage from the first raid. I was on my way up to the quads. Len was downtown on a parade. Before I got to the gun pits, I heard the quads open fire. This time, two Mosquitoes flew over the town and circled around for a closer look. It was the fastest plane the

British had. It was faster than the Typhoon, and could outrun our Focke Wulf 190 by a mile.

Our quads normally did not bother much with the Mosquitoes because their speed made it difficult to get a range on them. But these two seemed to be cocky, so we let loose with all eight barrels. That meant that we were throwing up 6,000 rounds per minute, a fearful curtain of fire. One Mosquito flew into this storm of bullets and was blown to smithereens in an instant. The two Napier engines fell into the garden of the hospital. The rest of the plane just burned to ashes. The pilot was found in the cemetery, where Uncle Herman had a grave dug. The other Mosquito, probably with vital information on his camera plates about our town defenses and the armor parked around, got clean away.

No doubt the photographic plates would show a good many defensive installations, AA batteries and, above all, the town crammed to the brim with retreating troops. Tanks and other equipment were parked in open spaces without any attempt at camouflage. Our old improvised football field, the factory parking lot, was now temporary home to a Hanomag halftrack and a radio wagon. Soldiers were sitting around on wooden camp chairs playing cards and smoking pipes. The war seemed a 1,000 miles away.

That day was a repeat of the 13th, except that a good fighter escort and flak suppressors accompanied the bombers. A few twin engine Mitchell bombers came at lower levels to bomb the rail track that ran along the road below our position. Our quads threw up a tremendous fire as the Mitchells came into range. The 88mm in the field was furiously firing at the B-17s higher up, then our twin machine guns chimed in as well because the low-level flak suppressors had started to attack the AA defenses.

I had been on the way to the quads, but the sudden appearance of the dreaded fighter bombers made me jump into one of the roadside ditches the POWs had so conveniently dug for us in recent months. I had a quick peep over the edge of the trench, but seeing a Mustang with cannons blazing away making a beeline for the roadside trenches, I fell back. I heard the bullets hitting the ground nearby, and saw the shadow of the Mustang passing over me. Then he was gone.

I looked up again. This time there was no Jabo in my immediate vicinity, so I watched the bombs tumbling out of the open bays of the Mitchells, exploding somewhere near. A lot of firebombs were dropped as well, setting the town ablaze. Then another lot of HE bombs dropped to distribute the fires more evenly. Fighter-bombers were darting back and forth to catch anything that made an attempt to get out of the way. Not much did. The town center erupted in a huge continuous explosion, as gas mains and ammunition dumps went up with a deafening roar, sending a shower of red hot metal all over the rest of the town. A dud from a 150mm Nebelwerfer landed not five feet away from the trench I occupied. Luckily, it did not go off. Down in the town center it was hell. The steeple from our seventeenth century gothic cathedral was burning like a funeral pyre. The main roof had already caved in.

As I gazed in horror at all this destruction, unable to take my eyes off it, I almost paid dearly for neglecting to watch the sky around me. A Jabo roared over me, coming so fast that I forgot to see what type it was. He was not more than 50 feet above me. Had he seen me crouching in the trench? He did a sharp turn and came for another run toward me. This time I identified the plane as a P-47 Thunderbolt. Any second now I expected the wing cannons to riddle my position, but he passed overhead without firing a shot. Perhaps in the pilot's eyes I was just small fry, not worth a bullet. But there again, he might not even have seen me in that slit trench. I sighed a breath of relief when he was gone. Talk about a close shave!

All of a sudden, all was quiet up in the air. The attackers had gone. I can't remember how long it all lasted before the all-clear sounded. As fast as I could, I ran home to see if things were okay there. No harm had come to anyone at home. Mom was coming out of the recess behind the chimney where she had sheltered. Seeing that all was okay, I thought I would have a look downtown. It was another mess. This time the main street and the town park had been thoroughly plastered. The tramway rails were twisted, and huge craters, half full with water, were everywhere. Close to the big clothing store, a policeman and an air raid warden were blocking any further progress toward the end of Main Street.

"This way, son," the warden said. "Go up Peters Street. There's a delayed action bomb buried outside the store. It could go off any minute."

What in God's name was he doing there then, if there was a delayed action bomb in that hole outside the store? I hadn't gone 100 yards up Peters Street, when the thing went off with a huge bang, showering me with debris. I didn't bother going back to see what had happened to the warden. He had been standing ten yards from the impact site, and that was sure too close for comfort. The brewery, of all places, had received several direct hits, and the street was awash with beer. Some of the vats must have been damaged in the explosions, not that it mattered much. As far as I knew from Giant and the others at the quads, the beer nowadays was not worth drinking, and there were no takers for the stuff that was running in streams through the gutter.

A row of houses on Church Street was well ablaze, and no firefighting crew was in sight. Several firebombs were still lying on the pavement burning. There was no point trying to extinguish them with water—they required sand to stop them from burning. The most dangerous were what we called phosphorous bombs, the forerunner, in terms of damage anyway, of the Napalm bomb. On impact, they sprayed a generous dose of a liquid containing phosphorous, which has the nasty habit of burning when it comes in contact with air. The droplets burnt holes in the flesh with a greenish glow, and no amount of water could stop it from burning. The only remedy was to stop the air getting to it. It burnt until it exhausted its supply of liquid, which could be, if it happened to be on your skin, until it reached the bone.

I found Brother Len by the Old Market, where he was rescuing an old couple from a cellar. The house above was well on fire. A fire crew was in attendance but they had their hands full trying to save St. Mary's Church. The iron rails from the tramway, uprooted by the blast by several huge bombs, stood like a giant, two-pronged fork, high in the air. A street car was lying on its side with several dead passengers in it. Nobody as yet had found the time to take them out.

The living came first. The dead had to wait. Len came over to me, his hair singed, his hands and face black from soot, shaking his head. "You know that old couple we just pulled out alive from the cellar? They had been sitting in there since that last air raid, and couldn't get out. The trapdoor was blocked with rubble. We heard someone knocking under that mound and we investigated and found them both, well and in high spirits."

"How did they survive? I mean, food, drink or whatever?" I asked.

"That's the point." He said. "They had over 300 jars of canned peaches, strawberries, gooseberries, currants and other things in that cellar. That kept them alive."

I left Len to his work and walked along Main Street in a southerly direction. This brought me again by the clothing store where the delayed action bomb had gone off. I was getting curious. As I suspected, the warden had met the end of the road. There was also another body. Both lay covered with white bed sheets onto the pavement, a few yards from the crater. I identified the warden's boots sticking out from his sheet.

Just then my Hitler Youth group commander turned up on a bicycle. He dismounted and motioned me over. "What are you doing here?" he said. "You should be on your duty post or helping in the rescue."

"Sir, I was just with my brother by the Old Market, and he has things well in hand. In fact, he deserves a medal. He just rescued two old people from a house." I said.

"Leave the judgment of who receives awards to me," he growled. "You should be on your post up by the quads."

"For what, Sir?" I asked. "The Amis won't come back today. There are no leftover pickings here," and I pointed at the mess all around.

"Okay," he said, "then, make sure you are on your post tomorrow. Heil Hitler."

"Heil Hitler," I muttered and walked on.

I continued on Main Street toward the New Market and came across the most gruesome scene I had seen so far in the war. At the southern end of Main was the Lyceum, a kind of high school for girls aged 12 to 16, which was part boarding school. At the sound of the air alert sirens, the girls tried all at once to get to the public air raid shelter next door. As they were streaming out of the huge Greek-style portal, a half ton HE bomb dropped right in front of them onto the marble steps, killing 65 outright and wounding another hundred or so, many of whom later died of injury. The force of the half-ton bomb exploding five feet in front of the girls onto solid marble block steps was devastating. Some bodies were blown 200 yards along the street and onto the roof of a store. Others ended up in the city park, 300 feet away. One dead girl was found inside a nearby house in a bedroom. The force of the explosion had blown her through an open window into the room. It was a sight I will never forget.

Sick to death, I made my way home, hoping I had seen enough death and destruction for the day, but it was not to be. I passed the silk weaving factory. Once upon a time, in better years that is, it had been the biggest source of employment in town apart from Mr. Kersken's food factory. A bomb, or maybe several, had exploded square on the street in front of the main building, right on top of a huge underground water reservoir. The concrete ceiling or the reservoir had caved, in taking houses, several Wehrmacht vehicles and a score of people down with it. Some of the people were never found.

Opposite this was the barbershop where I used to get my hair cut. Rescuers were just then digging into the rubble and pulling bodies out. Two of them were the barber's sons, who were about my age. I had played soccer with both of them on the parking lot by the food factory. The pub next door to the barbershop had also received a direct hit from an HE. The early morning customers sitting there sipping their watery beer had all been killed. How many were killed in that raid? I can't remember, but I do know that they were all buried in a mass grave in the main cemetery. Today, over half a century later, it is still and always will be called the "Memorial Cemetery Plot," as a testimony to the senseless loss of life.

Not many survivors blamed the Allies for the raid, apart from the few diehard Nazi cronies still about. Times and beliefs had changed a lot since 1939. People, although not openly, blamed the whole system, the senseless war, and Goering's failure to keep his promise to shoot down any allied plane flying over Germany. Some even blamed the local Party members. Many of them had already packed their bags, fled east and crossed the Rhine by "Nacht und Nebel" (night and fog), as the saying went.

On my final stretch home, having left behind the last smoldering ruins, I passed our local soccer stadium. Aircraft sounds made me look up. Two British Typhoons were circling above. Well, were there to be leftover pickings? I was a mile from the quads, with no chance of getting there undetected. I thought that maybe they were just looking at the good work big brother had done earlier. Better safe than sorry, I thought, so I continued home, but kept a wary eye on the Typhoons.

From past encounters, we all knew that these particular fighter-bombers were hard-hitting customers, packing up to eight air-to-surface rockets in addition to their machine guns and cannons. Although the two planes were slowly circling in range of our quads, I heard no firing from them. The crew was either still collecting their wits from the heavy raid, or was out of action for reasons unknown to me. Lower and lower the Typhoons came, still searching about two miles off. I didn't like the look of things. I had the funny feeling that those two guys were in fact looking for leftovers, despite my earlier judgment to the Hitler Youth guy.

A huge bus came crawling uphill, black diesel smoke belching from his exhaust. The Typhoons had just about completed another turn and came toward me. I frantically waved my arms and hands to the driver and pointed skywards behind his truck. He understood and immediately came to a stop, jumped from the cab and came running over to me. The planes were now about 500 feet up, about a mile and a half away, their noses pointed in our direction.

"Looks like they mean us," the driver shouted, as he glanced over his shoulder at the Jabos.

"There's an air raid ditch, Sir," I said, "just opposite the stadium doors. We'd better hurry."

We jumped into the five-foot deep ditch, peeping over the rim. As luck would have it, the Typhoons had no rockets. They had probably fired them at some other target, but their machine guns and 20mms were very much in evidence as they came diving toward the bus. As if by magic, holes appeared in the wooden stadium gates. Dirt flew into our faces. We made ourselves as flat as possible in the trench to avoid being hit by the deadly, accurate fire. With a roar and rush, the Typhoons came over us. Then, circling round the factory chimney, they came for a second run. This time it was the bus they were after, and it went up in flames when the fuel tank took a 20mm tracer. Then there was silence. The planes had gone. Only the crackling of wooden sideboards burning on the truck could be heard.

"Those no-good bastards!" the driver shouted. "Three years I had that truck and never, in all that time, have I taken a scratch. Now look at it! Just you look at it!"

"It just shows you, Sir, things happen in war," I said.

He looked at me, but said nothing. We climbed out of the trench. An awful smell was hanging around, but not from the burning truck— it was me. Someone had used the trench as a convenient toilet, depositing his contribution in a neat heap smack in the middle of the trench. When the Typhoons came streaking toward us, I had jumped right into the pile, then flattened myself down into it for good measure when the planes fired at the trench. What a mess! I was covered in crap from ass to appetite with no way to wipe it off. I ran home, avoiding people as best as I could, but some still held their noses as I hurried by. Mom couldn't stop laughing when she saw me, and marched me straight to the rainwater barrel outside. My uniform was dipped into a steaming cauldron of boiling water.

Len came back at suppertime, black as a chimney sweep. His uniform was singed, but he was proudly sprouting a KVK 2nd Class rib-

bon on his tunic. The local defense commander had issued a citation for
bravery to his whole group, and each one had been awarded the medal
for rescuing several people from burning houses. He also brought a canvas bag full of canned peaches he had saved from destruction when he
rescued the old couple. "Spoils of war," he said with a grin.

He was learning fast, I thought. A few weeks earlier, it would have
been beneath his dignity to take anything from a burning house. He
would rather have seen the stuff rot or melt. We all savored a few slices
of the peaches and went to bed. I lay awake for a long while, still seeing the dead schoolgirls by the Lyceum. Then I wished the Allies would
come soon to end all this misery, but it was not yet time for deliverance.

The next morning I was up early, feeding the rabbits. Then the postman knocked. He gave Mom a letter for Brother Len. Mom thought it
had something to do with his Hitler Youth business and put it aside. Len
had already gone to town to report to the guardroom and quartermaster for a new uniform. I made my way up to the quads. The men were
busying themselves taking stock. From up here we could look over the
whole town from end to end. The skyline surely had changed since yesterday. Fires were still going and a grayish brown cloud hung high
above the city. The high steeples of several churches had gone, as had
some of the chimneystacks and two tall apartment buildings. POWs
were already busy at work clearing the thoroughfares so the military
traffic could flow eastward to the Rhine. As far as we knew, the Rhine
Bridge at Urdingen was still standing, and there were also two crossings
at Düsseldorf, 15 miles away.

"Now let's take stock of our situation here," Giant said. "No damage as yet has been done to our guns, despite a few close calls by rocket-firing Typhoons and other fighter bombers. Our ammo is at a dangerously low level for the first time since we've been here. We need food
for our guns and food for us. We've got 16,000 rounds per barrel left.
That's just about 20 minutes firing for each gun. As for food for us, I'm
sure there is some sauerkraut left somewhere. All communications have
broken down due to the air raid and have not been restored of yet.
Someone has to go to headquarters in town to see the captain and take
a message to him. Feeling fit to run, boy?" he said to me.

"Sure do, Sir, You just give me that message and I'm on my way."

Giant scribbled something on a page of his message pad. Then he
noticed that I was not in uniform. I told him of my mishap yesterday
and that it was not yet dry. I had no spare uniform. "Okay, don't worry,

boy,' he said. "Here is the leather case with the message and a message for your personal use."

"Personal use, Sir?" I asked.

"Personal protection," he said. "If anyone stops you, show him this message and tell the person that I will personally see that he is punished if he delays you."

I looked at the message and read: "I hereby authorize Hitler Youth Gehlen to proceed on the shortest possible route to Battery HQ of the 64th Light Flak to deliver a message of utmost urgency to the commanding officer, Captain Heinseler. All personnel are hereby advised to give Hitler Youth Gehlen every assistance possible so that this message reaches its destination. Any infringements on his duties in the course of delivering this message will be treated as an act of treachery against the defenses of the Reich and will be punished. Signed: Lieutenant Roland, CO, 64th Light Flak Battery A&B."

He had even put the official flak stamp over his signature. "Wow, that gets me even to the Führer!" I said, after I had digested the writing.

"It's all meaningless, boy," he said, "but it might help in case some crony wants to stop you. Now on your way. We need ammo and plenty of it. Tell the captain."

I dashed off toward the town, keeping the usual eye on the sky. I knew where headquarters were, near the main post office. POWs were busy clearing rubble from pavements. The roads had already been opened. On the corner of H and F streets, a group of people stood around gawking at a dead POW. He had been clearing away some beams and had touched a live high voltage cable, dying instantly. The other POWs were somewhat reluctant to carry on with this dangerous work, but two SS guards with leveled machine pistols yelled at them and the poor guys continued hacking away at a piece of masonry.

A policeman stopped me at the corner by the New Market. "No entry here, boy," he said.

"Why not?" I asked.

"It's none of your damn business, but I will tell you nevertheless," he said. "Some highly explosive incendiaries are lying up ahead waiting for disposal. So beat it, boy."

Incendiary bombs lying on the ground are harmless. They will burn only if they hit the ground. Some break up on impact and are duds. Not dangerous at all. They do not explode by themselves, as I told the policeman.

"Ah, so we have a know-it-all here," the policeman roared. "Now listen to me, you-out-of-uniform Hitler Youth nuisance!"

Before he could utter another word, I stuck Giant's message under his nose and told him to read it very, very carefully. He read it, straightened his back and said, "In that case, excuse me, boy. I didn't know the urgency of your business, so please proceed, and Heil Hitler."

Same to you, I thought. I passed a few incendiary bombs, hexagonal in shape and about two feet long. They were mean-looking devices, made of some sort of aluminum and magnesium alloy that burns easily when the phosphorous is released on impact. I reached headquarters, where a guard corporal politely asked me what my business was. I told him that I had an urgent message for the captain, and the guard directed me to his office. Just as I was about to enter the office, the captain came from a hallway on the other end of the building.

A grin was on his face. "Well, well, who's here then? Hello, boy!" he exclaimed, patting my shoulder. I gave him Giant's message and added that there was only 20 minutes worth of firing left in the ammunition stock.

"Tell the lieutenant that I will personally see to it that the ammunition gets up there in the morning," he said, adding, "I will send a Demag halftrack with three tons around 8:00 AM, or even earlier. I hate to think what could happen if three tons of 20mm gets clobbered by a fighter-bomber. Tell him to have all his men on standby for unloading and to let them have their breakfast afterwards. I want that Demag back in one piece before 9:00 AM. Things will be getting busy after that time and that halftrack is the only one we have. It serves the 88s as well. Got all that?"

"Yes, Sir," I said, and I made a smart turn and walked out. Then I realized I had forgotten the obligatory "Heil Hitler," but so had the captain.

A light snow was falling when I got back to the quads. "That will keep the Jabos off our back," Giant remarked after I gave him the captain's message.

"Thank you, son," he said, "and God bless you. You're more reliable than the telephone around here. Okay, you guys, now listen all. It looks like the weather is closing in on us. That also will take care of any further molesting by our enemy. I can make out six evening passes. Who wants to go into town for a romp?" he shouted.

"Count me out, Lieutenant. There's nowhere to go," K-2 answered.

"Lousy lot you are," the lieutenant said, waving six blank passes around. "You can have an evening out, but nobody wants it. What has come over you?"

A corporal from B gun said it all, "Romp where and what, Lieutenant? There ain't much to romp," and he pointed at the ruins of the city where just now another Blindgänger ("blind walker") went up. This was the common German word for a dud, or a bomb that somehow had failed to explode on impact, whereas a Zeitzunder was a time or delayed action bomb.

The corporal continued, "I'll stay here and play billiards in our mess bunker. I'd rather knock ivory balls around the billiard table than get blown up by a Blindgänger."

"What about stand-by crews for the cannons?" K-1 of B gun asked.

"Just send two men out and relieve them every few hours," the lieutenant said. "There'll be no flyers out in this foul weather I can assure you, and the captain won't be up here either. They still have good beer and cigars in the downtown officer's club. That is, if the club is still standing."

I told the sergeant that the club was indeed still standing. Naturally the poor civilians had borne the brunt. Their houses were burned and leveled, but the officer's club had gotten away without so much as a broken window. How about that for justice? I walked home through the light snow. A warm fire and a plate full of fried potatoes greeted me. Len was home and he opened the letter the postman had delivered that morning.

"What does it say, Len?" I mumbled with a mouth full of hot potatoes.

"It's a farce," he said. "These are my 'call-up papers.' I'm already called up. What have I been doing for the last year or so? Len threw the letter in the fire.

I couldn't help it, but I had to tell him that he had just destroyed an official document of the Wehrmacht's Recruiting Office.

"Who cares? So what?" he said. "Who's recruiting whom or what? Have you heard the latest news from the front? The Allies have finally crossed the Roer River and the swamp, and are now, at this moment, advancing on Erkelenz and Wegberg."

"That," I said, "does not surprise me. All I'm worried about right now is how we can save our skins and Mom and Baby Fred. You know what I'm getting at, Len?"

"Of course I do," said Len, "and that's why I burned that call-up document. I'm off in the morning to the POW camp to do my normal duties. Nothing more, nothing less, and I shall continue to do so, until someone comes to tell me to go home and stay home. Then I'll smash this K98 rifle against a tree, burn my uniform and walk home in my underpants."

Len left at 6:00 AM. I didn't know then that we wouldn't see him again until early March. I was up at 7:00 AM, had an ersatz coffee and a sandwich, and told Mom that I had to be at the quads early. It was snowing, so there was no danger of any low-level attack, but somewhere, thousands of feet above the snow clouds, the big bombers were still trekking eastward, unmolested by flak. We had no radar in operation to determine the height, and besides, 88mm ammunition was a scarce commodity. We did not fire at planes we could not see.

True to the captain's word, at 7:30 the Demag turned up, spitting and puffing black smoke. It brought the ammo, but not exactly the amount we had asked for. It had also brought some long-awaited decent food. There was half a pig in a case, a box of 50 cigars, eight bottles of the finest booze, twelve loaves of good white bread, a pack of sugar and some dried milk, and a pound packet of ersatz coffee.

Gunny almost had tears in his eyes when he surveyed the lot. "My, oh my, Christmas has either come late, or very early this year. I wonder where the captain got this from?"

"Search me. I got no clue," Giant said.

"I got an idea where all that foodstuff is coming from," I said to Giant.

"So you do, eh?" Giant said.

"That first heavy raid we had a few days ago, remember?" "Well," I said, "an HE dropped on the Party headquarters that day, and you all know where the Party people are when a raid is in progress. They hide for 24 hours in their bombproof bunkers. That gave the captain and the guys from the Luftwaffe Field Division time enough to cart some of the Party goodies away to a hiding place. I saw a Luftwaffe truck leaving the smashed Party HQ just after the raid."

"Well, yes, that's it then. Good old Party men!" shouted Gunny.

"Good old brandy, too," said Giant. He took a big mouthful and burped with a "Heil Hitler" mixed in it.

"Hitler," K-1 said. "I heard he never touches the stuff, so I'll have his share too."

"Now, listen you guys," Giant said, putting the bottle on the parapet. "Let's get the ammo into the bunker first so the driver can take his Demag back. I need all hands except the cook. He can start on that half a pig and make us some decent stew. If the bad weather holds, we'll have a bit of a celebration then."

The ammunition was stowed away into the magazine in less than an hour—a record time by Gunny's calculations.

"I wish those guys would always work like that," lamented the gunnery sergeant to the lieutenant.

"Food and booze work wonders sometimes," the lieutenant said.

Luckily for us, the weather was on our side. With light snow and ground visibility almost nil, there was no way an intruder could sneak up on us. In this weather they could not get airborne and risk their necks in a low-level attack. After all the ammo was safely stored away and the Demag had departed, the celebration, as the lieutenant promised, went ahead. The cook had meanwhile made a super stew using almost a quarter of the pork. In came potatoes, carrots, turnips, leeks and a generous dose of dried spices and herbs. The sergeant from the twin machine guns said it was a meal fit for the gods. Mess cups were filled with brandy. The nondrinkers had to make do with the Kathreiner Ersatz Kaffee.

After a few brandies, the general mood was that Adolf Hitler was not really a bad guy after all. I suspected that they said that because some were already drunk, but more importantly, some of them were not. They toasted to each other, to the Führer, to Mussolini, to the SS and even to the Allies, of all people.

I was annoyed that they had toasted to that big fat mouth Duce. After all, he had never done any good for Germany. On went the eating and drinking. But by late afternoon, the first after effects of the unusually heavy meal and the booze started to appear. Men were forming a queue by the toilet.

"Good old sand pit," K-1 yelled. "Cheers, yeah, good old Wehrmacht toilet. With all this crapping going on we ought to have a crap master here in charge of the toilets. Any volunteers?"

Stalin, the halfwit Ukrainian replacement, was selected as the crap master. Proper toilet tissue was not available in those days, and men made do with cut up newspapers or cement bags. They decorated the Ukrainian guy with a gray cement bag paper still sprouting the "Reiner Portland Cement" logo. He stood by the toilet booths, half drunk, attempting to give orders: "Now then Soldaten, ve vant an orderly line here by ze Scheissen Housen. You all vill hav a turn for ze crapping."

I finally had enough. I had only a small helping of the stew and I felt okay, but I went home anyway. There were sure to be some hangovers next morning. Giant, in one of his generous moods, had given me a three-pound piece of pork as a departing present.

"Tell your Mom that this comes with the compliments of the National Socialist Party. I'll see you in the morning, okay?" Giant said.

"Thank you, Sir," I said, "and good night, too."

Mom was glad to get some meat. "We'll have Sunday roast for a change. I'm getting rather fed up with rabbit every week," she said.

"Mom, I need some vitamins," I said. "I've been stacking ammo boxes all day. Can I have a candy bar?"

"You sure can. There are some left that we brought back from Wiltz, but not many."

I thought it was high time the Allies arrived to replenish our candy bar stock. I wondered what was holding them up.

The Allies were indeed coming, slowly but surely. The retreating SS and army had fortified a few farms and a village here and there. A well-concealed Panther tank or a SPG could easily hold up the infantry advance. The Americans advancing toward our area had to bring up heavy armor to knock the strong points out. The 84th and 102nd had to have the British help out with armor. This was because the 84th advanced on the extreme left wing of General Simpson's Ninth US Army, bordering on Montgomery's 21st Army Group. The 84th and 102nd Infantry had their own divisional artillery, but tank support was provided by the British 5th Armoured, who had, of course, American Sherman tanks as a main weapon.

The next morning at the quads, it was business as usual. Hangovers and cobwebs were soon shaken out of sleepy heads when the weather cleared up around 10:00 AM. The late February sun came out and melted the light dusting of snow. The guns were fully manned and eyes were glued to the sky. Magazines were filled and piled up by the entrance to the ready room.

At precisely 11:00 AM, Ami fighter-bombers made their first appearance. Two Thunderbolt P-47s, searching for suitable targets, stayed well out of our range; not that it mattered much. The P-47s had armor plated pilot cabins, and our 20mm peashooter could not harm them unless we hit a vital part of the engine. Even their internal gas tanks were, by now, self-sealing but the thin-walled drop tanks were vulnerable to our tracers.

The two P-47s worked the railroad yard over for a while, but soon lost interest. There probably was not much left to shoot at after the air raids of the last few days. By midday, we heard a heavy mob coming from a westerly direction: Liberators, Fortresses and Mitchells, all protected by the usual swarm of fighters stacked between 15,000 to 20,000 feet up. This wasn't our fight. The planes were too high up, but the 88mms let loose as soon as they had the range. Other 88 batteries now joined in the circus, and the first Libby took a hit. It flew on for a few miles but then trundled to the ground and crashed near Krefeld. We saw no chutes, so there was total loss.

Then a B-17 Flying Fortress got hit by our sister battery of 88s over at Mackenstein. It broke in half, and we saw several parachutes floating down. The wreckage was scattered over a wide area. We even got our fair share of it. The tail of the plane came floating down like a wounded bird in a turkey shoot and ended up not 150 yards away from our guns. I ran over to have a look at the piece, but there wasn't much to look at. The tail end cupola was smashed to pieces and its twin machine guns mangled. It was only good for the scrap yard. The tail end gunner must have gotten out by chute. Nobody was to be seen.

I recovered a piece I thought was from a battery as a souvenir. I also found an open tin with a sausage still in it and, behold, a candy bar! Well, that was something amazing, I thought. Food survives falling 20,000 feet, and men get killed doing the same thing. It was high time for me to get back to cover. The crews, highballing in their heavies 20,000 feet up, had just about enough of the 88s and had probably asked for flak suppressors, who of course would respond promptly. With fighter bases only 50-odd miles out from us, the guys were with us in a few minutes, coming in like beads on a rosary. A few miles out, their formation broke up and each group selected their targets. It was obvious that the 88mms just down from us were getting a plastering from the Jabos, and our job was to stop the Typhoons from firing their deadly rockets.

Under good flying conditions, a good Typhoon pilot could fire a brace of rockets into a field kitchen a mile out—and the Typhoon pilots were all good. Other planes like the Thunderbolts made it their duty to take care of the light flak, meaning us, and we were supposed to be protected by the twin machine guns. Protection on this scale went from the

88mms down to the ordinary rifleman who, if he had a chance, would take pot shots at anything that came within his range.

The 88s were fearsome weapons and hated by all the bomber crews. A German fighter could be seen and fired at if he came within range, but the 88s could not be seen, and a close shave from one of the HE shells could mean destruction of the plane. The chances of surviving were slim if the plane was on fire. It did not take a direct hit from an 88 to bring a plane down.

The sky over that part of the Roer area that morning was so crowded, it was like watching a flying circus. After a few minutes of full blast with all we had—that is, four barrels per gun—we switched to diagonal again, giving the other two barrels time to cool down. All hands stood by the guns, the loaders with magazines at the ready. The others were scanning the sky, but the action at that moment was several miles to the northeast. The cook had made a few sandwiches and a pot of Kathreiner coffee and was getting ready to announce "come and get it" when someone over by the twin machine guns shouted, "Enemy planes coming at four high!" This was right in line with the morning sun, so we heard them before we could see them. As they got nearer and under the glare of the sun, we saw two British-made Mosquitoes coming at full speed at our position. I dived into the radio bunker and peeped through a slit in the steel door. The Mosquitoes normally are not armed, or so we had been told, and are only used for fast reconnaissance. Their main defense is their fantastic speed, but these two guys surely had some shooting sticks on their planes, because bullets were flying all around the quads. Some were hitting metal parts, making clanking noises. Finished and gone in a second or two, they then circled and watched us from a safe distance. I heard someone screaming as I emerged from the cover of the bunker. It was K-1 on B gun. "Look, those bastards shot my right index finger off!" Blood was dripping onto the turntable of the gun.

"You don't need an index finger to fire that gun. You have pedals. Now keep firing!" the lieutenant was shouting.

"I can't turn the elevation wheel, Lieutenant."

"We'll buy you a wooden finger, but keep firing. Here they come again!" The lieutenant screamed.

They came back at us, spoiling for a fight. This time one had the guts to try to break our tracer curtain, and got hit by several 20mm rounds. The plywood plane blew into thousands of bits and pieces. The other one flew off toward the east, looking for easier pickings. No major damage had been done to our quads. There were just a few dents and scratches here and there, and of course K-1s missing index finger.

The whole attack had lasted about ten minutes. To me, it was more like two hours. We looked around for any other damage. Some B-23s had dropped a few HE bombs nearby, but we did not have time during the attack to see where they fell. The cycling track down the road had taken a few hits, but the railroad to the food factory was undamaged. All in all, four heavies and five bombers had been shot down in our area. We were credited with a Mosquito. The 88s had gotten the big bombers and a 37mm battery had scored well on the rest. We cleaned the place up a bit. I collected empty cases and bagged them, and K-1 was sent off to the hospital down the road to have his wound seen to. He wasn't very happy that he had to cycle the two miles to the hospital, but ambulances were not available. Then we changed barrels on the guns. A worn out barrel can be a disaster. Just a tiny infraction could reduce the firing ability of a barrel by 20 percent. No more low-level attacks came, but the 88s kept firing intermittingly at the bombers high overhead.

Later that day the captain drove up. He brought two guys with him that I had not seen before. In their late teens, they wore the uniform of the Kriegsmarine (navy). On their caps was a black band with silver stitching, Kriegsmarine Zerstörerflottile—Destroyer, or tin can sailors.

"I haven't much time now," the captain said. "I have to see to those 37mms. How was your day up here, Lieutenant?"

"Fine, Sir. Just a few attacks. Not much really. K-1 lost a finger, shot off clean by a Mosquito, but we got the culprit. Some men have a bit of diarrhea, and we changed barrels. Just a normal workday, Sir," Giant said with a hit of irony in his voice.

The captain grinned and said, "Just write a report later and I'll pick it up tomorrow. The Mosquito goes to your credit after confirmation."

"The 88 crew can verify that with no problem, Sir. Excuse me, but have you got a navy bodyguard now, Sir?" asked Giant, pointing at the two sailors.

The two Destroyer men were uneasily looking the position over and glancing at the sky. A few rounds from the 88s, 400 yards away, which were still firing at some stragglers, made them shudder. Nobody else took notice of the firing.

The captain laughed, "No, Lieutenant. The two sailors are reinforcements for you. You told me a while ago that you need more men. Give the two of them a few instructions. They're attached to you as z.b.V. (zur besonderen Verwendung, standby status, temporary assignment) until further notice."

I went into the ammo bunker with the two swabbies in tow. "He isn't a bad lieutenant," I told them, "but his nerves are a bit tender today. We just had an attack before you turned up. One of our cannoneers was wounded, but we shot a Mikki down."

"What's a Mikki?" one of them said.

"Mosquito, British, made from plywood," I replied, "with two Rolls Royce Napier engines, top speed around 600 kilometers per hour."

"Aren't you a bit young to be here on an AA position?" one of them asked.

"Not at all," I replied. "We have younger ones on 20mms in Krefeld. They could fire your sea-borne pom poms at anything within range. But come on, let's get them mags filled. We might have another raid today."

By 4:00 PM we had finished loading 60 magazines. The two sailors learned fast. Also, K-1 came back from the hospital, his right hand bandaged.

"That's it for me," he said. "I'm useless now."

"What was your job in civilian life?" I asked.

"I was an apprentice to a baker," he said.

"Well, your injury might stop you from getting your fingers in a pie," I said, "but why not become a professional soccer player? You don't need an index finger for that."

The mail truck came puffing and smoking up the hill on his weekly run. Times had been better in 1943 when mail was delivered every other day to the soldiers, but the mail carrier was nevertheless greeted with big applause. All got their fair share of letters and small parcels, except of course, Giant. His family was dead, and there was nobody else to write to him. Mrs. Helgers (not her real name), his new beloved, lived just down the lane, so there was no need for letters from her. There was also a leather case with some more or less official papers, new report sheets, inquiries about misdirected messages, and the ever-present news and propaganda material, which as usual was totally out of touch with the present situation. Mail call was always a diversion for the men from the drudgery of soldiering. They sat around and read the letters from home. Most news was bad by the beginning of 1945, but it didn't matter. Good or bad, any news was better than none at all.

Giant was going through the wad of official paper. "Hey, you guys, listen. I got some official news here. Gather around."

The men came closer, expecting something encouraging. Giant said, "Now this is official and comes right from the high command, the Führer's headquarters. Here, I'll read it to you: 'By order of the Führer, we are at this moment experiencing some hard times, but I can assure you all that final victory is just around the corner.'"

"What corner?" Gunny asked looking around.

"Shut up, Sergeant, will you? This is official." Giant said.

"I only asked a question, Sir. Sorry." Gunny apologized.

"You're not supposed to question a Führer order," Giant said. "Now, let's get on with it. As I was reading: 'victory is just around the corner.'"

Giant did not seem to hear Gunny's whispered statement about there being no round corners, so the lieutenant continued: "'The Allies are knocking on the door of our Fatherland and I must ask you all to do your utmost duty to preserve our National Socialist freedom, our homes, our Fatherland.'"

I could hardly hear Gunny's soft remark, "He's asking us now, not ordering us."

The lieutenant read on, "'Every soldier—in fact, every able bodied person, male or female—must be ready and willing to stop any further advance by the Bolshevists and Imperialistic aggressors. "No retreat" is our slogan. We will fight to the last round. We will stand fast. There will be no shirking of responsibilities. We will prevail. We will be victorious. Signed: Adolf Hitler.'"

"Well, any comments, now?" Giant asked.

No comments were forthcoming. The silence was deafening, until far out to the southwest, cannon fire could be heard like the roll call of a distant drum.

What a farce this Hitler order was. Who was going to get himself killed for the Führer now at ten minutes to midnight? It was now just a matter of surviving the last round. Of course, we could still be killed by a fighter-bomber attack, but that was different. We knew that the war was lost by now. Only a few diehards thought otherwise. We didn't know then that we had exactly six days to go before the war would be over, for us at least.

I asked Mom what she thought about the so-called "last stand" for our Führer. "You just stay out of trouble," she said. "If you have to go to the quads, at least you will have a concrete shelter you can hide in, but if and when the end comes to all this fighting, you come straight home, understood?"

Len's bed was empty the next morning. Mom said that he hadn't come home and she suspected he was with his unit somewhere manning the trenches surrounding the town. "Go down to the Hitler Youth center," Mom said, "and ask where he is. After that you can go up to the quads."

I was just putting my overcoat on when the alarm sirens went off all over town. I went outside and looked to the west. A fleet of high-level bombers was approaching with the usual swarm of fighter protection. The 88s were already in action. Our quads were silent because there were no low-level planes to be seen yet. The bombers came in over the town. Their bomb bays opened and out tumbled canister after canister of incendiary bombs. By the looks of it, we were on the receiving end of another raid. A second wave of bombers dropped HEs to spread the fires a bit more. It didn't matter much. The town was already a heap of rubble, so all the bombers achieved was a leveling of the ruins that still were standing.

Nevertheless, 88 people died in that raid. The hospital also took a direct HE hit, despite having a huge red cross painted on the roof. Amazingly, the food factory was again spared destruction, but it was a close shave. The railroad tracks were severed about a mile from the back gate. The factory was actually never damaged and operated until February 28. After March 5, it was occupied by the Allies and served as an ordinance depot for the victors until 1959.

I made my way to town to find out where Brother Len was, but the Hitler Youth HQ had taken a few firebombs and was burning. A few official-looking people were standing about, watching the fire. There was not a fire engine to be seen and nobody could tell me where Len was. One high-ranking Hitler Youth guy told me that his group had gone out toward Krefeld the previous day to dig trenches, but they had not come back yet. He also said that he had seen them marching out with a tool wagon and a field kitchen in tow, so they might be camping out. A Volkssturm group armed with Panzerfausts had marched with them. There was also some sort of party official there, busy burning papers he was taking from a large leather case. I thought it was funny.

Why not put the whole case into the flames? Wasn't there enough burning going on already?

I went home and told Mom the results of my inquiries and that there was no way we could check if Len was near Krefeld or somewhere else. There were no busses, no trains, just the Wehrmacht vehicles, and they were all hell bent to get to the bridges over the Rhine—that is, to the ones they knew were still standing. All Rhine bridges were supposed to have been blown sky high by the rear guards of the Wehrmacht. Some them were already down—the Allied bomber offensive had seen to that.

I lounged around by the kitchen window for a while. It was raining outside, a cold late February drizzle that would also give the quad crews a respite. I thought it pointless to go up there in this weather. What could anyone do on a day like this? My soccer mates were nowhere to be seen outside, and Len was not in yet either. There was no one to argue with. I went upstairs to my bedroom to look over my stamp collection. Brother Len also had a sizable album full of stamps. I found his hidden under the mattress, so I rifled through it and took some stamps that I didn't have in my collection. I hoped he wouldn't miss them on his return, but there again, he might never return, and then I could inherit all his stamps.

Mom called me down for supper. It wasn't much of a meal, but Mom always did her very best. We had fried potatoes with onions and a slice of hard black bread topped with some concoction that was supposed to be a paste from which to make soup. We had tried in vain to make a decent soup from the brownish, sharp-tasting stuff, but it would just not dissolve. It was something the NSV had invented in early summer 1944, and nobody knew what was in it. It was supposed to be very nourishing, but all we could do was spread it on black bread.

Black bread was something I could live without. On our bread ration cards, there were coupons for white bread and just bread. White bread, if you could call such a gray color "white," was rationed to one two-pound loaf per week. The black bread was rationed too, but our coupons entitled our family to eight pounds a week, including Aunt Carol's ration. Eight pounds sounds like an awful lot of bread, but the stuff was so tightly baked and heavy, just one slice felt like a stone in your stomach. The main ingredients were unground rye and barley, a small dose of flour, and unrefined molasses from sugar beets that held this whole concoction together so it wouldn't break into bits. I don't think any baking powder or yeast was used. When the loaf came out of the oven and was fresh, it could be sliced easily. The problem was that the bakery only made bread two days a week in order to conserve energy, or so they told us. The black bread was definitely not fresh after 12 hours in the bread bin at home. Once it reached this state, it was almost impossible to cut a slice off the loaf because the outside crust would go hard as a brick. We had a hand-operated bread-cutting machine, but even with the aid of this device, the black stuff was hard to cut. We usually ended up with an odd shaped piece and chewed for a long time to get it down. Our stomachs had to work overtime to digest the stuff. We always had plenty of ersatz coffee to help wash it down.

Early the next morning I made my way up to the quads. From the southwest came the sound of battle, the dull boom of artillery and the sharp crack of tank cannon fire. The steady staccato of machine guns could be dimly heard as well. Up by the quads, all was in an uproar. Overnight some men from an RAD detachment had cut down a whole line of poplar trees to the southwest of us. Now we had an unrestricted view almost to Hardt, five miles away. With the aid of binoculars, we could read the time on the clock tower of the Hardt Church. Even the small spire on the chapel on the grounds of the lunatic asylum was visible. In reality, it was not a lunatic asylum but the Josef Heim Hospital. Everyone referred to it as the loony bin because the inmates consisted mainly of soldiers who had gone loco in battle or been shell shocked, and a few real mentally ill patients.

"Why did they cut those nice poplars down?" I asked Gunny.

"They might need firewood or, and I have sort of a hunch," Gunny said, "they did it to give us a better field of fire."

"Planes wouldn't come that low, would they?" I asked.

"I don't think so," he said, "but we need a flat trajectory to fire at anything that can walk, crawl, run on wheels or tracks. Call it ground defense, if you like."

"Are our guns going to fire to the last round, and then we're all going to die for the Reich and Führer if it comes to the worst?"

"Hell no, boy," he said, "I suppose we'll cease fire one day, surrender, or run like hell eastward like the rest of our proud Wehrmacht. I'd personally prefer the second option. I don't know about the others. It's up to them, but I know my crew. They all realize the war is lost by now. Nobody wants to play hero around here."

Giant emerged from the radio bunker. "Message just came in. American tanks have been reported several miles southwest of Hardt.

No infantry as yet, but knowing the Amis, the foot-sloggers won't be far behind. Sergeant, call all the men into the mess room. I have something I want to say to all of them."

"Stand-by crews as well?" Gunny asked.

"You heard me. I want everyone in there," Giant said. "And don't ask me what we will do if we have an alert, okay?"

"Okay, okay, just asking and thinking," Gunny said.

The men came filing into the mess bunker and gathered around the billiard table. Even the machine gunners were present. Under normal circumstances, they were not under Giant's command, but alas, today's circumstances were not normal. They all realized that time was running out for the Third Reich, and that the future looked bleak and uncertain for them. They looked up to their commander as a sort of savior.

"Okay, Sergeant, all present?" Giant asked.

"Yes, Sir," came the reply.

"Alright men, relax," he began. "I have a few words I'd like to say to you now. Most of you have been with me and this battery since 1940. We've had good times and bad times. Some of our battery comrades have been killed. This is unavoidable in war. We all know it could be any of us next time around. You all know the Allies are about 30 to 40 miles away. There is nothing that will stop them from winning this conflict. Our Wehrmacht couldn't stop them on the beaches of Normandy. We surely will not be able to stop them now, not with what we've got left.

"The Führer's dream of winning the last round in this match with the V-2 weapon dissolved in 1943 when the Allies flattened Peenemünde. My family lived in Karshagen, a mile or so from the rocket station, and they died in that raid. Our Wehrmacht has retreated to the eastern bank of the Rhine. On the radio it was stated that the Huckingen Bridge was blown, so our retreat is cut off now. Between us and the advancing Allies are just a weak parachute division, some Hitler Youth units, the Volkssturm, and a few fanatical SS troops. As far as I know, there is no armor support for our troops up front. We're the only full strength unit that's left along with the 88s, who are in a fixed position like us and cannot move without trucks or halftracks and lifting equipment.

"I don't want to play the big hero now. There aren't any more Iron Crosses to be given. All I ask is that we give the remnants of our troops out there some sort of fire support. When they finally do pull out, then and only then will we cease fire. There's nothing we can do against tanks. We don't even have a Panzerfaust here. When we cease fire, I'll leave it to you to determine what to do, run east or surrender. Before that, we'll make sure the guns are made useless. Any questions?"

"Sir, how much time do we have?" the corporal asked.

"I don't know," Giant answered. "It depends on how fast the Allies overcome our resistance up front, but I'd say a day or so. American tanks could turn up on the horizon at any time."

As if to prove his point, we could already hear the explosions of artillery shells in the distance, maybe five miles away. It was nothing serious, but the guns were searching and probing, taking ranges, I supposed.

"Okay, men, back to your posts now," said Giant, dismissing the men. "Oh, and before I forget, good luck to all of you." He turned to me, "As for you, boy, you're better off at home now, and tell your Mom and Aunt to find a good place to hide, preferably with a solid roof over your head. As from this moment, you are dismissed, but don't look so worried. I'll see you when this is all over."

"But, Sir," I protested, "I want to come tomorrow. This bunker is much safer than our shelter at home and, besides, I'm part of the battery. The captain said so."

"The captain won't be coming up here again," Giant said. "I think I'm in charge now, but I can see your point about the shelter. Well, if nothing has happened by morning, if there is no artillery fire and no tanks are roaming around, you can come up. But I want you in that bunker when the shooting starts and things get serious. Is that clear?"

"Yes, Sir," I said, relieved. The thought of sitting in our flimsy shelter at home, surrounded by canned fruit, homemade briquettes and wood chips made me cringe.

When I got home I told Mom the things Giant had said. She was completely against me going up to the quads the next day, but I convinced her that the bunker was better protection than our shelter. Anyplace we were in now could become part of the front.

It is impossible to hide the fact that civilians in war always end up in the firing line. There is no escape. If they hide in their own shelters, they might be safe if a bomb drops across the road, but what if it falls directly on the house they are hiding in? I argued with Mom for a while and told her of the excellent bunkers we had up there. I told her that there was no public air raid shelter anywhere near us, so it was either our flimsy shelter or the bunkers by the guns, and I preferred the latter.

Mom had not yet decided what to do in a real emergency, but she mentioned that she, Aunt Carol and Baby Fred might seek shelter in the cellar under the food factory office complex. We compromised then. I was going to the flak bunkers, while she and the rest of the family would go to the factory shelter. Just then we heard the explosions of artillery shells not far off.

"There you are, Mom. It's getting closer by the hour," I said.

"Okay, I'll go to the shelter in the morning if things get bad," she said.

With this, I went upstairs to bed. There was no sleep to be had. I heard artillery fire off and on. Sometimes the explosions were far away, but the nearest round dropped into the field where the Fieseler Stork plane had met his end, and that was close.

At 7:00 AM, after having some weak coffee and a slice of black bread with homemade jam, I was on my way to the quads. Mom had meanwhile wisely packed some papers and other valuable items in a canvas bag and was ready to head for the factory shelter with Baby Fred and Aunt Carol. Several other local people had the same idea, and were also heading for the shelter. Mr. Vink, the air raid warden, was busy by the factory entrance, directing people to the shelter. Military traffic was still coming along the road from the west. Ambulances with wounded soldiers, trucks and trailers, an odd-looking tank destroyer with a twin 20mm atop, and horses pulling a light infantry support gun were among the traffic.

At the corner, where the road branches off to the quads and the sandpit, some German paratroopers wanting a lift were arguing with an army truck driver. During the night, somewhere to the west, their platoon had captured four Americans, probably a patrol that had stuck their noses out too far ahead. They all stood around, the Germans holding MP-40s at the ready. The GIs looked uneasy. A German corporal guarded the four prisoners while his mates were trying to convince the truck driver that they needed a lift to take the POWs for interrogation at headquarters, wherever it was.

As I walked up, my sparse English I had learned in Wiltz came back to me, and I tried saying something to the GIs.

They grinned at me and one said, "Hitler kaput, alles kaput."

"Quiet here. No talking to the POWs!" the German corporal shouted and waved me on with his machine pistol.

Knowing my superiority—that is, being a low-grade flak helper with Giant's blessing—I ignored the corporal and tried to speak to the GIs again. The corporal got the idea that I knew what I was saying and that the prisoners did too.

I did a smart about turn and walked on, "Alles kaput, Sieg Heil kaput," I heard the GIs saying behind me.

"Ruhe hier! Quiet here, stop talking!" the corporal was shouting and raving.

Up by the quads, there was a bit of traffic congestion when I arrived. During the previous night, a Maultier Ford halftrack had turned up with a 37mm AA gun on board. The Maultier was a converted two-ton truck that had tracks attached to the rear instead of wheels. The back loading platform was used for anything from carrying ammunition to soldiers to a mounted antiaircraft gun. A Panzerwerfer with ten 150mm tubes mounted atop had also arrived. The Panzerwerfer was a sort of mobile rocket launcher that was installed on a Puma armored reconnaissance eight-wheel vehicle. This thing turned up with another halftrack, a light Tatra infantry carrier with nine men aboard.

Giant was talking to the new arrivals, but our quads were fully manned and ready to fire if anything alien tried to sneak up on us. The lieutenant first went over to the Tatra driver, who explained to him that he had orders to reinforce the local AA defenses on the southwestern side of town.

"Well, you won't be much good with that Panzerwerfer as an antiaircraft weapon," Giant remarked.

"No, Sir," he said, "but our orders are also to assist the infantry that are pulling out of Hardt. If the Amis try to outflank them, our Werfer plus your AA guns can do a lot of damage to their advancing infantry."

"What if the Amis decide to send a bunch of tanks in first, before showing us their infantry? Your Panzerwerfer is useless then," Giant said.

"Well, yes, Sir," he said, "but we can try to help our men. Those 150mm rockets of ours are feared by the Allies."

"How much ammo do you have for that contraption?" Giant asked.

"Contraption? Sir," the Tatra driver corrected him. "I beg your pardon, this is a highly effective weapon."

"Okay, okay. Panzerwerfer, or whatever then. How much ammo?" Giant asked.

"We have ten rounds in the tubes now," he said. "There's not much room in the Puma, so we had to stash another 20 rockets in the Tatra. In effect, this means we have three salvos, but our rockets cannot be fired in a salvo of ten at one time. They have to be electrically ignited one at the time. The firing speed is about two seconds per tube."

"Hmm, impressive." Giant said.

"It is, Sir," he agreed. "A few well placed rounds can send infantry packing and looking for a way around us, out of our range. Trouble is, Sir, the rockets stray an awful lot, sometimes 400 yards from the aim point."

"What is the effective range?" Giant asked.

"Effective, Sir, about 6,000 yards, give or take a few, depending on elevation, wind velocity and terrain," he said. "We can go beyond that for annoyance, but accuracy is practically nil, unless we are just lucky."

"Good luck is all we need, Herr Feldwebel," Giant said. "Put your Werfer battery over there in the bushes and camouflage the position. We had some American 105s probing during the night. Our range finder told me that their artillery fire came from the vicinity of that church spire you can see in the distance, to the left of the trees."

The Werfer NCO looked through his binoculars and said, "It's too far off for accurate counter fire, but I can give them a scare if you like, Sir."

"Okay, but wait for them to open fire first," Giant said. "That will give you a rough idea of their position. You have your own observer, I see. Tell him to keep a sharp lookout, and if you get the coordinates, send a few rounds over."

"Will do, Sir," the NCO said.

Giant then turned his attention to the guy in charge of the Ford Maultier with the 37mm cannon. He was a sergeant in his mid-twenties, proudly displaying a flak medal and an Iron Cross ribbon in his buttonhole. He and his three companions gathered around the lieutenant.

"Coming to reinforce us, too?" the lieutenant asked.

"Sergeant Lennartz, Sir, 67th AA Battalion. Yes, Sir, we're supposed to report here to the local AA commander, but nobody can tell us who is in charge."

The sergeant spoke with an unmistakable French accent. "You French?" asked the lieutenant.

"No, Sir. I'm from Diedenhofen, Alsace-Lorraine. Our people speak French and German," he replied.

"Okay, Sergeant," Giant said, "I'm in charge here. The higher-ups have gone, departed, run away, or whatever—you understand?"

"Yes, Sir. Deserted, I presume," said the sergeant.

"You can call it that, Sergeant," said Giant. "What is your ammunition situation for this 37mm?"

"Nonexistent, Sir," he replied.

"You have no ammo for this thing?" Giant yelled.

"No, Sir," he replied. "Our ammo trailer took a bazooka round yesterday outside the town of Hehler and blew up. Luckily, our halftrack was parked far enough away. We had two killed and four wounded. We expected to replenish our ammo stock here."

"Look Sergeant," Giant explained, "we fire 20mms, not 37s, and those big brothers of ours out there can't help you either. They fire 88 mms."

"What now, then?" the sergeant asked, a bit disappointed.

"Sergeant, the nearest 37mm batteries with ammo are that away, five miles to the north of us. You'd better get a move on before the fighter-bombers have you," Giant warned.

"We can't, Sir," he explained. "We have no gas left. You haven't got a few gallons to spare by any chance, have you?"

"No, we have not, and anyway the Puma and Tatra run on diesel," Giant said. He was getting really upset about the whole affair.

The Maultier Halftrack, with the 37mm gun, pointing at a 45-degree angle skywards, stuck out like a sore thumb on top of the hill, inviting any enemy plane that happened to be within a four-mile range to come in for a closer look. It was a dead certainty that the halftrack was going to receive a working over.

"Who gave you orders to come up here, Sergeant?" Giant asked.

"Division Headquarters, Sir. They gave us orders to proceed to the 64th's position southwest of town. What they did not give us, Sir," the sergeant was really working himself up now, "was gasoline and 37mm rounds. I've had it up to here," the sergeant cut across his mouth with his right hand. "Sir, give me enough ammo and a defensive position, and I can show you what my men are made of. I did not make sergeant for nothing and I got my medals for combat, not for pencil pushing in some obscure office."

From the southwest came the sound of artillery firing. Four geysers of dirt and smoke rose up about a mile in front of our position.

"Did you get that?" Giant shouted at the Werfer observer, who was intently scanning the horizon with his binoculars.

"Yes, Sir," shouted the observer, "about 7,000 yards. A battery of 105s somewhere behind the Josef Heim Hospital. There's a big cluster of trees there and I think that's where they are."

The lieutenant turned to the Werfer Feldwebel, "Can you get a few rounds over without hitting the loony bin? Say a bit to the left of it?" He was watching the area through his glasses.

"We can, Sir," he replied. "But we have ten rounds in the tubes. The rockets are fired by a two-second interval automatically. All ten will go off. You want me to fire all of them?"

"What happens if you take five rounds out of the tubes? Can you still fire the others left in there?"

"We sure can," he said, "but it takes a while to remove the rockets and rewire five so they go out in the right sequence."

"Well, do that," Giant said, "and tell me when you're ready."

It took a few minutes to get the Werfer ready. Then the Feldwebel called the lieutenant and reported. "We're ready, Sir, on your command."

I had already dived into the ammo bunker and was watching the proceedings from a safe distance. The lieutenant shouted "fire," and with an almighty screech the 150mm rockets left the tubes at two-second intervals, trailing white smoke behind them. Seconds later, we heard the explosions a few thousand yards off. No visible effect of the explosions could be observed from our position, but the 105s ceased firing, probably alerting the fighter-bombers to the new menace from the German army.

If they had a good observer who could pinpoint the position of the Werfer, we knew we would be done for, so the whole crew of the quads and the twin machine guns were on high alert and scanning the sky. Those who were not detailed to man the quads were busy loading and stacking magazines by the ready room door. Even the two sailors had by now gotten the hang of things.

During the excitement, no one noticed the captain arrive.

"Well, Sir," the lieutenant said, "we thought you had left with the rest of the gang from HQ, but it's nice to see you are still here. It's getting a bit hot up here, Sir. We had some 105s searching for us. Nothing much, but we expect an air attack any minute. We have a Werfer up here to support our infantry around Hardt, plus a clapped-out Maultier halftrack with a 37mm gun—minus gas and ammo. The thing is parked

here on top of our hill and stands out like a memorial column for anyone to see for miles. Can you get some gas up here and a trailer with
some 37mm ammunition? We'll set it to some good use if you can."

He said, "I'll tell you something now, Lieutenant Roland. The ordinance quartermaster was given orders by the high command to blow up
his stores. That includes all ammunition. The brass has left for the eastern side of the Rhine. Whether they will get across or not, I don't know.
As far as I know, all bridges have been wrecked and are useless. What's
left of our glorious Wehrmacht on this side of the Rhine is trapped. My
advice to you now, and this time I speak to you as a friend, not as your
superior officer, is this; see that our poor devils around Hardt pull out
under your fire support—that is, if they attempt to do so, rather than
surrender. After that, well, it's up to you. I'm not your guardian, but
please don't try any heroics. That goes for the men as well.

"My only order is, if you feel the end is near, make the quads useless by whatever means. Sooner or later, the Amis will get here, and I
want the quads to be in absolutely useless condition when the do. I hate
the thought of being fired on by Americans manning my own guns. Got
that?"

"Yes, Sir. Are you pulling out, too, Sir?" The lieutenant asked.

The captain's answer was a chuckle. Then he said, "No, Lieutenant,
I'm going up to the 88s and see if there is any use for me there. My latest frontline information tells me that the Americans are trying to sneak
around the town to the west with a battalion of tanks. The 88s have a
good field of fire in that direction, and I can hold them up for a while,
at least until Hardt has been vacated. After that, well, I quit."

"What about that damn 37mm and the halftrack?" The lieutenant
asked.

"Blow it up, or whatever you want," he said. "Without ammo and
gas, the thing is useless."

"Okay, Captain," the lieutenant said, "I will do as you order. Hope
we meet again in the future."

I asked the lieutenant, "What now, Sir?"

"Now? I'll tell you what we do," he said. "We push that contraption of a 37mm and halftrack over the edge into the sandpit below.
Nobody wants to know, nobody cares anymore, and apart from our
captain, all the other officers have left like rats from a sinking ship. Did
I say rats?"

"No, Sir, you didn't," I said with a smirk.

"Okay, then, let's get organized while there is still time."

We went outside. Except for some small arms fire in the far distance and the occasional coughing of a 75mm tank cannon, the countryside seemed remarkably quiet, considering there was a war being fought not far off. Even aircraft were absent, despite the good flying weather. Giant called the NCO from the Werfer, whose crew was busy reloading the 150mm tubes.

"Herr Feldwebel," the lieutenant asked, "can your Puma push this two-ton Maultier over the edge into the sand pit?"

"Yes, easily, Sir," he replied, "but we're reloading at this moment and we have camouflaged our position. The Tatra can be camouflaged too. He's all of four tons of heavy metal, Sir. Why do you want it pushed to oblivion, Sir?"

"It's got no ammo," The lieutenant replied. "It won't move on an empty gas tank, and it attracts enemy planes, so please send the damn thing into the pit."

"It'll be a pleasure, Sir," came the reply.

"Okay, then, get moving," he said, "and when you've done with that, camouflage that Tatra as well. There are some nets somewhere around here, and make sure your Werfer is ready. By the sound of it, our guys around Hardt are having a hard time. We're going to make it a bit easier for them."

The sergeant in charge of the 37mm was only too pleased to get rid of the useless weapon. Meanwhile, the driver of the Tatra had started the engine and slowly crawled forward, his tracks clattering on the frozen ground. He directed his front armored plate against the side of the two-ton Ford, then slowly pushed the whole thing over the edge. The halftrack did two somersaults, then came to rest on its side, its 37mm barrel bent and twisted.

"Shall we throw a few hand grenades on it for good measure?" the driver asked.

"No need for that," The lieutenant said. "It won't burn or explode. If there is justice in this world, we'll come back here after the war and sell it to make razor blades and cooking pots," the sergeant answered.

Then the sergeant turned to the lieutenant, "Now that we're rid of our gun and Maultier, what are your orders? I mean, what are we supposed to do now? Are we under your command?"

"No, Sergeant," he replied. "I neither have the rank nor the authority to place you under any command. We are a Luftwaffe flak outfit, not a Heeres Flak Artillery or Infantry unit. We have too many men up here as it is, without your men clogging up the traffic. If you and your men want to be useful or play heroes, there is an 88mm battery just behind those houses in a field. Our captain will be up there shortly, but I can tell you now what his orders will be. He will probably tell you to go home, surrender, or whatever, but don't go east. The bridges over the Rhine are down. The Amis are almost halfway into our rear."

"What are you going to do then, Sir?" he asked.

"I will make certain that we support our infantry when they pull out of Hardt," said the lieutenant. "After that, I suppose it's goodbye Deutsches Reich."

"You going to pull out then, Sir?" he asked.

"No, Sergeant," he replied. "There is nowhere to pull out to, and besides we are in a fixed position with no means at our disposal to break camp and move. I'm not a person to command a last ditch defense. My wife and kids died for the Reich and Führer and they didn't get a hero's funeral either."

"I'm sorry to hear that, Sir."

"In that bunker there, Sergeant," the lieutenant said, "is a telephone. You can try to get through to Berlin. I doubt if you can, but if you do get through, do you know what they will tell you? Your orders are to stay put and die for the Führer. It's up to you."

"I see, Sir," he replied. "Well, I'm from Alsace-Lorraine, and I won't be able to get home ever again. The French are going to hunt me as a traitor. I'm not a married man. I've no family, Sir, nothing to lose."

"Well, Sergeant," the lieutenant replied, "go over to the 88s. The captain will surely give you some good advice. He's a fine man, that captain of ours. Now if you will excuse me, Sergeant, I'm busy—and good luck to you."

They shook hands, and the sergeant and his three men walked down the hill toward the 88 position.

"Right, then," the lieutenant said, and turned to the gunnery sergeant. "Gunny, get the men together. I have something more to say to all of them. Not in the bunker, outside here. It will only take a few minutes."

"Okay, Sir," he replied. Gunny went over to the quads and twins to call the men. They gathered around the lieutenant.

CHAPTER 19

The End of the War for Us

When all the men were assembled, the lieutenant spoke up: "What I told you yesterday regarding our intentions still stands. We will make sure that our men," and he pointed to the west, where the staccato of machine guns could clearly be heard, "get our full support to pull out safely. When they pull out, the Amis will no doubt follow them, with or without armor.

"The 88s will deal with tanks or tank destroyers. Our job will be to deal with their infantry, and help our troops to cross a four-mile wide-open stretch of ground. By the sound of it, part of the American armor is already closing in on the town from the north, and we will soon be outflanked. We will do our best to help our troops, but when I give the command to cease fire, you're all dismissed and can make your own way to the rear, or walk forward with your hands up. I will stay behind and blow the guns up. The sergeant can throw the twins into the sand pit. What you do is your business, but I don't want any miniature Stalingrad, okay? If you and your crew are determined to fight to the bitter end, then you can take the Tatra and Werfer out of here. Clear enough?"

"No sweat, Lieutenant," the sergeant replied. "I'll be glad when it's all over. I hear the Amis have corned beef and liver cheese on real white bread. I'd like to try some of that."

"You'll sure get plenty of time to try them as a POW," the lieutenant said. "Okay then, all back to your positions. The cook will bring the food to you men. Keep your eyes glued to the sky."

The men moved back to their posts. Giant went into the mess bunker and rummaged around in a trunk. I followed him, and soon the lieutenant found what he was looking for. It was a white bed sheet.

271

"We better make sure we have that ready," he said. "I don't want anybody to get hurt once we have ceased firing. You boy, can hide in here. A 105mm will not penetrate this concrete roof. You'll be safe inside."

"No thank you, Sir. Not yet anyway," I answered.

"Alright, he said, "but, if you have just the tiniest scratch on you after we cease fire, your mother will kill me."

"I will be careful, Sir, honest. I really will," I said.

"Okay, boy," Giant said. "I didn't mean to be nasty, but I kind of feel responsible for you up here. Your Mom is in a cellar at the factory. God knows where your Brother Len is, and your Dad might be a POW."

"Mom went to the factory shelter with Aunt Carol and the baby," I told him.

It was mid-morning now, cloudy but with good visibility. Surprisingly, there were no enemy aircraft to be seen. We did not know it then, but they were busy chopping the Reichswald to firewood, where the remnants of a whole German army had made a last stand in several thousand acres of pine trees. We could clearly hear track and engine noises to the northwest. Soon, we heard the crack of the 88s, then an explosion in the distance. A black oil smoke cloud drifted toward us. Our view was limited in that direction by houses and trees, but from the sound of it, the 88s had scored a tank or some other armor. Further west, another battery of 88s near Mackenstein Village joined the firing. Our only open field of flat trajectory was to the south and southwest, so all eyes and ears were trained in that direction. Our town was to our rear. To get at us from that direction, the Amis had to capture the town first.

Toward Hardt, we could see part of the road that led northwest to the town of Dulken, four miles away. We could only see about half a mile of the tree-lined road; the rest was obscured by farms and low-growing bushes. Just beyond the road was the St. Josef Heim Hospital. We could clearly see the red cross on the roof and the small chapel spire between the trees, and hear heavy infantry fire from that direction. Our men strained their eyes but, so far, had seen no movement. Another salvo of 105s came whistling toward our position. Three rounds exploded about 500 yards in front of us. The fourth hit the spire of St. Peter's Catholic church, and bricks tumbled to the ground. A window from the belfry hit the roof and lodged itself against the tower, a small spire containing a bell we used to call the "klepper" because of its funny clapping sound. The bell made a few ding dongs then all was quiet.

"Okay, let them have it, Feldwebel, whenever you're ready," The lieutenant told the Werfer commander.

With its characteristic earsplitting screech, ten 150mm rockets left the tubes at one-second intervals, arching high through the sky toward the distant target.

"Take another shot, Feldwebel," the lieutenant ordered. "Our infantry should know that they're not on their own."

It took several minutes to reload the tubes. Halfway through it, someone shouted, "Enemy aircraft, north 40 degrees!" Four P-47 Thunderbolts were screaming toward us.

"Now look what you've done," I said to Giant. "They are surely coming for that Werfer," and I dashed into the bunker and slammed the door shut behind me.

If they had bombs, and most of the time they did, I wanted to be out of harm's way. We knew that most of the P-47s carried 50- to 100-pound bombs, small fry really, with no penetration power, but they had a nasty habit of exploding into thousands of fragments. A foot of concrete overhead was the safest bet. The Thunderbolts veered to the left of us. They were probably unsure of where to search for the Werfer, but they sure as hell were out looking for it. The Puma was well camouflaged, protected from view by small pine trees and evergreen bushes, as well as the netting, which made it hard for a pilot to see unless he knew exactly where to look. Out of effective range, the Thunderbolts circled a few times, then made a dive toward the town of Hardt where they dropped their bombs onto an outlying farmstead. Then they were gone.

"We're reloaded, Sir. Shall we send another batch over?" inquired the Werfer commander.

"Go ahead, Feldwebel," said Giant. "The rest of you guys keep a sharp eye on the sky."

Another ten rockets left the tubes, one after another. But before the last one left the Werfer, Gunny shouted, "Enemy aircraft at two, range three miles!"

"Those bastards were just waiting for that Werfer to fire again," a crewmember of the Puma shouted. "They now see the smoke trails and have us in their sights."

The Werfer crew dived into a bunker. They knew full well that their rockets were absolutely useless against aircraft as a defensive weapon. From what we had seen a few minutes earlier, the Thunderbolts had already shed their load of bombs, but they still had their cannons. Luckily for us, their cannon aim was poor, and well off target. The four planes came on in perfect formation. Our quads and twins hammered away, sending streams of tracers up. The pilots were either green or reckless. They came in like beads on a string, one behind the other. A formation does not attack a flak position that can throw up thousands of tracers per minute. Moreover, they had no wingman for cover and no divers ional attack from ninety degrees out by another pilot. Experienced pilots always kept a wingman out of the melee as a safeguard.

What those P-47 pilots lacked in experience, they surely made up for in guts. Their cannons sent spurts of dirt and concrete spewing up not ten feet away, some hitting the steel doors. Even the abandoned Maultier down in the sand pit got a dose of bullets. The last P-47 in line flew right into the tracer curtain. Although armored around the pilot's seat, the unprotected engine took a full magazine of 20mms. The pilot realized he was in trouble and pulled the stricken plane up to about 1,000 feet then banked off to the right. Just to the southern side of the Hardt-Hehler Highway, then he bailed out, knowing he had made it to his own lines. The Thunderbolt came down in flames, hitting only a turnip bin in a field two miles away. It exploded in a ball of flame, sending frozen turnips flying all over the field.

"Lucky devil. He made it," K-1 called out, and the men slapped each other's backs.

The other P-47s had left by this time, so the Werfer crew emerged from their hiding place.

"Want to continue firing, Sir?" someone from the crew asked. "We have enough left for one more shot."

"Yeah, why not?" Giant said. "It'll be dark soon and those Thunderbolts won't come back today. Tomorrow is another day."

Another ten rounds were fired toward Hardt. It was all the Werfer crew had left besides their two machine guns. The answer soon came from the other side, four salvos of 105s. The nearest shell exploded about 200 yards away. Some hit roofs on the houses by the factory, sending broken roof tiles flying in all directions.

"Let's hope the people all took shelter in that factory cellar," the lieutenant said. He was naturally concerned since his girlfriend, Mrs. Helgers, lived right opposite the factory entrance next to the parking lot.

We could now hear small arms and machine gun fire again from the direction of Hardt. Then we saw some dark figures streaming out of town toward our position. Was our infantry pulling out, or were they Americans? When we saw one figure turn around and fire back, we then knew they were Germans leaving Hardt to the enemy. More men came running out of the last houses of Hardt. The fire intensified. What appeared to be American infantry were hard on their heels.

"Okay, we cover them now," the lieutenant shouted. "Fire!"

Four barrels went off in unison, tracers in a flat trajectory arriving at their targets in seconds. Several men dropped to the ground, some retreated back to the shelter of the houses. Two Sherman tanks suddenly appeared from out of nowhere. We had nothing to counter the armor and they probably knew it. In short succession, three 75mm rounds hit our parapets, sending dirt and shrapnel flying around.

"What the hell are our 88s doing?" Giant screamed. "They should take on those tanks!"

Our quads were still firing, if only to keep the enemy infantry at bay. Luckily, so far, nobody was hurt. Two more 75mms came whistling in about two feet above our heads, sailing over the parapet and exploding somewhere in town. At last we heard the sharp crack of our 88s, and seconds later the leading Sherman took a hit that sent the turret flying off.

"Jesus, what a lucky shot!" Gunny screamed over the din of the battle.

The Mackenstein 88 joined in the fray, but was firing in another direction. Another barrage of American 105s came raining down, but well out of our immediate area. We still had no casualties. Giant dashed over to the Puma. "Any more rockets left, Feldwebel?"

"Just two," he said. "That's it, Sir."

"Okay, send them over with our compliments," Giant said, "but make sure you don't hit the loony bin."

The last two rounds left the tubes, screeching towards Hardt. The lieutenant watched their trails through his glasses.

"What in hell is that? Cease fire, cease fire!" he shouted.

The quads and machine guns stopped their racket. All the men looked with puzzled expressions at Giant who was still observing an unbelievable sight up front. Out there, in the frozen fields by the hospital, strange-looking figures were aimlessly walking around or sitting on the ground. All were clad in snow-white gowns. The Americans had apparently liberated the loony bin, and the inmates, not realizing what was going on, were now wandering between the two opposing lines. All firing stopped. Both sides knew the rules of the Geneva Convention. Those were sick people out there. We could not fire at them unless they fired first, but the sick inmates not only had no weapons, they could hardly think for themselves. Barefooted and dressed only in flimsy hospital gowns, they were far from being dangerous combatants.

"The war is over for us," Giant said. "Those of you who want to surrender, get some white sheets and wave them and walk towards the enemy's lines. I'll take care of the quads."

The gunnery sergeant walked up to Giant, "I threw the twins into the sand pit, Sir."

"Good," Giant said. "What are your plans, Gunny?"

"If I get the chance, I'll make my way to Krefeld. I have a nice girl there and I can hide out, or the Amis can flush me out. I can't get across the Rhine now with all the bridges down. You see, Lieutenant, I can't swim."

"You should have thought of taking swimming lessons years ago, Gunny," Giant said. "It's too late now."

"Years ago we were winning this war, remember?" Gunny said. "There was no need for swimming lessons. I suppose you're going to stay around here, Amis or no Amis, and with your luck, you will probably get away and not be taken POW."

"I'll try my best, Gunny," Giant said.

"I will surely look you up when times get back to normal, Lieutenant. I know Mrs. Helgers. She's a good woman and I wish you the best of luck."

"Hope you call soon," Giant said, "and now get out of my way before I get too sentimental."

Darkness fell over our silent gun position. It was an eerie silence. Some crewmembers found bed sheets and tore them to bits to make white surrender banners. They shook hands with each of us and marched off into the unknown towards Hardt. Others wanted to hang around until daybreak, for fear of being shot by friend or foe. Giant draped a large white bed sheet over the parapet and secured it with a rock on each corner. Then he took four white phosphorous canisters from a box in the ready room and placed two under each quad near the loading chamber. He pulled the red cord hanging from the cylinder. They burst into a greenish white fire that ran along the metal parts of the gun, partly melting the steel and rendering the gun absolutely useless.

"Help yourselves to all the food that's left," he said to the men who wanted to stay behind to be taken POW.

"What about the ammo that's left in the bunker?" I asked Giant.

"Let the Amis take care of that now," he said. "No guns, no shooting, got me?" We shook hands with the rest of the men. Then the lieutenant turned around to me, "Well, boy, it's time to go home. We've done enough shooting. I never want to see another gun in all my life."

His eyes, for the last time, went over his beloved quads, the bunkers, the men. Then, without another word, he walked off toward the houses. I followed like an obedient dog.

"What are you going to do now?" he asked me. "Going home?"

"I reckon I have to," I said. "Mom is in the shelter at the factory with Aunt Carol and Baby Fred."

"I hope Mrs. Helgers has gone to the shelter too," he said. "I think I'll go up to her house first and change into some civilian clothes and burn this uniform. You might do the same. Get rid of all your Hitler Youth garb."

"You mean you already have some civilian clothes, Sir?" I asked.

"Well, don't tell anyone," he said, "but your Mom gave me your Dad's tram driver uniform. When the Amis start asking questions, I'll pretend to be a streetcar driver, a noncombatant, so to speak."

"But my Dad is a lot shorter than you. The uniform won't fit you."

"I'll make it fit, don't worry," he said. "Well, at least the coat. The pants are a bit short, but I'll stick them inside the boots. I have your Dad's Arbeitsbuch, too. There's no photo, so I might just get away with it."

"Mr. Vink is your size, Sir. He might lend you a pair of pants," I said.

"I wouldn't count on that," He said. "Vink is a Nazi Luftschutz member. Just don't tell anyone anything. Just pretend to be deaf, okay?"

"Yes, Lieutenant," I said.

"And drop the 'lieutenant.' From now on," he said, "I'm Mr. Roland or whatever, but no military rank."

We parted by the factory entrance. He made his way across the road to Mrs. Helgers' house, and I walked slowly to our home on the other side of the parking lot. Shards of roof tiles, masonry and a downed telephone wire were reminders that a 105mm shell had hit a house earlier in the day. It was pitch dark now, so I could not make out what had been hit. It was quiet, as if the end of the world had come. I could not even hear a distant gun or plane.

I entered the house by the back door, which we never locked. People trusted each other, and a burglary was very rare. Most people had nothing to steal anyway, and criminals in the Third Reich, if caught, were sent for re-education to a concentration camp. It was a harsh law by any standard, but people lived more safely in those days. Of course by saying we were "safe," I am forgetting the constant air raids and bombing. That was war and it was accepted. If a party headquarters took a direct hit from an HE, the attitude was, well, they have enough—they can afford to loose something. But if a criminal broke into someone's house, it was altogether different. If he got caught, and not many got away, it was two years at Neuengamme or even Buchenwald, and there was not much chance of getting out of those places alive.

I made my way through the dark hall. I fell over something, a cooking pot. The smell of cordite was evident. Mom always kept a candle or two on the windowsill for emergencies, and I found one and lit it. I was confronted by a good deal of rubble and plaster, but I could see no holes in the wall. Even the panes were still intact in the hall windows. I went upstairs, where things were a different matter. Aunt Carol's rooms were a shambles. I soon discovered what had happened. A 105mm artillery shell had come through the roof into my bedroom and gone through the wall into Aunt Carol's bedroom, entering her wardrobe from the back, where it had exploded. Her dressing table and clothes were all in shreds. Windows were blown out and all the legs were missing from her bed. The mattress hung partly out of the window.

I decided to leave the attic alone for the night. There was surely a hole in the roof somewhere. I went back downstairs. Next, I took my Hitler Youth uniform off and changed into normal clothes. I made a small bundle of the uniform, pants, and belt, and took the cover off the cesspit. An infernal stink rose from the hole, but I had to get rid of my Nazi stuff somehow, and I reckoned that the Amis would not empty our septic tank to see if Hitler was hiding in there. I threw everything into the mire and pushed it well under with a pitchfork for good measure. I deposited my Hitler Youth knife in there as well. Next came my air rifle with the swastika stamp on the side. I thought about throwing the radio in there as well since it had two telefunken tubes in it with eagles and swastikas stuck on the glass, but decided against it. The Amis would surely not open the back of an innocent-looking radio. Then I realized we had several hospital towels with a swastika and eagle, Nazi newspapers, and an alarm clock with a swastika. Hell, I thought, what else? I might as well set fire to the whole house to rid the place of Third Reich items. No, let the Amis do it if they find the things, I thought.

It was freezing cold that night and I was thinking of lighting a fire, but not knowing in what shape our chimney was after the 105mm hit, I had second thoughts. I would have gone to the shelter in the factory, but it was dark and the place was probably locked or guarded by Mr. Vink, who might take me for an Ami and put a bullet in my brain.

"I wish someone would drop a bomb," I said out loud. But my wish was not granted. Inside our parlor, I sat on a sofa, thinking. What was going to happen now? What would peace be like? I had no idea what peace was. Ever since I could remember we had been at war. Six years now had passed since the first shots were fired. I started school in wartime, lustily shouting my "Heil Hitler" each morning at assembly, just like the rest of the kids and teachers. I wondered if school would ever start again, and if so, what would be shouted at the morning assembly. Surely not "Heil Hitler" or "Sieg Heil." Perhaps there would be no more school now. To me, all teachers seemed like Nazi Party members. They might all end up in prison camps, I mused, or else the Amis will give us American teachers.

Then I thought of the better side of life—peace, that is. No more bombs, no more fighter bombers to dodge, no more falling into ditches full of crap. At this point, I must have fallen asleep. I awoke with a jolt when I suddenly heard the staccato of a grease gun, or was it a machine gun? I could hear it was very near, and peeped through the window. It was just getting daylight, and I could dimly discern a line of American soldiers in the shadow of the overhang. A GI had his grease gun at the ready. He fired another burst around the corner without exposing himself. I kept on watching, but they could not see me. After a while, the line of infantry resumed their advance toward downtown, cautiously hugging the walls of the houses along the road. I went back to the sofa to wait for better light. I didn't fancy the idea of getting in the way of a trigger happy GI. As the saying goes, in the dark, all cats are gray and the same size.

I fell asleep again, dreaming of Jabos and Panzerwerfers, of Kübelwagens, and a West Wall bunker that I was defending with my rifle against a tank. The tank roared at me full speed and then stopped.

I woke up. It was bright sunshine outside and the driver of a huge Sherman tank was just cutting his engine off outside on our pavement. It was as good a parking area as any. At least he kept the road open to the moving military traffic.

Someone knocked on our front door. I went to open it, expecting to be shot or at least taken prisoner. But there stood a six-foot tall GI with a tanker helmet on his head and a mess cup in his hand saying, "wasser, wasser (water) für coffee, understand?"

I remembered the few English words I had learned in Wiltz and repeated to him, "water, water for coffee?"

"Yeah, yeah," he replied.

I pointed to the tap in the hallway. The water was still running, but there was no electricity. He filled his mess tin with water and walked out. I followed him to see how things were shaping up and to see if it was safe to look for Mom. An American lieutenant walked up to me. No other civilian was in sight. He addressed me in broken German: "Nix people here. Where are all people?"

"In the cellar," I said in German, and I pointed over to the factory.

"Okay, you're coming with me. We see people in cellar," he said, and turned around and shouted something to another GI, who turned out to be fluent in German. He picked up his grease gun and the three of us made our way to the cellar steps. The lieutenant hammered on the locked steel door with his hand gun, and the other GI shouted in German to open the damn door or else. What he meant by "or else," I could imagine, as he was holding his submachine gun at the ready. The door was unlocked from the inside and opened, and there stood Mr. Vink, the warden. In the diffuse light of the staircase he thought the GI was a German soldier, and he saluted with a smart "Heil Hitler".

I held my breath. Any second now the grease gun would let loose on poor Mr. Vink. But the lieutenant stepped in and said, "Nix Heil Hitler. Hitler gone kaput!" (Hitler, at that time, was still very much alive and not kaput.)

Mr. Vink tried to explain his mistake, but the German-speaking GI cut him short. "Shut your mouth Nazi. Get out with your hands up."

Mr. Vink did as he was told. We then walked into the cellar. It was normally the room where the empty wine barrels were washed and dried. A kerosene lamp tried its best to light the huge room. About 300 people were sheltering in there, sitting on blankets and boxes, most with fear in their eyes. The soldier slowly swung his grease gun around, from left to right and back, finger at the trigger. The lieutenant motioned him to point the gun at the floor, his eyes looking at the assembled civilians.

"Any German soldiers in here?" the lieutenant asked.

The German-speaking GI translated. A hundred replies of "nein, nein" (no, no) went up. "We civilians, we nix soldaten," an elderly man explained.

Then I saw Mom standing with Aunt Carol next to Giant, looking ridiculous in Dad's tramway uniform. Baby Fred was in Auntie's lap. Giant had the foresight to take the eagle and swastika off the peak of the cap. I went over to Mom, but the lieutenant followed me and looked Giant up and down.

The GI with the grease gun raised his weapon. "You in uniform. You a soldier?"

"No, no, Sir. I'm the local streetcar driver, not a soldier at all. Just driving trams you know. Bimmelimmelimm!" Giant answered, imitating the bells on the tram.

"Yes, bimmelimmelimm. And why not soldat?" the lieutenant asked.

"I was wounded in '42, back in Kharkov, Ukraine, shot in the lower stomach. I can show you the hole it made," said Giant, and he started to drop his pants.

"No, no, that's okay," the lieutenant replied, then turned back to the others again. His speech, translated by the GI with the gun, was short and to the point. "We have occupied your town now. For all of you, the war is over, but bear in mind that hostilities will continue between Germany and the Allies until the present Nazi government is subdued or surrenders unconditionally. You will remain in this shelter until my superior officer decides what to do. Perhaps in another hour he will address you. I don't have to remind you that we expect your cooperation in all matters. You have been in this shelter for 24 hours now. Another hour or so will not make much difference. Good morning."

He and the guy toting the grease gun left the cellar, but left the door unlocked. Mr. Vink was the only occupant taken by the Americans.

"I didn't know you were shot in the gut at Kharkov, Lieutenant," I said.

"I'm not your lieutenant anymore," Giant said, "so be careful what you say. And that stomach wound, I only made that up just now. I knew he wouldn't let me drop my pants in front of all these people. Ha!"

"What if they check on you later?" I asked.

"We'll cross that bridge when we get to it," Giant replied. "I might have some decent civilian clothes by then."

"I know just the place to get you a first-class civilian suit." I told him.

"Tell me," said Giant.

"You know they took Mr. Vink just now and like I told you, he's your size." I said. "I'll tell the Americans that he and his wife were high Nazis. They're going to take Mrs. Vink in as well. Then, I'll sneak through their back door and get you Mr. Vink's finest striped suit, shirt and tie. They're going to lock both of them up and maybe throw the key away. He doesn't need a suit anymore. What about that?"

"Don't you dare," Giant said. "Mr. Vink is a good man. He was only an air raid warden and he has probably saved many lives."

"I was only joking, Mr. Roland," I said.

"Ahhh, now you're learning," Giant replied.

I then told Mom and Aunt Carol about the damage at home. Mom took it well. "As long as we're all alive, I don't care. I hope Len is alright. You haven't seen him?" she asked.

"No, Mom," I replied, "but knowing him, he'll be fine. He's probably gone into hiding until the storm blows over."

A muffled voice came from somewhere in the far dark corner of the cellar. "Let me out of here! Can anyone let me out?"

The voice came from a huge upturned wine barrel. Giant walked over and easily lifted the heavy thing and turned it on its side.

"Heck," Giant said. "What did you do, change clothes under the barrel?" A figure stood up clad in a white gown with red-stenciled lettering on the back, "St. Josef Heim." At first I thought it was one of the liberated patients, but then I recognized the face in the semi-darkness.

"Gunny!" Giant said. "What are you doing under there in that loony outfit?" We all slapped backs, shook hands and asked questions.

"Okay, okay, folks," Gunny said. "Take it easy. I'll tell you the short of it."

"Make it snappy, Gunny," Giant said. "The Amis will be back any minute to release us all, and we have to find a way to get you out of this loco outfit."

"Don't worry," Gunny said. "I figured that one out already. Well, I was going to Krefeld after we quit the guns, but got lost. In the darkness, I stumbled across a dead patient, frozen I guess. I thought Krefeld was a bit too dangerous to get to just yet, so I took this dead guy's gown off and came to the shelter. The dead guy didn't mind me taking his only clothes. Under that barrel, I changed from uniform into this white rag. Now, let's get rid of the uniform."

We stuffed the flak outfit into an old air vent shaft in the darkest corner of the cellar. "What's next, Gunny?" Giant said. "You are sitting here in this shirt from the loony bin. When the Amis come back, you'd better play loco, or you won't get away with it."

"For the time being, call me Karl, Heinrich, or Maximilian, but not Gunny," Gunny said. "And as for playing loco, well, when we are released, I'll just start singing, making funny faces or shout "Sieg Heil."

"Not Sieg Heil," Giant said. "They might shoot you. Just keep quiet and grin. We'll look after you."

Another hour went by. Finally an American major entered the cellar, flanked by four GIs with rifles slung casually over their shoulders. All were chewing gum. The major was excellent in German. "Okay, folks. You're all free to go home and tend to your peaceful business. You all can consider yourself lucky to have survived this war. There are a few regulations you have to obey until a military commander for the town has been appointed. No fraternization with any member of the occupying forces.

"Curfew is 4:00 PM until 8:00 AM the next morning. I don't want to see any civilian in public during curfew times unless he or she has a reason to be out, and it better be a damn good one. Troops will arrest anyone who cannot give a proper excuse for being in public during curfew times. All ex-Nazi Party members must report to the military command of this town, as soon as it is established, for interrogation. And the Nazis among you had better show up. We'll get you sooner or later—there are plenty of informers around. I'm afraid we cannot supply you with food. We're a combat unit, not a Red Cross outfit. You'll have to do the best you can for the time being. If you know of any food stores around here, come and see the commanding officer. He has full authorization to utilize any store or depot containing food supplies. Please cooperate, and all will be well."

From the back of the cellar crowd came a voice singing, "Wie einst Lili Marleen."

"Who's that?" the major asked.

Mom stepped forward, "I beg the Major's pardon, Sir. This person is a relative of mine who was interned in the Josef Heim Hospital as mentally ill, Sir. Your people, I mean, your troops, yesterday liberated the patients without knowing their true conditions. Well, some froze in the fields, some found their way back home. My relative here was at Stalingrad, but luckily got out before the Russians closed the trap. He's been crazy ever since but otherwise harmless, Sir. The Nazis were going to gas all mentally ill patients, Stalingrad or no Stalingrad. I have to thank you and your troops for rescuing them from certain death, Sir."

"We do what we can to help, Madam," the Major said. "We want to have a good relationship with the German people after the war is over. I'm afraid we'll be here in your country for a long while to come."

"Thank you so much, Major, and may God bless you and your men," Mom said.

We all filed out of the dark cellar into a gloriously sunny morning, the first day of March 1945. Several Ami soldiers lounged around the steps looking people over but not doing any close searches. A suspicious GI walked up to Giant when he emerged in his tram driver's uniform, but since he could see no swastika or eagle emblem, he stepped aside to let him pass.

"Wie einst Lili Marleen, wie einst Lili Marleen," Gunny, a.k.a. Karl Heinrich Maximilian or whatever, sang as he emerged in his loco gown, drinking from a wine bottle he had found somewhere in the cellar.

A GI approached him, speaking good German, "You can sing 'Deutschland Uber Alles,' but no alcohol's allowed," he said, and took the bottle from him.

Gunny wrapped his arms around the GIs neck and planted a big kiss on his cheek. "Beat it, man! I'm not Lili Marleen," the soldier exclaimed, pushing Gunny forward into Mom's arms.

Mom pointed to her head, then at Gunny, "He's loco, brain kaput, Stalingrad."

"Okay, okay!" the soldier said. "Now just move on."

The roads were absolutely choked with military traffic. Dozens of tanks, halftracks, self-propelled guns and tank destroyers all were clamoring along the road, tearing the tarmac to shreds. Interspersed among them, trucks of all shapes and sizes rolled along, loaded with troops and pulling artillery pieces, as jeeps darted in and out of the huge column. Then came big gas tankers, water tanks, Red Cross vehicles, and fearsome-looking 155mm Long Tom artillery pieces on flatbeds, towed by huge tractor trucks.

"Well, well," Giant remarked, "I'm not sorry that we gave up, after seeing all this gear. What do you think, Heinrich?"

"Wie einst Lili Marleen," came Gunny's answer.

"Oh, I almost forgot that we got a loony with us. Now folks, let's all go home," Giant said, and he crossed the street between two tanks and entered Mrs. Helgers' house. She had spotted us down in the street, and had been waving from her top window. We later learned that she had hidden in her own small shelter for two days with nothing but a can of water. She had come out when she heard strange voices outside.

We took Gunny with us. Along the road toward us came a smart-looking group of soldiers as if on parade, rifles slung over their backs, wearing black berets with an orange, white and blue ribbon attached which identified them as members of the Free Dutch Brigade. We watched in awe as they marched by singing, "overall where the meijses are," and saluted the American officers who were standing around to watch the spectacle.

"Wie einst Lili Marleeeeeeeeeen...," came Gunny's voice.

"Will you shut up? You're putting it on too thick, man!" Giant called from across the road. He was leaning out of the window, his right arm around Mrs. Helgers. "They're going to take you back to the loony bin to recuperate!"

The Dutch detachment had stopped. The officer dismissed the men and we went into the house. Mom looked at the mess in the hallway. Aunt Carol went upstairs to inspect her once-proud bedroom. The bed was okay, if you could still call it a bed, even without legs. We recovered the mattress from the window, but the rest of the room was rags and firewood.

I told Mom not to start a fire in the stove, as I had to see what damage had been done to the chimney in the attic. But first, we had to get Gunny out of his ridiculous outfit. We figured that eventually someone would be looking around to see what had happened to the patients who had not died of cold. Someone might let the word slip that we had taken in a white-robed loony.

Gunny said he wouldn't mind hiding out with us until the left bank of the Rhine was clear, then somehow he would make his way to Krefeld, 17 miles away. We found him one of Granddad Willem's old overalls. They fit him perfectly, and with Granddad's cap on, he almost looked like a stonemason. Then we both went to inspect the chimney. The roof had a hole in it the size of a trash bin lid where the 105 had entered, but this could be easily fixed as spare slats and clay tiles were lying all around the attic.

The shell had also hit the chimney, knocking out a few bricks and leaving a fair sized hole before it went through the ceiling and into Aunt Carol's bedroom. The hole had to be fixed before we could light a fire. Gunny found a bag half full of lumpy cement in the outside shed. "It will do for now," he said, "but we need sand as well."

I told him that I could get some from the sand pit below our quad pits. There was sand enough there to build a new town. I grabbed a bucket and the two-wheel cart I used for fetching wood chips, and trundled down the road walking close to the factory wall. I didn't fancy getting run over by a Sherman tank. I saw the quads above the sand pit, dead now. One barrel was bent in a 30-degree angle but I dared not go up to have a closer look. I reached the sand pit. Two GIs were climbing over the Maultier with its 37mm and the twins all in a tangled heap. The GIs were searching for souvenirs. One guy had a small hammer and chisel, and was trying to get the metal eagle that was attached to the door of the Maultier. He looked at me, came over and said, "nix Gitler souvenirs?"

"Who's Gitler?" I asked.

"Sieggeil Gitler, kaput?" he said.

I must have looked puzzled. The other GI now approached me, "He means Hitler souvenirs."

"I nix have Hitler souvenirs. I came for sand," I said. "Sand, you know?" and I pointed at my bucket and the sand pit. "House kaput, alles kaput."

The funny-speaking GI spoke again, "Da, da, alles kaput, Gitler kaput, njemzi kaput."

"What does he mean?" I asked the other in German.

He must have understood because he answered, "He is Russky. Come to America und now soldat, gute soldat he is."

I thought I had seen it all in this war—Ukrainians, French, British, Dutch. All I expected now was General Yamamoto or the Japanese Emperor to come up the road. I filled my bucket with sand and went back. The parking lot was full of tanks, SPGs, and other hardware. GI's sat around chewing gum, smoking or playing their dice game. From somewhere I heard a voice singing, "Wie einst Lili Marleen." No, it was not Gunny this time. Some soldier was busy winding the handle on a portable gramophone, playing discs he had confiscated from somewhere, and they were all German songs.

"Wir fahren gegen England," came the cheerful sound of a hundred

Hitler Youth voices from this music machine.

"Hey, boy!" the GI shouted over to me as I passed.

"Gitler kaput, Njemzy kaput, Sieggeil Gitler," I answered, shaking my head.

Gunny was ready to work when I got in. He mixed the sand and cement while Mom and Aunt Carol cleaned up the house. Within an hour, Gunny had the hole in the chimney fixed. It would not have passed an architectural survey, but it was the best he could do, he said, and we were grateful. I told him he could be proud of his handiwork. Before the war, he used to be a butcher. "There is a hell of a difference between the two trades," he said. I agreed.

"Now, then, what about the hole in the roof, Gunny?" I asked.

"Well, from what I can see," he said, "those tiles are the same as the ones up on the shed, and it's better to let it rain in the shed than in the house."

And so we took a few from the shed. A dozen tiles did the trick. We cleaned up and went into the kitchen. "All ready to light the fire, Mom," I reported.

"Great," she said. "I can make us a nice stew now and make some coffee. I still have a very small tin with some real coffee powder left. We'll mix some Kathreiner with it."

"Heck, Madam, I'd almost forgotten we've had nothing to eat in the last 24 hours," Gunny said.

"I'll fix something, don't worry," Mom said, "and please, Gunny, call me Agnes. 'Madam' sounds so snobbish." Then she added, "What's your real name? Everybody calls you Gunny."

"It's hard to pronounce, Agnes," Gunny said. "My ancestors came, so I was told, from Finland. That was part of Russia then. My name is Pepe Vakkulinnen, but please stick to Gunny. I got used to the name when I was made a gunnery sergeant back in 1938 during the Czech campaign. I'll be off in a day or so to Krefeld once the dust of war has settled."

"If you do stay around in the area, please come to visit us once times are normal again. We all know that the war is lost and will soon be over, and with God's help, there will be better times ahead in the not-so-distant future."

"I will. I will visit you again. I have to come back anyway. I owe your husband a bottle of schnapps," Gunny said.

"Whatever for, Gunny?" Mom asked.

"Well, it was like this." Gunny explained. "When Lou was here on furlough two years ago, I was AWOL for a day, with Roland's permission. That day some high-ranking brass came up to the quads for an inspection tour. Your Lou took up my position and answered 'present' when my name was called. Lou just happened to be up there with us at the right time. The brass didn't know the difference, so all went well. Only the captain wasn't very pleased about it, so he gave me a dressing down the next day when I got back. But it went without brig time. A gunnery sergeant was too valuable to put in chains for a day. I promised Lou a bottle the next time he came home."

"Well, let's hope Lou is okay," Mom said. "We have no idea where he is. The last we heard he was with the 70th Infantry Division in Holland."

"The 70th?" Gunny asked. "I heard a rumor that some of them were transferred to Denmark last October after they mauled the Tommies and Amis at Arnhem and Nijmegen. If he's in Denmark, then he's pretty safe."

"Is Denmark is at war with us?" Mom asked.

"Of course," Gunny said, "but there's no fighting there. It's just like Switzerland and Sweden."

"Now let's get on with making dinner," Mom said. "You, boy, go and see to the rabbits. I bet they're starving hungry. Gunny, you can light the fire."

I told Mom that in order to make a good stew we needed meat, and the only meat we had was covered in rabbit skin, very much alive and waiting for hay in their hutches.

"Then kill one," she said. "The big brown buck. He's getting old and slow in his productive work. Must be the war. They suffered, too."

Gunny got into the conversation, "Agnes, let me do that. I'm a butcher in civilian life. I can butcher anything from elephants to bedbugs. A rabbit is no problem."

"Good. I'll light the fire myself and Willy boy here can help you," she said.

In no time the buck was killed, skinned and strung up on a ladder. Gunny dressed the carcass as skillfully as if he was doing a delicate job on the firing mechanism of the quads. Mom chopped up potatoes, beans and greens and put into the big cast iron pot. Aunt Carol contributed two canned jars of carrots and a handful of herbs. Last but not least, the cut up rabbit was added. Soon the whole concoction was boiling away and we were licking our lips in anticipation of warm, delicious food. Outside on the tank parked on our pavement, the Ami soldiers were munching cold hash and beans. One was aimlessly poking his fork into a can of cold corned beef. What a life! The loser lives on ambrosia, the winner eats cold beans and hash. There is no justice, I remarked to Gunny.

By noon, the stew was finally done. The iron pot was full to the brim. "Go and get Roland and Mrs. Helgers," Mom said. "There's plenty for all of us."

Giant was still hanging out the window looking at the might of the American army. A white bed sheet was still displayed on the ledge. He came over with Mrs. Helgers. It was a happy lot sitting around the table, each one with a steaming bowl of rabbit stew. The only disappointment was that a rabbit has only four legs, so the not so fortunate, and that included myself, had to be satisfied with a piece of rib cage. I wondered if we would be able one day to breed rabbits with eight legs, or even twelve, a sort of centipede rabbit. Then all could get an even share.

Just before 4:00 PM, the front door opened, and in walked long lost Brother Len, he who knew everything. There he was in black pants, a white shirt and an old coat a farmer had given him, but minus his Hitler Youth cap and knife. The knife, so he said, he had buried. The cap had been taken by an Ami searching for Nazi mementos. In Vorst, near Krefeld, where he had been detailed to antitank ditching, the Ami tanks had simply gone round the ditches. Then some P-47s had come and they waved at them with their white shirts. They in turn fired a farewell salute that killed two Volkssturm members.

Half an hour later, an SPG drove up manned by grim-looking GIs. They simply pointed the 75mm at them and told them to get out of that ditch. The Volkssturm men with weapons were taken POW. The others like Len, who were armed with dirty spades, were given a lecture by an American officer, and sent home with the warning to make it pronto because 4:00 PM was curfew time.

"So, here I am," Len said. "I smell rabbit stew. Any left?"

"Stew? Yes, we had stew and a bit is left. I'm afraid the meat is gone, but you're welcome to the rib bones. I saved them for you," I told him.

"Shut your mouth," Len said "I asked Mom, not you."

Life was almost back to normal, I thought, except that the war is over for us. Had I spoken too soon? An almighty racket started outside. Machine guns and twin 40mm were hammering away. I dashed to the window and saw a rare sight. Two German FW-190 fighters came low over the town, spraying cannon bullets as if they had an unending supply.

"Now we are getting shot at by our own Luftwaffe," Gunny shouted over the din.

"Yes, we shouldn't have wrecked the quads," I said. "The Amis would probably give you a medal if you had stayed at your post and could hit those FW-190s."

Through the window, Gunny was observing the performance of the American gunner on the 40mm twin that was mounted on an M3 chassis. "I wish they would let me have a turn on them. I would show them a thing or two," Gunny said.

"Go and ask that gunner," I told him. "Tell him you are a retired German flak ace with twenty destroyed B-17s to your credit. He might let you have a go on that twin."

"Yeah, or he might just have me locked up. No thank you," Gunny said. "On second thought, I've had enough of flak. I will concentrate on butchering pigs and cows. It's easier and less dangerous."

The firing stopped after a while. The FW-190s turned tail and flew to the east. No damage was seen, but I reckon the Amis weren't very pleased that the German Luftwaffe was still able to make an appearance, albeit a minor one. Mom dished Len a plate of rabbit stew minus the meat, but he was too hungry to notice. Afterwards, we all had a good wash in the zinc tub. Len was eager to go outside for an inspection trip, but we told him to wait. The curfew was until 8:00 AM next morning. He might get himself shot or arrested.

We sat by the window looking at the comings and goings. The Sherman tank was still parked outside our house. Four tankers sat on the engine cover smoking and talking. We lit a kerosene lamp and made sure that the blackout blinds were down. After all, we had just witnessed that there were still planes around that would fire at anything they thought was hostile. No shouting was heard from Mr. Vink, who was obviously still in custody for interrogation. The GIs had a different idea about the blackout. They simply shot a few rounds with their grease guns through some of the windows and confiscated the lamps if they saw too much light.

The night was full of traffic noise. High overhead, thousands of bombers made their way to the east unmolested. No flak barked at them from our area. We all went to bed in the knowledge that peace, after all, was not too bad. We had something to eat, Len was home, and Gunny and Giant were still around. We still worried about Dad, and hoped for the best.

I was up at 7:00 AM. Mom was already making coffee. Gunny was trying to get into a pair of Granddad Willems homemade clogs. He wanted to save his boots for better days.

"What size are these clogs?" he asked me.

"Any size," I replied.

"What's that supposed to mean?" he asked. "Footwear is divided into sizes."

"Not Granddad Willem's clogs," I replied. "He only used to make two sizes. They either fit or they didn't."

"Those clogs also look the same to me, boy," Gunny remarked.

"They are the same, exactly the same," I told him.

"You mean there is no left or right?" he asked.

"That's right," I answered. "Granddad was one of the old guard. He was around when clogs were made equal, no preference to a left or a right clog. It's a good idea. Saves a lot of time, money and complaints. You had two choices. They either fit or they didn't. Those you are trying on don't, so rummage around in one of his old boxes in the shed. There might well be a pair that fits you."

"I was under the impression that at one time your Granddad was an excellent craftsman," Gunny said, "but a pair of clogs with no right nor left beats me."

"Your impression is right," I told him. "He was a first-class craftsman. He built that factory across the road, brick by lousy brick, and after six years of war, mistreatment, bombing and abuse by countless individuals, it's still standing."

"Where did you learn all this?" he asked.

"I keep my eyes and ears open. And above all," I told him, "I'm never too slow to learn, or to adapt myself to a new situation, good or bad, Gunny."

Gunny went back into the shed. After a while he came back with another pair of clogs. "They seem to be better," he said. "I can get into them with room to spare."

"Put a handful of straw inside. It will keep your feet warm and it makes the fit better," I told him.

Later, a knock on the door made us jump up. It was still not 8:00 AM. Curfew was still on, so it could only be someone from the military. Three tankers stood outside, mess cups in their hands. One addressed Mom in reasonably good German, "Could we have some water for coffee, please Ma'am?"

I noticed he had said "please." I spoke before Mom had a chance, "Of course, Sir. Step right in. There is the tap in the hallway over the sink."

Mom came into the hallway and said, "Please excuse the state of our house, Sir, but we had some war damage and we are in the middle of cleaning up. We're not used to peacetime yet."

The tankers filled their cups. On the way out, the German-speaking soldier turned around and said, "My Dad was born in Greifswald, Pommerania, and emigrated to the States a long time ago. I'm from a small town in Wisconsin. That is a state in the U.S. That's why I speak your language. Anything I can do for you?"

"Well, Sir," Mom said, "we were warned not to fraternize with the military, but I wouldn't mind a satchel of your real coffee if you have any to spare. My husband is in Denmark as far as we know. We live here with a cousin, my sister-in-law and three children. We haven't got much."

The tanker smiled, "I'll get you some coffee." He went to the open front door and called over to the other tanker men to bring us a tin can of coffee powder. The GI came over and handed me a tin of Nescafe. I looked around for a bag or something to put some of the powder in, but he pushed the whole tin into my hand. "There you are, boy," He said. "Have it all, we've got plenty."

I stormed into the kitchen with my treasure. "Not a bad deal, Mom," I said. "A tin full of coffee for three cups of tap water. This tin will make hundreds of cups."

Len finally crawled out of bed at 9:00 AM. After breakfast, we gawked through the open window at the new changed world. The American hardware was impressive, even Len admitted. He pointed at the Sherman outside with its 75mm gun. "Not bad, not bad, but ours are better."

"We were better, Len—were better," I said. "We'll never go back to those times with our Wehrmacht. There won't be another German tank coming down that road unless it has been captured intact and is being driven by American tankers."

"A few of our Panthers and Tigers would send this mob packing," he remarked.

"Bullshit, Len," I said, making sure I pronounced it with an accent. "That stuff out there you see has murdered our Panthers and Tigers since last June. It has sent the Wehrmacht running all the way back to the Rhine. Once the Amis get across, Len, the war is over, kaput, fini. The Americans and the British are not an uncivilized lot. I was in Wiltz when the Ardennes fiasco started. They might not have the best armor in the world, but they have plenty of it and can afford to lose a few hundred. The Wehrmacht can't. If they lose five Tigers, they're bankrupt."

I walked up to the tanker who was sitting on a campstool brewing coffee. "You speak German?" I asked.

"Nope," he said.

"Gotta chewing gum?" I said in bad English.

"Nope," he said again.

"Any candy or chocolate?" I kept on.

"Nope," he said for a third time.

"You wanna make a deal?" I asked.

"What kind of a deal?" he asked, speaking a little German.

"Big deal, real big deal," I replied.

"Go on, boy," the soldier said. "Tell me more about this big deal."

"Okay," I said. "I give you Hitler medal for souvenir, you give me candy or ration box, okay?"

"Let me see that medal first. Then we'll talk about big deals," he managed to communicate.

The day before, when we had disposed of Gunny's uniform in that air duct, I had taken his shiny flak medal off his tunic. Now I produced it and showed it to the tanker. His eyes lit up as he handled the medal. As a tanker, he probably had not come in contact yet with flak men, only infantry with iron crosses or KVKs. This was something new to him.

"Okay, you have a deal," I understood him to say. "I'll give you three rations and a roll of candy. No chocolate, sorry. Take it or leave it. If I wanted to, I could confiscate that medal from you, but I'm an honest trader. What do you say?"

"I'll take it," I agreed.

He opened a hatch, climbed into the Sherman and came out with three cartons of rations and a few candy rolls. "There you are, boy, big deal," he said.

"Thank you, Sir," I said politely, "and good day."

"You're not a Jew, are you?" he asked.

"No, Sir," I said. "There are none left. Oh, there is Mr. Hersch, but he's not a real Jew. He thinks he is because they gave him a yellow star to wear on his coat, but the Party never arrested him. He is a very nice man, that Mr. Hersch."

"Glad to hear it, boy," the soldier said. "I'm Jewish, and I'm glad to meet you."

I went back over to Len with my treasures. "There you are, Len. Even American Jews are nice. They ought to hate everything German from what we've heard lately."

"Only rumors, that's what it is, rumors." Len said.

"I hope to God you're right," I said. "If not, those Party men that took all the Jews away will be arrested and shot."

Little did we know then that it was the Gestapo and SS who were mainly responsible. A few weeks later the real truth was forced down our throats—if need be, at the point of a bayonet.

Mom opened a ration box and a tin of real butter came out. "For our evening sandwiches. We ought to get some bread and milk from somewhere," she said.

"There's powdered milk in these cartons, Mom," I said, pulling a packet out, "also saccharine sweetener and gum."

"All we need is bread, but I only have half a pound of rye flour," she said.

Then I had an idea. I turned to Gunny, "Didn't that officer that came into the cellar yesterday mention that we could help ourselves from any store containing food supplies?"

"Yeah," he said. "I think I heard something like that, although I was playing loco at the time."

"Okay, Gunny," I said, "the food factory store under the canteen is a retail store, isn't it?"

"Yes, it is—or was," he said. "What are you getting at?"

I explained, "The store is obviously locked. It has provisions and supplies in it. We all know that, otherwise, they would have blown the place sky high a long time ago. Len, come on. We'll go and see that Ami officer. Gunny, get the two-wheel cart ready and give word to Giant and anybody else who cares. We're going to have us some fun."

It felt great giving orders for a change. It was something I had always dreamed of when I had to take them up at the quads or from the

Hitler Youth leader. Now the tables were turned.

We soon found a lieutenant in a command trailer parked by the factory. We explained the situation to him, saying there were babies in the neighborhood that needed milk and food and that the factory owner, Mr. Kersken's son, had probably gone over the Rhine. "And he was a Nazi, too," I added for good measure, but that was far from the truth.

"Is that so?" the lieutenant asked.

"Yes, Sir," I said. "You told us yourself yesterday that we could help ourselves to food stores or depots. We tried to get some food from the few small privately owned corner stores, but they have as much as we have, Sir—nothing."

"Okay," the lieutenant said, "I'll get two of my men to come with you to make sure everything is done in a decent manner. I want as many people as possible to have the benefit of the food. You can go ahead and alert your neighbors."

"We've done that already," Len said. "We were figuring you would stand by your word, Sir."

The lieutenant looked sheepishly at Len and said, "Yes, yes, I do."

He called to two GIs. "Go and open that store for the people. They'll show you where it is."

People had already gathered around the entrance when we got back. Gunny was there with the cart and Giant had an old potato sack over his shoulder. I just hoped there was enough food in there to go around. The crowd had swollen to about a hundred. The GI told everyone to step back so no one would get hurt by a ricochet. Then he set his grease gun to work. A few rounds later and the lock sprang open.

"Now, then, we will have an orderly line here," the other soldier said, but nobody could understand him. Nobody took any notice and everyone wanted to be first. They burst into the store like a tidal wave, nearly trampling the poor solders underfoot.

Sadly, there wasn't much food to be had. There was definitely no flour, sugar or bread, but we found plenty of dried prunes, scratchy pumice soap, ATA scouring powder and other stuff not made to eat. Len found a large can of prunes in syrup and offered Gunny a ladle full. The ex-gunnery sergeant slurped it down, and then we left the mob to it. There was no point in turning the place over. There simply was not anything there to take.

"So much for your idea of robbing a food store," Giant said to me.

"I didn't know it was a pumice depot or whatever," I said. "The last time it was open to the public, they had bread, cheese, margarine and other stuff."

"That was a while ago," Giant said.

"No, Mr. Roland," I said, "it was the day before the second air raid, and the store was well stocked. I didn't see any pumice then. Look, there is the old unused nine pin bowling alley from the pub and I know the Wehrmacht used it as a storeroom for a while. I'm pretty sure I saw them unloading kommis bread there last weekend. I made a mental note where our bread was to come from if times got hard. Let's investigate. The pub is owned by the brewery. They were all Nazis for sure and have gone across the Rhine."

The back door of the bowling alley was made of wood. With one decent kick from Giant it flew wide open.

"There you are," I said. "All the bread you can eat and flour, too! Not wheat, I suppose, but rye and barley flour will do fine. We can't be too choosy."

"Well, well, look at that, and we were going hungry up at the quads while less than a mile away was a QM store full of food. Them no good bastards," Gunny lamented.

We formed a line there and then. Giant was the tallest, so he was first in line to grab the loaves from the huge pile. He handed them to Len, then he handed them to me. I handed the loaves to Gunny by the fence and he finally threw them across the road through the open kitchen window. There, Aunt Carol and Mom stacked them along the wall. We worked like greased lightning. It was really hilarious to watch, and some GIs standing around laughed their heads off watching us. Some even joined in the fun. The Amis were excellent loaf catchers. It was almost like a football game. The wide receiver was the champion. He could catch a loaf from Giant right across the road and make a touch down on Mom's windowsill.

More people joined the fun. The GIs began throwing loaves to anyone who cared to catch them, and there were many takers, believe me. Hunger can be terrible. You will do anything for a mouthful of food. The GIs didn't mind. It was not their food we took and therefore, none of their business. Besides, they probably would not have touched such hard, grayish-looking bread. You have to have a good stomach to digest rye or barley bread. Finally, we each loaded ourselves with a 50-pound sack of flour. Giant took two sacks and we all went home. The bread football game went on for another hour before supplies eventually dried up, but everyone had a share. People went home happy in the knowledge that they had something to eat in weeks to come. The bread went stale after a few days, but we lived on it anyway; better stale bread than no bread at all. Our stomachs could digest anything by now. In fact, we never felt healthier in all our lives.

I walked around the now empty bowling alley. The people had all left. It was almost curfew time. A forlorn and forgotten loaf, half crushed by hobnailed boots, caught my attention. I picked it up and threw it at the distant ninepins still standing like soldiers on parade. I missed. A half loaf of kommis bread is hardly a bowling ball. A few sacks of flour had been spilled across the once polished floor. My eyes fell on a small box on a shelf by the bowling counter slate. I opened it and discovered thousands of small pills. I licked one. It was saccharine—enough sweetener to last us a year or two. At home, the living room was almost half full of bread loaves, plus four sacks of flour, a can of prunes in syrup, two years' worth of saccharine and twelve bars of pumice soap. Not a bad day, I thought, not bad at all. We decided to store all the bread in the attic, the driest place in the house. No doubt the mice would take their share, too, but who cared. Mice had to live as well. We felt generous.

Supper was a feast of kommis bread, American ration butter and liver cheese, all washed down with real coffee, dried milk with saccharine added, and a roll of candy for dessert, thanks to Gunny's flak medal.

A few days passed peacefully. Curfew hours were extended from dusk to dawn, in fact, so we had more time in the afternoon to get around. Late one afternoon, Gunny and I sat on the bench in our garden looking at the military traffic going by. The Sherman tank in front of our house had gone. It was mostly truck traffic now. There were still dozens of trucks and M3s parked around. A few GIs were playing cards, sitting by a camp table across the garden.

A soldier walked up to the fence and bid us hello.

We said "hello" too.

The GI, who could speak a bit of German, asked, "Do you know of any frauleins around here?"

"Hmm, depends on what you're looking for," Gunny said.

"What do you mean?" the soldier asked.

"Well, little, tall, fat, thin, old, young," Gunny said. "They come in all shapes and sizes, you know."

"Something sort of mid-twenties and looking for a good time," the soldier said.

"I don't know of any offhand," Gunny said, "but I'll keep my eyes and ears open for you."

I nudged Gunny in the ribs, "What about that Margaret? The one who used to hang around with the 88 crew. She'll take anything now that the 88 guys have gone."

"Hmm," said Gunny, "if the gentleman here doesn't mind an ex-BDM girl, 28 years of age with a fat butt."

"Fat butt?" the GI interrupted Gunny. "How fat?"

"Well, something between a horse and a trash bin lid."

"Geeze, where does she live, tell me!" the GI exclaimed.

"Marcus Street 21, and she takes rations or Chesterfields as payment."

We told him where Marcus Street was. He then put four packs of Lucky Strikes into Gunny's hand and added, "and nix telling my comrades, okay?"

"Okay, Sir, and thank you. It was nice being of service."

"See, boy, another satisfied customer," Gunny said.

"Yeah, you got the Luckys and I didn't even get a candy bar," I said. "It's not fair. After all, I told you about fat Margaret in the first place, and you don't smoke either."

"I just started this minute," he said. "In fact, I got three packs left. Here is one pack. Give that to Roland in exchange for a candy bar."

I stuffed the cigarettes into my pocket and thought about starting smoking myself. It seemed that cigarettes were more valuable than candy bars.

The electricity came back on a few days later, although we still had to observe blackout regulations. Mr. Vink had finally been released. If he had ever been a Nazi, it was not a big deal for the Americans. They put him to good use. He was made official stoker for the boiler house in the factory, which was probably the only large building complex in town left undamaged. The Amis had made a truck park out of it. The soldiers now billeted in the offices and had set up shop between writing desks, typewriters and waste paper baskets. We even got our radio going and heard all the news and both sides' opinions. We still received some German stations outside of the Allies' reach, but we also got some new stations intended to give the German people now under Allied rule an honest picture of how things were going.

The war was far from over, as we were again reminded a few days later. Early on that March morning, a flight of twelve German twin-engine bombers came over, escorted by a few ME-262 jet fighters and some FW-190s. All hell broke loose around town. Every conceivable gun that could throw a shell into the air went into action. Even the soldiers who had nothing more than M-1 carbines were firing at the fighters. The bombers were too high. There were no Allied fighters to be seen. This happened quite often, I thought. If you do not need them, they show up, if you're in trouble, none are there to help you out. The bombers came in and dropped their loads haphazardly all over town. None fell near us and only a few minor military targets were hit. The 84th Infantry lost two cooking stoves from shrapnel damage and the 102nd lost a couple of trucks, but that was all. The rest of the damage could not be determined as the bombs exploded in parts of the town that had been leveled by the Allied attack two weeks earlier.

News reached us later that morning that our school had taken a hit. Now that was interesting. After all, a ruined school means no lessons for the foreseeable future. The school had been closed anyway. The Allies were still too busy trying to find out which teachers were Nazis and which were not.

Sadly though, the school was undamaged, but a delayed action bomb did drop outside the school onto the road. The stabilizers were lying a few yards away, twisted and bent. Of course, I did not know the difference between a time bomb and a dud then, but a few kids had gathered around the hole looking into the hellish device, whose top could be seen about two feet deep in the ground. I didn't like the look of things and told the kids that we had better get away fast. Delayed action bombs, German or Allied, have a nasty habit of going off at the most unexpected time. There were no bomb disposal teams around and the Amis had more urgent things to do than clearing Germany of unexploded ordinance.

Some of the kids, including myself, decided to go and tell Mr. Vink. After all, he had been a warden and ought to know what to do next. We drifted away and I walked back toward home. About six kids foolishly stayed behind, throwing rocks from a ten-yard distance into the hole. A terrific explosion shook the ground. I turned around and saw dust and debris flying high into the air. I ran back as fast as I could, but three kids were dead, blown to bits. The others were badly burned. One had his face horribly scorched. Another, who had stood with his back to the hole when the device went off, had his back completely burned. The last one had gotten away with a few minor scratches and sat on the pavement with tears streaming down his blackened cheeks. A few minutes later, a military ambulance turned up and took the dead and injured to the hospital. The school's windows were all broken. One of the teachers came by on his bicycle shortly after the explosion. We had not seen a teacher for a few weeks, and I saluted him with a smart "Heil Hitler," as we had been accustomed to doing since 1938.

"Shush, shush! Do you want the Amis to hear you saying that?" he said.

"Okay, then, good morning," I said, "or not so good morning. If you came to be of any help, you're too late. The Amis have taken care of things." I gave a report of the things I had witnessed to the teacher, and he said that he would go to the hospital and find out who the injured children's parents were.

Another silly accident happened a few days later. One of our neighbors' sons, Helmut, found an American hand grenade, the pineapple type. The Americans had a habit of leaving a lot of ammo and hand grenades lying around and forgetting about them. Helmut pulled the ring and the grenade blew both of his hands off. Only a quick blood transfusion at the hospital saved his life. In those days, although all the factories and most shops were closed, the hospitals stayed open. The doctors and nurses, with limited medicine at hand, worked miracles. Helmut is still alive today, half a century after World War II, and works as a gardener with a pair of wooden hands.

By the beginning of April, the weather had gotten warmer and days were getting longer. Curfew times were now only a few hours in the dead of night. Still, the military traffic rolled eastward but it was mostly truck business or railroad. Even the tanks had a better time, being carried piggy back on huge low loaders. Attacks by the German Luftwaffe had ceased altogether. There were still a lot of Allied planes in the skies—bombers and fighters, and now and then large swarms of C-47 transports. Absent were the once-dreaded fighter-bombers. One morning in early April, Gunny said he would try to make his way to Krefeld. The curfew was still on at night and a seventeen mile walk to his girl's place would surely get him running into one of the patrols that controlled all comings and goings. Mom told him he could use Dad's bicycle, with the reminder that he had to bring it back one day when times were better. We all knew the war was almost over. The Allies were on the Elbe, and the Ruhr was surrounded and on the verge of collapsing. The German commander, Model, had taken his own life rather than surrender. Gunny promised to bring the bike back as soon as he was able to do so. We all shook hands. Giant was especially moved to see his old fighting companion leave.

"There goes a good friend," Mom said.

"Yes, and a good handyman, too," I answered. "Now I'll have to do all the work around the house."

Brother Len had found a job as a farm hand. The factory where he had started his apprenticeship had still not reopened. For him now, it was pulling weeds between rows of turnips and sugar beets. His wages were twenty worthless Reichsmarks per week plus six ham or bacon sandwiches a day. It made us wonder where the farmer kept his pigs. We never located them, despite the fact that Len and I looked everywhere.

CHAPTER 20

V-E Day &
Dad's Homecoming

Finally in May, V-E day, as the Allies called it, arrived. The war was really over. All the guns around town let loose a last victory barrage. Soldiers were dancing in the streets. "Hitler kaput! Germany kaput!" they yelled.

Bottles of beer and spirits miraculously turned up from haversacks, halftracks and the depths of tanks. Festivities went on for 24 hours. Some soldiers got dangerously drunk and started firing their automatic weapons at anything that looked remotely like a left-over from the Third Reich—flag posts, enameled party signs, street signs and, in some instances, innocent people. The local US commander put a stop to it before things could get too far out of hand. Military police arrested any soldier who was found drunk and in possession of a gun.

Toward the end of the war, the Allies decided that the part of Germany we lived in would be allocated to the British, so it was called the British Zone, even though the United States had conquered our area with the Ninth US Army under General Simpson. Under the Yalta Agreement, the Americans had to move out, and so they did. One day in early summer, the US Army packed their bags and left the field to the new arrivals, the British army and the Royal Air Force. Only a skeleton crew of US personnel stayed behind, but that included the town commander.

The British immediately occupied the food factory and turned it into an ordnance depot. The Royal Engineers, service corps, and other units were billeted in the office buildings the Amis had vacated. German labor was hired after a security check and employed as loaders, drivers and translators. A company of ex-Latvian patriots, who had fled their country fearing the wrath of the not-so tolerant Russian army, was put in

303

charge of guard duties, and patrolled the compound around the clock with loaded weapons.

We now set to the task of sorting out the legacy of the departed US Army. Another winter was coming. Soon we would have to grow our own food. The garden had been neglected in times of plenty and was now overgrown. Len and I decided on a clearing operation, but didn't get very far. Between some currant and bramble bushes, we discovered a stack of 75mm tank cannon rounds, fused and in good order. There were 22 in all.

"What now, Len?" I asked.

"We keep them," he said.

"Keep them? For what, might I ask you?"

"Well, just in case," Len argued.

"In case of what?" I said. "This is 75mm fused tank ammunition, and it'll blow us and the whole neighborhood to kingdom come if it goes off. The war is over and lost. There is no black market for that sort of stuff. So let's get on over to the British at the factory and get a disposal team here. They'll surely do something about those rounds. Having a stack of live 75mm tank rounds on their doorstep is not every army depot commander's wish."

"Okay, okay. Don't rattle on," Len finally agreed. "I'll organize something. Just hold on."

"Forget it. I'll go and see the British guard by the factory gate," and I left Len standing alone.

I walked up to the Tommie, "You speak Deutsch?" I asked.

"No," he made me understand, "but just hold on. I'll get someone who can translate."

I watched him go into a small office and talk to somebody on the telephone. A few minutes later, a sergeant with a globe and a flash badge on his beret, obviously someone from the Royal Electrical and Mechanical Engineers (REME), came up to me.

"Yes, boy, what's the matter? Can I help you?" he asked.

"Sir, we found twenty two 75mm live tank cannon rounds in our garden," I explained. "We want to do some planting. Any chance of removing them before we start digging?"

"Hell, boy," he said, "there are millions of live rounds lying around this country, and we're doing the best we can to clear the mess up. Just come back in a few days. Meanwhile, stay at least 400 yards away from them. Twenty-two 75mm rounds have a hell of an explosive power."

"Four hundred yards? Sir," I explained, "the rounds lying in our garden are roughly 130 yards from your gate."

His jaw dropped a full inch. "Hold on, boy," he said. "I'll get the captain. You just don't move, okay?"

After I had waited a few more minutes, an Austin jeep drove up with a captain, the sergeant and two corporals in it. "Come on, jump in, boy. Show us where those rounds are," the captain said.

"No need to drive there, Sir," I explained. "They are just over there in our garden. We found them in the brambles."

I took the four Tommies into our yard and showed them the stack of 75mms. Len was watching from a few yards away.

"Jesus, if they had blown up, your house, the neighborhood and part of our depot across the road would have been a goner. Thanks for telling us," the captain said.

"I found them first!" Len shouted, hoping to get a pat on the back.

"Yeah, and you were going to sell them as souvenirs," I said under my breath, so that the Tommies could not hear me.

Len took me away from the inspecting soldiers. He still wasn't convinced. "We could have buried them here," he said. "There might be another war coming one day."

"And you would love it too, and be the very first one to shout 'Sieg Heil,'" I told him in no uncertain terms. "While you were away digging silly no-good antitank ditches, I was up at the quads in the gun pits taking artillery and tank fire. I know what one 75mm can do, never mind twenty two of them. Maybe there are even more lying around. So forget it. And if you don't mind, let's clear out of here until they have been removed. When that is done, you better get your spade ready and dig this garden or we're gonna live on moldy kommis bread and saccharine this coming winter. You ought to be good at digging, having dug miles of useless antitank ditches."

The British ordnance team came an hour later and removed the deadly rounds. We watched from a respectful distance. The disposal went without a hitch, so we could finally start thinking about growing some food.

School started in July. Our old class teacher visited us to give us the news. I thought I could have gone on without school for the rest of my life. I couldn't think of anything that I wanted to learn. I was under the impression that I knew enough as it was, without doing another few years at school. Our teacher was cleared by the de-nazification team that had been set up by the Allies. A few of the old teachers were gone—they had retired, died in air raids, or had just had enough of the whole system. Others, who had been Nazi Party members, were told in unmistakable terms to get a shovel and clear away the rubble, to clean the streets or else. What was meant by "or else" we never found out, but quite a few ex- teachers and other high officials could be found in town throwing shovels full of debris onto dump trucks. For months on end, the rubble of the leveled town was carted to a dumpsite several miles north, where eventually it accumulated to a 60-foot high mound covering 22 acres. A soccer stadium was built over it a few years later.

School was not too bad when it started again after the war. The whole curriculum was in a mess. The old Nazi reading books and all that came with them had been banned, but new books had not yet been written, much less printed. Even writing paper was scarce. We used anything we could put our pens to. Leaflets from the new parties that had sprung up like weeds after a thunderstorm were very much in demand because the back of them was blank. We used the only leftover book from the Nazi time, the local train timetable book, for reading lessons. Not many passenger trains were running, and those that did were never on time anyway. Chalk for the teacher's blackboard was so scarce at one time that an order came out to do away with the horizontal stroke in the middle of the number 7 to save chalk. Ink was dished out in drops once a day. Pencils were used to the last stub.

Worst of all was the toilet tissue situation. Five hundred seventy kids in our school alone used a lot of paper, so it was newspaper, billboard leftovers, or just plain cement bags. Some people who worked for the British took the rolls of toilet tissue from the depot toilets, but the military police soon put a stop to that. Each tissue roll had a printed warning and "Government Property" stamped on it. Workers leaving the depot were strip searched, and if any military item was found, they were arrested and dismissed.

We were warned repeatedly, by teachers not to mess around with any ammunition, bombs or other dangerous materials that were still lying around. It was expected that sooner or later something nasty would happen. One day in early August it did. After school, some kids started a small fire along the railroad embankment. The grass was bone dry, and the wind soon spread the blaze over several hundred yards. Twelve railroad cars parked on a nearby spur line caught fire. They had stood there ever since the end of the hostilities, and nobody knew what was in them. It was assumed that they were empty cars, but six of them were full of ammunition. In fact, they contained 80mm and 150mm rockets for the Nebel and Panzerwerfers. The other six cars were loaded with boxes of apples and tomatoes, which by this time had all rotted.

The British, who were in charge of the railroad system in their zone of occupation, also had no idea of the contents of the dozen cars. Nevertheless, they sent a "Green Goddess," or British army firefighting truck, to fight the blaze. Before it reached the scene, the first railroad car containing a thousand or so Werfer rockets blew up, followed a minute or so later by the other cars. The fire fighters, who were 200 yards from the disaster, got away without serious injuries, but were showered by thousands of rotten apples and tomatoes. The rockets took off in all directions, crisscrossing town and causing quite a few deaths and injuries. Some landed as far as eight miles away, much further than our Puma had fired the same rounds back in February. The area near the railroad track bore the brunt of the explosion and the destruction was enormous. After that episode, the British made an all-out effort to rid the town and county of all explosives.

We still found enough ammunition after the clean up to have started a guerilla war. One day, Brother Len found a muslin bag the size of a 16-ounce can of beans. He showed me the bag, and on closer inspection, we found it contained gunpowder sticks about the size of matches but hollow, resembling miniature macaroni. They were harmless on their own, but if they came in contact with an open flame they would explode with a violent flash. I took a few and kept them in an empty cigarette box, and we buried the rest in a field.

That day, a Saturday, we explored some old unused air raid bunkers that still dotted the countryside. We were covered in mud from crawling through airshafts and foxholes. Mom wasn't very fond of washing muddy clothes without detergent. Warm water and elbow grease was all she had to keep clothes in a reasonable state. When we got in and she noticed our state, she flew into a rage.

"Get that dirty stuff off right now and have a bath. No supper for you two tonight," she scolded.

I undressed, and Mom went through my pockets. It was one of her long-standing habits to throw anything that was not to her liking in the fire of the cooking stove. She found the box that contained the gunpowder, and without opening it, she threw it into the fire. My warning not to do so came too late. A second later, the evening supper of beans and potato stew covered the kitchen walls and my body. Mom's hair was singed and a blister was coming up on her forearm.

"Now look what you've done!" I shouted, licking the stew off my face and picking a potato from the floor, "I was going to tell you about that box, but you didn't give me the chance."

"I'll give you a chance. No dinner tonight or tomorrow. No playing either. It'll be garden work every day next week after school."

Either I was getting too old for the carpet beater, or Mom was getting even older. The dreaded beater did not come out.

It was mid-August now. In normal times, we would be in the middle of our summer school holidays, but times were not normal. Because we lost almost a year of lessons due to air raids and occupation, we had three hours of school lessons every day, and another three hours in the afternoon helping the farmers out in the potato fields by picking off zillions of Colorado beetles from the bushes that threatened the heart of the German food chain. Potatoes have always been a German staple, war or no war.

We were given a roll of candy for each small glass jar full of larvae, beetles or egg nests. We became real experts in separating the good from the bad insects. Ladybugs, for instance, were considered good guys. At the end of picking for three hours, the teacher handed out the candy rolls. The jars were emptied into an open tin can containing gasoline and duly set on fire. If this potato pest had come a year or two earlier, the Nazis surely would have made something out of them—cooking fat or explosives or axle grease for Tiger tanks.

I walked home that day clutching the three rolls of candy I had received for my effort. Nearly home, I saw an ex-German POW coming slowly uphill. He was still wearing his uniform, except that all Nazi emblems had been removed. It was a common sight in the first year after the war when thousands of soldiers had been released from POW camps after clearance by the Allied de-nazification team. They were given a slip of paper as a release notice, three ration cartons and 20 cigarettes, and told to go home somehow. By train, truck or even on foot, the once proud Wehrmacht soldiers came home.

Something seemed to be familiar about the POW coming up the hill. Then I recognized him. It was Dad, covered in dust, with his once shiny tank destroyer uniform in tatters. I ran indoors, almost taking the doorframe with me. "Mom, Mom, Mom! Dad's coming up the road! Honest, no joke, Mom! Come quick!" I yelled.

She dropped the hot iron she had just taken from the stove onto the floor. Her face went white and she was unable to move. She sat down, tears streaming down her cheeks. The door opened and there he stood. At long last, Dad was home for good after seven years as a soldier. I cannot remember what we did or said in those first minutes, but after a while, I dashed outside and told everyone who cared to listen that my Dad was home. Soon the house filled up with all sorts of people— friends, relatives, and nosy neighbors who had never set foot over our doorstep before. All were welcomed. Giant came running over. Mr. Vink left his boiler room after hearing the news, graciously released for an hour from his duties. Even Mr. Hersch made an appearance. Everyone came to shake hands with our Dad.

We went to bed late that night. I said to Len that now that Dad was home, we would get the garden done in time for certain. The next morning I skipped school. I wasn't in the mood for picking Colorado beetles, candy or no candy. Len took the day off as well, and Dad told us what had happened since we had last seen him in early 1944.

In late summer of that year, the Canadian army, which was advancing through north Holland, had bypassed the Dutch Island of Walcheren, where my dad was at the time. Only a narrow causeway connected the island with the rest of the country. The Canadians had left the island alone because the Germans had blown the dykes. Most of the land on Walcheren was below sea level, and the German army had turned the once beautiful farmland into a bottomless morass where no army could successfully operate. Tanks and guns simply disappeared into the quagmire, never to be seen again. Bombs dropped from planes did not do much damage either, for they exploded far too deeply inside the soft ground to cause any damage.

The Canadians tried to isolate Walcheren and carry the war further east toward the German Reich. But the Germans, having the wisdom to blow up the dykes, shut the Canadians out. This created a dilemma as well, for they had also blocked themselves in. There was no way out unless they could close the holes in the dykes and pump the water out. Given their circumstances, this was beyond their capability on the island, especially because the weather in northern Europe is usually bad at that time of the year.

The fall of 1944 was unusually wet in that part of Holland. Some German units, however, managed to fight their way along the narrow causeway to the mainland. Toward the end of September, they almost managed to stop the British from reaching the Nijmegen Bridge during the Market Garden fiasco. There, on that narrow, straight road to Arnhem, with soft ground on either side unsuitable for heavy armor, the roles were reversed. The British came to a dead stop. The Tiger tanks of the 11th SS Panzer picked the British-manned Sherman tanks off the road one after another. There was no way the armor could move. Ahead, wrecked tanks blocked the road. The rear was a nine-mile traffic jam, creating a "shooting gallery," as the Tiger crews named it.

For the rest of the German army on soggy and flooded Walcheren, there were a few fishing boats and an assortment of pleasure vessels. There was also a rusty torpedo boat of 1916 vintage and a minesweeper group. These were all commandeered by the army high command, who told the sailors to get them out of there with the boats. The navy didn't like the idea of taking orders from the Wehrmacht, but war is war and they had no choice. British corvettes and destroyers patrolled the sea lines along the Dutch coast, but had to stay at least four miles offshore because of treacherous sand banks. The German boats, with a much shallower draft, loaded with men but no heavy weapons, sneaked away by night, hugging the Dutch shoreline 100 yards off.

Just off the West Friesian Islands, a British corvette captain suspected something and opened fire with a four-incher, sinking one boat and damaging another. Later, the British pursuers had to call it a night when they came in range of German 150mm coastal artillery of that outgunned their little four-inchers. Some German boats made it into Leeuwarden waters. The bad news was that the Allies weren't too far away on land and would, in all probability, reach the area soon.

Several boats continued their journey and made it to Sylt, one of the north Friesian Islands, where the soldiers were trucked over the causeway linking the island with Germany proper and to an army camp near Aarhus in Denmark. Dad was among them. Here they sat the war out doing nothing. They had left all their weapons behind on Walcheren, and there was no way to re-equip the army sitting useless in Denmark. Their carbines and an odd machine gun they had somehow managed to acquire were installed in watchtowers around their camp, more as a show than a deterrent.

The Danish population cooperated by leaving the Germans very much to themselves. Food supplies were adequate, enough to last for a few months, so nobody worried much. Air raids were seldom: there were no worthwhile targets for the bombers, and Denmark, unlike the rest of the countries Germany had fought over, had never been a battle-field. So, in effect, the Germans made themselves POWs without ever seeing their captors. At war's end, it was the Danes who accepted the German surrender in Denmark, not, as many history books tell us, Montgomery. He appeared on the stage a few days later when all was over and done with.

Not a shot had been fired by either side and the Danish people, tired of war but grateful for a peaceful cessation of hostilities in their country, agreed to feed the German POWs for the duration of their intern-ment. The screening of several thousand POWs took time. The British did not hurry. Their system was slow but efficient. They separated offi-cers from NCOs and enlisted men and interrogated each and every one of them. Those found without soldier's books or dog tags were trans-ported to another camp until their true identity could be established.

Many Nazis were caught in this way, but it also caught the odd sol-dier who had lost his dog tag or ID book. Most went to POW camps in England or Canada, where some had to stick it out for several years. Dad's youngest brother came back in 1948. That was my Uncle Wilhelm, who lost his family in the first air raid on the town. Not only had he lost his dog tag, he was also a member of the Waffen SS, which did not set very well with the British.

Dad showed the British officer his ID card, dog tag and some letters from Mom he had saved, so his interrogation lasted only seven minutes. Three days later he was given a travel pass, ration cartons and two packs of Senior Service Cigarettes. The Red Cross also issued him a per-mit to seek help or shelter in any Red Cross establishment on his way home. Home was 500 miles away, and it took him almost three weeks to cover the distance. He had already marched 2,000 miles through Russia, so 500 miles on home soil was easy, he said.

With Dad's return, we all could start rebuilding our homes and lives. School was not so bad after that. It was time to start winter prepa-rations in earnest: there was still some kommis bread in the attic, along with a 50-pound bag of flour and, of course, the saccharine. Then there were the rabbits. We had seven, and soon there would be more. They were breeding like, well, like rabbits.

Those first days in March 1945, when, for the first time in their lives, many Germans came in contact with Americans, were days full of fun and exploration for the ex-Hitler Youth. The easy going and casual behavior of the GIs pleasantly surprised us. They marveled for days over the fact that some cars and trucks ran on wood, or more precisely, on wood gas. This, too, was an invention of Nazi times. Gunny had one of these "Holzvergasers" to run his scrap and black market business. The system was simple; a steel cylinder attached to the side of the truck, or in the trunk of the car, converted smoldering wood blocks into combustible gas. Five pounds of wood was good for 30 to 35 miles; trucks, depending on weight, could make 15 miles. So a cylinder with the capacity of, say, 50 pounds of wood blocks gave you 300 to 350 miles on the road. There were even "Holz Tank Stellen," wood gas stations where the driver could get a 50-pound sack of wood blocks for less than an American dollar. There are still a few of these vehicles left in Germany now, though they only run on special occasions like car shows or parades.

Another puzzle for the GIs were the tractors the food factory used for moving heavy trailers over short distances. They were a sort of shunting tractor. The vehicle was driven by an electric motor fed by huge lead-zinc batteries that had to be recharged every night. One recharge was good for about 25 miles. The Americans, who thought they knew everything there was to know about trucks and tractors, used them for pleasure rides until the batteries ran dry, usually on a busy road full of rolling military traffic. They would often leave them there, in turn creating huge traffic jams. The Americans commandeered M3 halftracks to tow the tractors to the nearest electrical outlet for a recharge, but that didn't work. They needed 440 volts for recharging from a special charger unit. They also tried generators, but it was to no avail. When all else failed to get the tractors rolling under their own power, they towed the whole lot into a field next to the cycle track and set them ablaze.

"If we cannot drive them, nobody else gets them," was the motto.

Looting by the Americans was unheard of and was strictly forbidden. Penalties were severe if a soldier was caught. The exception was Nazi mementos. A proclamation printed in German was given to every household and plastered all over town. Lt told us to report any forced entry into a private house to the commanding officer. This did not stop us kids from making privately conducted deals with the GIs for anything that took their fancy, whether it was a cuckoo clock, Granddad Willem's Meerschaum pipe, or a pretty local female who had no qualms about spending an intimate and lustful hour with a generous American soldier. The girls generally had plenty of previous experience with the former German soldiers. To them, a soldier was a soldier, whether German or American. They all wanted the same thing, only the payment had changed since March 1. In place of worthless Reichsmarks, it was Chesterfields, Lucky Strikes, Nescafe, Nylon Stockings or chocolate, and the Americans had plenty of all of them. It was amazing to see how fast the local economy changed from Reichsmarks to US rations. Of course, all this wheeling and dealing was officially forbidden by military law for soldiers and German civilians alike, but it's impossible to keep tabs on thousands of people, even in the best circumstances.

We soon learned that Dad's Iron Cross 1st Class, awarded to him for taking a T-34 tank on single-handed and almost getting himself killed, was worth 200 Chesterfields. The 1941-1942 Russian Front Winter medal was only good for five C-rations. The GIs had gotten wind of the fact that millions of these medals had been awarded, which reduced their value accordingly. Mothers' certificates of Hitler as a Godfather for a 3rd child, along with the medal was a good bet to get a pound of Nescafe. Metal cap eagles with swastikas fetched only two chocolate bars, but then, when we were in need of a decent piece of candy, we often took the offer. We searched the house and dumps for Nazi stuff—anything with a swastika was currency. When we tried to trade Granddad Willem's World War I medals to a tanker crew in exchange for three pounds of candy, Mom put her foot down.

"Those are World War I mementos, not Nazi stuff, and they are not going anywhere. Is that clear?" Mom told us.

"Yes, Mom, but, but...." we argued.

"No buts, take Len's belt buckle or go and fish for your Hitler Youth knife out of the cesspit. That will get you some candy, alright!" Mom suggested.

The thought of rummaging through our septic tank for the dagger was enough to put me off candy bars for a while. I went over to Giant and asked him if he had anything to spare in the way of Nazi medals.

He turned his pockets inside out, "Search me, boy, my medals and eagles have gone to the USA, like your stuff. If we only had known this a few weeks ago, we could be millionaires now."

Right by the turn to the factory, the Todt Organization years ago had put up a concrete pillbox. It was never manned, and eventually the Nazis used it as a convenient place to placard some slogans. "We march to Victory, the Führer says so," was one; another read, "Our wheels will run to victory." There were also some printed portraits of Hitler stuck to the sides. The GIs had drawn some extras on the Führer's face. One picture showed Hitler with huge ears and whiskers that made him look like Mickey Mouse. On another, he looked like Charlie Chaplin. We really admired those works of "fine American art."

The pillbox was a nuisance right on the sharp turn. The long barreled M40s on their motor carriages had a pretty difficult time negotiating the corner, and it took some hard maneuvering to get them past this useless edifice. The Amis therefore decided to remove it, break it up, and dispose of it, but nobody had reckoned with German efficiency and craftsmanship. The Nazis had gained plenty of experience, building a 2,000 mile-long line of concrete fortifications all the way from Norway to Spain, and pillboxes were one of their specialties. Any GI in a front-line rifle company that fought inside the Siegfried Line could vouch for that.

For a day or so jackhammers rattled, but the pillbox was reinforced with steel and the hammers barely scratched the surface. The US Army brought up a huge M32A, an armored recovery vehicle that could lift 20,000 pounds with the attached crane and had a powerful nine- cylinder radial engine. A steel cable was lowered from the jib and secured around the pillbox. The M32A operator gave the full power signal—no deal, the thing would not budge. Blasting it to bits with dynamite was out because of all the surrounding buildings. Mr. Vink, by now reduced in rank to an ordinary civilian, had a better idea. Since the captain's men were unable to move the bunker, why not make the road wider? The captain's face lit up. The job only involved rooting up 50 yards of hedging, and the road was made wider in no time. The pillbox stood there for another decade, but was finally dug up with its foundation and now rests 20 feet below the municipal soccer stadium.

We also admired American efficiency and ingenuity. A huge bomb crater in the middle of the highway was no problem: a bulldozer did the trick in short order. The Germans had always used POWs to do their dirty work. Germany had always prided itself on how well and fast her bridges had been built across rivers, but building a bridge in peacetime and in combat are two different things. Meticulous and slow was the German way to make the bridge last forever, but in warfare, a bridge has to be built in hours, not in days or months, and there is no need for watchtowers on the ends or fancy ornaments. The reinforced, solid granite rock watchtowers on either end of the Remagen Bridge did not hold up the Americans' dash across the Rhine.

New slogans appeared and replaced the Nazi-dominated media and advertisement. The end had come for "Save soap for our Wehrmacht." It was now, "Use pumice soap for a healthy body." Healthy? I was not so sure of that. The stuff took the skin off if you rubbed too hard. Cigarette ads were everywhere. Tobacco was grown in gardens, then dried and cut with the breadslicer. The end product was then rolled into any sort of paper and sold as cigarettes for 20 Pfennigs each. US cigarettes were still the best currency. We even invented a little song and the GIs loved it: "For just one pack of Chesterfields, the Amis drive my sister wild." They rewarded our singing with a banana or an orange.

With the blessing of the Allied Control Commission, those political parties that had been banned by the Nazis in 1933 were permitted to compete for new members, although voting as such was not yet allowed. The old Socialist Party was one of the first to re-establish itself in town. They even formed a new youth movement called the Red Falcons. The Allies mildly tolerated all this, until one day there was an athletic competition arranged between soldiers and Germans. The Falcon leader had his boys lined up outside the stadium. When they marched in goose-stepping as they had done under the Nazis, the organizer, a US Army major, put an end to it.

Basic commodities people take for granted today were unobtainable. Even decent cigarettes were hard to come by. For lack of stockings, women used to paint their legs with a concoction made from walnut shells and diesel oil. It was advertised as 1A+ Leg Paint. Nylon stockings reached Germany with the coming of the Americans, but you either had to be a Chesterfield millionaire or a beauty queen with American connections to get them. Slowly the word "Yankee" crept into the German vocabulary. To us, a Yankee was an American, regardless of whether his home state was Maine, Arkansas, Alabama or New York. If by chance an American introduced himself as a Texan, to us he was a Yankee Cowboy. If he was from Tennessee, he was a Yankee backwoodsman.

Once the pubs were reopened, the soldiers flocked in, drinking the weak beer or bringing their own liquor, which they generously shared with anyone. Schutzen Clubs, an old German association going back several hundred years, were also permitted to re-open. Every year the club would have a weeklong festival when members would fire air rifles at clay pigeons. Each shot cost several German Marks, and he who finally shot the pigeon down would be Schutzen King for a year. All the participants would march around in unison from one pub to the next for days on end.

When the secretary of the local club approached the US control commissioner with a request to use their old rusty air rifles to shoot the pigeon down, the commander drew the line, so at the next Schutzen festival, the members smartly marched around town with shouldered walking sticks. The King was elected not by shooting skills but by the Reichsmarks he had in his pocket or his ability to out drink the rest of the members. All were happy, even the commissioner, who had been invited to watch the proceedings.

Dad got his job back as a tram driver. Roads had been cleared, tracks repaired, and overhead, new cables had been strung. Every half hour a streetcar came trundling along Main Street on the way to or from M-G. The company gave him a new uniform and he was on the day shift from 9:00 AM to 5:00 PM. The first tram left the depot at 6:00 AM, but the depot was seven miles away and Dad's bike was somewhere in Krefeld with Gunny, who was either dead or had forgotten us, so Dad had no way to get to the depot that early in the morning. Instead he walked down into town at 8:00 AM and took over from another driver an hour later.

Dad asked the local German supply officer if there was a chance of getting a used bicycle so he could do early or late shifts. The man in charge at the office, an ex-Nazi with a fat gut who munched bacon sandwiches and drank real coffee while everyone else lived on ersatz, flatly refused to even consider his request. Colonel McKay, the US officer in charge of town administration, heard about this fat-gut and made an example of him. Dad came home as happy as if it was Christmas day, proudly showing us his bike. It even had a front and rear light driven by a small dynamo, and a carrier where he could clamp his lunchbox. We stood around open-mouthed, as if it were a tank destroyer. He took the early shift the next week and the late one the week after.

Every second weekend, Dad had three days off work. Of course, the streetcars ran on weekends too, but the drivers took turns working weekends so everyone had some free time. One weekend in October when Dad had off was Giant's fortieth birthday. He invited everyone in the neighborhood to the pub for a drink. Even those of us who were still underage were allowed to come for a glass of apple juice, while the older folks sipped the still weak beer. Some had made their own moonshine and brought that along. This moonshine stuff, in fact, was secretly produced by the Latvians who guarded the depot. They had been made very welcome by the community, and some had found German girlfriends. Germany had lost three million men in the war, leaving no shortage of war widows and other single women.

By 8:00 PM, Giant's party was in full swing. A few British soldiers joined in from the depot, bringing rum and whiskey. There were no bad feelings at all. The war was over. A few toasts were made to our dead friends and then to Adenauer, who was canvassing in Cologne to become the Chancellor of a new Germany. We toasted to Clements and to the British Prime Minister, Atlee, and Truman and de Gaulle. There were also toasts to the Führer, but they were not said very loudly.

At 10:00 PM, the pub door burst open. In the doorframe stood Gunny, our long lost ex-gunnery sergeant. "Happy birthday, old man!" he shouted to a speechless Giant.

"Well, well, Gunny, how are you?" Giant asked. "Where do you live? Have a drink. Got married yet?" Question followed question and many glasses were raised.

Then Gunny walked over to Dad. "Glad to see you made it back, Lou. I borrowed your bike in April. Hope you don't mind."

"Not at all, Gunny." Dad said. "I got another bike, free of charge, compliments of the town commander, Colonel McKay."

"Well, Lou, I brought your bike back anyway. It's outside." Gunny answered.

"You pedaled all the way from Krefeld to bring the bike back?"

"No, no, Lou. I came in style," he said. "All of you, come outside and look what I have." We all tumbled through the door. Outside, in the light of gas lanterns, we now saw Gunny's so-called "style," an old 1941 Opel Blitz one-ton truck, ex-Wehrmacht, but painted black. On the side of the cab a wood burning "Holzvergaser" was attached. Gunny was proud of his truck and we all agreed that it was the finest German-made driving machine we had seen since the war. Dad's bike was on the back. He took it off and gave it to Dad with a big thank you. Dad looked it over and then he presented it to Brother Len. I had hoped to be the beneficiary, but Len had his old job back and needed a bike, so I gave my silent consent.

The birthday celebrations lasted well into the early hours. The fire in Gunny's wood burner had meanwhile gone out, as he had not refilled the cylinder on his arrival. He carried a good supply of blocks on the back of the truck. It didn't matter, he said. He was going to stay for the night. We took him home with us, leaving the truck at the pub, and gave him the spare room for the night.

Next morning at the breakfast table, we asked him what he was doing now. "Trucking," he said, "doing this and that, and collecting and selling scrap metal."

"Scrap metal? There are thousands of tanks and dead trucks and guns all over the country. You mean they pay money nowadays for this stuff?" I asked.

"Sure they do," he said. "Germany's industry has to recover somehow. Making pots and pans instead of guns is a start. What better way than using all that metal stuff that's lying around by the ton? Copper, zinc and brass are in demand. Some pay me in almost worthless Reichsmarks, others in demandable goods."

"What's demandable goods, Gunny?" I asked.

"Anything that doesn't look remotely like German Marks," he said. "Food, bike tires, gold teeth, broomsticks, church bells, you name it, I can get it."

"Black market, then?" I said.

"Hmm, yes. I guess so," Gunny said. "I traded two nice accordions last week for 30 pounds of flour and a packet of yeast. I got ten pounds of sugar for a roll of copper wire."

"Copper wire, Gunny?" I said. "Heck, there's a lot of that up in the quad pits, remember? You buried that thick cable when the generator was installed back in '42. You connected all the bunkers and even sunk a cable to run to the "big ear" and the searchlight. The 88s had some as well, running to the guns and bunkers."

"Well," he said, "I think we'll have a closer inspection up there after breakfast."

Giant came over the next morning, and after we gave him the details, he offered his spade, pickax and his services, and we made our way up to the gun pits. Nobody was around the sand pit, which was now used for recovering sand. It was Saturday and the area looked deserted. The quads were gone, scrapped I suppose, but the bunkers were still there, minus their steel doors. A musty smell hung around the place.

We knew the cable was buried about a foot deep. The area was overgrown with weeds and grass, but Gunny soon found the old cable trench. After a few minutes of digging we found the cable, and from then on it was easy. The soil was not hard or compact, so there was no need to open up the whole trench. The five of us just kept pulling one end and the cables came up. By noon we had about 200 feet of heavy insulated wire in a big heap. Gunny said he was going to get the truck fired up. Meanwhile, we should burn the insulation off. We lit a hastily built bonfire, and put the cable on it.

A huge black cloud drifted skyward from the burning insulation. The Green Goddess came up to see what was going on, but the fire-fighters soon left, satisfied that the fire was not getting out of hand. Giant and Len also recovered some wire from the 88 pits and dragged it across the field. More black smoke shot up, but by late afternoon we had several rolls of copper, plus brass fittings from the sinks and basins. It was a sizable load that Gunny threw in the back of his truck. He gave Mom a can of liquid soap to wash the mud and grime from our clothes. On Sunday morning, he was going to haul the wire to a collection yard at a smelter in Duisburg, which was open 24 hours a day every day. He made sure that his truck's wood fire kept on burning all night so he could have an early start. At 6:00 AM he was ready. "I'll be back tomor-row, folks, with the profits," he said, and with that he was off.

Tuesday, around noon, he was back with a smile on his face. We crowded around the truck that was filled with boxes and crates. Neighbors stretched their necks from windows to get a glimpse of what was going on as we brought the goods into the house. Giant was there, observing the event. The business Gunny conducted in Duisburg was well worth the effort we put into recovering the cables: three sides of bacon, a box with a dozen one-pound packs of butter, flour, powdered milk, sugar, tobacco, potatoes, cooking oil and candy bars. We all had our fair share.

Dad came home at 2:00 PM from his early shift. Gunny approached him with something wrapped in paper. "Well, Lou, it time I make good on my promise."

"Promise? What promise?" Dad said.

"Remember that day you shouted 'present' when someone called my name up at the quads, but I was AWOL?" Gunny said.

"It's been a long time, Gunny. I almost forgot," Dad said.

"Well, I didn't, and here is the schnapps I promised!" Gunny said, and he presented Dad with a stone bottle of Steinhäger.

Then they all marched off to the pub again to celebrate. Mom and Aunt Carol stashed the loot away. Winter was ahead, but it didn't look too bad right now. The garden had produced a good crop of vegetables.

Fruit was canned. The old shelter below the house was still cluttered with glass jars, briquettes and wood shavings.

Gunny left the next morning after handshakes and hugs. Sadly, we never saw him again. We had no address and did not know the name of his girl.

Giant married Mrs. Helgers one day in mid-winter. He got himself a job as a rural bus driver. Some outlying villages had no connection to rail or tram so this was a good opportunity for him to go into public service like Dad. Of course, Giant had a few things to explain to the authorities when he registered, since he had never applied for discharge papers from a POW camp. He never really was a POW, but the British, who controlled all registration and whereabouts of any person, questioned him for a day then let him off with a warning. Dad went to a few reunions of his old tank destroyer unit, but not many showed up. A lot of them lived behind the iron curtain, in the Russian Zone of Occupation.

The winter of 1945-46 was surprisingly mild. We had less coal and wood, but we kept reasonably warm. On the really cold days, we just shivered along with everyone else. We had enough kommis bread left in the cellar. It was a bit moldy, but who cared? In 1946, we heard that a lot of the high-ranking Nazis were being tried at Nuremberg, and we later learned that some were executed for crimes against humanity. Shortly after the war, the Allies made a film about the liberated concentration camps and the discovery of thousands of mass graves and emaciated living inmates. The film was shown in every theater and it was mandatory to go and see it. The Allies were determined to force the grisly pictures into the conscience of every German, and they did so at bayonet point if necessary. So for the first time, the German people, who had up to then dismissed the gruesome tales as hearsay, could see with their own eyes what Hitler's regime had in mind when he promised in 1938 to rid the world of Jews and undesirables.

The winter of 1946-1947 was the worst in people's memory but from then onward, life got better. Money was still worthless, but with the help of General Marshall's European Recovery Plan, things were shaping up. I often went up to the old quad pits in those days. The bunkers where we had hidden many times during attacks were overgrown. I met Giant there one Sunday morning after church. Was he searching for something? I don't know and he didn't say. We overlooked the town below us where only a few years before all hell had broken loose, as P-38s and Thunderbolts created havoc among the population. My mind wandered back to times when Jabos were circling above, to searching, probing, tracers shooting up, burning planes, parachutes, and the crack of the 88s.

My dreams of getting a medal finally turned into reality. I earned mine on a blood-drenched hill with the funny name of "Elaine" at a godforsaken place with an even funnier name, Dien Bien Phu. But that's another story.

EPILOGUE

Did what I learned from my wartime experiences help me later in life? You bet it did. At 11 years old, I knew how to fire a quad AA gun. This helped me tremendously ten years later, when Viet-Minh forces tried to overrun our position and all we had left was a brace of 50-caliber quads. I also learned to live on the scantest of rations and how to save on food in an emergency. This again came in handy in the early 1960s when I was stranded for two days with a broken down truck in Northern Queensland.

The two years following the end of World War II were in fact the worst for the population. Stores opened up in town that traded or swapped anything for food, from arc welders to zinc bathtubs, from xylophones to bedsteads. The rich got even richer (yes there were a few of them about in those days), and the "have nots" got poorer.

The ghosts of World War II still linger on in Germany and other countries that were turned into battlefields. Unexploded ordnance is still being discovered to this day. A farmer in the Hürtgen Forest area recently had a reservoir excavated and the backhoe tangled for several minutes with a buried 75mm antitank gun. The last World War II ruin in our town was leveled in the late 1980s. There is not much left now to remind people of the war, except the cemeteries with their rows upon rows of neat white crosses. In some fields you can still see the dragon's teeth, the useless antitank obstacles that were never removed. They have become a tourist attraction today. Deep in the underbrush, if you care to get your shoes soiled or clothes ripped to shreds, you might even find the remains of a West Wall bunker, probably inhabited by wild animals. The new German generation is reluctant to talk about World War II. To them, other events in recent history are far more important. You have to search long and hard to find a German born after 1950 who admits that his or her country was a part of that worldwide slaughter. Only the older generation, those that grew up in or fought in World War II, can tell you that Germany in the 1930s brought the war upon themselves, but the number of those still living is getting a bit thin now, as most are in their 70s, 80s and even 90s. They can also tell you how to make a tasty soup from cabbage roots and pancakes from potato peelings, or how to bake bread from rye and barley ground into a coarse flour with mother's coffee grinder, and remember carrot pudding sweetened with saccharine, and savory salads of dandelions, nasturtiums and lupin flowers.

Doctors traded their knowledge and the few medicines that were available for bread, butter and milk. There weren't many sick people to attend to; not as many as there are today, it seems. People lived on a healthy diet. They had no choice. Ever tried making cottage cheese from sour milk? We did. Or drink tea brewed from hand picked and dried broom flowers? It's delicious and healthy. Come to think of it, I might one day write a World War II recipe book. It is not a bad idea, just in case....

I met Giant for the last time in 1986 at the funeral of Brother Len, who died of liver cancer. Giant was then in his 80s, and still lifting the bottle and glass at the pub. My Mom died in 1968 in a tragic accident. The same butcher Mom worked for back in 1941 was also responsible for her death. He ran Mom over in his car while drunk. She died the same day in the hospital. He tried to run, but witnesses saw the incident and reported him to the police who caught up with him. He got two years in prison and was fined 22,000 Marks, which in those days was about $5,000. Dad followed her in death in 1976.

I turned my back on Germany in 1965. My job took me to many different parts of the world. I was on the Azores Islands when Dad died and did not make it to the funeral in time. The telegram about Len's death reached me in Austria, and I made it in time to see him buried. In 1994, I visited Germany again. By then Giant had died, and Mrs. Helgers followed him shortly afterward. I took a day to wander around the old haunts. I went up to the hill to see the old gun pits, but they were gone. The sand pit was in full operation and they had extended their excavation beyond the original pits I knew. The town had been rebuilt. The old food factory had been pulled down, and a park with a medium sized office tower stood on the spot where a half a century earlier people had sought shelter in cellars and Mr. Vink had shouted "lights out."

It was getting dark. I looked around. Was I searching for Gunny or Giant, for Kohn the K-1, for the captain? A breeze blew up. I shivered. I walked back to where our house had one time stood. It had been demolished in 1978 after Dad's death. Then I made my way through the new park where children were having a good time playing. Come to think of it, we never had a park to play in.

It has been a while since this manuscript was written, and it is now 2004 as I write these notes. Last November, after not seeing my home country for ten years, my American wife and I decided to go and visit relatives and friends I had there. Alas, the friends had all gone. They got older too, and died. On a Saturday afternoon, we paid our respects to Brother Len at the cemetery. We stayed at my nephew's house at a place Brother Len had built in the early 1960s. The next day, a blustery November Sunday morning, I stood outside, musing what to do before lunch. Inside, my wife and relatives was busy preparing a midday meal. I went inside, put my coat on, and walked across a narrow path toward the place were our gun pits had been in World War II. Yes, I found the spot all right. Even the sand pit had finally closed, and the site was a tangle of underbrush and thorns, impossible to penetrate. A sign said "Nature Reserve. No Entry."

What a change. Sixty years ago all hell let loose here in that spot, now it was a nature reserve. I searched for the old cycle track that I knew was somewhere around there, and I eventually stumbled upon it. The concrete surface was gone, and trees and brush grew everywhere. A small heap of bricks I found had once been the ticket booth, and then I found the bomb craters—yes, they were still there, albeit shallower after 60 years. A middle-aged man with his son and dog came walking along the path. He looked at me a bit suspiciously, but I bade him a good morning.

"It's not a very good one," came his reply," but it's better than sitting inside. You live around here"?

"I used to," I said, "60 years ago, up there," and I pointed to the top over the overgrown sand pit.

"Where up there?" he asked. "Was there ever a house there? I was born around here in 1965, and I never knew there were houses up there."

"Well," I said, "you wouldn't know it now, but back in '44 and '45 me and a few more fanatics defended this part of the Fatherland from up there. We had a flak position up there, two quads and a 20mm. Ever seen one?"

"No, of course not," he said, "but that must have been a hell of a time you had in those days."

"Hell of a time, yes, I suppose you could call it that," I answered.

"You must have been mad," he replied. "I have read a lot about World War II—mad, I would say."

"The world went mad," I told him. "For six long years—not only me, the whole world," and I walked down the hill to have a warm lunch.